WHITE RIOT

ONE WEEK LOAN

WHITE RIOT

PUNK ROCK AND THE POLITICS OF RACE

————◆————

EDITED BY
STEPHEN DUNCOMBE AND
MAXWELL TREMBLAY

VERSO

London • New York

First published by Verso 2011
© Stephen Duncombe and Maxwell Tremblay 2011
Individual contributions © the contributors

1 3 5 7 9 10 8 6 4 2

Verso
UK: 6 Meard Street, London W1F 0EG
US: 20 Jay Street, Suite 1010, Brooklyn, NY 11201
www.versobooks.com

Verso is the imprint of New Left Books

ISBN-13: 978-1-84467-688-0

British Library Cataloguing in Publication Data
A catalogue record for this book is available from the British Library

Library of Congress Cataloging-in-Publication Data
A catalog record for this book is available from the Library of Congress

Typeset in Adobe Garamond by MJ Gavan, Truro, Cornwall
Printed in the US by Maple Vail

CONTENTS

ACKNOWLEDGMENTS

First we'd like to thank all the writers whose words make up this reader. This book is really theirs. We'd also like to spotlight two individuals who were critical in the genesis of *White Riot*: Elizabeth Esch, who floated the concept of this reader nearly a decade ago, and Joe Lowndes, who resurrected the idea a few years back and contributed so much to the project in its early stages. As with any endeavor like this, our deepest debt is to librarians and archivists: Billie Aul and Paul Mercer at the New York State Archives; Jenna Freedman at the Barnard Library Zine Collection; the staff at NYU's Bobst and Tamiment libraries; Chris Hubbard and the Kill from the Heart online zine archive; the Operation Phoenix Records Punk Zine Archive; Eric Nelson, Jack, and Cookiepuss the Cat at the ABC No Rio Zine Library; Andy Vande Vorde at the *Village Voice*; and Cissie Spurlock, Layla Gibbon, and Justin Briggs at *Maximumrocknroll*, who let us hang out and scan things at the house for a couple days. We'd also like to thank Mimi Nguyen for helpful points in the right direction, Ben Holtzman and Dewar MacLeod for leads early on, Bryan Waterman for his thoughts on Patti Smith, Brian Cogan for his prodigious knowledge of punk rock history, Vivek Bald for his film *Mutiny: Asians Storm British Music* and turning us on to Alien Kulture, Millery Polyné for his thoughts on race and popular music, and James Spooner for embracing the project. Several people and institutions also made this book possible. We'd like to thank the Gallatin School of New York University, the Gallatin Faculty Enrichment Fund, and the New School for Social Research Philosophy Department for helping support this project, Suzanne Wofford for her generosity, and the fabulous Linda Wheeler Reiss for her financial acumen and conjuring ability. At Verso we're indebted to Sébastien Budgen, Audrea

Lim, Mark Martin, John McGhee, John Yates, and especially our editor, Andrew Hsiao, who nurtured this anthology from the start and made us kill some of our darlings to keep its size under control. *White Riot* would never have happened without the support and encouragement of our friends and family: Alisa, Rayna, Juliet, Mom and Dad, Jean, Sydney and Sebastien, and band members past and present. Finally, we're thankful for punk rock and all the kids who continue to try and make it alright.

FOREWORD

It's 1988. I'm a biracial kid, in a white trash town sprinkled with black and brown gang affiliates. I'm the new kid at school, fluffy hair and a Powell Peralta T-shirt. My Walkman blares the one tape I own, Black Flag's *Wasted ... Again*. I just found out about punk rock this summer, but when Keith Morris screams, "I don't care," I know what he's saying. That's me!

I think to some extent all adolescents can relate to the angst of punk rock. For the kids, everything is black and white. You are this or you are that, you're real or you're a poser. Your ability to be yourself is what makes you real, but in truth every kid just wants to fit in. Life is complex, but when you're thirteen a slogan like "I don't care" makes the hypocrisy go away.

When I walked into school that first day a gangbanger named Troy asked me why I "wasn't a nigga like him." He showed me his jailhouse tattoo and keloided knife wound across his arm. Up until that day I thought gangs were limited to the Hell's Angels and the Mafia, but Troy thought I would somehow be an ideal candidate for the Black Mafia Crips.

Later that day I befriended another black guy. Travis. He was a real punk rocker. Spikes on his jacket, bleach spot in the front of his hair. A little white dude, Mason, with a shaved head and red laces in his boots, sat down next to us. We all ate lunch together. In one period, I learned about the Circle Jerks and Descendents, and was asked to join a band (never mind I'd never played an instrument). Mason also clued me in on another tidbit: he hated "niggers," but like Travis I "was cool."

That day I was asked to make a choice: punk or black. I'm biracial, black and white; I was born into duality. My mother raised me to believe I didn't have to be one thing. But when you can't explain, even to yourself, something as complex as navigating double consciousness, it's easy to regress into what you know. Nigger or nigga, it was unanimous I wasn't like Troy and his friends. For me the choice was clear.

Q. Are you black or punk?
A. I don't care, I choose PUNK FUCKING ROCK!

My freshman year of punk rock was like boot camp. I was beaten emotionally and occasionally physically into the arms of my chosen identity. I was continually questioned and challenged by everyone—skinheads, gangsters, teachers, and my parents—about my chosen identity. The more they questioned me, the more I had to prove. In no time, I had pierced myself, slashed myself, and shaved my head in a double Mohawk in order to show everyone that I was punk *first*.

A year later, by the grace of my wonderful white mother, we moved from that California truck-stop town to the Big Apple.

It was 1991. New decade, new me. Almost immediately I felt a sense of relief in this giant city. Living a few blocks away from Washington Square Park, I was instantly inserted into a world where skateboarders, punks, Rastas, street performers, and park weirdos hung out with relative ease. Kids were Puerto Rican and Asian and white and black, and it didn't seem to matter. No one wanted me to be a nigga or nigger or anything else. I was just another kid wearing a leather jacket in the summertime.

It's there where I met another black punk, Ryan. He was in a punk/ska band called Bushmon. Ryan was just old enough for me to look up to but young enough to enjoy having a fifteen-year-old to pal around with. Bushmon was playing one of its first shows, and Ryan used his one comp ticket on *me*. A month prior, angry skinheads were chasing me through a field of dust and tumbleweeds, and today I was on the guest list to see an all-black punk band on the Lower East Side.

Seeing Bushmon did something to me. Some of the complexity of double consciousness just got a little less murky. I didn't have to defend myself as a black punk. Dreadlocks swinging, brown sweat pouring from their faces, these guys validated me. For the first time in a long time I felt pride.

Dreadlocks were popular in those days and my spiked Mohawk followed suit. But it wasn't just black kids locking up. I got my first taste of black camaraderie while smoking pot and dissing our white buddies' struggle to dread. We'd laugh and slap five; no amount of egg white, beeswax, spit, and dirt could replicate what us brothas had.

Some of the guys in Bushmon were having similar feelings of pride. But for them Black Power was giving way to black rage. They were feeling hate for the white kids that I was yet to understand. "Power to the People," "Kill Whitey," "Down with Yacob." Ryan, with me as his loyal follower, was asked to make a decision.

Q. Are you black or punk?
A. PUNK ROCK! Fuck you for asking.

The party was over. Summer came and went and I was back in high school. A lot more black peers ushered in a new boot camp with a new set of identity-challenging drill instructors.

"How come you wearing tight pants? You gay?"
"Oh my God, look at them skulls. You a Satan worshipper?"
"Yo son, he got a ring in his lip! You black, right?"
"Oh, he got a white mom, that's why he act like that."

ARGGGGGG!!!!!! Black or punk, punk or black. I couldn't get away. It would be years before I found a way to properly answer the damn question.

Two years later, New York, with all its legendary punk and hardcore history, was failing me. I was getting tired of the tough-guy, drug-infested NYC hardcore scene. I was getting into politics: animal rights, feminism, DIY, Straight Edge. I needed to find people like myself, so I started to travel. Every weekend I was on a bus to somewhere. Middlesex College in New Jersey, the Cabbage Collective in Pennsylvania, the Middle East in Massachusetts. I was racking up serious Greyhound miles going to see bands and, more important, my newfound friends. This was a different breed of punk rocker. We had a network of kid-run concerts, kid-owned record labels, and kid-produced media. We debated the merits of peace versus militant action. We plotted and protested. It was empowering. It was also very, very white. In this politically conscious climate, no one would dare mention race. No one would dare ask me to choose. To be honest, it felt good. I was just another kid wearing the same dirty pants for a month straight.

It might be oversimplification to pinnacle another big change around one event but the summer of '95 sticks out. I was traveling with a band and we kept bumping into another band, Los Crudos. They were one of the most popular bands around, all Latino, superpolitical, and sang exclusively in Spanish—on purpose.

Tempe, Arizona, marked the third time I was seeing them this tour.

The kids rocked out, traded zines, joked around, and did what kids do, but there was one noticeable difference: everyone, and I mean *everyone*, was Chicano. Seeing punk in a brown context put things in perspective. I sat at the merch table and watched the show, the whole time thinking, "Punk rock is *really* white."

A week later I found myself in San Francisco and, wouldn't you know it, saw Los Crudos again. The night came and went. After all the bands left, some of us stuck around to help the promoter clean the venue. As I was sweeping stepped-on flyers and empty soda cans into the recycling bin I heard, "Why do they have to speak Spanish? I mean, who can understand them?"

I turned around to see the radical white feminist I had been crushing on through letters for a year. As I thoroughly tore her a new asshole to pack her privilege in, I explained that maybe she was not who they were talking to. That night, as my friends began to be a little more awkward/cautious around me, I was realizing that maybe it was time for me to make a choice.

Q. Are you black or punk?
A. Uh … fuck me.

Skipping ahead only a year, I found myself completely alienated from the scene. Maybe I was getting older, maybe it just wasn't speaking to my needs anymore, but one day I was out. No longer punk but not any more black.

With the passing of Y2K, I was five years deprived of the punk scene that raised me. Still, I was clinging to my eighth-grade motto more than ever. Without punk rock and still no black community, "I don't care" was the only thing I could hold on to. But I did care. I needed answers. I was pissed at the black community, I was pissed at my punk family, I was pissed at myself. All these years I had let everyone push me around, and the only thing I had to do to release all this anger was to make a choice.

Punk rock is about questioning everything. Making your own damn rules.

In 2001, I picked up a camera and I talked with every black punk in pre-social-network America I could find. I found eighty and I found myself.

Reading *White Riot: Punk Rock and the Politics of Race*, I found a lot of other punks trying to decide what it means to be punk *and* black, white, Asian, Latino, or whatever.

I've made my choice.

Q. Are you black or punk?
A. Both (and yes, FUCK YOU).

James Spooner lives in Los Angeles. He is the director of Afro-Punk, *a tattooer, a dad, proud to be black, and still punk as fuck.*

ONE

WHITE RIOT?

STEPHEN DUNCOMBE AND
MAXWELL TREMBLAY

Black man gotta lot a problems
But they don't mind throwing a brick
White people go to school
Where they teach you how to be thick

White riot—I wanna riot
White riot—a riot of my own
                    —The Clash, "White Riot"

Stephen Duncombe

White Noise was the name of my first band; it was 1980 and I was fifteen. Some friends and I heard the Ramones and, intuitively understanding punk's guiding DIY ethos, figured that we could learn to play at least as well as they did. "Blitzkrieg Bop," with its simple three-chord musical structure and politically more complicated appropriation of Nazi tactical terminology, was the first song we learned. We picked up a few more cover songs, wrote some of our own, and soon began playing out at bars and VFW halls, carrying notes from our mothers so we could perform in places that served alcohol. We were never very good (I was a particularly bad guitarist) but we were enthusiastic and willing to play anywhere at any time for little money and free drinks, so we ended up opening for some of the big punk bands on their East Coast tours. I never gave much thought to the name of our band at the time. We *were* White, and the music we played and enjoyed *did* sound like noise, so … White Noise! Now, thirty years later, I think a lot more about that name.

I wasn't a racist, at least no more so than any other middle-class White kid growing up in the United States. In fact, probably less so: I was raised in a progressive household with a father who had been a civil rights worker in the South in the early 1960s and helped organize Martin Luther King, Jr.'s "Ministers' March" later in the decade. I was sympathetic to the politics of racial equality and all that, yet when it came time to name our band, I was the one who came up with White Noise. Why?

I, like many White people growing up after the 1960s in North America and Europe, grew up acutely aware of my race. In this way I think we were different from previous generations of Whites who had been allowed the dubious privilege of thinking of themselves, at least on a day-to-day level, as raceless. Blacks, Latinos, Asians, and other "minorities," of course, didn't have this luxury. Whether through legal restriction, social exclusion or physical violence, non-Whites in the West were, and still are, continually reminded of their race. "The problem of the twentieth century," the great W. E. B. Du Bois wrote, "is the problem of the color-line";[1] he might as well have added the problem of the previous few centuries too. But the "problem," as Du Bois points out, was always perceived to be that of the racial Other. To be White was to be uncolored, the norm from which all others deviated. Whiteness was universal.

But not in my world. Until I was a teenager I was raised in New Haven, Connecticut. For people who don't grow up there, New Haven is thought of, if thought of at all, as a small genteel city in a wealthy White state, home to one of the world's most elite universities. My New Haven was a bit different: a combat zone with warring parties marked by race and class. The city, like many cities in the northern United States and across the United Kingdom during the 1960s and '70s, was in the process of deindustrialization. Winchester Arms, a major employer, downsized and eventually closed after a bitter strike. With Winchester went thousands of blue-collar jobs once held by African and Italian Americans; other factories and jobs followed. The trial of the Black Panthers' "New Haven Nine" was held in 1970 and one of my first vivid memories as a young boy was watching armored personnel carriers of the National Guard rumble down my street to stem the expected riot. And in the center of the city was Yale University: its faux Gothic walls enclosing lush green lawns where I watched privileged students read books, toss frisbees, smoke pot, and protest injustice. Surrounding Yale was a predominantly Black slum.

Racial tension was palpable and, at that time, divided between Black and White. The poor Blacks hated the poor Whites, who they understood as having racial advantage in securing whatever blue-collar jobs were left in the city. The poor Whites hated the poor Blacks, who they perceived as criminals or parasites living off the government. And both groups hated the Yalies, who could afford to sit above it all and mouth liberal platitudes about racial harmony. As is often the case, us kids suffered the brunt of the strife. A race riot in my neighborhood high school ended up in a lunchroom stabbing. Walking home from my elementary school I was taunted and beaten up by gangs of Black kids who minutes before had been sitting in the same classroom as me. I learned to cross the street or run away when I saw kids of different races. There was never a moment when I was not aware that I was White. Still, blackness held an attraction for me. I lived on a racially mixed block and before we learned to segregate ourselves I had Black friends. Black was cool. Black kids danced at their birthday parties. Black kids backed each other up in fights. Black kids didn't wear Sears Toughskins. *Soul Train*, Afros, "Kung Fu Fighting," dashikis: to my young White eyes Black was very, very cool.

And then we moved. We moved to a White suburb where I could go to the local public school and not worry about being stabbed in the stomach with a fork (instead I would be threatened by White jocks). It was 1977 and punk rock had already started in the clubs of Manhattan and the pubs of London, but now isolated in suburbia I knew nothing of that. The kids in my new school listened to Southern rock, heavy metal, and the Grateful Dead, but I—and the band of freaky White kids I hung out with—couldn't relate to that music and the styles and attitudes that went along with it. We found what we were looking for in Black music, Black rebel music: Bob Marley and Parliament/Funkadelic. By identifying with Black culture we felt we were different from the White preppies and jocks and stoners that surrounded us. Our borrowed cultural color marked us as "not them." We were the teenage, suburban version of Norman Mailer's "White Negro."

Discovering punk a couple years later was like a homecoming to a home I hadn't known existed. It just felt right, and its anger and immediacy spoke to me as no music ever had. It was freak music, it was rebel music, it was outsider music. But the people I saw playing it, and the people I knew listening to it, were White. Here was a music that was *mine*. I had never been able to identify with the other options of White cultural identity available: they all seemed integrative, to accept the world as it was. Punk, on the other hand, insisted there was something wrong with society (exactly what was left hazy) and therefore the only ethical posture was that of an outsider; "I'm Against It," as the Ramones song goes. My personal alienation was given social expression. In punk I found the outsider identity I desired, without borrowing a (Black) culture and a history that was so evidently not my own. As ridiculous as this might now sound, as a punk I imagined I could be White and not-White at the same time. White Noise was both a recognition of my race and an imaginary rejection of it.

I left high school early and moved out to Southern California, lured by 72-degree weather and the burgeoning U.S. hardcore punk scene: Black Flag, Fear, the Vandals, Circle Jerks, Suicidal Tendencies, TSOL, and the Adolescents. It was the birth of a new kind of punk, fast and aggressive. It was the music of pissed-off White kids who had no ostensible reason to be pissed off. After all, what was there for them to be so upset about? It was the Reagan '80s and White privilege was—again—officially recognized and legitimized. Southern California's economy was rebounding, and many of the hardcore bands were coming out of Los Angeles's prosperous suburbs to the south. Yet these White punks were still angry. Hardcore wasn't guilt-laden lamentations over luxury's disappointments; it was adrenaline-fueled rejection of the affluent society and the punks' often privileged place within it. It felt just about right for me.

But thinking back to that time, it's not the lyrics to a Black Flag or Suicidal Tendencies song that haunt me, but the words to "White Girl," a tune by LA's seminal prehardcore punk band X. Like many X songs, "White Girl" is a poetic Bukowskian lament about love and loneliness and being an LA outsider, the lines sung alternately by Exene Cervenka and John Doe. It's the chorus that gives the song its name, and it's this chorus that still gets to me: "She's a white girl / I'm living with a white girl." Why would a band of White people, singing to a mainly White audience, find it necessary to point out the whiteness of the character in the song?

Because it isn't assumed. The girl could be White, but just as well might not be. Whiteness was no longer a given (though still emphasized). This new racial awareness was partly the result of simple demographics. "We're gonna be a white minority," Black Flag sang, and by the early 1980s Whites were approaching minority status in LA (Latinos and Anglos being the primary ethnic axis). Whereas once being White was the assumed default, the "of course" that therefore didn't need to be mentioned, it was now just one of many hues in the multicultural landscape of the New America and the New Europe. This decentering created a "problem" for Whites. They were now compelled to understand their ethnicity as no longer an unproblematic universal and instead a subject position in need of definition. Whiteness was, of course, always such a positioning. What changed, among White punks at least, was the forcing of this subject positioning

into popular consciousness. You now had to name yourself as White …
and figure out what the hell this meant.

You can read the political landscape of the United States and the United
Kingdom in the 1970s and '80s through this problematic. Thatcherism
and Reaganism represented a determined effort to return to the fantasy
of White universality: a time when only that which was not-White—
Margaret Thatcher's infamous "alien cultures"—needed to be named and
defined. Thankfully, it's a lost cause. The ideas and programs of Thatcher
and Reagan successfully dominated the political and economic agenda
for decades to come, but the racial program, while still having a powerful
purchase on the conservative imagination, was an exercise in nostalgia
doomed to demographic extinction. Among White people, punks probably realized this sooner than others.

Punk offered a space for young Whites growing up in a multicultural
world to figure out what it meant to be White. What was so exciting
to me at the time was the very incoherence of the definition. Against
the solidifying reactionary definition of whiteness—traditional, patriotic,
and (in the United States) God-fearing—punk's whiteness was open and
undecided. We recognized that being White now had to be defined, but
had no firm agreement on what that definition might be. It was an *inchoate whiteness*. Whiteness was an identity, a subjectivity, a culture to be
embraced, distanced from, reconfigured, and redefined, but in all cases,
something to be acknowledged. As Dick Hebdige claims, punk, in its first
incarnations, was an attempt by young Whites, dissatisfied with the world
they were born into, to grab and forge a new ethnicity for themselves.
What form it took was up for grabs.

One form was conscious White racism. It was there from the start, in
the Ramones'—albeit ironic—appropriation of "blitzkrieg" and the Nazi
regalia sported by Sid Vicious and other punk personalities. In White
Noise we sometimes appeared on stage with swastikas penciled on our
skin with eyeliner (which, to complicate things, we also applied to our
eyes). For us, the swastika was nine parts shock value. The 1970s marked
the beginnings of the postmodern playhouse we live in today, where
seemingly anything can be appropriated, recouped, and made safe. In
the swastika we were looking for something, anything, that would resist
appropriation and commodification; its political content was meaningless
to us. But not for all of us, not entirely. Our lead singer was flirting with
something else, that tenth part that still carried the original meaning of
the sign.

The lead singer of White Noise was my best friend. We smoked our first cigarette together, rode on a skateboard team together, and discovered punk rock together. We also came from different worlds: I was decidedly, if not comfortably, middle class; he was the third son of a working-class single mother. His mother worked long hours as a nurse and his older brothers joined the army and the police force, the latter being a "career opportunity" my friend would take up himself. He was a great guy, but could talk easily about "niggers" and "spics." He was obsessed with the Vietnam War and killing "gooks" and once wrote a song about it that, to my present shame, we played out. He shaved his head and wore combat boots. White Noise, a simple acknowledgement of our obvious whiteness to me, may have meant something different to him: White Power.

I ended up moving in another direction. Listening to bands like the Clash, Stiff Little Fingers, and the Dead Kennedys, a new definition of whiteness began to make sense for me. Proclaiming my race did not mean rejecting others, or pretending they didn't exist. Likewise, acknowledging my whiteness, with all its sins and privileges, didn't have to mean denying my race and donning the culture and skin of another. In recognizing that my whiteness was not universal, and in understanding that it was merely one race among many, each with its own struggles and histories, I discovered the possibility of cross-racial *solidarity*. Through punk I attempted to embody what the rock critic Jeff Chang, writing about the Clash, calls "a radical whiteness."[2]

Having a (White) riot of my own meant that I could more easily embrace other cultures. One of the reasons my early teenage transition from Bob Marley and Parliament to punk rock was so easy was because so many punks held reggae and P-Funk in such high esteem. "Rejected by society. Treated with impunity. Protected by their dignity." It was a "Punky Reggae Party" Marley promised, and we welcomed the comparison. But comparison presupposes distinction and difference. I still remember one night's trip out to hear the reggae great Freddie McGregor at a small venue where, I recall vividly, my band of punk rock buddies and I were the only White folks there. In retrospect there *must* have been other White people there, but we were having our "(White Man) in Hammersmith Palais" moment and reality was not going to get in the way. Just as we saw punk as pure White people's music, it was important for us to see reggae as pure Black people's culture. That night, as we smoked weed and listened to McGregor's soulful style of roots reggae, we were emissaries of radical whiteness.

"This isn't *white* reggae," Joe Strummer once explained, introducing the Clash's cover of the reggae classic "Police and Thieves." "This is punk *and* reggae. There's a *difference*. There's a difference between a ripoff and bringing some of *our* culture to *another* culture."[3] "Punk *and* reggae," not one culture subsumed by the other, but both standing side by side, shoulder to shoulder. You could see this antiracist punk ideal played out all over the place during that first wave of punk: in the Rock Against Racism rallying cry of "Black and White Unite and Fight," or even the name of the Specials' record label: Two-Tone. The ideal of solidarity is a good one, a union of common interest with an understanding of individual or group difference. It's so much better than that liberal claptrap we were all brought up with where all difference is subsumed under the name of universalism and what is "universal" ends up looking a lot like the interests of those who are the most powerful. But cross-racial, cross-cultural solidarity brings with it a big problem: it reinforces cultural and racial distinction. In recognizing distinction, even if the goal is to bridge the difference, you inevitably end up creating fixed, contrastable, and partially *essentialized* categories. In order for Black and White to Unite and Fight, to stand shoulder to shoulder in solidarity, each category has to be discrete and assigned a dissimilar character proper only to itself.

This distinction holds for cultural forms as well. If your ideal is "punk *and* reggae" then they have to be distinct and mutually exclusive to start with, not just musically but racially, and there's never much doubt that punk is White and reggae is Black. The twain may meet but they will never meld. You are always a White man in a Black Hammersmith Palais, or conversely, a Black, Latino, or Asian person in a White punk club. This may be a realistic description of the racial segregation that happens in musical scenes, but by accepting distinction as a fundamental axis and then making solidarity the basis for some sort of antiracist punk project, punk essentially inscribes itself as indelibly and essentially White. And once punk is indelibly White, the genuine contributions of Black, Latino, Asian, and other punks of color tend to get erased. White Noise. White Riot. *Whitewashed.*

Maxwell Tremblay

I'm sure my reaction to Steve's band name is akin to that of many contemporary readers, namely: Sweet Jesus, you really couldn't do *that* today! The punk scene Steve describes arose from a context wherein punk's political ambitions remained undecided and ambiguous. Like listening to the Descendents reference "fucking homos" today, hearing about a punk band named White Noise drives home exactly how different the prevailing discourse in punk, in the United States and Britain, after Reagan and Thatcher, has become. The "inchoate whiteness" Steve felt, in the context of related racial identifications on the Left and Right, still crops up here and there in unexpected ways. However, progressive, primarily anarchist leftism has firmly settled in as punk's political operating principle, with an assumption of necessary antiracism as its corollary.

Now, how did we get there?

I suppose some backstory about my own initial steps into punk might aid in tracking this long, strange trip, and help explain why what was so obviously an identity option for Steve became unavailable to me a mere fifteen to twenty years later. Like more '90s-weaned punks than would probably like to admit it, I came to the music through two inauspicious avenues: the mainstream rock heavy hitters who aesthetically fit the bill (your Rancids, your Green Days, your Nirvanas, et al.) and a couple kids from my San Francisco private elementary school with "strange" T-shirts who I thought were objectively cooler than me and ergo wanted to be like. My experience of race, as refracted through both my school and the larger San Francisco Bay Area environment where I grew up, was mostly a matter of banal multiculturalism: equal parts shallow hippie fantasy and pernicious tokenization. This was the soil from which a quasi-punk version of myself began to emerge.

And I don't think I was atypical in this regard. Indeed, this is one of the chief peculiarities about getting into punk rock in the late 1990s, particularly in San Francisco. Across the Bay, at Berkeley's famed punk collective 924 Gilman Street, for instance, you would intermix with middle- and working-class kids from Berkeley, Oakland, and their outlying suburbs, but on our particular peninsula, punks were, to an alarming degree, as White and private school educated as me, to the extent that a friend used to adorn his homemade shirts and tapes with the initials "P.S.P.R."—Prep School Punk Rock. We were all hormonally raging against parental and scholastic authority during one of our economic stratum's most lucrative boom periods, while mainstream "punk" rock at that moment was performing alienation and at the same time becoming all the more commercially successful for it. This is not to say that there weren't punk folks in the Mission District, protesting against the gentrification that would push them, eventually, across the Bay, but that generation was giving way to a newer round of kids who were noticeably squeaky-cleaner. Their contradictions were my contradictions, including the most interesting contradiction of all: that my ability, implicitly at first and then more and more apparently as I got older and (hopefully) a little wiser, to even partially claim membership in a community that was ostensibly anti-establishment and at least ideologically proletarian derived directly from privilege, both race- and class-based.

But none of this was very clear to me at the time. The bands were loud and said "fuck" a lot, and I felt marginally more interesting playing and listening to the music. Race didn't seem like a factor; this was the '90s, the (glaringly inaccurate) assumption was that racism was a thing of the past, that we could all just hang out as individuals. My original dalliances with primarily apolitical pop-punk reflected and thrived on this same overwriting of the specificity of whiteness in favor of hollow universalism. However, as I followed a not-uncommon trajectory from pop-punk to political melodic punk to hardcore, crust, and thrash (with a brief and ill-advised sidestep into emo), punk rebellion took on content as well as form. The primarily anarchist politics that framed how punks saw themselves came into clearer focus, and with them the constitutive rejection of what Joel Olson of *Profane Existence* calls "the white supremacist, patriarchal, capitalist world order." That is, the more one identified as "punk," the more one was expected, as part of a larger political project, to reject one's inherited whiteness. Thus, whether by pseudo-libertarian elision or politically motivated rejection, one could not be even "inchoately" White—only punk. To be in a band called White Noise, as Steve was once, would have been even more unthinkable—unless you were a Nazi. Whiteness, rather than being in need of defense, had become wholly indefensible; there was no recognition, only rejection.

More important, of course, than the amount of shit a young punk would get these days for starting a band so ambiguously named is the difference this flags between the kinds of narrative possibilities White punks could tap into between the generations. For Steve, White punks could be oppressed and oppositional—that is, to quote Minor Threat, be "guilty of being white" and, like X, lash out at "every nigger and Jew, every Mexican that gave her a lot of shit, every homosexual and the idle rich"; they could take the right-wing nosedive into racist White Power; or, as Steve discovered for himself, they could remain self-consciously White, but refashioned "radically" and in solidarity with oppressed peoples. But by the time I knocked on punk rock's doors, the first two options were shut. Sure, you still got quite a bit of inchoate White male rage from certain corners of the scene, most notably the straight-edge community, and the odd Nazi band cropped up here and there. However, anything that smelled even faintly of misinformed or blatantly racist bullshit was usually called out either on stage or in print. Door number three—solidarity with the oppressed—was the one most of us ended up walking through, probably for the best.

But the terrain was different. In the previous generation, the Clash had called for "punk *and* reggae"—that is, punk as specifically White in solidarity with specifically Black culture, like the Weather Underground or the White Panther Party. My generation of punks inherited the ideals of racial solidarity and the overarching leftism, but didn't filter these through any kind of self-aware whiteness, reclaimed and remade, but rather through *treason*: to whiteness, to the very privilege that allowed us to "discover" punk rock in the first place. Now, none of us were as explicit about this as, say, the folks from the Chicago hardcore band Racetraitor, but you could see it all over the various and sundry microscenes we had in the Bay Area: the crusties, the fastcore kids, the Hickey-inspired weirdos. If you had asked any of them, I would wager that they wouldn't have told you they thought of themselves as "White punks." They saw themselves as punks, and whiteness was something to be obliterated, wholesale. This denial permeated everything, to the degree that the White singer for one of my bands referred to burritos he didn't particularly like as "honky burritos" (something I must admit I instinctively still do). Not quite "kill White culture," but it's on a certain continuum. And this rejection of whiteness by young White punks wasn't unique to the Bay Area. From *Punk Planet* and *Profane Existence* to the tiniest little perzine, issues were debated, points contested, and opinions revised. However, the position that White people were "honkies" but White punks were something different provided a fundamental premise upon which all reasonable punks could agree.

This new punk hegemony had consequences good, bad, and weird. On the one hand, this sense of a universal subcultural citizenship encouraged punks to further build up the alternative, do-it-yourself infrastructure begun by earlier generations of punks. Whereas earlier generations of punks had been DIY mostly by necessity—seriously, who the fuck else was going to release Black Flag's *Jealous Again* 12-inch EP?—putting out records, setting up shows, publishing zines, and establishing all manner of punk cultural production completely outside of the jurisdiction of the corporate world became, by the 1990s, the scene's *sine qua non*. If you didn't get that, why were you bothering in the first place? When this was done right—well, hell, it worked like gangbusters. The perseverance of 924 Gilman Street in Berkeley, where I had the privilege of playing several times, and the zine *Maximumrocknroll* in SF, where I started out as a "shitworker" writing record reviews, speaks volumes about the potential of punk rock as alternative culture.

And yet, even in the midst of this increasingly insular and rejectionist cultural sphere, White folks predominantly occupied the positions of prestige, both at shows and on zine staffs, whether it was acknowledged or, more often, not. This became one of the noticeable problems of White self-rejection, founded in radical whiteness and eventually forgetting itself. Insisting that punk was more important than race didn't change the still-sizable degree of privilege Whites derived in mainstream and punk culture as a result of their skin color, language, and so forth. Even as explicitly identifying as a "White punk" became less of an option, the whiteness of punk failed to significantly change.

However, it did accommodate, in its own interesting way, certain powerful divergences that shook the very foundations of the way punk saw itself racially, whether as White-ambiguous, White-Right, White-Left, or White-traitor. One striking intervention was Los Crudos, a powerful, ripping hardcore band any way you sliced it, but all the more significant for being a group of Latino punks from the Chicago area who sang in Spanish about issues specifically pertaining to their communities, and who spent as much effort in playing to different kinds of Latino and Latin American audiences as they did in playing to "the punx." Fronted by Martín Sorrondeguy, who later went on to serve time as *Maximumrocknroll*'s distribution coordinator and found the equally exceptional queercore band Limp Wrist, Los Crudos was one of the most universally adored bands of the late '90s—again, something upon which all reasonable punks can agree.

What Los Crudos signified, and why I think they remain important for both my own punk rock upbringing and Steve's, is that in the midst of a scene that went from explicitly defining itself as predominantly White to rejecting whiteness and advocating antiracism while going, to coin a phrase, "racially underground" in its unspoken racelessness, was a band for whom race, being Latino, was *as central if not more so than being punk*. At the same time, they were claiming punk infrastructure and punk history as their own. Los Crudos demanded that "raceless" White punks acknowledge the history of people of color in punk rock: Poly Styrene, the Brat, Alice Bag, the Zeros, Alien Kulture, Bad Brains, and all the nonwhite bands and fans that were there from the start.

It'd be nice to simply say, "White kids love Los Crudos, and we've got some people of color playing in bands—the raft is in good shape! Ask us again at the next fest." This is *precisely* what punk kids ended up saying, and it's bullshit. White punks spent the better part of two decades narratively defining and framing themselves as White rebels playing White rebel music—indeed, half of this anthology is devoted to unearthing the circumstances, stakes, and mistakes that made this possible—and now that whiteness was found to be irredeemable, they want to toss it off with a breakaway march and a facial piercing, and then trumpet their success by counting up the number of people of color who are on their side? Ye gods, what a mess.

This muddle started out as at least two steps in the right direction: as punk's political position hardened, there was a greater need, first, to distance itself from the dominant culture, and second, to reverse the essentialist gesture, to divorce "punk" from "White" in order to recognize the kinds of contributions a band like Los Crudos represented. But a familiar logic ensues: White rejectionism relies on "punk" as an ur-signifier, a kind of overarching identity position that was expected of those who listened to the music and contributed to the scene, around which we all could rally and whose honor we could all defend. From there, however, it's only a short slide to "punk" as a catchall term for the neutral position of the scene—and if critical race studies in the past few decades has taught us anything, it's to be wary of that which purports to assert itself as the "neutral." Behind that term, in most cases, lurks the specter of White privilege. You end up, as usual, with a bunch of mostly White men milling around a basement screaming about how much, say, Christianity and capitalism suck, man, but unwilling to talk about the fact that they're White—or male, for that matter.

This is what the zinester Mimi Nguyen meant, in 1998, when she wrote in *Punk Planet* that "'whitestraightboy' hegemony organizes punk." It's not just that punk is demographically White-ish, it's that the language in which it speaks about itself participates in an exclusionary discourse of whiteness and White privilege. As Steve points out, the dreams of solidarity of the earliest generations of White punks were predicated upon distinguishing and essentializing punk as White people's music, eliding the experiences and contributions of punks of color. In this newer iteration, the dreams of color-blind anarchism mix with the liberal multiculturalism status quo of the late-Clinton/Blair era to produce a far less self-aware variety of de facto whiteness, in which "punk" functions as a category of citizenship. According to the rhetorical framing of some of its most revered institutions (like Berkeley's 924 Gilman, with its commandments: "No Racism, No Sexism, No Homophobia"), the punk scene is meant to be "our" refuge from an unfeeling and unjust world, and "punk" as a des-ignator is meant to be salient prior to other differences. Punk is a category that we can all claim before or outside of our other cultural investments, in the face of which we should all be able to remove our various hats, place our hands over our hearts, and salute the (Black) flag. But to *whom* does that scene belong, and what kinds of identities are allowed inside its safe spaces? What gets left out in claiming such an overarching citizen-ship category? What are the boundaries of being punk? Punks of color take up and reappropriate punk cultural forms in order to construct and live a new kind of racial identity, taking those forms to their very limits. But what happens when they come up against these limits and find them intolerable, unlivable?

You get a race riot.

Arising through a cocktail of contemporary influences and develop-ments—Riot Grrrl, queercore, 1990s cultural studies, the explosion of personal zine culture—punks and ex-punks of color in the late '90s and early 2000s took up a structural critique of the scene, excoriating punk and punks not just for isolated incidents of racism, but for the very assumptions by which punk maintained itself in the first place. What Riot Grrrl did for punk misogyny, this new group of zinesters tried to do for punk's unspoken White vision of neutrality. In the process they produced perhaps the most vibrant body of zine writing in recent memory, drawing connections and building on one another's work, reprinting important essays and adding their own criticisms. Mainstream punk notions of politics, music, and community could scarcely stay the same.

And yet, by and large, they did. Nguyen began a "J'accuse" in *Punk Planet* by asserting that she was still "waiting for [her] race riot," and in many ways punk is still waiting. While misogyny and homophobia were by no means eradicated in punk, they were acknowledged openly, if sometimes opportunistically: a male friend of mine once quipped, "Every punk guy wants to be the male guitar player for Bikini Kill." The "White" in "whitestraightboy hegemony" has proven much more intractable. Yes, *HeartattaCk* did a special issue on "Punk and Race," *Maximumrocknroll* a volume on "Punk and Immigration," but it has proven too easy for most White punks to slip back into racial comfort. Traces of struggle remain—the recent British zine *Race Revolt*, for instance, reprints essays from the time—but the Race Rioters, seeing little change and pushed to the brink of punk's margins, largely moved on to other things: academia, activism, publishing, or other genres of music. And while I would be profoundly stupid to claim to have been burned by punk prejudice (I'm a whitestraightboy, after all), my own eventual migration away from punk and into the academic study of feminism and postcolonial philosophy was partially motivated by beginning to see the punk scene as these Race Rioters painted it: White, male, straight kids railing against the reprehensible dominant culture loudly to one another but largely unable to accommodate criticisms of their own assumptions. To queer the Minor Threat song title: "Screaming at a Wall," indeed.

Stephen Duncombe and Maxwell Tremblay

From its inception punk rock has tried, in myriad ways, to "solve" the problems of racial identity in an increasingly multicultural world. But punk didn't deliver, it couldn't deliver. As Johnny Thunders once sang, punk is "born to lose." Punk was and is a subculture, at best a haven in a heartless world, at worst the old world dressed up in a ripped T-shirt and sporting band badges. The problems of race and racism run deeper and wider than any subcultural scene; race as a concept stretches back for hundreds, if not thousands of years, and racism as an ideology and practice spans the entire globe. Employing one strategy or another, be it highlighting race or erasing race, calling out punk's racism or insisting that the scene is color-blind, punk forever looks for subcultural solutions to much bigger problems. As Stuart Hall, John Clarke, and others at the Centre for Contemporary Cultural Studies in Birmingham argued so many years ago, subcultures " 'solve,' but in an imaginary way, problems which at the concrete level remain unresolved."[4] It seems the more punks try to resolve issues of race within the scene, the more those solutions seem to elide them. Race isn't just a punk issue, and its resolution cannot take place in only a subcultural scene.

Perhaps punk has failed politically, probably necessarily so, but we're not ready to give up on it just yet. With eyes wide open we still see that punk has promise.

Not too long ago we walked over to ABC No Rio for its regular HC/Punk matinee show. For more than twenty years a volunteer collective has been organizing gigs (with the de rigueur lefty punk stipulation "We do not book racist, sexist, or homophobic bands") in the alternately freezing or boiling basement of this former squat on the Lower East Side. On this day it was boiling and we were outside catching some air on the sidewalk. Nearby was a group of young punks: leather, spikes, mohawks, heavy black boots, the whole bit. They were drunk, rowdy, loud, and thoroughly punk. Blink your eyes and it could have been 1977, 1987, or 1997. Except for one thing: these punks all spoke Polish. They were the teenage sons and daughters of the latest wave of immigrants to New York City.

We stood there wondering what punk meant to them. We're pretty sure it largely meant what it had to us: a language of rebellion and a community of belonging. But we're also pretty certain it meant something else. Punk, with its Anglo-American lineage and the dominance of English, must have also been something foreign to them, something alluring, something "Other." It, we imagine, was a way to rebel (against their Polish parents) to assimilate (into this new English-speaking world), and rebel once again (against mainstream America). It was a more complicated punk experience than our own. And what was these Polish punks' relationship to race? Punk, we've argued, is thoroughly racialized and inextricably structured around the articulation of racial identity and the struggle to "solve" problems of racism. So how do a bunch of kids who grew up—and were perhaps first exposed to punk—in a nearly homogeneously White country like Poland make sense of punk's racial identities? Rock 'N' Roll Nigger? White Minority? White Riot? Race Riot? What can these essential punk positionings possibly mean to them? These aren't questions whose relevance is limited to a handful of White Polish punks hanging out on the Lower East Side of New York; they are core questions for the future of punk rock.

HC/Punk matinees still take place every Saturday at ABC No Rio, but the most interesting developments in punk rock don't necessarily come from New York City nowadays, nor from London or Los Angeles. Arguably the most lively and important punk scenes in the world are in places like Mexico City and Jakarta, Indonesia. As punk rock followed the global flow of commodities and communication, it brought with it certain assumptions and projections about race and identity from the Global North. But—and this is an important "but"—this music and culture is then adopted and *adapted* by local punks to speak to their particular concerns. In this translation meanings change and punk takes on different accents. In terms of race, what "makes sense" in Britain or the United States has to make a different sense to be meaningful in a place like Indonesia where ethnic relationships do not revolve around a White/Black axis, and whiteness has limited relevance as an identity. Perhaps it is exactly in this process of adaptation and translation that punk stands its best chance of being something more than a "White riot." The migration of cultures and of peoples may be able to resolve concretely those problems of race that punk was never able to solve subculturally.

A little more than half a dozen blocks north of ABC No Rio, and about half that number of blocks east from where the famed punk club CBGB once stood, there is a memorial mural created by the local graffiti artist Antonio Garcia, better known as Chico. The memorial is for Joe Strummer, who died in 2002. It's a big picture of the Clash front man in classic punk black leather, and underneath, in all caps, is the famous Clash lyric "Know Your Rights!" But whose rights? As punk goes global the response to this question is played back in a variety of languages. This decentering of punk is made manifest in the mural itself: Chico frames Strummer in the red, yellow, and green stripes of the Rastafarian flag. Overhead the Puerto Rico–born graffiti artist quotes the British singer of "White Riot," in large spray-paint letters: "The Future is Unwritten."

The future does remain unwritten; the past, as usual, still demands some accounting for, and punk rock is no exception. Whatever punk's political failings may continue to be, the punk scene *has* engaged in extensive, lively, and contentious debates surrounding issues of racial identity. The trouble is, they have taken place in far-flung and diffuse modes of cultural production. As anybody who's ever spoken to a record collector or a zine librarian knows, punk has a very acute sense of institutional memory, bolstered and internationalized by the upsurge in online zine archives and digitized-vinyl blogs. However, with small runs of records and zines scattering to all corners of the earth, certain threads of discussion end up falling through the cracks—which is precisely why, say, the Race Rioter Krishna Rau can hammer punk on issues that dozens, including Greil Marcus and Lester Bangs, had criticized thirty years ago with the same force and urgency.

While we are both relatively illusion-free about punk's ability to "solve" issues of racial identity, we would hope that this volume begins to rectify and reverse this process of forgetting. You've heard us try to situate ourselves in relation to both punk rock and race, drawing out certain themes we witnessed in the course of our so-called punk rock lives; now it's time to let punk speak for itself. While we've both talked briefly about generational differences, the story we've assembled here can't quite rightly be called "historical." What you have, both in the preceding pages and the ones that follow, is not a linear progression of happenings in the life of a subculture—that is, we can't just say that, for instance, *first* you had your "White Negro," which passed into inchoate White nihilism, or that White punk anti-racism *then* gave way to non-White bands taking up the mantle of punk rock. Punk rock, like most sub- or countercultural forms, is far too messy for all that, and it exhibits its own peculiar—to use an expensive and totally unpunk term—"historicity." Ideas and forms are proposed, threads are picked up and dropped, challenged, and negotiated, and ultimately end up resurfacing in ways that both preserve their original spirit and fundamentally alter them. In that sense, we can think of each of the roughly seven threads we've touched on in this anthology as "tendencies": racial identity options opened up and made available in, through, and against punk rock. Each one persists in its own ripped apart, duct-taped-together, fucked-up way.

Now it's the task of whoever ends up reading this book to fuck the tendencies up again. We're not just here to survey the damage. To have these myriad punk rock identity struggles laid out before us is a way of seeing where we have been, of understanding what worked and what didn't, what kinds of oppressive exclusions were performed and what kinds of ingenious interventions were made ... and then to go on from there: to rebuild, rewrite, fuck around, get dirty. All of us with a relationship to the punk scene brought something to it and took something from it. Punk mattered, and still matters. There's something to it that, when it works, is incredibly effective. Take, for example, the efforts of punk-inflected political gestures like Reclaim the Streets, Food Not Bombs, the Icarus Project, or even the mass globalization protests, which applied punk style, strategy, and infrastructure to other forms of organization. "Punk" as an identity works in some contexts too, just as it fails miserably in others. Punk identity can no longer see itself as totalizing, but it can develop a notion of itself as partial, maintaining a relationship to its outside, and sustaining difference within and against itself. We're not all "just punk"; it's never been that simple, no matter what White liberal punk kids might argue. We all come to punk from different intersections of class, gender, sexuality, nationality, and, of course, race.

If punk is ever going to be the kind of subcultural form that truly undermines White privilege and develops an alternative way of living race in and against mainstream society, it has to be remade, again. It may look different, it may cease to be recognizable to those who currently carry its banner, but that's the risk and possibility of culture—if you care about it mattering to others, you have to accept that it may turn out differently than you planned. Because for all the ways the punk scene has fucked up and gotten it wrong, it *has* changed, shifted, adapted, and sometimes gotten it right. The future is unwritten.

TWO

ROCK 'N' ROLL NIGGER

Baby was a black sheep. Baby was a whore.
You know she got big. Well, she's gonna get bigger.
Baby got a hand; got a finger on the trigger.
Baby, baby, baby is a rock 'n' roll nigger.

Outside of society, that's where I want to be.
Outside of society, they're waitin' for me.
  —"Rock 'N' Roll Nigger," Patti Smith and Lenny Kaye

What was the Patti Smith Group thinking when they recorded "Rock 'N' Roll Nigger" in 1978? This was the post–Civil Rights, pre–Gangsta Rap era and the N-word was strictly *verboten*. "Because the Night," recorded on the same album and co-written by Smith and her fellow New Jersey native Bruce Springsteen, climbed to #13 in the United States and #5 in Britain, and became Patti Smith's most popular song. "Rock 'N' Roll Nigger," on the other hand, couldn't even be played on mainstream radio. The song made no commercial sense. But it did make sense in the logic of another tradition: the history of White outsiders and their identification with racial and cultural Others.

A long line runs from Shakespeare's Othello through Montesquieu's *Persian Letters* to Arthur Rimbaud's declaration "Je suis une bête, un nègre" and Norman Mailer's "The White Negro"; from going native in the bush to enjoying urban minstrel shows. For centuries White folks have donned blackface to say and do what they felt their culture would not allow. The impulse stems, in part, from a rejection of White culture; an understanding—be it social or political—of the oppression to which the White race has subjected the rest of the world, and the suppression to which they subjected themselves in the process. The flipside of this knowledge of oppression and suppression is the idealization of the freedom of the racial Other. They become everything White is not: rebellious, rhythmic, spontaneous, and sexually free; in short, gloriously uncivilized. By identifying with the Other's culture you make yourself an Other, free of the weight and guilt of "civilization."

But it is not necessarily the desire to be the racial Other that drives the White Negro, rather it is by othering yourself that you can become something else: a white who is not White. In this new position, so the thought goes, you can understand and sympathize with the struggles of Blacks, Latinos, Asians, Native Americans, and others, and with this understanding you can even join them in solidarity. By othering yourself you can build an alliance (largely imaginary, but perhaps not necessarily so) with the not-White world. As Smith sings, "Outside of society, they're waitin' for me."

Punk continues in this tradition. In the MC5's identification with Black rebellion in Detroit, British punks' attraction to reggae and dub, and Patti Smith's self-description as a "nigger," the White Negro lives on. It's easy to be critical of this tradition, and we certainly are, but it's important to recognize that the impulse is usually a worthy one: the identification with people of color is a struggle to create a whiteness detached from the banality and brutality of White history. And while this impulse often results merely in vague notions of aesthetic transgression, it at least has the potential, as we will see, to articulate itself politically. Ultimately, however, a White punk can take off the leather jacket and shave off the mohawk, and, facial tattoos notwithstanding, integrate back into society's mainstream, casting off the Negro and keeping the White. For White punks, like all the bohemians before them, being an outsider is a choice made by themselves, perhaps more existentially profound for being so, but nonetheless still a choice.

NORMAN MAILER, "THE WHITE NEGRO"

It may seem odd to begin a reader on punk rock with an author better known in more rarefied literary circles. In "The White Negro," however, Norman Mailer—author of *The Naked and the Dead, Barbary Shore, The Executioner's Song,* and many other works of fiction and narrative nonfiction—provides a potent

introduction to idealized oppositional whiteness. Appearing first in the progressive journal *Dissent* in 1957, this widely celebrated—and condemned—essay was an opening gesture of late-twentieth-century counterculture and establishes threads that will stay with us throughout this reader. Recoiling at the conformity and inhumanity of postwar American culture, Mailer finds refuge in "Hip," that is, an articulation of White identity meant to subvert the oppressive whiteness of society at large; by participating in the "black man's code," the White hipster becomes the titular "White Negro." But what are the implicit racial assumptions of such articulations? That is, in formulating an oppositional identity, to what extent do Whites fetishize and appropriate the "outsider" status of people of color, a status that has arisen out of specific conditions of economic and political inequality? With the distance of years, it seems easier to criticize Mailer for his assumptions yet the narrative of the "White Negro" reappears in myriad ways within punk's own attempt to articulate oppositional identities.

Probably, we will never be able to determine the psychic havoc of the concentration camps and the atom bomb upon the unconscious mind of almost everyone alive in these years. For the first time in civilized history, perhaps for the first time in all of history, we have been forced to live with the suppressed knowledge that the smallest facets of our personality or the most minor projection of our ideas, or indeed the absence of ideas and the absence of personality could mean equally well that we might still be doomed to die as a cipher in some vast statistical operation in which our teeth would be counted and our hair would be saved, but our death itself would be unknown, unhonored, and unremarked, a death which could not follow with dignity as a possible consequence to serious actions we had chosen, but rather a death by *deus ex machina* in a gas chamber or a radioactive city; and so if in the midst of civilization—that civilization founded upon the Faustian urge to dominate nature by mastering time, mastering the links of social cause and effect—in the middle of an economic civilization founded upon the confidence that time could indeed be subjected to our will, our psyche was subjected itself to the intolerable anxiety that death being causeless, life was causeless as well, and time deprived of cause and effect had come to a stop.

The Second World War presented a mirror to the human condition which blinded anyone who looked into it. For if tens of millions were killed in concentration camps out of the inexorable agonies and contractions of super-states founded upon the always insoluble contradictions of injustice, one was then obliged also to see that no matter how crippled and perverted an image of man was the society he had created, it was nonetheless his creation, his collective creation (at least his collective creation from the past) and if society was so murderous, then who could ignore the most hideous of questions about his own nature?

Worse. One could hardly maintain the courage to be individual, to speak with one's own voice, for the years in which one could complacently accept oneself as part of an elite by being a radical were forever gone. A man knew that when he dissented, he gave a note upon his life which could be called in any year of overt crisis. No wonder then that these have been the years of conformity and depression. A stench of fear has come out of every pore of American life, and we suffer from a collective failure of nerve. The only courage, with rare exceptions, that we have been witness to, has been the isolated courage of isolated people.

It is on this bleak scene that a phenomenon has appeared: the American existentialist—the hipster, the man who knows that if our collective condition is to live with instant death by atomic war, relatively quick death by the State as *l'univers concentrationnaire*, or with a slow death by conformity with every creative and rebellious instinct stifled (at what damage to the mind and the heart and the liver and the nerves no research foundation for cancer will discover in a hurry), if the fate of twentieth-century man is to live with death from adolescence to premature senescence, why then the only life-giving answer is to accept the terms of death, to live with death as immediate danger, to divorce oneself from society, to exist without roots, to set out on that uncharted journey into the rebellious imperatives of the self. In short, whether the life is criminal or not, the decision is to encourage the psychopath in oneself, to explore that domain of experience where security is boredom and therefore sickness, and one exists in the present, in that enormous present which is without past or future, memory or planned intention, the life where a man must go until he is beat, where he must gamble with his energies through all those small or large crises of courage and unforeseen situations which beset his day, where he must be with it or doomed not to swing. The unstated essence of Hip, its psychopathic brilliance, quivers with the knowledge that new kinds of victories increase one's power for new kinds of perception; and defeats, the wrong kind of defeats, attack the body and imprison one's energy until one is jailed in the prison air of other people's habits, other people's defeats, boredom, quiet desperation, and muted icy self-destroying rage. One is Hip or one is Square (the alternative which each new generation coming into American life is beginning to feel), one is a rebel or one conforms, one is a frontiersman in the Wild West of American night life, or else a Square cell, trapped in the totalitarian tissues of American society, doomed willy-nilly to conform if one is to succeed.

A totalitarian society makes enormous demands on the courage of men, and a partially totalitarian society makes even greater demands for the general anxiety is greater. Indeed if one is to be a man, almost any kind of unconventional action often takes disproportionate courage. So it is no accident that the source of Hip is the Negro for he has been living on the margin between totalitarianism and democracy for two centuries. But the presence of Hip as a working philosophy in the sub-worlds of American life is probably due to jazz, and its knife-like entrance into culture, its subtle but so penetrating influence on an avant-garde generation—that post-war generation of adventurers who (some consciously, some by osmosis) had absorbed the lessons of disillusionment and disgust of the Twenties, the Depression, and the War. Sharing a collective disbelief in the words of men who had too much money and controlled too many things, they knew almost as powerful a disbelief in the socially monolithic ideas of the single mate, the solid family and the respectable love life. If the intellectual antecedents of this generation can be traced to such separate influences as D. H. Lawrence, Henry Miller, and Wilhelm Reich, the viable philosophy of Hemingway fits most of their faces: in a bad world, as he was to say over and over again (while taking time out from his parvenu snobbery and dedicated gourmandise), in a bad world there is no love nor mercy nor charity nor justice unless a man can keep his courage, and this indeed fitted some of the facts. What fitted the need of the adventurer even more precisely was Hemingway's categorical imperative that what made him feel good became therefore The Good.

So no wonder that in certain cities of America, in New York of course, and New Orleans, in Chicago and San Francisco and Los Angeles, in such American cities as Paris and Mexico, D.F., this particular part of a generation was attracted to what the Negro had to offer. In such places as Greenwich Village, a ménage-a-trois was completed—the bohemian and the juvenile delinquent came face-to-face with the Negro, and the hipster was a fact of American life. If marijuana was the wedding ring, the child was the language of Hip for its argot gave expression to abstract states of feeling which all could share, at least all who were Hip. And in this wedding of the white and the black it was the Negro who brought the cultural dowry. Any Negro who wishes to live must live with danger form his first day, and no experience can ever be casual to him, no Negro can saunter down a street with any real certainty that violence will not visit him on his walk. The cameos of security for the average white: mother and the home, job and the family, are not even a mockery to millions of Negroes; they are impossible. The Negro has the simplest of alternatives: live a life of constant humility or ever-threatening danger. In such a pass where paranoia is as vital to survival as blood, the Negro had stayed alive and begun to grow by following the need of his body where he could. Knowing in the cells of his existence that life was war, nothing but war, the Negro (all exceptions admitted) could rarely afford the sophisticated inhibitions of civilization, and so he kept for his survival the art of the primitive, he lived in the enormous present, he subsisted for his Saturday night kicks, relinquishing the pleasures of the mind for the more obligatory pleasures of the body, and in his music he gave voice to the character and quality of his existence, to his rage and the infinite variations of joy, lust, languor, growl, cramp, pinch, scream and despair of his orgasm. For jazz is orgasm, it is the music of orgasm, good orgasm and bad, and so it spoke across a nation, it had the communication of art even where it was watered, perverted, corrupted, and almost killed, it spoke in no matter what laundered popular way of instantaneous existential states to which some whites could respond, it was indeed a communication by art because it said, "I feel this, and now you do too."

So there was a new breed of adventurers, urban adventurers who drifted out at night looking for action with a black man's code to fit their facts. The hipster had absorbed the existentialist synapses of the Negro, and for practical purposes could be considered a white Negro.

Norman Mailer, from "The White Negro: Superficial Reflections on the Hipster," *Dissent* no. 4 (Summer 1957).

JAMES BALDWIN,
"THE BLACK BOY LOOKS AT THE WHITE BOY"

James Baldwin, justly famous for his novels as well as collections of essays such as *The Fire Next Time* (a book that gave its name to an early 2000s political hardcore outfit), offers here a powerful rejoinder to Mailer's "White Negro." Baldwin takes his friend to task, unearthing the many privileges of whiteness that underlie his idealization of Black otherness. The picture of blackness

aspired to by Mailer and, even more ludicrously, Jack Kerouac and the Beats, is woven from centuries of stereotypes of Black male sexuality and rebellion, and the structure of the aspiration reveals itself to be mere atavism: nostalgia for a "primitive" origin underneath the oppressive constraints of "square" White culture. There's a lesson here for punk: when countercultural identification takes the form of racial fetish, it relies upon and perpetuates the very privileges accorded by the dominant culture it is attempting to subvert.

I was on the road—not quite, I trust, in the sense that Kerouac's boys are; but I presented, certainly, a moving target. And I was reading Norman Mailer. Before I had met him, I had only read *The Naked and the Dead*, *The White Negro*, and *Barbary Shore*—I think this is right, though it may be that I only read *The White Negro* later and confuse my reading of that piece with some of my discussions with Norman. Anyway, I could not, with the best will in the world, make any sense out of *The White Negro* and, in fact, it was hard for me to imagine that this essay had been written by the same man who wrote the novels. Both *The Naked and the Dead* and (for the most part) *Barbary Shore* are written in a lean, spare, muscular prose which accomplishes almost exactly what it sets out to do. Even *Barbary Shore*, which loses itself in its last half (and which deserves, by the way, far more serious treatment than it has received) never becomes as downright impenetrable as *The White Negro* does.

Now, much of this, I told myself, had to do with my resistance to the title, and with a kind of fury that so antique a vision of the blacks should, at this late hour, and in so many borrowed heirlooms, be stepping off the A train. But I was also baffled by the passion with which Norman appeared to be imitating so many people inferior to himself, i.e., Kerouac, and all the other Suzuki rhythm boys. From them, indeed, I expected nothing more than their pablum-clogged cries of *Kicks!* and *Holy!* It seemed very clear to me that their glorification of the orgasm was but a way of avoiding all of the terrors of life and love. But Norman knew better, had to know better. *The Naked and the Dead*, *Barbary Shore*, and *The Deer Park* proved it. In each of these novels, there is a toughness and subtlety of conception, and a sense of the danger and complexity of human relationships which one will search for in vain, not only in the work produced by the aforementioned coterie, but in most of the novels produced by Norman's contemporaries. What in the world, then, was he doing, slumming so outrageously, in such a dreary crowd?

For, exactly because he knew better, and in exactly the same way that no one can become more lewdly vicious than an imitation libertine, Norman felt compelled to carry their *mystique* further than they had, to be more "hip," or more "beat," to dominate, in fact, their dreaming field; and since this *mystique* depended on a total rejection of life, and insisted on the fulfillment of an infantile dream of love, the *mystique* could only be extended into violence. No one is more dangerous than he who imagines himself pure in heart: for his purity, by definition, is unassailable.

But *why* should it be necessary to borrow the Depression language of deprived Negroes, which eventually evolved into jive and bop talk, in order to justify such a grim system of delusions? Why malign the sorely menaced sexuality of Negroes in order to justify the white man's own sexual panic? Especially as, in Norman's case, and as indicated by his work, he has a very real sense of sexual responsibility, and, even, odd as it may sound to some, of sexual morality, and a genuine commitment to life. None of his people, I beg you to notice, spend their lives on the road. They really become entangled with each other, and with life. They really suffer, they spill real blood, they have real lives to lose. This is no small achievement; in fact, it is absolutely rare. No matter how uneven one judges Norman's work to be, all of it is genuine work. No matter how harshly one judges it, it is the work of a genuine novelist, and an absolutely first-rate talent.

Which makes the questions I have tried to raise—or, rather, the questions which Norman Mailer irresistibly represents—all the more troubling and terrible. I certainly do not know the answers, and even if I did, this is probably not the place to state them.

But I have a few ideas. Here is Kerouac, ruminating on what I take to be the loss of the garden of Eden:

> At lilac evening I walked with every muscle aching among the lights of 27th and Welton in the Denver colored section, wishing I were a Negro, feeling that the best the white world had offered was not enough ecstasy for me, not enough life, joy, kicks, darkness, music, not enough night. I wished I were a Denver Mexican, or even a poor overworked Jap, anything but what I so drearily was, a "white man" disillusioned. All my life I'd had white ambitions. ... I passed the dark porches of Mexican and Negro homes; soft voices were there, occasionally the dusky knee of some mysterious sensuous gal; and dark faces of the men behind rose arbors. Little children sat like sages in ancient rocking chairs.

Now, this is absolute nonsense, of course, objectively considered, and offensive nonsense at that: I would hate to be in Kerouac's shoes if he should ever be mad enough to read this aloud from the stage of Harlem's Apollo Theater.

And yet there is real pain in it, and real loss, however thin; and it *is* thin, like soup too long diluted; thin because it does not refer to reality, but to a dream. Compare it, at random, with any old blues:

> Backwater blues done caused me
> To pack my things and go.
> 'Cause my house fell down
> And I can't live there no mo'.

"Man," said a Negro musician to me once, talking about Norman, "the only trouble with that cat is that he's white." This does not mean exactly what it says—or, rather, it *does* mean exactly what it says, and not what it might be taken to mean—and it is a very shrewd observation. What my friend meant was that to become a Negro man, let alone a Negro artist, one had to make oneself up as one went along. This had to be done in the not-at-all-metaphorical teeth of the world's determination to destroy you. The world had prepared no place for you, and if the world had its way, no place would ever exist. Now, this is true for everyone, but, in the case of a Negro, this truth is absolutely naked: if he deludes himself about it, he will die. This is not the way this truth presents itself to white men, who believe the world is theirs and who, albeit unconsciously, expect the world to help them in the achievement of their identity. But the world does not do this—for anyone; the world is not interested in anyone's identity. And, therefore, the anguish which can overtake a white man comes in the middle of his life, when he must make the almost inconceivable effort to divest himself of everything he has ever expected or believed, when he must take himself apart and put himself together again, walking out of the world, into limbo, or into what certainly looks like limbo. This cannot yet happen to any Negro of Norman's age, for the reason that his delusions and defenses are either absolutely impenetrable by this time, or he has failed to survive them. "I want to know how power works," Norman once said to me, "how it really works, in detail." Well, I know how power works, it has worked on me, and if I didn't know how power worked, I would be dead. And it goes without saying, perhaps, that I have simply never been able to afford myself any illusions concerning the manipulation of that power. My revenge, I decided very early, would be to achieve a power which outlasts kingdoms.

James Baldwin, from "The Black Boy Looks at the White Boy," *Nobody Knows My Name* (New York: Vintage Books, 1993).

WEATHERMAN SONGBOOK, "WHITE RIOT"

Weatherman provides a template for punk's confrontational, performative politics, as well as its racial assumptions. Eventually renaming themselves the Weather Underground, they "brought the war home" in the late 1960s and early 1970s by bringing the violence of U.S. imperialism to American soil through spectacular bombings and raucous protests like the "Days of Rage" memorialized below. While punk's method is cultural, not military, both share a similar technique: publicly performing the ugliness of the very society they reject through shock tactics. In addition, punk's later aspirations of White solidarity with oppressed people of color mirror the aims, if again not the means, of Weatherman and their overseas comrades, the German Red Army Faction and Italy's Red Brigades (both of whom Joe Strummer memorialized on a frequently worn T-shirt). Weatherman set out, according to Bernardine Dohrn's own (pretty punk) words, to "build a fucking white revolutionary movement," while punk, at its most political, set out to be White revolutionary music. This short text comes from a songbook published by the group, which, like some of the work of their French counterparts in the Situationist International, *détourned* the lyrics to popular songs—in this case, "White Christmas." The key line here, for our purposes, comes at the end: the implication that whiteness, in its mainstream, square, complicit-with-capital-and-imperialism variety, can and must be remade, or it is doomed. And the first line, if the story is to be believed, gave the Clash the title to their song (and, subsequently, this anthology).

> I'm dreaming of a white riot
> Just like the one October 8,
> When the pigs take a beating
> And things start leading
> To armed war against the state.
>
> We're heading now toward armed struggle,
> With every cadre line we write.

May you learn to struggle and fight,
Or the world will off you 'cause you're white.

Anonymous, from "Weatherman Songbook" in *Weatherman*, ed. Harold
Jacobs (Berkeley: Ramparts Press, 1970).

JOHN SINCLAIR,
LINER NOTES TO MC5'S *KICK OUT THE JAMS!*

"Kick out the jams, motherfucker!" Coming straight outta Detroit in the late 1960s, the MC5 (Motor City Five, naturally) were, to many, one of the first manifestations of what would later, in the 1970s, crystallize around the term "punk." The Five famously played a gig at the tumultuous 1968 Democratic Convention, and their manager and spokesman John Sinclair founded the White Panther Party, a political organization started as a way for White youth to show solidarity with the Black Panthers. In the MC5, however, this solidarity took an explicitly libidinal form as well, rendering them a sort of proto-punk expression of what Mailer described in "The White Negro." But there is something else going on here as well: the repeated mantra that "there is no separation" is a call to arms against the atomization of modern life that later punks will take up in their commitment to a "punk rock lifestyle" that refuses to separate music from life (and a Do-It-Yourself ethos that refused to separate producers from consumers). Nevertheless, this critique is based in some of the same racist (and sexist) assumptions of "free men" carried over from Mailer's vision of hip culture. This proto-punk lineage compels punks to ask: What kind of liberation are we after, and upon what is it predicated?

The MC5 is a whole thing. There is no way to get at the music without taking in the whole context of the music too—there is no separation. We say the MC5 is the solution to the problem of separation, because they are so together. The MC5 is totally committed to the revolution, as the revolution is totally committed to driving people out of their separate shells and into each other's arms.

I'm talking about unity, brothers and sisters, because we have to get it together. We are the solution to the problem, if we will just be that. If we can feel it, LeRoi Jones said, "feeling predicts intelligence." The MC5 will make you feel it, or leave the room. The MC5 will drive you crazy out of your head into your body. The MC5 is rock and roll. Rock and roll is the music of our bodies, of our whole lives—the resensifier, Rob Tyner calls it. We have to come together, people, "build to a gathering," or else. Or else you are dead, and gone.

The MC5 bring you back to your senses from wherever you have been taken to hide. They are bad. Their whole lives are totally given to this music. They are a whole thing. They are a working model of the new paleo-cybernetic culture in action. There is no separation. They live together to work together, they eat together, fuck together, get high together, walk down the street and through the world together. There is no separation. Just as the music will bring you together like that, if you hear it. If you will live it. And we will make sure you hear it, because we know you need it as bad as we do. We have to have it.

The music is the source and the effect of our spirit flesh. The MC5 is the source and effect of the music, just as you are. Just as I am. Just to hear the music and have it be ourselves, is what we want. What we need. We are a lonely desperate people, pulled apart by the killer forces of capitalism and competition, and we need the music to hold us together. Separation is doom. We are free men, and we demand a free music, a free high energy source that will drive us wild into the streets of America yelling and screaming and tearing down everything that would keep people slaves.

The MC5 is that source. The MC5 is the revolution, in all its applications. There is no separation. Everything is everything. There is no thing to fear. The music will make you strong, as it is strong, and there is no way it can be stopped now. All power to the people! The MC5 is here now for you to hear and see and feel now! Give it up—come together—get down, brothers and sisters, it's time to testify, and what you have in your hands is a living testimonial to the absolute power and strength of these men. Go wild! The world is yours! Take it now and be one with it! Kick out the jams, motherfucker! And stay alive with the MC5!

John Sinclair, liner notes for *Kick Out the Jams!* (New York: Elektra Entertainment, 1969).

STEVE WAKSMAN,
"KICK OUT THE JAMS!: THE MC5
AND THE POLITICS OF NOISE"

In this essay Steve Waksman brings the resources of early twenty-first-century American studies to bear on the racial and gender dynamics of the MC5. Waksman argues that the Five's conception of resistance "betrays the sort of primitivization of blackness, and of black masculinity in particular, that has characterized so many of the attempts by white European and American men to escape or transcend the constrictions of 'their' culture." What makes this primitivization so important is that it arises precisely out of a desire for solidarity gone interestingly awry, a desire that will come into play in fruitful ways as we move later into the "Punky Reggae Party." Additionally, Waksman connects the Five and the history of white countercultural appropriation of blackness to a complex analysis of the long tradition of blackface and minstrel shows, arguing that the transparent racism of applying dark-skin makeup subtly shifts into the adoption of coded signifiers that make a spectacle of otherness. Such adoption also carries over into punk rock, as tattoos, piercings, and mohawks come to signify the subculture's radical separation from the "straight world."

Rock 'n' Roll, Dope, and Fucking in the Streets

John Sinclair issued his "White Panther Statement," the official declaration of the formation of the White Panther party, in the November 14–27, 1968, issue of the *Fifth Estate*. Drawing his inspiration from the combined influences of the Black Panthers and the Yippies, he outlined a movement of "visionary maniac white mother country dope fiend rock 'n' roll freaks" who were to parallel the Black Power movement in African-American politics with their own brand of cultural revolution.[1] Stating the party's opposition to the "white honkie culture that has been handed to us on a silver plastic platter," he especially emphasized the centrality of rock 'n' roll music to the group's platform. "Rock and roll music is the spearhead of our attack because it's so effective and so much fun," proclaimed Sinclair, who further cited the MC5 as the best example of the "organic high-energy guerilla bands who are infiltrating the popular culture and destroying millions of minds in the process."[2] To conclude the statement, he called attention to the absolute centrality of black politics and black music in the formation of the White Panther program.

> The actions of the Black Panthers in America have inspired us and given us strength, as has the music of black America, and we are moving to reflect that strength in our daily activity just as our music contains and extends the power and feeling of the black magic music that originally informed our bodies and told us that we could be free.
>
> I might mention Brother James Brown in this connection, as well as John Coltrane and Archie Shepp, Sun-Ra, LeRoi Jones, Malcom X, Huey P. Newton, Bobby Seale, Eldridge Cleaver, these are magic names to us. These are men in America. And we're as crazy as they are, and as pure. We're bad.[3]

This reverence for African-American masculinity was essential to the White Panther program, and also to the music of the Five. A program from an MC5 concert dated May 10–11, 1968, betrays the pervasive presence of "black magic music" referred to by Sinclair. Among the fourteen songs on the program, six are covers of songs by black performers, while one is an original jazz piece dedicated to Archie Shepp, one of Sinclair's "men in America" and a saxophonist who was part of the Black Power movement.[4] The six covers are themselves interesting for the way they are distributed among different styles of African-American music: "Upper Egypt," originally by Pharoah Sanders, and "Tunji," by John Coltrane, drawn from the same free jazz terrain that Shepp occupied; "Stormy Monday Blues," by T-Bone Walker, and "Bad Sign (Born Under a ...)," by Albert King, which were blues numbers; "I Put a Spell on You," by Screaming Jay Hawkins, and "I Believe It to My Soul," by Ray Charles, soul or rhythm and blues pieces. What linked these disparate styles for the Five was their high energy, and a sensibility that represented to the band a subversion of the "white honkie culture" and an affirmation of a new aesthetic and political order founded upon the celebration of bodily pleasure.

That this return to the body was to be led by "pure" black men and that one of its goals was to reconstruct white men as sexually charged "rock 'n' roll guerillas" does not speak well for the Five's revolutionary vision. Indeed, it betrays the sort of primitivization of blackness, and of black masculinity in particular, that has characterized so many of the attempts by white European and American men to escape or transcend the constrictions of "their" culture. Frantz Fanon has described how black maleness has been reduced historically not only to a body but to a penis, which is in turn amplified to superhuman proportions. Marianna Torgovnick, in turn, has discussed the ways in which "the idiom 'going primitive' is in fact congruent in many ways to the idiom 'getting physical.'" Fascination with the primitive "other" works to overcome "alienation from the body, restoring the body, and hence the self, to a relation of full and easy harmony with nature or the cosmos, as they have been variously conceived."[5] In this relationship, white men colonize the body of the "other" to resolve the split between mind and body that has been enforced by the civilizing process.[6]

Indeed, Sinclair and the MC5 seemed to believe that it was only through the appropriation of black masculinity that white men could become any kind of men at all. The Five's attitude paralleled that branch of 1960s radicalism that claimed the consumer-driven technocratic order had emasculated American manhood. Although Barbara Ehrenreich, among others, has called attention to the "androgynous drift" of countercultural masculinity,[7] Todd Gitlin has discussed the strong masculinist impulse that underlay so much of the New Left and the counterculture. Describing a 1967 SDS meeting that was crashed by members of San Francisco's anarchistic Diggers, Gitlin recalls the confrontational display enacted by Digger Emmett Grogan:

> He leaped down, kicked over the table, smashed down a chair. He knocked down a woman and slapped around some others, or went through the stage motions—accounts disagree. "Faggots! Fags! Take off your ties, they are chains around your necks. You haven't got the balls to go mad. You're gonna make a revolution?—you'll piss in your pants when the violence erupts. You, spade—you're a nigger, what are you doing here? Your people need you …" Grogan unrolled a scroll of wrapping paper, declaimed a poem by Gary Snyder called "A Curse on the Men in the Pentagon, Washington, D.C.," including the line, "I hunt the white man down / in my heart."[8]

The masculinist program of action performed by Grogan strongly parallels that of the MC5 with its denigration of passive, tie-wearing men, who came to stand for white masculinity in general. Gitlin goes on to explain how, as the movement turned toward a "revolutionary vision," the Black Panthers ascended to models of action for white men in the movement.

> If revolution was imminent, the black underclass, rioting in the streets, were the plausible cadres. Who seemed to represent those specters better than Huey Newton, Bobby Seale, and Eldridge Cleaver, these intelligent brothers in black leather jackets, James Dean and Frantz Fanon rolled into one, the very image of indigenous revolutionary leadership risen from the underclass and certified in prison?[9]

Where Gitlin provides substance for noting the connections between the MC5's fascination with black manhood and that of the political and countercultural movement at large, his allusion to the specter of the rioting black underclass should also force us back into a recognition of the specificity of this fascination within the context of Detroit. The Detroit riot of July 1967 was among the deadliest of the 1960s, with a death toll of over forty. Local authorities witnessed the event with fear, but radicals like John Sinclair adopted a far different perspective. Writing in the *Fifth Estate* during the immediate aftermath of the "Rebellion," Sinclair described the action as a ritual of purification, and went on to assert: "No, baby, it's not a 'race riot,' or anything as simple as that. People just got tired of being hassled by police and cheated by businessmen and got out their equalizers and went to town ... Oh it was Robin Hood Day in merry olde Detroit, the first annual city-wide all-free fire sale, and the people without got their hands on the goodies."[10] Sinclair's imagination was clearly stoked by the spectacle of unrest, yet his rejection of the simple classification "race riot" was likely more than a rhetorical flourish; Gitlin provides corroborating evidence that the events in Detroit were an integrated affair.[11] Furthermore, Eric Ehrmann, in profiling the MC5 for *Rolling Stone*, described a pact between the city's white and black militants "to stick up for each other," a pact that Sinclair himself was instrumental in engineering.[12] Given the dispute between Sinclair and Black Panther William Leach, one hesitates to conclude that there was a secure alliance between Detroit's countercultural enclave and the black community. If nothing else, though, what we can locate in Sinclair's words is a desire for a connection to exist between the two communities, a desire that became in the "White Panther Statement" a longing to participate in the black revolution itself, and to follow an aesthetic and political path that black men had already charted.

Given the political context of the time, Chuck Eddy's "half-truthful" association of the MC5's music with a riotous Detroit gains in symbolic truth-value what it might lack as a statement of fact. If the Five's music was not literally produced during the riots, it certainly gained much of its definition from the racial unrest that characterized Detroit during the mid-to-late 1960s. The MC5's music certainly can be taken as a response to the political imperative felt by Gitlin, Sinclair, and other white activists during the 1960s in the face of black political activity, an imperative articulated by Gitlin with the simple question: "What does Whitey do?"[13] Yet this perspective only takes us so far in understanding their music, which arose out of a broader mix of influences than any reference to the riots can explain. Furthermore, the band's and Sinclair's attraction to black music predated the riots, and was rooted in patterns of racial and sexual desire that extend well beyond the 1960s.

Insight into these patterns can be gleaned from Eric Lott's study of minstrelsy, *Love and Theft*. Seeking to move beyond the notion that blackface minstrelsy arose solely out of twin white impulses to denigrate blackness and capitalize upon that denigration, Lott locates in the form evidence of a "profound white investment in black culture" that cannot be explained as mere racism.[14] More specifically, Lott identifies in minstrelsy "a gendered pattern of exchange, a kind of commerce between men" motivated by a "complex dynamic" in which white performers' tendency to dominate black maleness "coexisted with or indeed depended on a self-conscious attraction to the black men it was the job of these performers to mimic."[15] The putting on of blackface also involved putting on a particular style of masculinity, one in which the qualities thought to belong to black men—"cool, virility, humility, abandon, or *gaité de coeur*"—were transferred.[16] According to Lott, the sexual envy that motivated this homosocial exchange betrayed a sort of homoerotic desire on the part of white men; the desire to have the black man's qualities slid easily if uncomfortably into the desire to have the black man, with the ambivalence between economic and sexual possession residing in the word "have."

Although Lott's analysis is centered upon minstrelsy as an antebellum form, he makes a convincing case that these modes of homosocial exchange laid the foundation for the subsequent history of relations between white bohemians and African-American culture. The MC5 and the many legions of other white musicians who drew from African-American culture no longer literalized the putting on of blackness through the application of blackface, but did adopt other signifiers to mark the exchange (especially hair, in the case of the Five).[17] However, I would argue that it was primarily by strapping on electric guitars, and in their use of technology more generally, that groups like the Five most clearly reproduced the logic of blackface. In his original liner notes for *Kick Out the Jams*, John Sinclair outlined a philosophy based upon the principle "Separation Is Doom," in which he stressed the Five's status as a "*whole thing*":

> There is no way to get at the music without taking in the whole context of the music too—*there is no separation*. We say the MC5 is the solution to the problem of separation, because they are *so together*. The MC5 is totally committed to the revolution, as the revolution is totally committed to driving people out of their separate shells and into each other's arms

I'm talking about *unity*, brothers and sisters, because we have to *get it together*. We *are* the solution to the problem, if we will just *be* that. If we can *feel* it, LeRoi Jones said, "Feeling Predicts Intelligence." The MC5 will make you feel it, or leave the room. The MC5 will drive you crazy out of your head into your body. The MC5 *is* rock and roll. Rock and roll *is* the music of our bodies, of our whole lives—the "resensifier," Rob Tyner calls it. We have to *come together*, people, "build to a gathering," or else. Or else we are dead, and gone.[18]

Consider alongside this statement of purpose the MC5 song "Come Together," alluded to by Sinclair. Bearing no resemblance to the Beatles song of the same name (which was, in any case, released over a year later), "Come Together" was an explicit expression of the band's program of union through the musical enactment of orgasm. As with "Rocket Reducer No. 62," the song is characterized above all by an excess of volume and noise and by its unchanging harmonic structure: a single note struck for several beats, followed by two massive power chords, repeat throughout the course of the song without interruption. No guitar solos here; the band operates as a "whole thing" while Rob Tyner intermittently shouts vocals punctuated by the line "Together in the darkness," a line multiply inflected by the sexual and political command of the song's title. Any sense of variation comes from subtle shifts in the level of loudness; the thunderous density of the band's attack eases as Tyner announces that "it's getting closer … God it's so close now" with a voice that sounds pained with anticipation. The volume rises once again while the song rushes into its concluding gasp toward togetherness, ending with a progression of chords that ascends and then lunges back downward while becoming increasingly out of tune, the blur of the drums and the whirr of the feedback further contributing to the heightened disorder that immediately precedes the song's finish.

The prioritization of volume in this song, the way in which loudness was to provoke bodily excitement and changes in the level of noise provided the friction, if you will, that was to bring this excitement to its climax, lead us further into the MC5's aesthetic and political program. More specifically, it is here that we come to the Five's principles of high energy music as a tool of cultural revolution. For the band, the revolutionary potential of their music lay in its presumed ability to drive people "into their bodies," to provoke what Rob Tyner called "purification and resensification on all levels. Resensify you back to your meat, because that's the way you take it in. Your meat is your senses, because your senses are made out of meat. And if you don't keep in contact with your meat ... that's why all these straight people are so fucked up, man, 'cause they let their meat loaf—and it just rots, it rots."[19] Rock 'n' roll as an assault upon straight society might seem like the most naïve sort of sixties idealism, yet there is also in Tyner's statement a powerful recognition of civilization and its discontents. Here the primitivism that underlay the band's reverence for black manhood comes back into play: if straight, civilized society required the dissociation of mind and body and the sublimation of physical pleasure, the Five would counter this system with a sonic assault on the senses that would, ideally, rid the body of its civilized trappings and return it to a purity of sensation that had long been lost.

Bodily pleasure, then, was not an end in itself for the MC5. Instead, the band's music was motivated by an impulse very similar to that described by Norman Mailer in his notorious essay, "The White Negro." According to Mailer, the white negro, or hipster, is a sort of psychopath seeking to resolve "those mutually contradictory inhibitions upon violence and love which civilization has exacted of us."[20] Refusing the negative associations of psychopathy, Mailer finds the hipster/psychopath especially adapted to the tensions of modern life, and defines the project of the hipster in terms that foreshadow the Five's own brand of sensual politics:

> What characterizes almost every psychopath and part-psychopath [and thus every hipster, according to Mailer's logic] is that they are trying to create a new nervous system for themselves. Generally we are obliged to act with a nervous system which has been formed from infancy, and which carries in the style of its circuits the very contradictions of our parents and our early milieu. Therefore, we are obliged, most of us, to meet the tempo of the present and the future with reflexes and rhythms which come from the past. It is not only the "dead weight of the institutions of the past" but indeed the inefficient and often antiquated nervous circuits of the past which strangle our potentiality for responding to new possibilities which might be exciting for our individual growth.[21]

Like Mailer's hipster, the MC5 sought to escape the reflexes and rhythms of the past for a new mode of response. The desire to restore the body to a condition of purity, then, was not only a longing for primal return but also a vision of new possibilities for the future. Blackness, meanwhile, is crucial to this scenario; for both Mailer and the Five located the model for these potentials of bodily experience in the "super-sensuality" of black men ...[22]

Steve Waksman, from "Kick Out the Jams! The MC5 and the Politics of Noise," *Instruments of Desire: The Electric Guitar and the Shaping of Musical Experience* (Cambridge: Harvard University Press, 1999).

PATTI SMITH,
LINER NOTES TO "ROCK 'N' ROLL NIGGER"

Patti Smith remains one of the most influential punk singers of all time, and her third album, *Easter*, released in 1978, contains both her most famous tune, "Because the Night," and her most infamous, "Rock 'N' Roll Nigger." In the track, Smith envisions a redefinition of the word "nigger," framing it as a badge of honor for anyone "outside of society," including Jimi Hendrix, Jackson Pollock, "Jesus Christ and Grandma, too." For Smith, being a "nigger" was first and foremost about aesthetic transgression and mutation—a position she extends to the conventions of language itself in the liner notes we present below. Art's (and punk's) transgression sets one apart from society, marks one as "other," and this is a phenomenon that, for Smith, transcends one's given race or religion. As she writes:

nigger no invented color it was MADE FOR THE PLAGUE the word (art) must be redefined—all mutants and the new babes born sans eyebrow and tonsil—outside logic—beyond mathmatics poli-tricks baptism and motion sickness—any man who extends beyond the classic form is a nigger—one sans fear and despair—one who rises like rimbaud beating hard gold rythymn outta soft solid shit-tongue light is coiling serpant is steaming spinal avec ray gun hissing scanning copper head w/white enamel eye wet and shining crown reeling thru gleem vegetation ruby dressing of thy lips puckering whispering pressing high bruised thighs silk route mark prussian vibrating gushing milk pods of de/light translating new languages new and abused rock 'n' roll and love lashing from the tongue of me nigger.

Patti Smith, from liner notes to *Easter* (New York: Arista Records, 1978).

DICK HEBDIGE,
"BLEACHED ROOTS: PUNKS
AND WHITE ETHNICITY"

Published in 1979 at the height of punk's mainstream saturation in the United Kingdom, Dick Hebdige's *Subculture: The Meaning of Style* **remains one of the founding texts of cultural studies. Applying the semiotic theory of, among others, Roland Barthes to the developing cultural phenomenon, Hebdige in this section examines the dynamics of race as they manifest themselves in British punk. In Britain, punk arose partly through a rejection of commercially successful white glam rock and an encounter and subsequent identification with Black reggae and dub. In reggae's explicitly political and oppositional language and themes, punks found ways to articulate a version of their own outsiderdom, to remake their own White ethnicity in opposition to the dominant culture of '70s Britain. There's a problem, however, with this cross-cultural identification: White British punks have a different cultural language, a different future, a different past, and a different skin color than their Caribbean and Caribbean British counterparts. As such, Hebdige argues in an oft-quoted sentence, "at the heart of the punk subculture, forever arrested, lies this frozen dialectic between black and white cultures—a dialectic which beyond a certain point (i.e., ethnicity) is incapable of renewal, trapped, as it is, within its own history, imprisoned within its own irreducible antinomies."**

… Punk's guttersnipe rhetoric, its obsession with class and relevance were expressly designed to undercut the intellectual posturing of the previous generation of rock musicians. This reaction in its turn directed the new wave towards reggae and the associated styles which the glam rock cult had originally excluded. Reggae attracted those punks who wished to give tangible form to their alienation. It carried the necessary conviction, the political bite, so obviously missing in most contemporary white music.

Dread, in particular, was an enviable commodity. It was the means with which to menace, and the elaborate free-masonry through which it was sustained and communicated on the street—the colours, the locks, the patois—was awesome and forbidding, suggesting as it did an impregnable solidarity, an asceticism born of suffering. The concept of dread provided a key to a whole secret language: an exotic semantic interior which was irrevocably closed against white Christian sympathies (i.e., blacks are just like us) while its very existence confirmed the worst white chauvinist fears (i.e., blacks are nothing like us).

But paradoxically it was here, in the exclusiveness of Black West Indian style, in the virtual impossibility of authentic white identification, that reggae's attraction for the punks was strongest. As we have seen, the clotted language of Rastafarianism was deliberately opaque. It had grown out of patois, and patois itself had been spoken for centuries beneath the Master's comprehension. This was a language capable of piercing the most respectfully inclined white ear, and the themes of Back to Africa and Ethiopianism, celebrated in reggae, made no concessions to the sensibilities of a white audience. Reggae's blackness was proscriptive. It was an alien essence, a foreign body which implicitly threatened mainstream British culture from within[1] and as such it resonated with punk's adopted values—"anarchy," "surrender" and "decline."

For the punks to find a positive meaning in such a blatant disavowal of Britishness amounted to a symbolic act of treason which complemented, indeed completed, the sacrilegious programme undertaken in punk rock itself (c.f. the Sex Pistols' "Anarchy in the U.K." and "God Save the Queen," Jordan's rendition of "Rule Britannia" in Derek Jarman's film *Jubilee*). The punks capitulated to alienation, losing themselves in the unfamiliar contours of an alien form. In this way, the very factors which had dictated the skinheads' withdrawal in the late '60s facilitated the punks' involvement a decade later. Just as the mod and skinhead styles had obliquely reproduced the "cool" look and feel of the West Indian rude boys and were symbolically placed in the same ideal milieux (the Big City, the violent slum), so the punk aesthetic can be read in part as a white "translation" of black "ethnicity."

This parallel white "ethnicity" was defined through contradictions. On the one hand it centered, however iconoclastically, on traditional notions of Britishness (the Queen, the Union Jack, etc.). It was "local." It emanated from the recognizable locales of Britain's inner cities. It spoke in city accents. And yet, on the other hand, it was predicated upon a denial of place. It issued out of nameless housing estates, anonymous dole queues, slums-in-the-abstract. It was blank, expressionless, rootless. In this the punk subculture can be contrasted against the West Indian styles which had provided the basic models. Whereas urban black youths could place themselves through reggae "beyond the pale" in an imagined elsewhere (Africa, the West Indies) the punks were tied to present time. They were bound to a Britain which had no foreseeable future.

But this difference could be magically elided. By simple sleight of hand, the co-ordinates of time and place could be dissolved, transcended, converted into signs. Thus it was that the punks turned towards the world a dead white face which was there and yet not "there." Like the myths of Roland Barthes, these "murdered victims"—emptied and inert—also had an alibi, and elsewhere, literally "made up" out of Vaseline and cosmetics, hair dye and mascara. But paradoxically, in the case of the punks, this "elsewhere" was also a nowhere—a twilight zone—a zone constituted out of negativity. Like André Breton's Dada, punk might seem to "open all the doors" but these doors "gave onto a circular corridor."[2]

Once inside this desecrated circle, punk was forever condemned to act out alienation, to mime its imagined condition, to manufacture a whole series of subjective correlatives for the official archetypes of the "crisis of modern life": the unemployment figures, the Depression, the Westway, Television, etc. Converted into icons (the safety pin, the rip, the mindless lean and hungry look) these paradigms of crisis could live a double life, at once fictional and real. They reflected in a heightened form a perceived condition: a condition of unmitigated exile, voluntarily assumed. But whereas exile had a specific meaning, implied a specific (albeit magical) solution in the context of Rastafarianism and Negro history, when applied metaphorically to British white youth it could only delineate a hopeless condition. It could neither promise a future nor explain a past. Trapped in the paradox of "divine" subordination like Saint Genet,[3] who "chooses" the Fate which has been bestowed upon him, the punks dissembled, dying to recreate themselves in caricature, to "dress up" their Destiny in its true colours, to substitute the diet for hunger,[4] to slide the ragamuffin look ("unkempt" but meticulously coutured) between poverty and elegance. Punk, having found an adequate reflection in the shards of broken glass, having spoken through the holes in purposefully torn tee-shirts, having brought dishonour on the family name[5], found itself again at the point from which it had started: as a "lifer" in "solitary" despite the fierce tattoos.

These contradictions were literally re-presented in the form of punk's association with reggae. At one level, the punks openly acknowledged the significance of contact and exchange, and on occasion even elevated the cultural connection into a political commitment. Punk groups for instance, figured prominently in the Rock Against Racism campaign set up to combat the growing influence of the National Front in working-class areas.[6] But at another, deeper level, the association seems to have been repressed, displaced on the part of the punks into the construction of a music which was emphatically white and even more emphatically British.

In the event, certain features were lifted directly from the black West Indian rude and Rasta styles. For example, one of the characteristic punk hair-styles consisting of a petrified mane held in a state of vertical tension by means of Vaseline, lacquer or soap, approximated to the black "natty" or dreadlock styles. Some punks wore Ethiopian colours and the Rasta rhetoric began to work its way into the repertoires of some punk groups. The Clash and the Slits in particular wove reggae slogans and themes into their material, and in 1977 the reggae group Culture produced a song describing the impending apocalypse entitled "Two Sevens Clash," which became something of a catchphrase in select punk circles. Some groups (e.g., the Clash, Alternative T.V.) incorporated reggae numbers into their sets and a new hybrid form—punk dub[7]—grew out of the liaison. From the outset, when the first punks began to congregate at the Roxy Club in London's Covent Garden, heavy reggae had occupied a privileged position inside the subculture as the only tolerated alternative to punk, providing melodic relief from the frantic *Sturm und Drang* of new wave music. Partly for reasons of expediency (i.e., in the early days there was no recorded punk music) and partly through choice (because reggae was obviously "rebel music") the more esoteric Jamaican imports were played regularly in many punk clubs in the intervals between live acts.

The punks' open identification with black British and West Indian culture served to antagonize the teddy boy revivalists, and the ted/punk battles played out every Saturday afternoon along the King's Road in the summer of 1977 provided spectacular evidence of the fundamental tension between the two subcultures. As early as 5 July, Rockin' Mick, a 19-year-old teddy boy (fluorescent socks, black suede creepers and jacket emblazoned with the legends "Confederate Rock" and "Gene Vincent lives") was expressing his disgust for the punks' lack of patriotism to an *Evening Standard* reporter, adding, "We're not against the blacks, let's just say we're not with them ..." (5 July 1977).

However, despite the strong affinity, the integrity of the two forms—punk and reggae—was scrupulously maintained, and far from simulating reggae's form and timbre, punk music, like every other aspect of punk style, tended to develop in direct antithesis to its apparent sources. Reggae and punk were audibly opposed. Where punk depended on the treble, reggae relied on the bass. Where punk launched frontal assaults on the established meaning systems, reggae communicated through ellipsis and allusion. Indeed, the way in which the two forms were rigorously, almost wilfully segregated would seem to direct us towards a concealed identity, which in turn can be used to illuminate larger patterns of interaction between immigrant and host communities. To use a term from semiotics, we could say that punk includes reggae as a "present absence"—a black hole around which punk composes itself. This can be extended metaphorically to wider issues of race and race relations. Thus we could say that the rigid demarcation of the line between punk rock and reggae is symptomatic not only of an "identity crisis" peculiar to the punk subculture but also of those more general contradictions and tensions which inhibit the development of an open dialogue between an immigrant culture with a strong "ethnic" character and the indigenous working-class culture which technically "encloses" it.

We can now return to consider the meaning of that uneasy relation between rock and reggae characteristic of punk. We have seen how punk's belligerent insistence on class and relevance was at least partly determined by the ethereal excesses of the glam rock cult, and that the particular form this insistence took (the vagrant aesthetic, a singular music) was also indirectly influenced by the subcultural styles of the black immigrant community. This dialectical movement from white to black and back again is by no means solely confined to the punk subculture. On the contrary … the same movement is "captured" and displayed in the styles of each of the spectacular post-war, working-class youth cultures. More particularly, it runs through rock music (and earlier, jazz) from the mid-'50s onwards, dictating each successive shift in rhythm, style and lyrical content. We are now in a position to describe this dialectic.

As the music and the various subcultures it supports or reproduces assume rigid and identifiable patterns, so new subcultures are created which demand or produce corresponding mutations in musical form. These mutations in their turn occur at those moments when forms and themes imported from contemporary black music break up (or "over-determine") the existing musical structure and force its elements into new configurations. For instance, the stabilization of rock in the early '60s (vapid high school bop, romantic ballads, gimmicky instrumentals) encouraged the mods to migrate to soul and ska, and the subsequent reaffirmation of black themes and rhythms by white r&b and soul bands[8] contributed to the resurgence of rock in the mid-'60s. Similarly, at the moment when glam rock had exhausted the permutations available within its own distinctive structure of concerns, the punks moved back to the earlier, more vigorous forms of rock (i.e., to the '50s and mid-'60s, when the black influences had been strongest)[9] and forward to contemporary reggae (dub, Bob Marley) in order to find a music which reflected more adequately their sense of frustration and oppression.

However, here as elsewhere in punk, the mutation seems deliberate, constructed. Perhaps, given the differences between them, there can be no easy synthesis of the two languages of rock and reggae. The fundamental lack of fit between these two languages (dress, dance, speech, music, drugs, style, history) exposed in the emergence of black ethnicity in reggae, generates a peculiarly unstable dynamic within the punk subculture. This tension gave punk its curiously petrified quality, its paralysed look, its "dumbness" which found a silent voice in the smooth moulded surfaces of rubber and plastic, in the bondage and robotics which signify "punk" to the world. For, at the heart of the punk subculture, forever arrested, lies this frozen dialectic between black and white cultures—a dialectic which beyond a certain point (i.e., ethnicity) is incapable of renewal, trapped, as it is, within its own history, imprisoned within its own irreducible antinomies.

Dick Hebdige, from "Bleached Roots: Punks and White Ethnicity," *Subculture: The Meaning of Style* (London: Routledge, 1988).

THREE

WHITE MINORITY

> We're gonna be a white minority
> We won't listen to the majority
> We're gonna feel inferiority
> We're gonna be a white minority
>
> White pride
> You're an American
> I'm gonna hide
> Anywhere I can
> —"White Minority," Black Flag

How to make sense of Black Flag's "White Minority"? Is the 1980 hardcore song a racist call to arms that Whites are becoming a minority in Southern California, or is Black Flag parodying White fears? Is articulating whiteness though punk rock a racist gesture, or an honest acknowledgment of a racial identity in an increasingly ethnically heterogeneous society? Who is the "we," the "you," and the "I" of the song, and who is the audience supposed to identify with? Finally, are the answers to all these questions complicated by the fact that the lead singer and drummer for Black Flag at the time were both Latinos and the producer of the song was black? It's hard to make sense of the racial politics of "White Minority" through the simple prism of White/Other or racist/antiracist ... and that's exactly what makes the song, and the context that produced it, so interesting.

In the mid 1970s to early 1980s, concurrent with the rise of punk rock, White supremacy in the United States and Britain was being contested politically, culturally, and demographically. Whites in these countries could no longer live the fantasy of universality, wherein White is the given and everything else is Other, particularly not in cities like Los Angeles, New York, and London. No longer assumed as universal, whiteness began to be articulated as a conscious subject position. But this position was unsettled and volatile, finding versions of itself expressed in both the rising tide of liberal political correctness as well as the conservative revolutions of Thatcher and Reagan. Distancing themselves from both these options, punks staked out a terrain of whiteness that attempted to defy simple categorizations like liberal or conservative, tolerant or bigoted.

In punk, whiteness became something to be discussed and demonstrated; its definition, however, remained elusive. This undecided and oppositional quality of punk whiteness led cultural and political critics, from both ends of the spectrum, to define punk's racial politics in ways that made sense to them, but punk itself eluded such easy categorization. For the first wave of New York and London punks, symbols of starkly racist whiteness were mobilized for shock value; for the hardcore band Black Flag, whiteness was something to be ridiculed; for Minor Threat and the Fuck-Ups, whites were under attack; for bands like X, the White race had become merely one among many; and for Sham 69, race took a backseat to categories like youth and class. Punk whiteness at that moment and under these circumstances was inchoate and ambiguous: it was self-conscious, dejected, oppositional, and anxiety-ridden, with its political content still up for grabs. Yet it's important to remember that race, even hazily defined, has salience: redefining whiteness didn't release punks from the White race's place and privilege.

Nevertheless it's an opening. Forced to acknowledge their own racial history and specificity, it's a moment of opportunity for White punks to forge an oppositional whiteness against dominant definitions. In this context, Black Flag's lyrics, "We're gonna be a white minority / We won't listen to the majority," take on new meaning.

STEVEN LEE BEEBER, "HOTSY-TOTSY NAZI SCHATZES: NAZI IMAGERY AND THE FINAL SOLUTION TO THE FINAL SOLUTION"

In this selection Steven Beeber makes the provocative claim that punk, in its early New York iteration, was an extension of characteristically Jewish cultural tropes, and further, that without the historical experience of the Holocaust, punk rock as we know it

simply would not be. The locus of both of these arguments lies, for Beeber, in the New York punks' appropriation of Nazi imagery and, in particular, the swastika. Situated in the context of proto-punk provocateurs like Lenny Bruce, New York punk comes out as a struggle over the meaning of Jewishness. This, interestingly, takes the question of "race" out of the traditional White/Other binary, constituting "a rebellion against the Jewish desire to be taken seriously by the predominant culture." The singularity of this as a cultural moment cannot be overstated, since, as we will see, the use of the swastika in the British context turns out to be something interestingly different from "Jewish revenge." However, this intro-duces a valuable new thread: a subtle turn from a sincere White appropriation of non-White cultures into an aesthetics of shock, in which appropriations of extreme whiteness are refigured as ironic signs of a countercultural ethnic identity that isn't quite White.

Author's Note: *According to rumor, the following scene is true. While I can make no definitive statement as to its veracity, I heard it from at least two highly placed sources who prefer to remain nameless. Understandably.*

In a bedroom somewhere in the East Village, Chris Stein and Debbie Harry are making love, a Nazi flag beneath them, its red backdrop in perfect counterpoint to her blonde hair.

Meanwhile, in another apartment nearby, Dead Boys lead singer Stiv Bators and his Jewish girlfriend Cynthia Ross are doing the same, her equally blonde hair splayed out against the black swastika in the middle, its bent arms radiating around her face in *sieg heil*–like salutes.

And not far from there, Stiv's bandmate Cheetah Chrome is similarly engaged on his Nazi-flag bedspread with his half-Jewish girlfriend Gyda Gash, her dyed-blonde hair free from its vintage *Feldkommandant's* cap that goes so well with her matching tattoos of a Jewish star and the word *STIGMATA*.

Is it surprising to find so many punk principals involved in the same pursuit? Everyone knows that the punks were attracted to the dark side, and that they liked to shock their audiences both onstage and off. But what to make of the fact that in each of these instances, one of the par-ticipants is Jewish—at least in part? Both Chris Stein and Cynthia Ross had Jewish parents, and Gyda "Braverman" Gash had a Jewish father and Catholic mother.

Moreover, what to make of that other punk couple, Sid 'n' Nancy, he of the swastika T-shirts and she of the Jewish family in the Philly suburbs? Or of the five Jewish guys in the Dictators who played "Master Race Rock"? And don't forget early punk champion and child of Holocaust survivors Genya Ravan, or Dictators' press secretary and fellow child of a Holocaust survivor, Camilla Saly. Or Lou Reed and the iron crosses shaved into his hair, Jonathan Richman and his song about trains going through the Jewish suburbs of Scarsdale and New Rochelle, and Daniel Rey (Rabinowitz) and his band Shrapnel. Is there something sinister at work here? Something horrific? Something camp, perhaps? Say, concentration camp?

As we'll see, it's a mixture of all of these things. While the various punk responses to the Holocaust range from the mocking to the shocking to the world-rocking, as in the impulse to identify with the oppressors, each is in its own way an attempt to deal with this tragedy that affected the punks' lives whether they like to admit it or not. No Holocaust, no punk. As many a Jewish parent had pointed out to his or her dismissive child, it didn't matter whether you were religiously Jewish, culturally so, or completely apathetic about the link—it didn't even matter whether you were Jewish at all: if you had one Jewish grandparent, that was enough to get you gassed in Nazi Germany. Christ, even one *great*-grandparent could do it sometimes. You could scream and cry all you wanted, but it made no difference. The field of red and the white circle surrounding the black swastika in the middle would get you. It would put the agony to your ecstasy. Its purifying fire would burn you to your very core.

Even if you weren't worried about what might have happened to you in Nazi Germany, the Holocaust had an impact on you as a Jewish punk. As Andy Shernoff observed, it made you embarrassed that you were descended from a people who had allowed themselves to be so victimized. That's why he and others were so proud when Israel beat the combined forces of four Arab nations in the Six-Day War, and why folks like Chris Stein collected Nazi memorabilia even after they made it as stars. It was not to glorify their oppressors but to show that, as Debbie Harry explained, "he had won, the Jews had won."

Of course, the thrill of breaking taboos did play a part. When Chris Stein and his best friend, Glenn O'Brien—editor of *Interview* magazine and for a number of years in the late 1970s co-creator and host with Chris of the local cable access show *TV Party*—were on their way home from the airport, where Chris had just picked up a specially delivered ceremonial sword of Himmler's, Chris suggested that they should stop at a synagogue to "see how everyone would react." O'Brien says, "He seemed to think that it would be funny to stop at a synagogue. He had a weird gleam in his eye." ...

The combined elements of horror and satire that undermined the social order were as Jewish as they were New York as they were punk. ...

In both *MAD* magazine and the comedy of Lenny Bruce—not to mention to a lesser degree in the spiels of contemporary Jewish "humorists" such as Mort Sahl and Shelly Berman—this loud, irritated funniness that satirized social proprieties and institutions was fed by a larger distrust of governments, legal systems, and even history. Bruce attacked everything from the Catholic Church to the liberal Democrats of the Kennedy administration to the "authorized" purveyors of the story of the Holocaust in an effort to make his audience look below the surface, because he felt that civilization was drowning in hypocrisy. Whether he was simply attempting to make light of the *Shoa* so as to ease its horror, or attacking those who had begun to use it to promote a political agenda (chiefly in Israel), Bruce employed humor to undermine the accepted norms, a Jewish response throughout millennia of living on the fringes of society that was exaggerated all the more in the period following the Holocaust.

As distance in time provided the psychological and political safety to address the Holocaust more directly, it, like any other historical event, was interpreted variously, sometimes for competing purposes. Intellectuals such as Hannah Arendt saw in it an example of the "banality of evil"—the ability of shallow bureaucratic humans to commit murder dispassionately whether they were Jewish or not. Zionists saw in it a rationale for the establishment and defense of Israel, a Jewish state that would put the safety and interests of Jews first. Bruce saw the Holocaust as merely another in a long line of crimes against humanity perpetrated by humans of every stripe. In one of his most controversial bits he makes an analogy between (1) the Holocaust, (2) the Allies' fire-bombing of Dresden, and (3) America's use of atomic bombs in Japan. As he says, affecting an exaggerated accent in the spirit of Dr. Strangelove: "My name is Adolf Eichmann. And the Jews came every day to what they thought would be fun in the showers. People say I should have been hung. *Nein*. Do you recognize the whore in the middle of you—that you would have done the same if you were there yourselves? ... Do you people think yourselves better because you burned your enemies at long distance with missiles without ever seeing what you had done to them? Hiroshima *auf wiedersehen*."

Clearly not everyone's cup of methadone, but for a generation that was increasingly hearing—in after-school Hebrew classes, synagogue sermons, and movies such as *The Pawnbroker* (1965)—about the evils done to its people at the hands of others, it was a message that was felt, absorbed, and to a certain degree openly acknowledged. For if one is raised to see the Nazis as the enemy and the Jews as the good guys (not to mention the victims), when it comes time to rebel, who are you going to side with? Especially when it is the nature of your people to examine the position of the outsider, the maligned other rejected by the status quo, the enemy of the state? If you're a Jew, and the Jewish and non-Jewish powers-that-be tell you the Nazis are bad, then aren't you going to want to mess with that dynamic a bit? Like Lenny Bruce, aren't you going to want to throw it in their faces for shock value at the very least? Aren't you going to want to upset them as much as you can—just as a generation made up of your older siblings had done by adopting the rhetoric and slogans of the communists so despised by all (including Jewish parents who were often embarrassed by their own parents' socialist pasts)? Furthermore, aren't you going to want something even stronger, considering that most of those former radicals were already becoming fine, upstanding New Age Yuppies? Where had all the Yippies gone with their self-right-eousness, their revolution, their hopes for a brighter future? There was no future. And you, their younger siblings, were tired of hearing about the fascist state of Amerika. You were ready to attack *everything*, while perhaps buying bulletproof vests for the cops. You were ready to adopt the look and attitudes of the fascists, no matter how complicated, simpleminded, or ill-guided your motivations might have been.

This trend emerged in the late 1960s, in England, the only place where a swastika might be as disturbing to non-Jewish parents as to Jewish ones. Here, with the Rolling Stones, the first widely circulated images of rock stars in Nazi uniform appear. Brian Jones and his German girlfriend, Anita Pallenberg, did it first, followed by Keith Richards, now the para-mour of the lovely Anita, Keith Moon of the Who, and Ozzy Osbourne of Black Sabbath, to name just a few. All these bad boys of the British Inva-sion shared a historical background that had been turned upside down by the war. As any historian—or moviegoer (see John Boorman's *Hope and Glory*, 1987)—knows, before the Second World War the sun never set on the British Empire, vast swaths of the globe colored in that most royal of colors, pink. When the Germans finished off the job they had begun in the First World War, however, draining the British of their capital reserves and the will to fight uprisings across their domain, the empire all but crumbled overnight. Suddenly, England was reduced to a single, ration-hungry, bombed-out, gray island that throughout the 1950s was ruled by gangster youths and hooligans, many of whom, being Jewish, were not even "real" Brits (more on this to come). In reply to an upper-crust gent's indignant comment, "I fought the war for your sort," one of the original Brit invaders, Ringo Starr, said, "I bet you wish you hadn't won."

It isn't such a leap from here to Johnny Rotten's screaming "Belsen Was a Gas," while his loutish bassist Sid Vicious carved swastikas into his chest. With two hundred years of world domination destroyed by the Nazis it's not surprising that the wild—and perhaps disappointed—children of those who "won the war but lost the peace" might rebel in the very way that would hurt their parents most—by identifying with the enemy and in many cases adopting the same enemy's philosophy. ...

Before we get into New York punk's connection to Nazi themes, let's look back just once more—this time at pre-punk America. The Rolling Stones, among the first to adopt Nazi regalia on a large scale, were here imitated by less well known yet ultimately equally influential bands such as the Stooges, adored by punk impresario Danny Fields, and later, the Blue Öyster Cult, so important to the burgeoning New York rock scene.

In the case of the Stooges, the impulses are closer to those that emerged in England—economic dissatisfaction at the closing of auto plants around their native Detroit. Like the Dead Boys of Ohio, another punk Rust Belt band, the Stooges came from largely Slavic and German communities devastated by the loss of economic stability. Think Michael Moore without a camera (or liberal education) to fall back on, and you might have some idea of the types who made up the Stooges and later on the Dead Boys. These dead-end kids were the stooges (punks?) of industry, with nothing to look forward to in the postindustrial, postwar era. They were suddenly as obsolete as Henry Ford's Model T—and Ford itself was rapidly losing ground to that other Axis power, Japan. Meanwhile, they saw Jewish families in well-to-do suburbs around Detroit like Farmington Hills and West Bloomfield and their anger boiled over. As Ron Asheton says in the revised edition of *Please Kill Me* (1997), describing Iggy's—and later his—propensity to date Jewish girls, "He had this whole thing of hooking up with rich Jewish girls. He had this really rich Jewish girlfriend whose name was Alex. And Alex had a sidekick named Georgia. Iggy started bringing them over, and he'd be so fucked up that they started digging on me, because I had all the Nazi stuff. They became like psycho-Nazi-rich-Jewish-girls. So I usurped Iggy. That's when I got to understand Iggy a bit more—of how he was using these people ... so I would end up using them and their limousines."

The Stooges' embrace of Nazi imagery was based on economic resentment and a simple desire to align themselves with the darkest, most frightening, and shocking forces imaginable, and the "psycho" Jewish rich girls who gave themselves to the Stooges shared the latter impulse. ...

And yet, where other earlier bands were at least in part out to scare you with their ominous references to the Nazi past, there was something new in the attitude of the emerging punks. They took the frightening elements of history and turned them on their heads in the manner of Mel Brooks's *Springtime for Hitler* play in *The Producers*.

They were camp.

Susan Sontag, the New York Jewish feminist and intellectual of the 1970s with whom Richard Hell had a notable meeting (see Bockris's collection about the overlay between the Beats and the Punks, *Beat Punks*), explains in her essay "Notes on 'Camp'" (1964), "third among the great creative sensibilities [after tragic-or-comic seriousness and the seriousness of 'cruelty' such as that displayed in the work of Kafka] is Camp: the sensibility of failed seriousness, of the theatricalization of experience. Camp refuses both the harmonies of traditional seriousness, and the risks of fully identifying with extreme states of feeling."

So Nazi imagery in punk is anything but disrespectful—that is, it's anything but disrespectful to Jews because it is instead disrespectful to the Nazis. It is Jewish revenge incarnate, rooted in comedy. When the punk bands used swastikas in a camp way, they were making clear the "failed seriousness" of those symbols and the risks—in this case *extreme* risks—of "fully identifying with extreme states of feeling" like those of the ultrapatriotic National Socialists. Better to be ironic and detached than to trust unreliable emotions, pretending that they're inarguable truths to be acted on.

Of course, there was that element of rebellion discussed previously, just as there was an urge to shock for shock's sake. After all, what could be more rock'n'roll—or theatrical—than to use shock techniques to grab the attention of the audience? Yet one cannot discount the element of camp "play" inherent in the performances of bands like the Dictators and the Ramones. Later, Shrapnel, the Daniel Rey/Rabinowitz band, featured a cardboard German tank as part of its stage act, and the Sic F*cks featured those Italians possessed of shiksappeal, Tish and Snooky, backing up bandleader Russell Wolinsky on songs such as "Spanish Bar Mitzvah" while wearing nuns' habits adorned with swastikas. As much as they might have been intending to shock, as much as they may have enjoyed breaking taboos long established by their cultures, they were clearly also reveling

in tearing down the symbols of oppression—and oppressive seriousness. In doing so, they were not only attacking the Nazis, but the moral
imperative toward seriousness that the Nazis' Holocaust had seemed
to demand—and not just from the Nazis, who were long dead, after
all, but from their own Jewish community and parents with their self-
righteousness and Never Again sloganeering a few decades too late.

As Sontag herself recognized, the relationship between camp and Jewishness—at least in twentieth-century America—is a close one, the two
states emerging from similar origins. As she says in "Notes on 'Camp,' "
"The peculiar relation between Camp taste and homosexuality has to be
explained. While it's not true that Camp taste *is* homosexual taste, there is
no doubt a peculiar affinity and overlap. Not all liberals are Jews, but Jews
have shown a peculiar affinity for liberal and reformist causes. So, not all
homosexuals have Camp taste. But homosexuals, by and large, constitute
the vanguard—and the most articulate audience—of Camp. (The analogy
is not frivolously chosen. Jews and homosexuals are the outstanding creative minorities in contemporary urban culture. Creative, that is, in the
truest sense: they are creators of sensibilities. The two pioneering forces of
modern sensibility are Jewish moral seriousness and homosexual aestheticism and irony.)"

Sontag, writing in 1964, apparently didn't foresee the inversion of
"Jewish moral seriousness" that would soon take place in an emerging post-Holocaust Jewish generation—an inversion that would in fact
lead to something we could almost call Jewish camp. Still, she seems to
have anticipated it in her description of camp and Jewish sensibilities:
"The reason for the flourishing of the aristocratic [camp] posture among
homosexuals also seems to parallel the Jewish case. For every sensibility
is self-serving to the group that promotes it. Jewish liberalism is a gesture
of self-legitimization. So is Camp taste, which definitely has something
propagandistic about it. Needless to say, the propaganda operates in
exactly the opposite direction. The Jews pinned their hopes for integrating
into modern society on promoting the moral sense. Homosexuals have
pinned their integration into society on promoting the aesthetic sense.
Camp is a solvent of morality. It neutralizes moral indignation, sponsors
playfulness."

Again, Sontag is right on the mark—at least for the period in which
she was writing. And yet, even as she spoke, a new generation of Jews
was expressing a new sensibility and so heading in a new direction. This
sensibility—less moral than comic—was in many ways a rebellion against
the Jewish desire to be taken seriously by the predominant culture via

the acquiring of a *Bildung*, just as to a certain degree it was a rebellion by the mostly Eastern European Jews who made up the punk movement against the German Jews who largely embodied that desire. Unlike their older *brothers* and *sisters*, the punk Jews no longer wanted to work toward the betterment of the world in the most earnest ways. They wanted to enjoy that world and show their comfort in it. They wanted to be able to make a joke, even a bad, unsophisticated one. Hence, the Dictators' self-proclaimed worship of cars and White Castle burgers and the Ramones' self-professed love of trash TV and slasher films. Hence, too, these bands' comic songs of questionable taste, such as "Master Race Rock" (Dictators) and "Blitzkrieg Bop" (Ramones). If you weren't going to laugh, what were you going to do?

Both these bands—and others later, such as the Angry Samoans ("They Saved Hitler's Cock")—embraced the aestheticism and irony of camp. As did many who helped create punk from behind the scenes, such as Danny Fields, Howie Klein, and Seymour Stein, all of whom also happened to be homosexual. As Legs McNeil and Gillian McCain make clear in their oral history of New York punk, *Please Kill Me*, the breakdown, or rather, reconfiguration of gender roles was integral to the scene, which was not only highly focused on new definitions of what it meant to be Jewish, but also on what it meant to be a man or a woman, especially in a traditional, heterosexual sense.

In keeping with this is one final aspect of Sontag's take on camp, where she states that "the experiences of Camp are based on the great discovery that the sensibility of high culture has no monopoly on refinement. Camp asserts that good taste is not simply good taste; that there exists, indeed, a good taste of bad taste." While this is clearly relevant to punk's embrace of previously maligned three-chord rock (not to mention Jewish-American culture's embrace of so-called debased forms, such as blues and jazz, as expressed in low-high-culture landmarks, such as *Rhapsody in Blue*, *Appalachian Spring*, and *West Side Story*), what is also implicit here is camp's discovery that the sensibility of high culture can do much more than exclude—it can also malign. If camp sees the "good taste of bad taste," it also sees the bad taste of the so-called good. Hence, Jewish camp's mocking use of Nazi symbols such as swastikas. Once the height of Kultur in wartime Germany, these symbols of the Third Reich were that no longer. Indeed, when associated with governmentally approved culture of all sorts—including Nixon's Vietnam-era Amerika—they provided a dark kind of beauty. That is, if one equates beauty with revelation. Or truth.

It was almost enough to make Dylan stop frowning while singing "With God on Our Side," and Lenny Bruce stop grinning while holding up a tabloid rag's absurd headline "Six Million Found in Argentina." It was as if they could both stop trying so hard to make it all go away through earnestness or absurdity.

After all, hadn't it been enough to make Chris Stein and Debby Harry roll over on their flag of mass graves and kiss each other goodnight before drifting off to sleep?[1]

Steven Lee Beeber, from "Hotsy-Totsy Nazi Schatzes: Nazi Imagery and the Final Solution to the Final Solution," *The Heebie-Jeebies at CBGB's: A Secret History of Jewish Punk* (Chicago: Chicago Review Press, 2006).

EDWARD MEADOWS, "PISTOL-WHIPPED"

In 1977, the *National Review*, that bastion of intellectual conservatism founded by William F. Buckley, turned its restless eyes to a vibrant and strange music scene in the United Kingdom which it called "New Wave." What it found is startling: in British punk's nihilism, its use of Nazi imagery, its oppositional rage against mainstream culture and politics, the Review located "right-wing political protest." They got it wrong,[1] yes, but their reasons for doing so should give us pause, and tell us much about what kind of racial and political identifications occurred during this particular moment in punk's history. There was, at that time, a sympathy for Britain's leading racist/fascist political party, the National Front, on the part of certain bands, such as the explicitly Nazi-identified Skrewdriver and the often misunderstood Sham 69. (Paul Weller of the Jam announced in 1979 that the band planned to vote Tory, but later insisted it was merely a publicity stunt dreamed up to differentiate themselves from the majority of punk bands, who tilted left.) But more important than the conservative politics of a few punk bands was the widespread dissatisfaction with a status quo represented by the Labour Party in politics and progressive, "hippie" rock in the cultural sphere that manifested itself through punk as nihilism and what could be called a "formal" oppositional stance (rage at everything and everyone). That the *National Review* misread these signs as a coming conservative cultural movement says as much

about the confusion of political and cultural commentators who were trying to fit punk into simple binaries as it does about the confusing politics of punk rock.

> God save the Queen,
> A fascist regime.
> God save the Queen,
> They made you a moron.
> God save the Queen,
> She ain't no human being,
> And there's no future
> In England's dreaming.
> —"God Save the Queen," the Sex Pistols

The Sex Pistols' "God Save the Queen," which is the national anthem of British New Wave rock circa 1977, hasn't got a single filthy word in it. Yet the record's banned on all the radio stations and barred from every retail store. The Sex Pistols are prohibited from performing in England (they're exiled to Amsterdam). Still "God Save the Queen" is in the top five on the hit lists, and Labour Party MPs stand foaming at the mouth, swearing to "destroy New Wave before it destroys the nation."

But the wimpy MPs have got it backwards, any New Wave punk will tell you. It's the bleedin' Labour Party that's destroying the nation. New Wave rock music is music of working-class rage—at the empty promises of the welfare state, at the eternal dole and the double-digit inflation and the double-digit unemployment, all of which leaves young working-class Brits holding the empty bag. It's easy to sing of peace and love when you're pulling down $100,000 a night on tour. It's fun to play the dirty hippy when you know all the time you can shave off the hair tomorrow and go to work in Pa's law firm. Peace and love? The New Wave answers back with a song of its own, titled "Hate and War."

New Wave, descended from New York punk rock, is just now blossoming in England. The music scene is fresh, exciting, a renaissance to recall the rock explosion of the Sixties. But New Wave is the very antithesis of the now jaded and faded Progressive rock—the Beatles, the Stones, and all that. New Wave is best described as industrial-strength hard rock—the hardest of hard rock, mean, no-frills, four-chord rock, amplified till it burns your ears off. New Wave musicians and their fans don't go for kinky sex, nor any bleating whiny protest lyrics, nor any hokey drugged mysticism. They go right for the jugular. The music is charged with the energy of depraved political anger. And the fashion is to be as utterly unfashionable as one can be. New Wave kids stroll along King's Road wearing short hair, heavy black eye makeup, razor-blade earrings, and tee-shirts that say, "Hitler Was a Punk Rocker." The more devoted fans wear swastika pendants and safety pins through their cheeks.

The anti-chic of New Wave finds clearest expression in the vicious, snarling song lyrics, in the nasty satires New Wave bands do of "rich-kid" hippy rock, even in the names of the groups. There's the Clash and the Damned and the Adverts and the Stranglers and the Unwanted and the Stiffs. The short-haired, trashily dressed anti-stars of these groups go by such names as Johnny Rotten (lead singer for the Sex Pistols), Richard Hell, Rat Scabies. And Gloria Steinem would be appalled. New Wave bands are aggressively chauvinistic towards women; female New Wavers don't do much for the cause either. The hottest all-girl New Wave band goes by the name of the Slits. Another all-female group calls itself Snatch. And, if any fur-lined radical-chic fat-cat rock critic for *Rolling Stone* magazine should leave the safety of his chauffeured Rolls to enter a New Wave rock club and survey the scene, he's likely to get laid out quick. In the words of one New Wave fanatic, "If there's one thing that makes me take up arms, it's bored rich-kids treating my life as this week's trend."

Of all the New Wave bands, only the Jam has yet officially aligned itself with the Conservative Party. But most of the groups lean toward the (Neo-Nazi) National Front. This, of course, is just too awfully embarrassing for the trendsetters who'd love to neatly package New Wave and hawk it in the U.S.A. They lust to rip New Wave off, turn it into a trend, commercialize it, use it up, and make a killing in the process. But right-wing rock is utter blasphemy to your average cocaine-sniffing Manhattan-posh rock writer. He can't handle it, so he dismisses it as a passing fad, or he ignores it altogether. However, money is to be made, and every American record company has its scouts in every London punk club, searching for New Wave acts to sign.

And the vultures follow the jackals: pop psychologists are crawling out of the woodwork to "explain" this terribly sick, sick New Wave movement. A Harvard sociologist is already skulking among London's New Wavers, interviewing the poor dears for a trendy new book, which will doubtless decry the sad failure of these angry kids to see and understand the fruits of state socialism. But the kids see and they understand. When you finish school and can't get a job so you have to live at home with your parents and go on the dole, when you haven't got a hope of any future at all, then you're backed up against the wall. And if you're young and ripe, you're not about to keep quiet, to maintain the stiff upper lip of your frightened parents, as Britain goes down the bleedin' toilet.

Actually the New Wave movement could be a healthy development, a purgative for the self-delusions of British life. The time for decorum may be past, and the punk kids have thrown British reserve to the winds. Why should you stand around being subserviently decent when your nation is dying and your future is dying with it? What better time to point the angry finger, to offend those who, in the name of propriety, acquiesce in the political and economic failure of a nation? If the working-class, out-of-work youth weren't spending their energy on their hard new music, they'd be venting it in more vile ways. Music is their only void. And, as the rock of the Sixties did for its generation, New Wave gives the kids, the damned, something that's their own, a sense of community, of shared adversity. There's something touching about it all.

It's not likely that New Wave will sweep America. For, despite all the bland denials of appalled American rock critics, New Wave is, at base, right-wing political protest. And American kids haven't got so much to protest about: unemployment and inflation are worrisome problems here in the States, but nothing like the British disaster, and not nearly so directly traceable to the bankrupt policies of state socialism. No, the New Wave is born and bred of rage against the Labour Party, the Board of Trade, the unions, and long-haired hippy-dippy-chic rich-kid poseurs who don't have to worry because they've got it made. Peace and love? Hate and war! It's not pretty, but then it's not meant to be.

Edward Meadows, "Pistol-Whipped," *National Review*, November 11, 1977.

ROGER SABIN,
"'I WON'T LET THAT DAGO BY':
RETHINKING PUNK AND RACISM"

Perhaps one of the most significant articles on the relationships between punk rock, race, and politics, this work emerged in 1999, as the mainstream music press's celebration of the "twentieth anniversary of punk" began to subside. Such context is important, for in this essay Sabin argues that the historical and, we might even say, mythological reconstruction of the alignment between late-1970s British punk and antiracist political movements is sketchy at best.

In the inchoate White rage of the British punks, Sabin finds ample evidence of White racism, from National Front affiliation and brazenly prejudiced song lyrics to more symbolically ambiguous gestures like the now-familiar punk appropriation of the swastika. Sabin's argument is bold and necessary, but it can create a binarism that punk may not always fit into. What to do, for example, with Sham 69, who aligned themselves socially with the National Front and politically with Rock Against Racism? Nevertheless, Sabin's work lays the groundwork for a critical understanding of punk and race and generates continuing questions, namely, why are moments of punk rock racism so, well, whitewashed?

Histories of British punk, 1976–1979, have been unanimous about the movement's relationship to racism. Whether these histories be in the form of academic texts, commercial books, magazine articles, or TV and radio accounts, the conclusion has always been the same: that despite some posturing with swastikas, punk was essentially solid with the anti-racist cause. Its alliances with the reggae scene on the one hand, and the twin organisations of Rock Against Racism (RAR) and the Anti-Nazi League (ANL) on the other, are taken as irrefutable evidence of this, and have enabled historians to co-opt punk into a more long-term tradition of countercultural—left-wing—dissent.

In this chapter I want to question this orthodoxy, and to challenge some of the underlying assumptions about punk's political leanings. By taking a fresh look at sources from the time—music papers, lyrics, political literature, and especially those repositories of unguarded comment, fanzines[1]—I'd like to take issue with the twin ideas that punk somehow transcended the societal forces that gave birth to it, and that it can be judged as being ideologically commensurate with the 'politically correct' standards of the 1980s and '90s. Thus, I want to show how the movement's involvement with anti-racism has been exaggerated, how its political ambiguity left ample space for right-wing interpretation, and how its overtly racist aspects left a legacy for the fascist music scene of the post-punk era.

First, an unavoidably brief word about the background to race relations in the late 1970s,[2] a period more tense in this regard than at any point since the Second World War. This was thanks in no small part to the rise of the National Front (NF), the biggest of Britain's fascist parties. By 1976, after doing increasingly well in local elections, it was the fourth-largest political party in the country (though still a long way from gaining a parliamentary seat), and was concentrating its efforts on a campaign in the run-up to the general election which involved making its presence felt in areas of high non-white populations by a series of high-profile street-marches. The party additionally had a policy of recruiting from subcultures, and especially from punk—more about which later.[3]

Racism was "on the map" in other ways, too. The Conservative Party, then in opposition, proved itself anxious to steal the NF's fire by making race a key issue. The Labour government itself was far from non-racist, and made little effort to tackle racism in other organs of the state (especially in the police and the courts), or indeed in the employment market and in schools. Racism was an issue in the media in a sense that it had never been before, with pundits like Enoch Powell of the Conservatives and Martin Webster of the NF invited to contribute to debates in newspapers and on radio and TV (typically compromising the media's self-image of "neutrality"). Culturally, racist gags were everywhere—from TV shows like *Love Thy Neighbour*, *Mind Your Language*, and *The Comedians* to the "Best Jokes" series of books available in every high street bookstore (*Best Jewish Jokes*, *Best Pakistani Jokes*, *Best Coloured Jokes*, etc.).[4]

Against this background, the need to create a myth that punk was somehow anti-racist was understandable, and the process began almost as soon as the movement itself did. Most journalists on the music papers, for example, considered themselves to be "left wing," and many hailed from the same tradition as the countercultural publications of the previous musical era (*Oz*, *IT*, *Frendz*, etc.)—some, like Charles Shaar Murray, had also written for them. Thus, there was a caucus of journos who were pro-punk and eager to claim it for their own political world-view. Such names at the two big "inkies," *NME* and *Sounds*, included: at the former, Murray, Julie Burchill, and Tony Parsons; and at the latter, Jon Savage, Vivian Goldman, and Garry Bushell.[5] *Sounds*, by far the most punk-oriented of the two, even went so far as to devote an entire issue to the racism debate (25 March, 1978).

Reporting of punk in the mainstream press tended to follow the lead of the inkies. True, early on there was something of a moral panic in the tabloids, but once the "Filth and the Fury" headlines had played themselves out, the press was content to borrow stories—and this meant parroting the anti-racist line. In time, many of the music writers themselves would be poached. Meanwhile, high street bookshops began to stock the first histories of punk, invariably written by those same rock journos.[6]

The 1970s also saw a significant contribution to the anti-racist myth from academia. Even before the last power chords of punk's first wave had died away, Dick Hebdige's *Subculture: the Meaning of Style* appeared (1979), taking a semiotic approach to the movement, and making a case for seeing the history of British subcultures since the war as a response to the influence of black youth styles. This point was particularly relevant for punk, he argued, because of its associations with reggae, and since, "at the heart of the punk subculture, forever arrested, lies this frozen dialectic between black and white cultures …"[7] The book was extremely influential (to the point where it has been re-issued almost annually), and would become a set text in the developing field of Cultural Studies.[8]

The process of mythmaking continued into the 1980s. The music press, now dominated by the *NME*, continued to romanticise punk in retro-spect, with prominent socialist journalists like Steven Wells and X Moore taking up where the first crop of writers had left off. Once more the main-stream press, including the new "style press," followed suit, especially at the time of punk's 10th anniversary (1986–87), when celebratory special issues and supplements abounded. TV and radio were also quick to air retro documentaries. But whether the image was of a photo-spread of a punk band juxtaposed with a shot of a "Stop the Nazis" poster, or of footage of the Vibrators segued with that of an ANL march, the impres-sion was the same.

The 1980s saw another important book on the issue, David Widgery's *Beating Time* (1986), a history of RAR (and to a lesser extent of the ANL as well) written by one of its founders.[9] Although making no secret of the fact that these two organisations were specifically socialist, and had backing from the Trotskyist Socialist Workers' Party (SWP), it put punk at the center of the story, claiming that it was a natural (class) ally of socialism, and therefore an ideal conduit for combating the fascist tide. According to Widgery, "Punk expressed a political moment" in terms of anti-racist activism.[10]

Finally, the 1990s have seen the myth brought up to date, with yet more retrospectives (notably during the latest anniversary, 1996–97) which have been no more critical than their predecessors: indeed, they tended to can-nibalise them quite shamelessly. Meanwhile, the market in punk nostalgia, especially compilation "Best of" CDs and videos, has boomed, though sometimes edited of "controversial" and racist material. And, of course, there have been more histories—over 30 at the last count, if you include band biographies—the vast majority of which have been content either to avoid politics, or to repeat what has been said before.

The myth has therefore taken on its own momentum over the years, acquiring layers of respectability along the way. Even if, to be fair, some of its shortcomings have been taken into account by the better histories that have been published,[11] nevertheless it has solidified into an orthodoxy—the "historical truth." But history is nothing if not a selective presentation of the facts, and if we take it upon ourselves to foreground less "PC" evidence from the period, a totally different picture begins to emerge.

Punk and Anti-Racism

"Don't Back the Front"
—song title, Desperate Bicycles, 1977

Before looking at punk's relationship with reggae and RAR/the ANL, there is an area that requires more urgent consideration, not least because what punk didn't say about (anti-) racism was often more important than what it did. Specifically, punk's biggest failure in the political sphere was its almost total neglect of the plight of Britain's Asians. For it has been forgotten over time that the focus of attention for the far right in the late 1970s was directed primarily at them, and not, as most accounts assume, at British Afro-Caribbeans.[12] There were specific historical reasons for this, having to do with the bursts of immigration from 1976 onwards as Asians (with British passports) were expelled from Uganda, Kenya, and Malawi. These unfortunate people had typically experienced racism before—hence their exile. Now, in their new homes in Britain's inner cities, they would face more.

The racist backlash was immediate. The NF, newly energized by the "crisis," systematically redirected its propaganda away from its traditional enemies (Jews foremost among them) to Asians. New leaflets explained the threat from their "rapid family growth," uncleanliness ("filthy Asians" being a stock phrase), and above all from their "stealing" of jobs at a time of high unemployment. The only answer, the NF claimed, was to "Stop all immigration and start phased repatriation." The Conservative Party, for their part, began to speak "on behalf" of the white working class (an unprecedented move for them until this point) and called for much tighter immigration controls: Margaret Thatcher, leader of the party, even expressed her sympathy for whites who felt like they were "being swamped."

One result of this heightened atmosphere, and especially of NF fear-mongering, was an exponential rise in the number of street attacks on Asians (a phenomenon known as "Paki-bashing"—though, of course, only a few of the victims were ever from Pakistan). Firebomb attacks on Asian homes similarly became commonplace. Today, figures are hard to gather, not least because most incidents were never reported; but it is a certainty that the majority of racist murders in the late 1970s were of Asians.

What was punk's response? The most striking impression is one of silence. In general, articles in music papers and fanzines didn't mention the Asian situation, punk musicians didn't talk about it in interviews, and punk lyrics didn't acknowledge it. This could have been because of ambivalence, or even hostility, towards Asians. Or, more likely in most cases, it was because the issue wasn't a "hip" one. Asians simply didn't have the same romance as Afro-Caribbean youth—especially in terms of the latter's reputation for being confrontational with the police—and what was equally problematic, they had no music comparable to reggae with which punks could identify. As fellow "rebel rockers" they were a dead loss.[13]

On the very rare occasions when journalists did raise the subject, the response could be surprisingly unsympathetic. Thus, in a *Record Matter* interview with the Clash, the band are busy outlining their anti-racist views when the subject of anti-Asian violence arises, and manager Bernie Rhodes chips in: "There's a lot of Pakis that deserve it ..."[14] He's soon corrected by other members of the group, but the idea that such a comment could have been made about Afro-Caribbeans is unthinkable. ...

Even for the more committed punks, there is the question of how far anti-racism was perceived in the same way as RAR/ANL. The aim of these organizations was to combat *all* racism, but for many punks the cause was thought of in terms of anti-racism towards Afro-Caribbeans rather than towards other ethnic groups. This comes back to our previous point about the anti-Asian problem: thus, the Clash's manager may have had problems with "Pakis," but he was happy enough to allow the band to play on the same bill as Misty in Roots. The audiences reflected this contradiction, and despite RAR's efforts to put on gigs in areas of high Asian populations (e.g., Southall), writer Simon Frith is right that their methods had "an offputting effect for Asian youth."[15] Other RAR-supporting bands were equally capable of making racist gaffes about Jews, Hispanics, Arabs, you name it (e.g., Joy Division, Sham 69, the Art Attacks, and Adam and the Ants—see below).

Also, within the punk camp, there was sometimes open hostility to RAR/the ANL. Often this had to do with punk's broadly anti-authoritarian ethic—expressed both as an untheorized hatred of being told what to do and in more sophisticated anarchist terms. In short, there was a resentment of being seen as the "authentic voice" of anything, and a distrust of being used (especially as a tool in a socialist revolution)—a feeling that was quite justified, as the Widgery book makes unintentionally clear. There were other objections, too. For instance: the image of RAR/the ANL as "middle-class," "hippie," and "for students"; the way in which RAR included other musics under its umbrella which did not chime with punk (jazz, soul, etc.); the fact that the carnivals were festivals by any other name (how hippie could you get?); and the "fakeness" of *Temporary Hoarding* (closer to traditional left-wing newspapers than punk fanzines, despite its pretensions).

Leading punk figures were not slow to make their feelings known. Mark Perry of ATV and *Sniffin' Glue* put it this way: "RAR preach against the NF but on their badge is the red star, which has caused as much trouble and animosity as the swastika. I don't need to be told by a commie organisation to love blacks ... the SWP and NF are as bad as each other ..."[16] J. J. Burnel of the Stranglers called RAR/the ANL "racist," adding, "the standard left-wing pose is easy, not futuristic."[17] And though Johnny Rotten gave an interview to *Temporary Hoarding*, the Pistols pointedly never played an RAR gig.

Punk and Racism

> Y'know what they said
> Well some of it was true!
> —The Clash, "London Calling," 1979

If punk's attitude to anti-racism could be contradictory and eclectic, then there is also plenty of proof of openly racist behaviour within the subculture. To begin with, some punks were attracted by what the far right had to say. Indeed, part of the NF's late-1970s offensive was to attract youth to their cause, and to this end they looked to subcultures—and particularly to the hip one of the moment. NF newspapers like *Bulldog* tried to put a fascist spin on punk songs and to claim leading figures—including the openly hostile Johnny Rotten—as their own, while NF shops began to sell punk clothing.[18] Martin Webster was similarly very happy to do interviews with the music papers—notably the "racism" issue of *Sounds* mentioned above—and made clear his aim to recruit what he called "robust young men" to the NF, chiefly for the impression they would make on marches.

To a limited degree, the strategy worked. Such recruits as were made came from both punk *per se* and from the resurgent skinhead movement, which was an integral part of it.[19] Plus, a fair deal of money was made from the sale of NF badges and paraphernalia. There were other, minor manifestations of support. For example, there were fascist fanzines (such as *The Punk Front*), fascist clubs (at which, reportedly, the favored dance was the goose step [*NME*, 1978]), and a few fascist bands, who made no secret of their links with the NF and other far-right parties, and who actively encouraged fascists to come to their gigs. These included a clutch of bands based in Leeds, among them (according to *Sounds*) the Dentists, the Ventz, Crap, and Tragic Minds, who played songs with titles like "White Power," "Kill the Reds," and "Master Race." In March 1979 they linked, with NF backing, to form "Rock Against Communism" (RAC)—an obvious riposte to RAR, and also the name of a regular column-cum-insert in *Bulldog*. How many gigs were played under this manner at this time is not known, but certainly a few.[20]

Was this fascist stance a pose? For some bands and fans, undoubtedly—just as anti-fascism could be. We have seen how some top stars had expressed their disaffection with RAR, and it was not surprising that some punks took things further: soon it became fashionable to flirt not just with the NF, but with other factions like the British Movement (BM) and Column 88. Conversely, for some involved with fascist rock, their engagement was unquestionably sincere: they saw it as an opportunity to express a view on what was wrong with the country—to "tell the truth" (very punk) about the "race problem." In other words, it's worth bearing in mind that political commitment was not the sole province of the left.

Less focused politically, there were other forms of racism within punk. For example, prejudice did not begin and end with Asians. There were other blind spots, and anti-semitism could be one of them. Take Siouxsie and the Banshees' often-quoted lyric that there were "too many Jews for my liking" (from "Love in a Void"). Hardly a cryptic message, and made less so by the singer's penchant for wearing swastikas, goose-stepping and right-arm salutes on stage, not to mention songs that included "oi-oi-oi" *sieg heil*–type chants (e.g., "Make Up to Break Up"). In 1977, Siouxsie tried to justify the line by saying it was really about "too many fat businessmen"—which did not make things any better, but came perilously close to echoing the NF's view that "Zionists" controlled the economy.[21]

Other anti-semitic evidence is not hard to find. Take, for instance, Rat Scabies's (of the Damned) dismissal of Dick Manitoba (of the Dictators) as "a fat Jewish slob."[22] Or the Clash's constant ribbing of their Jewish manager—the above-mentioned Rhodes. Or Sid Vicious, provocatively and idiotically wandering around the Jewish quarter of Paris in his swastika T-shirt (as filmed for *The Great Rock 'n' Roll Swindle*).[23] No wonder the fans could sometimes get confused: as one writer from the fanzine *Ripped and Torn* explained, "I wore a swastika and an iron cross ... it was starting to interest me ... I was starting to stand up for the insults people made about the Nazi stuff. You know, people would say 'fucking Jew hater,' and I'd stick up for Jew killing ..."[24]

Racism was directed at other ethnic groups, too, though this was not as common. One cringeworthy example of anti-Hispanicism was the Adam and the Ants song "Puerto Rican." The "tongue-in-cheek" lyrics run: "You get off on his greasy hair ... / you got a small apartment and central heating / Why go waste it on a Puerto Rican? / ... Gonna strike a matchstick on his hair / ... Girl, you're gonna make me cry / I won't let that Dago by."[25] The Ants were another band who messed with swastikas, and who never really threw off criticisms of what Adam called "the Nazi thing." Other punk targets included Arabs (e.g., the Art Attacks' "Arabs in 'arrads"), the Chinese, and the Irish. The latter, it seems, were automatically amusing, and doubly so when bands themselves were from Ireland: as one *Sounds* review of the Radiators from Space put it: "Irish punks? Will it start 'One, tree, faw, two'?"[26]

The examples go on and on. Moreover, the fact that racism of this kind was so prevalent, especially in the context of the contemporary political situation, must raise questions about other aspects of punk—and especially its ambiguity. The flirtations with Third Reich imagery, for example, merit a fresh approach—despite the stock dismissals of it by punk historians as simply a manifestation of the punk desire to shock, to "say the unsayable"—sometimes unsatisfyingly theorised as some kind of postmodernist triumph of style over content.[27]

The wearing of swastikas, for example, certainly did contain an element of "shock," but that word could encompass within it many meanings. For instance: two fingers to the "peace and love" ethic of the hippies; the same to parents, who were of an age to have experienced the war; a nod to the "camp" S&M aesthetic of films like *The Night Porter* and *Cabaret*; an ironic symbol of living "in a fascist regime"; or simply a nice bit of hip (anti-) fashion. But it could also very possibly mean some degree of sympathy with fascist aims—as our quote from *Ripped and Torn* demonstrates. We can't know which motivation was more important at any point in time, or in any geographical location,[28] but it does seem reasonable to argue that there was a fair amount of disingenuousness in what was going on. To put it another way, with racism at such a pitch in society, and the NF actively recruiting from subcultures, many punks would have been well aware of the "mixed" signals they were putting out.

The same line of argument could be applied to bands who were fond of other kinds of Nazi imagery, or who wrote ambiguous lyrics. We've noted the example of the Banshees already, but there were many more. Joy Division, famously, chose their name for its holocaust connotations, dressed like Nazis, and had a Third Reich–fixated singer who, on their first recording, can be heard asking the audience "Have you all forgot [sic] Rudolf Hess?"[29] Less prominently, one can think of "satirical" songs such as the Models' "Nazi Party" (as in "I wanna form a ..."); the Vibrators' "Nazi Baby"; the Cortinas' "Fascist Dictator"; and the Spitfire Boys' "Mein Kampf"; and group names like Martin and the Brownshirts, London SS, and Stormtrooper.

Apart from the Nazi material, other punk symbolism and lyrics were up for grabs. The Union Jack, for instance, also a ubiquitous fashion item, could be worn ironically (especially around the time of the Jubilee, e.g., the Pistols, Clash), could be a homage to the mod era (e.g., the Jam and their fans), or, much less commonly, could be a statement against American influence (and American punk). But, similarly, it could be a symbol of the NF: by 1977, the party had pretty much made the flag its own. Furthermore, in terms of song lyrics, anybody who used the word "white" could be asking for trouble. The Clash's "White Riot" and "(White Man) in Hammersmith Palais" were indistinct enough to be left open to interpretation, while, later on, the Stiff Little Fingers song "White Noise" had similar problems (none of the three was intended to be racist, but all became *Bulldog* favourites).

The issue of ambiguity had other implications. If punk's outward appearance could be problematic, then so too could some bands' treatment of openly fascist fans. Most bands, especially in the "lower divisions," could not afford financially to actively put off this element ("cos fascists are money," to re-phrase the Pistols). Others were ambivalent for different reasons. Sham 69, for instance, an RAR-supporting band whose following was closely associated with the NF, had a policy of welcoming "kids" of all political persuasions to their gigs in a spirit of working-class solidarity and revolution. This could lead to some confusion, and was compounded by Sham 69's statements to the press. Thus, in a typically contradictory interview with *Sounds*, singer Jimmy Pursey explained during the course of outlining his anti-racist philosophy that "Some of the fans are NF or

BM … but they come from places where the black population is way over the limit …"[30] Other Sham 69 bloopers included employing a (reportedly) racist crew; inviting NF-ers onto the stage to dance and backstage afterwards for a drink; and playing "Land of Hope and Glory" as an intro tape. Their fascist fans, for their part, felt vindicated by the band's behavior, and continued to come to gigs (the Sham 69 chant became: "What've we got? Fuck all! National Front!").

One final point: What is particularly interesting about this welter of evidence concerning punk's racist leanings (intentional or otherwise) is how much of it has been "edited out" of history over the years. Sometimes this happened very quickly: for example, the Banshees' offending lyric was swiftly changed, while the Models' "Nazi Party" never made it onto vinyl (nor did the offerings of the neo-fascist Leeds bands, to the best of my knowledge). More often, things have been toned down more recently, both to conform to the anti-racist myth (for the political reasons outlined above), and because of commercial imperatives. Thus, "Puerto Rican" mysteriously disappeared from the Ants' Strange Fruit session compilation (1991) (it evidently didn't square with Adam's subsequent career as a teenybop star), and the track that included Ian Curtis's outburst was never collected on any of the "definitive" Joy Division compilations. Even in fictionalised accounts, things have had a tendency to change: in the movie *Sid and Nancy*, for example, Sid's T-shirt becomes a hammer and sickle.

The same "editing" has taken place on a more subtle level in recent histories of punk where ex-stars are taken at their word (especially true of the 1990s boom in band biographies). These are characterised by an uncritical acceptance of denials of any interest in the far right, of explanations given without context (Siouxsie saying she wore the swastika purely out of "high camp"[31]), and of devious excuses (Joy Division's label boss saying that they were merely "making a connection with those oppressed by fascism."[32] To be fair, many punk stars distanced themselves very swiftly from any mistakes they may have made in their early career, and some, admirably, went on to do valuable work for the anti-racist cause (the Banshees and Joy Division among them). But those who reinvented themselves after the fact were simply being dishonest, and were complicit in further clouding our understanding of the punk moment.

Conclusion

The story of punk and racism, 1976–79, is thus one of selective anti-racism, casual racism, pseudo and genuine fascism, naiveté, confusion, and ambiguity—a story overlain by vast differences in experience in different parts of the country, and changes over time. It's a complicated relationship, and not one that lends itself easily to analysis. Moreover, there are difficulties with placing it in the context of racial politics in general. It could be argued, for example, that racism within punk was mainly verbal and symbolic, and therefore had little effect on power relations in the spheres that really "mattered"—unemployment, housing, etc. But this is to ignore the fact that such behaviour "normalised" a set of assumptions about society—assumptions which had a huge effect on social relations—just as they do today. (The lyrics and remarks surveyed above, for example, rely on stereotypes—social constructs which themselves socially construct.)

Accepting that such racism did have an "effect," should we be surprised that punk was so compromised? As we've noted, mainstream culture was racist, and punk was bound to pick up on this to some degree. After all, the movement was born out of the same political recession that had produced the rise in far-right activity, and subcultures have historically mimicked their parent cultures as well as rebelled against them. Also, the fact that punk was so "young" must have been a factor. Band members were often not out of their teens, while fans were younger still (in researching this chapter, for example, it was noticeable how juvenile-looking the fanzines were). This meant that a significant proportion lived at home with their parents, in an environment where any racist views might arguably have been absorbed by osmosis (where, as Jimmy Pursey said at the time: "9 times out of 10, you're gonna believe in the same things that your dad believes in."[33]

Indeed, if punk was reflecting the racist *zeitgeist* in this way, we might expect similar controversies in other youth subcultures. And to a degree, this was true. Within heavy metal circles, for example, there was debate over the wearing of Hell's Angels–style Nazi regalia (iron crosses, swastikas—again!), the "SS" lightning strikes in the Kiss logo, and dodgy lyrics (e.g., Ted Nugent's "Stormtroopin'"). And within the rockabilly scene, about the use of Confederate flags and "inappropriate" 1950s lyrics. This is not to mention the racist and/or fascist outbursts of those more mainstream rockers, Eric Clapton, Rod Stewart, and David Bowie.[34]

So, even if conclusions are difficult to arrive at, we can say that, on balance, punk was probably no more or no less racist than the society that birthed it. To argue that any subculture was, or is, any more "progressive" politically than the mainstream culture it complements is highly contentious, and punk certainly exhibited no fundamental, gravitational pull to the left. To put it in more dramatic terms: sure, punks were angry about lengthening dole queues, the privileges of royalty, the anguish of boredom, and police brutality. But they were also angry about "Pakis" moving into their neighbourhoods, Arabs buying everything in Harrods, Puerto Ricans nicking their girlfriends, and there being too many Jews for their liking. This aspect to the movement existed, and was very vibrant. To underplay it by ignoring punk's historical context is not only a failure of investigative rigor, but a disservice to those who fought against racism at the time. …

Roger Sabin, from "'I Won't Let That Dago By': Rethinking Punk and Racism," *Punk Rock: So What? The Cultural Legacy of Punk* (London: Routledge, 1999).

JIMMY PURSEY OF SHAM 69, INTERVIEW IN *SOUNDS*

Sham 69, as hinted at above, stood at an important crossroads in the development of punk rock and the politics of race. One of the first in this generation of publicly exposed punk bands in Britain, Sham 69 were overt in their explicit working-class identification, in opposition to some of the more art-school-derived affectations of other similar groups. In this interview from 1978, the year the group released its debut album, the lead singer, Jimmy Pursey, talks about race and class in a surprisingly nuanced manner. Pursey has a very explicit understanding of the political intentions of his work—to play for working-class and poor kids, to get them to ask questions of themselves without giving them any easy answers—and yet refuses to characterize himself as a leader, or politically align himself with any particular cause or standpoint. He evinces more than a little casual racism, and refuses to reject his racist fans in the name of the "kids" being "united," but also campaigns against racist violence and describes a personal intervention he made with a blatantly racist fan ("what about the white kids that've beaten up your sister?"). He understands the poison of racism, and yet has a very visceral sense of the kinds of economic and social factors that

can lead one to, consciously or unconsciously, embrace racist positions. In fact, one might argue that his position regarding race here
approaches "oppositional whiteness" from a place of *empathy* and
solidarity in opposition. At the same time, however, what is at the
center is a notion of the unity of the downtrodden, and we need
to ask to what extent such an idea leaves one too apologetic for
certain kinds of racism.

SOUNDS: Your position as a "youth leader" … what do you think of
that?

JIMMY PURSEY: I don't see m'self as a leader, not because I don't fink I'll
ever be a leader in the sense that I'll have thousands of people following
me. If you tell someone to do something, or you tell 'em not to do it, that's
when you become a leader, right? Now the people that follow Sham 69,
we don't give 'em no orders, and we don't give them no answers. We're
just sayin', "We done it," or "We done certain fings that them songs
are about," and it's up to you to decide for yourself, after hearin' wot
we've got t'say, if you think it's right to kick the shit out of some bloke,
or if you think it's right to support the Communists or the Nazis or
whatever …

Our aspect of what punk was supposed to be about is just getting up
onstage, singin' about fings that've 'appened to you in your life, an' also
keepin' the crowd in wiv wot you're doin' … writing songs about the
audience, they're payin' their money to come and see you, right? You
gotta give 'em everything you can' an' that's what we try to do … every
time we go out we try to give the best.

Like you got Tom Robinson and his political thing about anti-Nazis.
Now, you're gettin' a lotta kids that're sayin' "That's it! I'm anti-Nazi."
They're not thinkin' what they're anti-against, they only know the word
"Nazi." If Tom Robinson said, "I'm anti-cowboys," quite a few of 'em
would be anti-cowboys! They should think before they start, because
what they're doin' is creatin' another barrier between them and some
more kids. They should start sayin', "Well, let me fink about it first
… lemme fink if that's wrong or not." I mean, that is a political fing,
an' if you build up something that's really big an' political, you build
up two sides. At the moment they're building up two sides, an' that
is horrific.

SOUNDS: A lot of people say to me that they wouldn't go to one of your
gigs because there's always skinheads there, violence, people getting
beaten up. Is that an accurate description?

PURSEY: No … but it's a description of some of the gigs that have been held in the past. Because they are the real McCoy. This is what it was supposed to be about, these are the kids you were supposed to be singin' to, not the geezers flashing their trousers down the King's Road at £35 a time. It was supposed to be about the kids that were comin' outta the gutter type places, tower blocks, shitty streets, East End of London, Manchester, Liverpool, Glasgow, don't matter where it was, they were the kids you were supposed to be playin' to. An' if you don't wanna play to them, you might as well just jack it in. An' I'm not gonna jack it in, 'cause I believe in them kids, an' most of them are great kids. 95% of 'em are. The 5% that do fight are kids that've gone along with another guy … they probably go to football with them geezers on Saturday directly just to 'cause a bit of bovver. Some of 'em are also National Front or British Movement. But, it's the situations where they come from.

Listen, if your dad is a conservative, or a liberal or a Communist or whatever, nine times out of ten you're gonna believe in the same things that your dad believes in, up to a certain age. And they come from places where the black population is well over the limit. So if you're livin' in them type of situations that's why your gonna start thinkin' that way. An' a lot of them kids have come up an' told me, "It's because this black geezer done my sister, like, y'know?" And I've turned round and said, "Yeah, what about the white kids that've beaten up your sister?"

SOUNDS: If you see violence in the audience, do you try and stop it?

PURSEY: Every time. I said at the LSE that this was the last gig I'd do if there was any violence. I'm totally against violence, that's what most of the songs are about. But you've got to play to them kids that cause the violence in the first place. I can't turn round and say, "You can't do that," they've got every right to do anything they want to do. All I can say to 'em is, "Look, please, I don't want you to do it." …

SOUNDS: Do you think there's any special virtues in the working classes?

PURSEY: Yeah, I think they fight harder. All the time they feel they're being put down, and they fight against that to prove that they're just as good as anybody else. Why do you think most good rock'n'roll bands come from hard areas?

SOUNDS: A lot of rock'n'rollers, if you look in their backgrounds are actually fairly middle class.

PURSEY: Well … what I'm sayin' is usually the best bands originate from that type of situation. My favourite bands … Small Faces, John

Lennon, Jimmy Cliff. I did like the Clash. I do jive on about a lotta bands at the moment, but it gets me down because I feel I'm fighting a little losing cause with all these other bands around me.

I feel that we're the only band trying to do something and everybody else is shitting on the kids around us. When I last saw the Clash, Joe Strummer said to me: "Y'know, we're not really a punk band anymore, we're trying to get away from that type of thing." That's what give 'em their bread and butter! It gives me my bread an' butter an' I'm not gonna ever deny that I'm in a punk band. We're in a punk band and that's it. If the band's gonna die it's gonna die as a punk band, not as a fuckin' pop group." …

Sandy Robertson, from "Sham 69: Son of Sham," *Sounds*, April 29, 1978.

BOB NOXIOUS OF THE FUCK-UPS, INTERVIEW IN *MAXIMUMROCKNROLL*

"You can't judge a book by its cover." So claims Bob Noxious in this 1983 interview conducted by the influential *Maximumrocknroll* founder Tim Yohannan. It's hard to see how the band could be judged otherwise: the Fuck-ups sang a song called "White Boy in the Mission," which—with none of Black Flag's satire—bemoaned becoming a White minority (in a largely Latino San Francisco neighborhood) and warned that "White boy gonna get a gun, white boy gonna kill." Noxious, the vocalist, also performed with a shirt emblazoned with a swastika and slogans proclaiming "White Power" and "Niggers Beware." Indeed, it's harder to comprehend how they could be interpreted otherwise. Yet Noxious insists that his obvious racism is justified because "That's what punk is being about, I guess. You gotta be offensive to somebody." As punks moved into the inner city in search of cheap living quarters and practice spaces, that "somebody" was often someone poor and non-White, and punk's trademark nihilism —"I'm against it"—could find a target in their new neighbors. Furthermore, Noxious insists that as a White punk living in a largely Latino neighborhood, he is the one that is oppressed and "treated violently." Whiteness here is still "punk whiteness," or oppositional whiteness, but in the case of Bob Noxious it is in opposition to other minorities as well.

MAXIMUMROCKNROLL: The Fuck-Ups are more than a band, right?

BOB NOXIOUS: They're actually a train of thought. You know, like the Fuck-Ups are now becoming an institution almost.

MRR: To you, what do the Fuck-Ups stand for?

NOXIOUS: Youth, and rebellion, and getting off people's backs. Doin' what you feel is right, not takin' any shit. Pretty much it's a group of people with the same way of thought. I don't see us having a goal, just playin' music, havin' a real good time, basically comin' and doin' the things we want to do, you know ... in our clubs, with the kids we want to be with. ...

MRR: Do you feel like you've been misunderstood or ...

NOXIOUS: Basically, a lot of people who listened to us at first ... you can't judge a book by its cover. And people, when they first heard our record, they thought, basically, that "White Boy" was a racist, anti-black song. What it is—it says right in the song—"White boy, you're a minority," and that's how we feel, you know. The San Francisco punks, which is what we're singin' right here, is there's not too many of them and they've got to unite. I think that's basically what the song says.

MRR: It also says, "White boy gonna get a gun, white boy gonna kill." What's that all about?

NOXIOUS: That's the anger built up deep inside everyone. Some people are gonna relate to that; some people jump right off and say, "Well, hey, you know, what is this? This is wrong to say things like that." Well, you know, you go to war, fuck, you're gonna have a gun. That's just a bit of the anger in all of us, I guess. Everybody lets it out.

MRR: The anger inside you—where does it come from?

NOXIOUS: Mostly, just being oppressed. Not really oppressed, as in a sense of I'm not a boat person, where I've come to another country. It's like, you take a lot of shit in your life, and you wanna do what you wanna do, and that's the way I feel. I don't have a whole bunch of anger, but everybody's got that side of them.

MRR: I was one of the people who took that song "White Boy" in a more racist sense, partly because I remember you used to have a T-shirt that said "Kill Niggers" or something like that.

NOXIOUS: It said "Supreme White Power." No, "White Power." Then there was a swastika, and then on the back it said "Niggers Beware."

MRR: So what was that all about?

NOXIOUS: I think everybody knows what that's about. I kinda wore it ... I thought the shirt looked real good. I was ignorant.

MRR: In what sense?

NOXIOUS: In the sense of … I didn't wear it for that sense, "Niggers Beware." I liked the way the swastika looked and stuff like that.

MRR: Then it didn't sum up your feelings on the subject.

NOXIOUS: Oh no. I don't think we even played "White Boy" that night.

…

MRR: In "White Boy," you're talking about punks being a minority versus the rest of society, right?

NOXIOUS: Yeah, pretty much.

MRR: Why the "White" part? In other words, what I'm saying is …

NOXIOUS: Why isn't it "Black Boy" or something?

MRR: No, what I'm saying is why isn't it "Punk Boy" or something? So, it's about being in the Mission (a district of S.F. that's heavily Chicano, Filipino, etc.).

NOXIOUS: You're not always a punk though. I don't have to label myself as being that. You know, "White Boy," when we wrote that, it's just, "Well, I'm white, and that's just the way I feel." That's what I told you about being a minority in your own area, where you live and shit like that.

MRR: Is there any sense on your part, that people who live in the Mission

…

NOXIOUS: That's where the song is. When I walk out of my house, there's about a hundred Mexicans and Chicanos.

MRR: Most of the people who live over there are pretty much forced to economically, right? They're not the "voluntary poor."

NOXIOUS: Oh no, we got a real good deal on a little storefront. It's the best thing we could have.

MRR: So along comes this punk culture into the …

NOXIOUS: Neighborhood.

MRR: Right, and in a sense, in relation to this "gang" thing, there's a certain arrogance to that way of thinking. And then you come marching in. There's bound to be some kind of collision, going into their ghetto territory.

NOXIOUS: That's what punk is being about, I guess. You gotta be offensive to somebody. …

Tim Yohannan, from "Interview: The Fuck-Ups," *Maximumrocknroll* no. 8 (Berkeley, September 1983).

BLACK FLAG,
INTERVIEW IN *RIPPER*

No band remains more emblematic of **LA hardcore punk** than **Black Flag**—in fact, you might even say that the band still provides the aesthetic blueprint for the contemporary **American punk scene.** For a band so confrontational, so contentious, none of their songs has proven to be more so than **"White Minority,"** from their 12-inch EP *Jealous Again,* released in August 1980. The song has been characterized, for instance, as a **"fascist, racist rant,"** and came under further scrutiny from zine-writing punks of color in the early 2000s.[1] Indeed, it seems to be articulating the same kind of White rage as Bob Noxious's Fuck-Ups. The track, however, with lyrics written by the White guitarist and **SST records** founder **Greg Ginn,** was sung by two consecutive Latino lead singers: **Ron Reyes,** who appears on the recording, and later **Dez Cadena. ROBO,** Black Flag's drummer, was also Latino, and **Spot,** the album's producer, was Black. This in and of itself would obviously not disqualify the song from racism, but in this 1981 interview with **Tim Tonooka** of the seminal zine *Ripper* the band has a chance to explain itself. They characterize the track as an exaggerated satire of xenophobia, and the very hyperbole illustrates the ridiculousness of such fears. So what is it about the song and its presentation that encourages subsequent generations to read it as racist?

RIPPER: What do your parents think of what you're doing?

GREG GINN: They try to think about all the good parts.

DEZ CADENA: Mine are into it, because I get to go all over the place and travel. I'm only 20 and it's a good learning experience or something.

HENRY ROLLINS: It's furthering our careers in life as young Americans growing up.

CHUCK DUKOWSKI: Mine wish I was a doctor or a lawyer. They wish I was real conservative and they go, "Do you really know what you're doing? Do you understand that the more recognition you get for this thing, the less future you have?"

RIPPER: What was that Manson trip (Creepy Crawl) you had going for a while?

GINN: It was devised by Raymond Pettibon (Greg's brother, and Black Flag's artist). It was basically a series of flyers and other stuff, just on the Manson theme, and the various things you can do with that.

CADENA: It was a fun topic to joke around with.

DUKOWSKI: And he's a real current symbol with a lot of impact on a lot of people. You take that to a place like New York, and it's really alien to them—the whole young, healthy, and virile thing with this whole sick side, and the potential that he had to STRIKE. It's not like I take Manson very seriously. But there is something going on there that was interesting to hook into a little bit. And I am into the Creepy Crawl concept to the end.

RIPPER: Would you like to explain that concept?

DUKOWSKI: Creepy Crawl is fear. Fear is a real strong emotion in people. It goes both ways. When you go into a situation, you experience it, and the whole idea is to RIDE it—to use the adrenaline you get from that and direct it. And that within yourself is part of the Creepy Crawl. What you do to other people with it is make them feel this experience of fear. You threaten a lot of their values, and the potential for something to happen that they don't understand, or they don't have control of in their existing mental framework, makes it useful to throw them off balance and thus open people up to where you don't have as prejudiced an attitude.

GINN: That's part of what we try to do as a band.

ROLLINS: If it's done right, you can have a lot of impact.

DUKOWSKI: If you can knock 'em out of their standard way of looking at things, with a strong emotion like fear, then you've got open minds.

GINN: But not just fear. Sometimes you can just BLAST 'em. We read an article in *BAM* about Carlos Santana, and he said, "In general, people like to be punched, they don't like to be blasted." Well, we like to blast.

RIPPER: Now that you've become widely known, what kind of effect do you think you've had on the general public?

GINN: A lot of people have the wrong idea about us. That's something we continuously have to fight. People think we're into promoting some kind of violence. The general public is starting to get the idea, because we've been able to counter some of the bad publicity with a more accurate representation. But we still got a while to go.

RIPPER: What do you hope to accomplish when you tour England and Europe in December?

GINN: Not very much. We think we can accomplish a lot more in the US as far as making an impact with the culture. We're more interested in playing in the US really, although we will go over there.

RIPPER: I've heard a number of different people's ideas of what your song "White Minority" is about. What's your explanation of it?

GINN: The idea behind it is to take somebody that thinks in terms of "White Minority" as being afraid of that, and make them look as outrageously stupid as possible. The fact that we had a Puerto Rican (Ron) singing it was what made the sarcasm of it obvious to me. Some people seem to want to take it another way, and somehow think that we'd be so dumb to where a Puerto Rican guy would sing it and it would be—I don't know how they could consider that racist, but people took it that way.

DUKOWSKI: It's one of those things. It's like the flyer for this gig (a naked superman flying through the air with a hard-on). It draws out people's existing attitudes. If someone is afraid that they're racist or something, then they're gonna call it racist.

GINN: Or they would like to say, "Oh, Black Flag—racists." It's people that don't like us, basically.

DUKOWSKI: If someone *is* racist, they'll use it for an anthem, for a while, but it's so polarized, that if you do it for a little while, it starts to get a little bit ludicrous.

GINN: It throws that attitude out and makes people think. To me, that's what it does. It doesn't preach, but it makes people think.

DUKOWSKI: The fact that there is a controversy means it accomplished its goal.

GINN: It's not a kind of song that has a long-term emotional impact or value to us. We don't even play it all the time.

RIPPER: What is your song "No Values" about?

GINN: It's not *about* anything. It comes from just feeling like what's in the song, rather than some kind of political thing. It's an emotional concept of a feeling at a certain time.

RIPPER: Would you say that describes most of your songs?

ROLLINS: Yeah. Our songs are personal. They're not about issues. They're about what's in our heads.

GINN: Yeah. "White Minority" is different than that. ...

Tim Tonooka, from "Interview: Black Flag," *Ripper* no. 6 (San Francisco, 1981).

GREIL MARCUS,
"CRIMES AGAINST NATURE"

In what is ostensibly a review of the Adolescents' self-titled album, the legendary rock critic and music historian Greil Marcus gives what is perhaps the most succinct and incisive critique available of LA punk's articulation of whiteness. Marcus, who would later invest much time and ink analyzing U.K. punk in _Lipstick Traces_, understands punk's movement to Los Angeles as a transition from Johnny Rotten's subversive and ultimately leftist antagonism to Sid Vicious's pure nihilism. With an assist from his fellow critic Robert Christgau, Marcus argues that punk's rage has moved from being directed at "those in power" to "the other" and "the powerless." He remains unconvinced that punk's embrace of racist tropes could be explained away through camp or ironic appropriation. When Marcus writes, "Contempt for and a wish to exterminate the other is presented here as a rebellion against the smooth surface of American life, but it may be more truly a violent spectacular accommodation to America's worst instincts," he astutely understands that punk rebellion against society at large may be encouraged and fostered by the very privilege it attempts to rage against.

> Father, Mother and Me
> Sister and Auntie Say
> All the people like us are we
> And everyone else is they
> —Rudyard Kipling, "We and They"

The Adolescents are five young men from Orange County who, if their songs are to be believed, hate everything. Neat and trendy: they hate children, homosexuals, girls, politics, their so-called peers, and science class. It's the revenge of the wimps: who else would think to take it all out on an amoeba? "A one-celled creature, a one-celled thing / It hardly knows it's alive / You're better off dead."

So why does their music sound so good?

The thirteen cuts on _Adolescents_ don't quite stand out from one another, and the feeling isn't exactly that of moral discovery, but the feeling is as convincing as it has to be: you don't _just_ laugh. The I'm-mean-and-pissed-and-confused voice of singer Tony Cadena isn't leagues away from those of better-known flag-wavers of lumpen Los Angeles punk—Ron Reyes of Black Flag, Lee Ving of Fear—but it's got its own momentum, because the Adolescents are such a tight, musically precise band. I like the way Cadena turns the Ramones' signature kick-off—that tiresome "one-two-three-*four!*"—into actual lyrics without losing the hurricane beat, but it's a hard trick to give a singer the rhythm he needs to pull that off, and the Adolescents have it down cold.

The Adolescents are also terrific at disguising their skill. They make finely crafted numbers with fairly complex structures sound like found objects, found noise, found rage—the result of too many days spent brooding, cultivating resentment, masturbating (a big theme here). With a British postpunk band like the Gang of Four, Delta 5, or the Au Pairs, an equally harsh, intense music plainly announces itself as thought-out, a matter of a confrontation with a situation that leaves you changed: the point is to acknowledge the process, investigate it, make it real to others. (If punk says, "Life stinks," postpunk says, "Why does life stink?") The Adolescents work in the long, rich tradition of the American's opposition to the effete, overcivilized Old World—a tradition in which Mark Twain's *A Connecticut Yankee in King Arthur's Court* and Henry James's *The American* remain the basic texts. The Adolescents are frankly barbarians, and they create (an essentially effete activity, as opposed to, say, arson) in order to deny the claims of the alternatives.

Which hardly disposes of questions about contradictions between the Adolescents' primitivist, mindless pose ("We're just a wrecking crew / Bored boys with nothing to do. ... I could care less about the queers—they suck. ... I'm just a victim of society / A slob") and their well-constructed music, between their mindlessness and the jolt their music can deliver to the skeptical listener. The answer may be at once simple and ambiguous: rock 'n' roll based in strong feeling works. It may be in the nature of the music, the terms of which were originally worked out by the earliest blues singers, black men who took a half step away from the feudal constraints of turn-of-the-century Mississippi, men for whom the public expression of rage—against anyone, including their wives and lovers—was a sign of freedom. But strong feeling isn't intelligence. For years women have had to deal with the contradiction, the ugly paradox, of finding themselves captivated by unmistakably sexist rock 'n' roll—and it is specious and sentimental to think that good art is "good": that, say, Nazi rock that is both powerful and seductive is out of the question.

What, then, is the strong feeling that underlies the Adolescents' music? In 1977 Robert Christgau wrote that punk was the first of the U.K.'s many rock-based teenage subcultures to direct its rage where it belonged: against those in power. L.A. punk, which is a U.K. punk spin-off that has chosen

Sid Vicious (prophetic thug) over Johnny Rotten (thuggish prophet) as avatar, jumped that track; perhaps because those who make L.A. punk are so often tracked to become those in power, to enjoy money and mobility without purpose, L.A. punk directs its rage against the other, the power-less—and that is a stance no less American than a happy barbarianism.

What this means is not ambiguous. Whoever is not formally like you is an irritant, and therefore the enemy, and therefore a crime against nature. In 1981 this stance is a glamorization of the disinclination to think, or a glamorization of the urge to hit what is vulnerable: to a boy, a girl may function as a crime against nature (his nature); to a white, a black; and so on down the line. Black Flag may explain its "White Minority" ("Gonna be a white minority / All the rest will be the majority / Gonna breed infe-riority") as an ironic joke on American racism, or as a steely expression of realism, of what people happen to think—but if a politician told us that "something has to be done about the queers, kikes, greasers, dykes, and niggers who are taking over our country," no one would be looking for the irony, and the politician's explanation that he was just trying to "shake people up" or "expose their hidden bigotry" wouldn't be taken seriously. The opening lines of X's searing "Los Angeles" ("She had started to hate / Every nigger and Jew / Every Mexican that gave her lotta shit / Every homosexual and the idle rich") tell us not that the subject of the song has her hangups but that the objects of her rage are types, not like us, deserv-ing of the contempt they get: crimes against nature. The song has enough musical bite to make any nigger, Jew, Mexican, homosexual, or idle rich want to hear the tune again, and then think, "That's not me, I'm not like that" (like *what?*), and that is the true black hole of the number, and of L.A. punk: attacked, one may side with one's attacker, and accept the terms of the attack.

Revenge on the other—how else explain the Asian-American punk in Penelope Spheeris's Los Angeles punk documentary, *The Decline of Western Civilization*, who graciously informs the camera he wouldn't kill a Jew ("Maybe a hippie …")? The kid isn't going to kill anyone, but that's not the point; the point is the attitude, that the question even comes up, and Spheeris's disclaimer that swastika-chic among L.A. punks simply reflects a lack of knowledge about the past doesn't wash any more than that of Black Flag or my imaginary politician. The punk doesn't think he's better than the Jews, or even hippies—they're just … *not like him*. That's why the question comes up.

Spheeris's movie is wonderfully shot and cut: the opening moments— L.A. punks slamming the shit out of each other with such stylized fury it takes a minute to figure out what's going on—rank with the giant bowling ball sequence in *Raiders of the Lost Ark* for thrills and impact. But that hatred for the other keeps taking you out of the film. Black Flag is more than likable and more than funny in interview segments, but "White Minority" is what it is. Fear's queer baiting and woman baiting are obviously calculated, their "I Don't Care About You" more delightful than it has any right to be, but the band remains repulsive. Contempt for and a wish to exterminate the other is presented here as a rebellion against the smooth surface of American life, but it may be more truly a violent, spectacular accommodation to America's worst instincts. This is the secret Spheeris tells in spite of herself, no matter how much she's cleaned up the scene for public consumption (no heroin, no deaths, no violence against those who don't want it).

This idea—if you want to call it an idea; the idea behind almost every one of the Adolescents' songs (the amoeba is not like you or me)—may well be invigorating: negations usually are, for a time. Certainly, L.A. punk brought Spheeris to life as an artist. A friend of mine saw the movie, laughed her head off, went back to see it again, got the soundtrack L.P., and found herself interested in pop music as she hadn't been in years. The action in *The Decline* convinced her that something is going on that knows no limits, and that is a metaphor anyone can use for any purpose, just as those founding Mississippi bluesmen used an attack on their wives and lovers to touch a hatred of their masters, a hatred of those they could not attack head-on.

That is the source of the power of L.A. punk, of the Adolescents' mastery of the form, of their borrowed but appealing detestation of anyone perceived as not like them. The difference is plain: in 1910 a Mississippi bluesman who called for the death of the man who ran his plantation would have found groundhogs delivering his mail. The Adolescents can say what they please. The freedom of Los Angeles punk may be inspiring, it may convince many their world is still to be made, but it costs those who use it nothing. They won't be the ones to pay the piper.

Greil Marcus, "Crimes Against Nature," *Ranters and Crowd Pleasers: Punk in Pop Music 1977–92* (New York: Doubleday, 1993).

DANIEL S. TRABER,
"L.A.'S 'WHITE MINORITY': PUNK AND THE
CONTRADICTIONS OF SELF-MARGINALIZATION"

In an academic essay that has proven a classic in the ever-emerging field of "punk studies," Daniel S. Traber picks up on some of the insights provided by Marcus, while examining the degree to which the punks' position of self-marginalization might contribute to the foundation of an effective politics. Importantly, he identifies the subversive potential of punk's oppositional stance, and admits that it has set up a vast infrastructure of bands, record labels, venues, and zines that can sustain itself in the shadow of the dominant culture. However, the flipside of this potential for Traber is its reliance upon the continued existence of that dominant culture in order to define itself as oppositional. For all punk's transgressions, it keeps the boundaries firmly in place: mainstream/alternative, dominant/Other, and, importantly, White/minority. Alongside these oppositions, punk defines itself in the search for authenticity that fetishizes poverty (what Traber calls the "sub-urban") and in a rage that is characteristically American in its individualism. What emerges is a picture of punk as an angry critique of bourgeois conformity articulated in a profoundly White bourgeois register.

Part of popular music's allure is that it offers fans tools for identity construction. Lawrence Grossberg argues that musical choices open sites for people to negotiate their historical, social, and emotional relations to the world; the way fans define and understand themselves—what they believe and value—is intertwined with the varying codes and desires claimed by a taste culture associated with a specific genre.[1] An example of claiming social and cultural difference through music occurs in *Dissonant Identities*, Barry Shank's study of the Austin music scene. In explaining her impetus for joining the punk subculture, a fan states, "[I]t really had something to do with just wanting to do something different. With in a way being an outcast but then being accepted. … And you were sort of bound together because the other people hated you. I think that [*sic*] might be a part of the attraction, too, is being in a minority. Being in a self-imposed minority."[2] This tactic of self-marginalization to articulate a politics of dissent is central to the Los Angeles punk scene from (roughly) 1977 to 1983.[3] To resist meta-narratives they found static and repressive, in order to form an independent sense of self, a small fringe group of youth pursued a life based on that inner-city underclass denied access to the American dream, an identity I will call the "sub-urban."

The racial and class facets of the sub-urban identity are deployed by L.A. punks to re-create themselves in the image of street-smart kids who are skeptical about the trappings of bourgeois America. In doing this they hoped to tap into a more "authentic" lifestyle—equivalent to "real," "hard," "tough," all those qualities associated with life on city streets—than the one they thought themselves being forced to replicate. However, it is the contradictions in punk's practice of tapping into the aura of the Other that will be the crux of this essay. Underpinning punk's appropriation of otherness is the theory that social categories are fluid constructs that can be accepted, rejected, or hybridized at will, and this belief disrupts the notion that identity is fixed, that there is anything natural or concrete about one's subjectivity. But in using markers classified as subordinate, this voluntarist self-exile is laden with the baggage of preconceived social categories. Punks unconsciously reinforce the dominant culture rather than escape it because their turn to the sub-urban reaffirms the negative stereotypes used in the center to define this space and its population. I consider punk rockers who move into the sub-urban site, but I am also interested in the general celebration of this identity by those who remain at home. While noting the specific positive effects of this border crossing, I analyze punk's lofty subversive goals as a paradoxical mixture of transgression and complicity for reasons the participants overlook.

I will elaborate on the theory of the underclass later; for now, I want to address labeling this space as "sub-urban." The term is more than a pun on the words suburbia, for sub-urban denotes an existence unlike the typical depiction of city life's everyday difficulties. It is important at the onset to emphasize that the sub-urban is multiracial (poverty is not just a "nonwhite" problem), but it does constitute a very specific class position, one that must confront the utmost levels of poverty, hunger, inadequate housing, and the constant threat of physical danger and death. Sub-urbanites are forced to negotiate their environment simply by surviving it as best they can, and it is this "extreme" way of life that punks of the period chose for their hard-edged bohemianism. I do not wish to trivialize the circumstances many of these kids faced, such as dysfunctional homes, being kicked out by their parents, or the economic downward mobility middle-class families suffered during this period; still, we will see that a good number of the earliest punks present themselves in a way that is rooted in the often romanticized existence of the down-and-out.

The choice starts to lose its thrust as a commentary on the parent culture's own litany of naturalized beliefs upon closer examination: that success is the result more of hard work than the privilege accorded to race and class (is it not such privileges that give them the option *not* to succeed?); that material wealth is synonymous with freedom (how can it be thought otherwise when these subjects have the freedom to come and go?); that their way of life constitutes the highest level of progress (then why else reject it by going "downward"?). Punk's adoption of marginality as a way to experience "real life" proves to be a belief in something transparent, thus they manipulate their identities in the name of choosing one they situate as less contaminated by middle-class illusion and conformity. This dissent and social critique are further contradicted and weakened since L.A. punk remains complicit with America's dominant social values by privileging the individual.[4]

Although problematizing L.A. punk's strategy of rebellion, I want to emphasize that their self-marginalization is not lacking in subversive promise. The punk movement did not achieve an outright transformation of society's dominant truths, but it did at least change the minds of many people. It established a permanent alternative to the corporate apparatus of the music industry by returning to a system of independent labels (originally used to distribute the postwar "race music" that influenced the white rockers of the 1950s). It also enabled a form of political community as witnessed by the numerous punk scenes throughout the world that share their music and ideas. Nonetheless, the foundations of L.A. punk's politics are shaky, and its liberatory spirit needs to be reconsidered. This subculture claims to desire dissonance and destabilization, but it depends on boundaries and regulatory fictions staying in place to define itself as oppositional. This does not mean the subversive energy completely dissipates, but it cannot be theorized as a trouble-free dismantling of identity categories because it relies uncritically on the dominant for its difference and forces the subordinated into the role of being an alternative. Punks are actually uninterested in abolishing those restrictive lines of cultural and social demarcation, and any act of denaturalization in this gesture starts to appear accidental. Instead of tearing down the boundaries, they use them to sustain a false sense of autonomy—like those in the center, without the Other they cease to exist.

In making this argument I do not strive to give an account of the way "it really was" in the L.A. punk scene. Instead, I aim to make sense of the way we are *told* it was by interrogating the narratives, discourses, and practices used to position Los Angeles in the punk movement by considering how participants and their supporters voice the merits of becoming like the sub-urban Other. ...

L.A. punks intend to transgress the fixed order of class and racial hierarchies by crossing the boundaries of their inherited subjectivities as privileged white youth.[5] The animosity they direct toward straights is commonly traced to their socialization experience: "Many punks had come from social situations where they had been the outsiders. Having escaped suburbia, having been outcasts, they now had their own group from which they could sneer and deliver visual jolts to the unimaginative, dumb, suburban world."[6] For many kids, the subculture's sense of anger and unrest came out of southern California communities where post-sixties children were searching for something to pierce the boredom of their lives and express their sense of social and political marginality. The ability to choose your own narrative, to live according to a worldview that you have authorized for yourself, is an act of self-empowerment, and the ideology of punk advocates just such a reinscription through an identity different from the majority. In *Subculture* Dick Hebdige describes how these subjects desire to annihilate their past: "the punks dislocated themselves from the parent culture and were positioned instead on the outside ... [where they] played up their Otherness."[7] L.A. punks react against the image-conscious mentality of Los Angeles by presenting a contrary image: celebrating ugliness in contrast to beauty, depression instead of joy, the sordid over the morally approved; in short, opting for the city's gritty underbelly over its glamorous face. It is by using a version of L.A.'s own tricks (e.g., making themselves into something to be looked at, the logic of self-(re)construction, a belief that history can be erased and rewritten) that they attempt to open a space for social critique.

Their strategy of segregating themselves from the status quo in an antithetical style extended itself beyond fashion and music for the core L.A. fans. In early 1978 a run-down apartment complex named the Canterbury Arms became the living quarters for several punks. Craig Lee (guitarist for the Bags) lists a catalog of their new neighbors that relies on racial and class markers to indicate its stark difference from home: the hotel was "occupied by black pimps and drug dealers, displaced Southeast Asians living ten to a room, Chicano families, bikers from a halfway house, in addition to various bag ladies and shopping cart men."[8] In discussing the Canterbury with Jeff Spurrier, Trudie repeats Lee's roster of marginal figures: "When we first moved there, the whole building was full of criminals, SSI people, hookers, bikers, and pimps."[9] This site constitutes a form of existence delegitimated in dominant American political discourses and the popular media. Greil Marcus's review of X's *Los Angeles* acknowledges punk's interest in and sense of connection to the darker realms of urban life ignored by many white middle-class Americans. In his opinion, X's songs express "an insistence that those horrors [of the urban down-and-out] have made the people who live them and who sing about them better than those who don't: not just tougher and smarter but morally superior, if only because they've seen through the moralism other people only pretend to believe in anyway."[10] Particular signifiers of race and class are used, often mapped onto each other, in establishing this rebel credibility to invent an inner-city subjectivity denoting genuine otherness.

Land and location are central to L.A. politics as they maintain the spatial hierarchy that allows some people access to the "good life" while keeping others out. For middle-class punks to banish themselves from "paradise" is a transgression of the American dream. Even as their parents fought battles over taxes, property values, and neighborhood boundaries to prevent the influx of inner-city populations, this subgroup of youth (who were the public justification for their parents' politics) rejected the planned utopias to live among the very people the folks back home claimed to be protecting them from.[11] It is a choice about a certain way of life: immersing oneself in urban decay and the asceticism of harsh poverty. This border crossing becomes, quite literally, an act of deterritorialization (to use Deleuze and Guattari's term for escaping repressive social structures) in that changing one's physical environment facilitates a change in the ideological framework of one's personal psychic space. The lifestyle works as an inverse form of social mobility; in their own social formation punks earn status by becoming tougher and going "lower."

One L.A. punk divulges the code: "Everyone got called a poseur, but you could tell the difference: Did you live in a rat-hole and dye your hair punk and wreck every towel you owned and live hand-to-mouth on Olde English 800 and potato chips? Or did you live at home and do everything your mom told you and then sneak out?"[12] Here austere living is configured as virtuous because it is a sign of honesty and devotion to the subculture's values. A similar example of this occurs in Penelope Spheeris's 1980 documentary *The Decline of Western Civilization* (hereafter *Decline*) when Chuck Dukowski, a college student, narrates becoming a punk as his "search" for an answer to the meaning of life: "I did this because I felt like to set myself aside and make myself different, maybe, maybe, [the answer] will just come to me." All the more suggestive is that he delivers this conversion narrative from a room brimming with signifiers of extreme poverty. As the camera pans to follow Ron Reyes (the Puerto

Rican singer for Black Flag, adding a nonwhite subject to the picture) giving a tour of his apartment, we see the rest of the band and a few hangers-on (all of them white) lounging on decrepit furniture, drinking cheap beer, surrounded by walls covered with spray-painted band names and profane slogans. It turns out that Reyes pays $16 a month to sleep in a converted closet since he owes money to all the utility companies. This scene establishes a connection with the "just getting by" life(style) of the sub-urban subject. Reyes's attitude about his living conditions teeters between realizing there is something troublesome here—he shows how some people actually live in America—and exhibiting a resigned, dignified posture—this is how "we" live as compared to "you."

Another voice on using self-marginalization to achieve a sense of hard "realness" comes from the eighties. From 1981 to 1986, Henry Rollins was the singer for Black Flag. In *Get in the Van* Rollins explains why he was attracted to the lifestyle of the band upon first meeting them:

> They had no fixed income and they lived like dogs, but they were living life with a lot more guts than I was by a long shot. I had a steady income and an apartment and money in the bank … The way they were living went against all the things I had been taught to believe were right. If I had listened to my father, I would have joined the Navy, served and gone into the straight world without a whimper.[13]

Rollins later describes his new life after joining the band and moving to Los Angeles:

> I was learning a lot of things fast … Now the next meal was not always a thing you could count on … Slowly I came to realize that this was it and there was no place I'd rather be. As much as it sucked for all of us to be living on the floor on top of each other, it still was better than the job I had left in D.C.[14]

Rollins defines himself in terms of his origin in middle-class stability, but also as proudly contesting that existence to live a life beyond the wall the bourgeoisie has built around itself. By adopting a life in contradistinction to his natal social environment, this kind of punk articulates the discourse that autonomy can be achieved by disengaging from the ruling social order.

All this locates punk's self-marginalization physically and philosophically, but where do they stand historically in relation to their identity as an Other? And how will that affect our reading of their attempt at transgression? The domestic and foreign battles of the late sixties were a difficult time for Americans trying to make sense of their country's future, but the post-Vietnam years saw the United States transform into a demoralized nation deeply wracked by uncertainty and instability. The historical record proves a daunting one indeed: a lost war, Watergate, feminism and Black Power's continued attacks on the status quo, soaring inflation and interest rates, oil embargoes causing a decrease in real wages, deindustrialization and downsizing, and hostages in Iran. These are just a few of the problems leading to the feeling that America's day was past. This was instrumental in the upsurge of neoconservativism from the New Right and the Moral Majority, culminating with Ronald Reagan sweeping into office on his antiliberal platform of *laissez-faire* economics, tax cuts, and anticommunism.

Research on the economic problems of the middle class in this period—such as Katherine Newman's and Frederick Strobel's—reveals the collapsing expectations experienced by late baby-boomer professionals as well as those of the lower class and lower middle class whose once secure manufacturing jobs were disappearing. The "median individual income declined 14 percent between 1972 and 1982" and inflation had affected over half the population as real wages decreased.[15] Additionally, postwar subsidies like the Federal Home Loan program and G.I. Bill, which enlarged a white middle class, had ended, and the tax burden had shifted from corporations to the lower and middle classes.[16] California, home of the 1978 tax revolt, was a key player in these events. Mike Davis reports that Reagan's plan for helping the rich get richer was successful in Los Angeles, where affluence tripled, but "ensured an erosion of the quality of life for the middle classes in older suburbs as well as for the inner-city poor."[17]

Since punk emerged from this social matrix, it is tempting to trace the appropriation of a sub-urban identity to this story of decline and stagnation or to frame it as an act of negation meant to minimize the pain of lost suburban dreams by claiming not to want them. Such an interpretation is inaccurate.

L.A. punk's common discourse, as expressed in the music and participants enunciations, presents a rationale grounded in privatized issues, e.g., feelings of personal alienation or repelling conservative attempts to control individual consciousness (there are exceptions, of course, like the Dils and the Minutemen, who openly voice Marxist ideas). Rick Gershon makes this case in stating (perhaps overstating), "Although people were doing their homework and reading their *NME*s, clearly it wasn't representative of any sort of economic or political situation in L.A."[18] This is not to claim that punk was apolitical or quietist, for it was hardly interested in making nice with the pop masses and corporations. Certainly we can interpret the waning of the middle class as a catalyst thrusting some punks into an understanding of class politics, making their border crossing a response to the conditions of late capitalism; however, to draw a straight cause-and-effect line between these two is misguided. It is rare to find in L.A. punk anything like an outright lament for the loss of white privilege, while critiques of suburbia's very values and desires are ubiquitous. These punks do not resolve their problems by deciding to work harder; instead, they say "fuck it" to the whole idea of desiring a suburban middle-class lifestyle. L.A. punk more often frames itself in language intimating they engage in this practice to rebel against the bourgeoisie, not to bemoan their dwindling opportunities to join it. We also cannot ignore how punk is commonly framed by its fans and performers alike as a response to the standard teen complaint of "nothing to do," not as a voice demanding the reinstatement of lost privileges. The extreme conditions of a sub-urban life are not ones many of them are *forced* into by their parents' financial problems, so by turning away from suburbia they challenge America's cherished shibboleths of prosperity and progress.

Clearly there are political motivations behind self-marginalization in punk, but its initial and fundamental concern is that of a privatized quest to differentiate one's self from the status quo, as a person free of any control outside him/herself. Of course, individualism and its attendant notion of freedom are not fixed. Eric Foner's recent *The Story of American Freedom* examines how eras and groups have their own functioning definitions of what it means to be free and to have rights, and these meanings are thoroughly tied to the distinct needs and interests of historically placed people. Still, the most evident source of punk's definition of individualism is classical liberalism's defense of the sovereign individual: no person or institution has the right to determine what you can say, think, feel, or do as long as you do not inhibit another person's freedom. This idea is one of the most prevalent threads running through American literature and culture. Likewise, self-marginalization as a strategy to achieve this individualism is just as prominent. The crusade for individualism, for escaping the authority of society, is fulfilled by taking up residence in the forest or following Huck Finn's advice to light out for the West's unexplored frontier. In 1977—when punk had developed into a recognizable cultural event—there is no longer a frontier to which one can escape (as Californians know all to well) and the individualist is left searching for a new territory that will provide refuge from the structures of late capitalism. What punks want, then, what they need from their definition of freedom, is a way to understand themselves in relation to the larger social body.

References to one's necessary freedom from coercion are overwhelming in their number and variety in punk rock, but they are hardly deployed in the name of upholding the "free market" doctrines of contemporary individualism. Rather, they are concerned with free will and autonomy in thought, values, and identity and being unencumbered by external constraints. In *Decline* Malissa tells the interviewer that punks are striving "to be accepted any way we want to." And Jennipher advises the audience that "everyone shouldn't be afraid to be as different as they want to be." This autonomy of conscience and action also gets distilled through a logic of artistic originality as the right to be unique instead of a conformist adhering to clichéd form. The earliest scene makers became disenchanted as the punk scene shifted to the hardcore style. The Weirdos' John Denny opines, "[Punk became] more macho, jock, aggressive. The whole individuality thing began to dissipate, and it just became more fascistic."[19] That is ultimately the passkey for grasping how individualism functions in punk subculture: one is either independent and unique, or acquiescent and ordinary.

Paul Fryer's critique of U.K. punk dissent mentions this "insistent championing of individuality," yet he foregoes a deeper analysis that would also complicate punk's pursuit of marginality as an act engaged in the negative impulses of liberal individualism.[20] The paradox is that as punks maneuver to enhance their self-identity as autonomous beings their appropriation of otherness starts to resemble one of liberalism's guiding tenets of "property in the person," which characterizes what C. B. Macpherson calls possessive individualism. The self becomes the property that they protect and aggrandize with the Other manipulated and objectified as a means to that end, thus, denied his/her own individuality and freedom. The ultimate implication of this negligence is that punk unwittingly repeats the ideological patterns of the dominant culture by privileging the importance of the self and self-interest, thus treating the Other as an object to be used for their own desires. Despite the call to be free from external influence, what L.A. punk shows is that without critically questioning our notions of the individual we take those discourses of the center with us everywhere we go. And this finally weakens punk's transgressive potential, for the individualism at punk's core forecloses the possibility of collective action that could more effectively challenge the problems they are protesting.[21]

This spirit of resistance in L.A. punk quite befits the whole subculture's initial ethos of negation. They scream in the face of authority, be it for political justice or just to have fun, by using their music and style. The antiestablishment attitude toward musicianship (three chords being enough), audience participation (demolishing the boundary between performer and audience), and cultural production (the DIY ethic) is intent on positioning punk as the antithesis of corporate-controlled rock and pop as an extension of its social politics. ...[22]

[A]s the U.K. variant of punk traveled back to America, Los Angeles is one of the places where the Clash's call to have a "white riot" is taken up enthusiastically, and it is by fitting themselves into public discourses surrounding nonwhites that they hope to realize their version of white insurgency.

The impulse behind this self-fashioning and its class politics is the rejection of a specifically conceived racial identity; namely, whiteness as a specific social, economic, and cultural formation. In denying the benefits of their race, these kids are in effect attempting to critique the entire system upon which the United States was founded and truly functions. Elaine K. Ginsberg explains the political benefits whites gain by choosing nonwhite marginality in their identity construction: "the decision to 'pass' as [an Other], to self-construct an identity perceived by a white majority as less desirable, disrupts the assumptions of superiority that buttress white privilege and self-esteem. [Consequently,] challenging racial categories threatens those whose sense of self-worth depends on their racial identity and the social status that accompanies it."[23] Additionally, Eric Lott's work on the racial logic of blackface minstrelsy as "love and theft"—simultaneously a desire for and racist disparagement of black culture—locates this form of entertainment in the "American tradition of class abdication through ... [a] cross-racial immersion which persists ... in historically differentiated ways, to our own day."[24] This situates L.A. punk as a link in that chain, and by turning to the sub-urban this treason is amplified by going against the dominant white social class buttressing suburbia. But in setting its sights on this particular form of whiteness—based on a conflation of racial and class categories—an unintended contradiction develops as punk drifts toward essentializing both whiteness and nonwhiteness by ultimately situating a version of bourgeois middle-class whiteness as the norm against which all is compared (which also perpetuates a stereotype of whites), such that it is sustained as the nation's dominant ideology. This paradox will be addressed more fully later; for now, I want to establish how whiteness is defined and deployed by these subjects.

In *Another State of Mind*, a 1983 documentary/tour film on L.A. hard-core, it is notable that during this later phase of the subculture's history the kids interviewed all pick out preppies, rather than hippies (the earlier middle-class youth group punk targets), as the opposite that helps them grasp their identity as punks. In other words, preppiness is the alternate subjectivity open to them. Like punk, preppiness is itself a distinctive way of life—clothes, behavior, and worldview—but one immersed in a notion of affluent whiteness. Now, one can find nonwhite preppies and those who do not wholly subscribe to tenets of conservatism and elitism, but in punk's social landscape it is a style thoroughly associated with "acting" and "looking" white as well as "acting" and "looking" wealthy. In punk, whiteness is configured as the subject position of the center, and punk's border crossing calls attention to its "invisible" ideology that permeates society and evaluates as an inferior "Other" all that does not meet its standards. By associating whiteness with the suburb, punk comments on the (mis)representation of white racial and class subjectivities, i.e., the invisibility of whiteness and the attendant privileges it is awarded.

This can be interpreted as a move toward fulfilling David Roediger's claim that "consciousness of whiteness also contains elements of a cri-tique of that consciousness and that we should encourage the growth of a politics based on hopeful signs of a popular giving up on whiteness" by "exposing, demystifying and demeaning [its] particular ideology."[25] The Black Flag [lyric] about being a "white minority" both labels whiteness as a specific race and resists the homogenizing pressures of that culture—to be bourgeois, mundane, conventional, in a word: uncool. As the lyrics propose, the only viable alternative for white kids uninterested in the American dream is to reject the privilege of their skin color by emulating the lifestyle of marginalized subjects—safe from outside control to the extent that they can remain hidden from and ignored by the larger society like other "oppressed" social groups.[26] So if, as Roediger argues, the "very claiming of a place in the US legally involved ... a claiming of white-ness," punk's cultural practice becomes even more politically weighted as a refusal of the ruling perception of legitimate Americanness itself.[27] The rewards of whiteness are rejected in their new identity through a con-scious "disaffiliation," to use Marilyn Frye's term, from the racial and class groups in which they are supposed to desire membership. ...

This chosen life of social marginality depends on its relation to what the suburban bourgeoisie decides to include and exclude from the center. The cultural practice of punk's subject formation comes to take on another quality: a colonial appropriation of the sub-urban life through a specific "look" and behavior. Punk's border crossing can be read as a commodification of the Other that aestheticizes identity for capital in a symbolic economy of signification. Some are bothered that punk's counterhegemonic power ultimately cannot escape cooptation in the material economic system, but the truth is they employ the same logic against those they intend to posit as the newly privileged element. They exploit the sub-urban to produce a product marketed through the channels of their own bodies and cultural production, and while I do not accuse them of a "failed rebellion" because they cannot get outside that system, I *do* reject treating this contestation as if the agents were completely aware of the contradictions within which they move. There is simply too much being invested in this public image that wants to be taken quite seriously as a cultural intervention.

The most obvious way to problematize this appropriation is by considering the option of (re)escape waiting for some participants back home. Although one must be wary of generalizing the disparate economic statuses and life options of white L.A. punks, we must also recall that this rebellion, as framed by middle-class punks, is a rejection of the desires and social values *causing* the sense of economic anxiety their parents and mainstream peers feel. These kids left a parent culture that believed their lifestyle could survive if the proper political steps were taken—hence the sweeping turn to conservatism—so there is still a sense of hope for the future. And those values that attempt to maintain a middle-class lifestyle, which punks ran from, are still waiting for them. Besides, any transition away from a sub-urban life will seem all that much easier because the next level appears all that less grim. Even the Chicana Alice Bag of the Bags, who left her East L.A. barrio to live in the Canterbury, has a better place to run as the first phase of L.A. punk is dying in late 1979. Disheartened by the changes in the subculture, she "moved back home and had quit [the punk scene] and was getting ready to go back to school."[28] By contrast, for "true" sub-urbans this life is one with very real threats of hunger, disease, and death that are firmly rooted in a systematized inequality from which they are unable to easily free themselves.

Admittedly, this border crossing increases the aura of "credibility" attached to punks because they *are* living this life, but that status is just another essentialist version of true identity. Postmodern parody and decontextualized signifiers cannot adequately account for this cultural practice because these subjects *want* context—they move *into* the sub-urban and are utterly invested in it, otherwise they are mere "poseurs." This pursuit of authenticity, no matter how sincere, is as insulting a gesture as playacting when compared to those who cannot escape. That they would freely opt to live like oppressed groups formed by historical and social conditions they cannot claim says much about the political dedication of some punks, but it also speaks to how people of their social status understand their relationship to the notion of freedom. As Grossberg proposes, mobility and access can be configured spatially, for where one is placed on the map of social totality "define[s] the forms of empowerment or agency ... available to particular groups."[29] Such places are constituted in a way that can offer either emancipation or further repression—a large number of punks enjoy the former. The crushing realities of racial and/or economic subjugation are trivialized in their search for autonomy. They become mere adornments for differentiation to be discarded when no longer useful to the new subjectivity—just one more brand in the supermarket of identities. Punks attempt to be associated with a group that is ignored and swept away form public acknowledgment, like Ralph Ellison's "invisible man" (forced to disappear despite his very real presence, a condition the Black Flag epigraph treats positively), but that oppressed status is complicated by being presented in a way that requires, that begs for, the shocked gaze of the conservative masses.

If we return to the Canterbury apartments, that physical and social space chosen for its qualities of extreme otherness, only seven months after a contingent of punks moved in, we find a growing tension between the "real" sub-urbans and the new initiates. Craig Lee describes the changing state of the hotel and the negative reaction of the non-punk residents to their neighbors:

> The halls smelled like shit, someone constantly pissed in the elevator ... one girl was raped at gunpoint, cockroaches were everywhere, and another girl had an angry neighbor throw a pot of boiling soup on her face. Racial tensions were high. The basement rehearsal room had been padlocked, little fires were breaking out and punks started to flee. What had been envisioned as L.A.'s equivalent of the Chelsea Hotel [in New York] was no longer hospitable to kids playing Wire and Sham 69 full blast at four in the morning.[30]

The punks treated the Canterbury the way they thought it deserved. They behaved like spoiled kids who refuse to clean up after themselves and showed no respect for a place some are forced to live in because they lack a choice. This is more than the "snotty teen" pose punks affected. Here we see them using the sub-urban identity but refusing the possible multiple desires of people in that habitus. The sub-urban subject is exoticized, forced into a preexisting stereotype that further stabilizes a monolithic view of marginality. Gayle Ward's account of this problem (with reference to Janis Joplin) is accurate: it "borders on a reactionary romanticization … and a reification of the notion of racial [and class] difference."[31] The belief that this form of self-fashioning endows one with authenticity in contradistinction to the smiling mask of white middle-class life is based on the same uncritical acceptance of the racial logic found in Norman Mailer's "The White Negro": "the Negro knows more about the ugliness and danger of life than the White."[32] Lee does not elaborate on the cause of the "racial tensions" at the Canterbury, but one might assume they grew out of a feeling that the punks "don't fit in" here and have no respect for "us."

Any conceptualization of punk identity that equates the suburban and sub-urban as having comparable opportunities for subject (re)formation is problematic. "True" sub-urbans have considerably less control over their life choices, least of all over the identities they can afford to wear or the places where they can show them off. Punks ignore how some have the freedom to explore different identities while ontological mobility is restricted for others—"white subjectivity [is equated] with a social entitlement to experiment with identity."[33] Denaturalizing both suburban and sub-urban identities is a worthy objective, but then what? This is not a plea for returning to a naïve conception of authenticity, it simply acknowledges that suburban punks crossing racial and class lines come from a position where they are allowed to speak and act, where they have more options. All identities are performances of approved categories (ways we are either taught or adopt) so punks are trying on a particular subjectivity to accomplish a transgressive goal. Yet something lingers, something that intimates complicity, when kids coming from comfortable lives earn hipness by playing dress "down"—a version of symbolic capital acquisition in the economy of youth culture.

By framing these practices of signification within an economic metaphor, we see that punk exhibits a colonizing impulse in its border crossing. It exploits the condition of sub-urbans by mimicking a "way of life" others must negotiate in order to survive. What can be considered the sub-urban's labor (i.e., what they "do") in the economy of signification is to look and act "poor," and this is turned into a form of prestige by punks: *being* different by *acting* poor, which is all the more troublesome since they believe there is such a way of behaving that is then totalized. Acquiring symbolic capital is how the appropriation of otherness "pays," and it becomes the imperializing gesture in punk's tactic of escape. Representing themselves as the same tears down the barriers of difference but as a by-product of self-aggrandizement. Punk's immersion in social disenfranchisement belies the more problematic ramifications of self-marginalization when considered a subject position for less or nonmarginalized kids to don and denude at their leisure. This is a re-othering because those in the margin are made to conform to preconceptions that are a product of the center. Punks totalize their chosen marginal subjects according to their own narrative of honorable poverty; they force the Other into a fixed identity to empower themselves. The assumption that the life of the underclass is open to appropriation objectifies them in a model of emulation, while conveniently ignoring how these people may want to escape from the degradation of this life.

By treating them as an exploitable object enabling punks to achieve their own desires, this re-othering allows the center to continue speaking for the Other. By eliding the heterogeneous hopes existing in the sub-urban, they silence the marginal subject's own viewpoint on marginality. By proposing that they have joined a different cultural formation by adopting a certain lifestyle, punks further naturalize that subject position in a binary relationship to suburban life that is also (re)naturalized. The power of whiteness is recentered and buttressed as the norm through a logic of stereotyped racial and class difference—those sought-after characteristics of otherness that are actually products of dominant white discourses—to give a substantive meaning to their cultural practice. I wish to avoid duplicating the punks' theft of voice, but it is highly dubious that anyone located in the sub-urban—for a reason other than free will—would consider this life a just and good consequence of the unequal distribution of wealth.

This incongruity between positive social intentions and negative ideological underpinnings rarely appears in the enunciations of L.A. punks. The result is that living on welfare becomes more like a game than a necessity, daily navigating danger is a source of excitement rather than terror. Although punk situated itself as a self-conscious reaction to the commodification ubiquitous in late capitalism—realizing that even as it berated corporate rock it could not sell its product without replicating its processes—it appears neither capable of, nor interested in extending, that critique to its own cultural practices at this level. Too many suburban L.A. punks seem to believe they can achieve an identity free of their past personal history by moving to this social space and positioning themselves as a taste culture on the boundaries of mainstream consumption. Ironically, it is this system of differentiation that limits the effectiveness of punk's politics. Those subjects adopting a sub-urban "lifestyle" are, in essence, duplicating the methods of the group they publicly vilify to realize their rebellion. They leave the parent culture to form their own "lifestyle enclave" by producing an identity different from others according to certain patterns of belief, dress, and leisure activity, all framed as a vanguardist movement occurring in underground venues for people of the same inclination.[34] To escape the group mentality, they build their own group; one purposefully designed to appeal to certain types of people while keeping others out. As a subculture of secret meanings and codes for dress, bodily movement (be it dancing, walking, or posing), and attitude, the identity produced is an exclusionary one; therefore, in the end they are not unlike their parents. Although intended to function as a counterhegemonic alternative to the center, punk remains less a threat to institutions of authority than merely another option because it must maintain the center's standards to position itself.

On a more directly political level, punk's rejection of radical collectivity—to limit any suppression of the individual—keeps its own revolt locked within the very system it claims to be protesting.[35] Of course this critique is not utterly foreign to punk. A key theme in the work of Crass is the call for a collective politics reaching beyond the subculture, but their demand for collective thinking signals its overwhelming lack. Taking a hard anarcho-punk stance, Craig O'Hara complains, "Many Punk anarchists have been content to stay within their own circle and have rejected the possibility of widespread anarchy. This attitude is referred to as a conception of 'personal' anarchy ... This idea echoes the epitome of bourgeois culture."[36] Yet it is really "Punk" itself that replicates the dominant by using the same basic ideology and social patterns as the parent culture. The transgressive potential of their strategy for rejecting America's reigning ideologies is enervated since it is quite complicit with such beliefs. And this is due to that stringent faith in the primacy of the individual—one of the key discourses America and Americans use to justify coercive and oppressive acts—so central to punk's conceptualization of resistance. Any economic and social injustices punk rails against are an effect of the logic of individualism. An ideology rationalizing the withdrawal into private concerns—be it financial or spiritual or aesthetic fulfillment—by advocating self-interest is the one taken up as the foundational tenet of punk politics.

Punk's discourse finally becomes an extension of the parent culture's belief system; an unconscious affirmation of the materialism and political self-interest this "counterculture" claims to oppose. And it is in this light that punk's ability to work as a form of dissent needs to be reconfigured. Zygmunt Bauman's critique of floating identities proves apt. Such multiple subjects "favour and promote a distance between the individual and the other and cast the other primarily as the object of aesthetic, not moral, evaluation; as a matter of taste, not responsibility."[37] The late capitalist alienation these subjects feel is due to their investment in a version of autonomy that perpetuates that sense of isolation by privileging an insular individuation over a collectivity that will allow the inclusion of non-punks. They force themselves into a solipsistic cocoon wherein they cannot affect the conditions they claim make them unhappy, and this adds the finishing touches to their sense of alienation. As a music and culture produced by postmodern subjects, punk may best be understood in terms of a Foucauldian micropolitics: the localized effect of crossing boundaries contains the potential to spread. This possibility is severely limited, though; punk is too far in the margin, due to its own actions and those of society at large, to be heard by the kind of mass audience a more subdued music can (or is allowed to) reach. Perhaps, however, that is all that can be asked of it.

My intention has not been to police ontological boundaries of race and class as they have been traditionally demarcated. The point is hardly that punks fail to achieve a thing called authenticity, a "true" and whole self; nor is it that they fail to meet an impossible injunction to exist in either "pure 'autonomy' or total encapsulation."[38] The point is to ensure that people deploying "subversive" narratives and practices maintain the skepticism that initially prompted the decision to transgress. Punks prove themselves highly adept at criticism, including themselves, but more typically of those positioned as outside themselves. Yet I have shown the borderline that could not be crossed in Los Angeles, the discourse they refused to treat with critical vigor. For those punks who join the sub-urban and those simply celebrating it as the Other of suburbia, their means of self-construction remain entrenched in the logic of individuality as it is practiced by the enemy: the bourgeoisie they claim to reject. Despite the possibilities for engaging in denaturalization, their contrarian version of "reality" and the "good" succumbs to the illusion of a whole self, and the home where they choose to cultivate that subjectivity is based on stereotypes circulated by the dominant power formation. Although attempting to create a free self on their own terms, L.A. punks forgo critiquing their complicity in denying freedom, thus getting further entwined within the system they despise to the point that the paradox becomes so accepted—like the unseen whiteness in the center—that it is rendered all the more invisible to themselves.

Daniel S. Traber, from "L.A.'s 'White Minority': Punk and the Contradictions of Self-Maginalization," *Cultural Critique* no. 48 (Spring 2001).

VIC BONDI, DAVE DICTOR, AND IAN MACKAYE, ON "GUILTY OF BEING WHITE," IN *MAXIMUMROCKNROLL*

Along with Black Flag and Bad Brains, Washington, D.C.'s Minor Threat was one of the templates for contemporary hardcore. Like Black Flag, they also managed to release one of the most infamous songs in the history of punk rock, "Guilty of Being White." Where "White Minority" was ambiguous and satirical, "Guilty" is shockingly sincere and tenfold more problematic. The singer Ian MacKaye has gone on to be a hero of independent music, doing pioneering work with the bands Embrace and Fugazi, as well as spearheading Dischord Records. At nineteen, however, MacKaye, responding viscerally to being a "white minority" attending D.C. public schools, was pleading to not be "blame[d] for slavery ... [a] hundred years before I was born," and to instead be treated as an individual, outside of the politics of race—a position he has since characterized as "antiracist." In this roundtable discussion, MacKaye, the MDC vocalist Dave Dictor, and Articles of Faith's Vic Bondi go over the complexities of the song, its intentions and interpretations, in the context of an overarching treatment of the role of politics in punk. MacKaye clearly taps into some of the oppositional White rage we have previously identified (see his comments about hating *everybody*), but interestingly, he advocates not a specificity of oppression, and opposition, that would be "White," but rather the dissolution of race as a category of social interaction and political salience altogether. As he asserts, he sees not races, but individuals. The problems with such a position are clear—one cannot merely wish away the historical and economic realities of racism's lineage—but it will prove to be a persistent one as punk moves forward.

VIC BONDI: What does "Guilty of Being White" mean? That's a song that can be misconstrued.

IAN MACKAYE: Not at all, I don't think. But I'll explain it. I live in Washington, D.C., which is 75% black. My junior high was 90% black. My high school was 80% black, and throughout my entire life, I've been brought up in this whole thing where the white man was shit because of slavery. So I got to class and we do history, and for 3/4 of the year slavery is all we hear about. It's all we hear about. We will race through the Revolutionary War or the founding of America; we'd race through all that junk. It's just straight education. We race through everything, and when we'd get to slavery, they'd drag it all the way out. Then everything has to do with slavery or black people. You get to the 1950s, they don't talk about nothing except the black people. Even WWII, they talk about the black regiments. In English, we don't read all the novelists, we read all the black novelists. Every week is African King's Week. And after a while, I would come out of a history class, and this has happened to me many times, like in junior high school, and you know that kids are belligerent in junior high, and these kids would jack my ass up and say, "What the fuck, man, why are you putting me in slavery?" To me, racism is never going to end until people get off this whole thing. It's going flim-flam, back and forth. When will people just get off the whole guilt trip … First, all the white people were like "Fuck the niggers," and all of a sudden, it's "The black man is great. We love him. We're going to do everything for him," all the time. It's never going to get anywhere, because one generation it'll be the KKK, the next generation it'll be the Black Panthers. Now we see the KKK come back in again, more popular. I think the best way we're going to have to deal with it is that if I am able to say "nigger" without everyone gasping, and if I'm able to say that word, because I don't have any problems with that word. I say "bitch," and that means a girl asshole. I might say "jock," which means an athletic asshole. But you say "nigger," which means a black asshole, everyone flies off the handle. That's where the racism thing is kind of fucked. That's where the whole thing gets out of hand. I think it'd be great if people could come down from that … I'm sure you know about the racism thing.

BONDI: I live in Chicago [where there was recently a racially charged Mayoral campaign.].

MACKAYE: You just got over the most ugly fucking thing. And it's ridiculous, man, for either side to feel like that. I mean, I'm white, fine. A hundred years ago, I was not alive. Twenty-five years ago, I was not alive. So whatever happened a hundred years ago, I am not responsible for. No more than, since I'm Scottish, I should be responsible for the Celtics or whoever we fucked with then. Or the Egyptians should feel bad about the Israeli people. People have got to get off the guilt wagon. And I'm just saying I'm guilty of being white—it's my one big crime. That's why I get so much fucking shit at school, that's why I cannot get on welfare in Washington, most likely. That's why when we took the PSATs, when Jeff checked off the black box, he got awards, he got scholarships, he got all kinds of interest, but when he admitted he was white, all that was gone. Just like that. It's ridiculous. I don't think it's fair.

BONDI: You seem to totally not have any sense of group identity whatsoever. In this country ... well, go ahead. You talk first and I'll go from there.

MACKAYE: Take my position, Dave. Remember my position.

DAVE DICTOR: I understand what you're saying you're doing as an individual who's part of a fucked-up system where to reverse the problems that they set in, you know, there's such a bad self-image given to black people and their history has been almost wiped out. I'm not going to lay onto you that you accept the guilt part, but just what happened to the black people that got kidnapped out of Africa and shipped over here is really horrible, it's really scarring. They're trying to give a sense of identity and you know all that. A lot of bad things that have happened in the urban city situations have been at the expense of urban white people because all the rich people left and took all the money out to the suburbs and sent their kids off to private schools and out of the hellhole of public education in bigger cities. What I'm just trying to say to you is that it's okay not to be guilty of being white, because I'm not saying you should feel guilty for being white, but don't you be guilty of being ignorant about how there is still a lot of oppression of black people in this country. A quarter of black men will go to prison by the time they're 60 years old. The economic and the educational opportunities for black people in this country are statistically worse than they are for white people. You could say, "Well, is it the chicken or the egg? Is it because they're fucking up so bad that they're not doing nothing, or is it that society's fucking up so bad that they just can't do nothing?" I might say it's part of both. That's just sociologically how I feel about that. You're just expressing an emotion about how you feel towards something, and that's OK.

MACKAYE: But it's simpler than that. I'm making a statement that I think the whole thing boils down to race. I would prefer to see the whole thing out of the way. There sure was a time when the Irish or the Jewish people in this country were getting a lot of fucking shit and just because they were white they had one good thing going for them. Things worked out eventually where the Irish people were just a part of this country. Whereas before, they were always made fun of, they were ostracized and treated like shit in general.

BONDI: There's a difference. Irish people came over here voluntarily and black people didn't. When you come over to America and you get shit, you're, "Great, but anything's better than what I had. I'll do anything I can to get my shit together here," and you're socially motivated towards it. Black people were never given that option. That kind of choice was never demanded of them. There's talk about socializing black people into American society, assimilation like other ethnic groups have been assimilated. The difference is that their set of standards in coming to this country wasn't the same.

MACKAYE: I understand what you're saying. The point is that there are still ugly feelings. The main thing is that they're a different color, and that's the worst part. But what is guilt going to lead to? Dave?

DICTOR: I don't think guilt is good at all.

MACKAYE: No, I'm saying if someone made you constantly feel guilty, what do you think that may result in?

DICTOR: A resentment …

MACKAYE: Thank you. And what would that resentment lead to? You just go right back. They're going to beat me over the head about African kings and stuff to the point where I'm going to say "Well, fuck the African kings. And fuck the black people too. Fuck all this shit. I've had it, blah, blah, blah." Guilty of being white. Well, fine. I'm not going to play it like that. It's an unfortunate thing, but when I'm in Washington, D.C., I'm the minority, so I have a totally different view.

BONDI: You can make the argument though, Ian, that it's not going to change. If you say, "Fuck this guilty shit, I ain't gonna feel guilty. It's not my fault." They're going to say, "Well, who the fuck's fault is it?" It's like, well, it's nobody's fault; it's history. But the situation is that they're still left with the remains of their historical past. Black people as a group still do not have the opportunity that white people as a group in this country have. What affirmative action and all that in the '60s tried to do is instead try to set the clock a little bit ahead towards more of a point where we can accept each other as equals but different.

MACKAYE: That's fine with me. I understand, but I guess what it basically boils down to is that you guys talk social and all that and if I can deal with people as individuals, not black and white, which is the way I do. Even though if I'm walking down the street and I see a whole lot of black kids coming up the street, I know from my experiences, I know that there can be trouble. I know someone can say, "Oh, you've been bred to hate black people." But if I'm walking down the street and I see a bunch of rednecks coming down, I know even more that my ass is about to get fucking kicked. But people don't jump on me for hating rednecks, even with college kids, a group of anything.

BONDI: But you would not hate rednecks period because a group of rednecks jump your ass.

MACKAYE: That's the whole point. I work on an individual level. I could say, "I hate hippies," but that's baloney. I don't. I know plenty of great people who may consider themselves hippies. And one thing that used to cause a lot of controversy was I used to say, "I hate everybody. I hate black people, I hate white people. I hate everything. I like individuals." Just blow the whole generalization, across-the-board business out. I can't do it. Even the whole cop thing. "I hate cops." Well, I may agree with some of the cop thing, but what it stands for. I certainly don't hate all cops. I know cops who I like on an individual level, and I can understand why people can be resentful towards cops. But that's not the way I work.

BONDI: Well, how do you work in situations where you're going to have to recognize some sort of group situation? Example: how do you feel about the good ol' U.S.A. and the way the good ol' U.S.A. system works? I mean, there you can't deal with that on an individual basis, right?

MACKAYE: But, the way I would answer that is that I don't. Probably the big difference is that I grew up in Washington, D.C. When you grow up in Washington, D.C., you are beat over the head with politics and you will hear no end of politics on both sides. All my life I've heard politics and for me, I pick up *The Washington Post* and I read it. I don't read it for any actual information. My most interesting things are little tidbits about weird things happening like guys getting impaled on sticks. Because every front page, I've been reading for ten years, whoever's in office, it's the same story, it's the same fucking plot lines, and I've been desensitized to politics to the point where I don't have any interest in politics.

BONDI: It still affects you, nevertheless.

MACKAYE: Yeah, but I don't think it affects me to the point where it really constricts me that much.

BONDI: But it sort of works in a circuitous route, because the thing about Jeff putting himself as black on his test and getting all his things because he was black. That's the result of a political decision.

MACKAYE: I know. That's why I said "Guilty of Being White" is a political song, is a political statement. I don't know, maybe I'm wrong, but if we could at least try and treat everyone as equals. It seems to me that if you give the black kids a little help, I think it will just go in a circle. I think someone will end up being resentful and it's not going to work out. When you help out a bunch of people and you don't help the other bunch of people—in that case it should help them all out. …

BONDI: Would you say that just being resentful that you're being fed this black stuff when you don't want to be is an example of being desensitized, because maybe you're not going beyond it to look at the reasons behind it or the ramifications of it?

MACKAYE: But the point is it's always down to the black people have been shit on by the white people, that's what it all boils down to. And that now the white people owe the black people. So the white people owe the black people, that's what the song says; I'm guilty of being white, that's my only thing. But, I will say again, that it may be really horrible, but I am not white people, I am me, and I don't appreciate my schooling, my life being threatened, I don't like being beat up for white people.

DICTOR: I don't want you to like being beat up for white people. A song that someone else does, it's the Fuck-Ups, and *Maximumrocknroll* will hate me for talking about them, but I like them to a certain degree, and one of the songs they do is "White Boy in the Mission." It's about how being left in the inner city as a poor white person, you are a minority within a minority. The minority being a Spanish part of town, you are a poor white person, a minority in the minority. I think that's kind of where that's almost coming from. In D.C., the white person left in that urban situation, left to fend for himself in those public schools, is a minority. They are the ones getting fucked over because all the money and all the riches got taken out of that neighborhood and it really is trillions of dollars that is tied up in banks and lending institutions that really should be going into investing in the earth with more of a thought-out economy of how this money will be spent and the resources that it will provide. And that's not happening, so that resentment, so Ian's feeling reverse discrimination. And other people are, and for those, that feeling is a valid thing.

BONDI: I'm not disputing that.

DICTOR: I'm not disputing it either. I'm just saying, we're all being ripped off, and that situation is rich white people that have left the cities to be as terrible as they are. When you say blame, those are the people we've got to get to change things. …

I know a lot of the people that write us letters are the kind of people that are pretty ... well, they're individualistic, but at the same time, they're almost coming at it from a loner's perspective.

MACKAYE: Same with me. Almost every time, they're always like "I'm the only one."

BONDI: Yeah, you get those letters from kids in New Jersey that are like, "There's nobody around here. I'm the only one with a skinhead."

MACKAYE: "I'm the only Chippewa punk who's 'straight edge.'" Actually, for me, the problem is that I get letters—long, real personal letters—from both guys and girls. I have so much mail, and I can't keep up with it, because I have to write real letters to all those people. I think it's a personal level where I start, and that it may have social ramifications, but only in the sense that it's still a personal choice. It's all personal; it's all individuals' decisions. I don't want to change a group of people. Actually, I don't even want to change people. I don't like the idea of me going out to change or open people's eyes. I don't like that idea. I don't want to come off like I'm incredibly great. I prefer to sort of spin a few tales and see if maybe they can pick up on them.

BONDI: What about you?

DICTOR: You know, it's semantics almost. Change implies that you are a voodoo doctor or something like that.

MACKAYE: Or that you're a higher being.

DICTOR: I do like affecting people.

BONDI: Well, so does Ian.

MACKAYE: Definitely. ...

Vic Bondi, Dave Dictor, and Ian MacKaye, from "Rap Session," *Maximumrocknroll* no. 8 (Berkeley, September 1983).

LESTER BANGS, "THE WHITE NOISE SUPREMACISTS"

Lester Bangs, gonzo music writer extraordinaire, got punk very early on and at a seemingly intuitive level, and as such produced some of the most penetrating, incisive, and, perhaps most important, funniest assessments of the genre. Here, in a 1979 piece from the *Village Voice*, Bangs brings the full force of his characteristic Benzedrine-fueled pacing—and whiplash-inducing shifts in subject— to rabbit-punch punk for its racism. Subtly weaving together many

**of the themes we've presented so far, Bangs sees the punk appro-
priation of racism as shock value, used to rebel against bullshit
liberalism and the status quo. But he also refuses to let the punks
get away with it, as he argues, over and over again, that words and
symbols are never detachable from their histories of hate. As a document itself, however, there's something disturbing about this early
piece of punk criticism. If this is one of the *first* times that punk is
called out for its predominant whiteness and creeping racism, a
mere two to three years into its existence, why must it happen, as
we shall see later on in the text, again, and again, and again?**

The other day I was talking on the phone with a friend who hangs out on
the CBGB's scene a lot. She was regaling me with examples of the delights
available to females in the New York subway system. "So the train came
to a sudden halt and I fell on my ass in the middle of the car, and not only
did nobody offer to help me up but all these boons just sat there laughing
at me."

"Boons?" I said. "What's boons?"

"You know," she said. "Black guys."

"Why do you call them that?"

"I dunno. From 'baboons,' I guess."

I didn't say anything.

"Look, I know it's not cool," she finally said. "But neither is being a
woman in this city. Every fucking place you go you get these cats hassling
you, and sometimes they try to pimp you. And a lot of the times when
they hassle you they're black, and when they try to pimp me they're always
black. Eventually you can't help it, you just end up reacting."

Sometimes I think nothing is simple but the feeling of pain.

When I was first asked to write this article, I said sure, because the
racism (not to mention the sexism, which is even more pervasive and a
whole other piece) on the American New Wave scene had been something that I'd been bothered by for a long time. When I told the guys in
my own band that I was doing this, they just laughed. "Well, I guess the
money's good," said one. "What makes you think that the racism in punk
has anything special about it that separates it from the rest of the society?"
asked another.

"Because the rest of society doesn't go around acting like racism is real
hip and cool," I answered heatedly.

"Oh yeah," he sneered. "Just walk into a factory sometime.
Or jail."

All right. Power is what we're talking about, or the feeling that you don't have any, or how much ostensible power you can rip outta some other poor sucker's hide. It works the same everywhere, of course, but one of the things that makes the punk stance unique is how it seems to assume substance or at least style by the *abdication* of power: *Look at me! I'm a cretinous little wretch! And proud of it!* So many people around the CBGB's and Max's scene have always seemed emotionally if not outright physically crippled—you see speech impediments, hunchbacks, limps, but most of all an overwhelming spiritual flatness. You take parental indifference, a crappy educational system, lots of drugs, media overload, a society with no values left except the hysterical emphasis on physical perfection, and you end up with these little nubbins: the only rebellion around, as *Life* magazine once labeled the Beats. Richard Hell gave us the catchphrase "Blank Generation," although he insists that he didn't mean a crowd with all the dynamism of a static-furry TV screen but rather a bunch of people finally freed by the collapse of all values to reinvent themselves, to make art statements of their whole lives. Unfortunately, such a great utopian dream, which certainly is not on its first go-round here, remains just that, because most people would rather follow. What you're left with, aside from the argument that it beats singles bars, is compassion. When the Ramones bring that sign onstage that says "GABBA GABBA HEY," what it really stands for is "We accept you." Once you get past the armor of dog collars, black leather, and S&M affectations, you've got some of the gentlest or at least most harmless people in the world: Sid Vicious legends aside, almost all their violence is self-directed.

So if they're all a bunch of little white lambs, why do some of them have it in for little black lambs? Richard Pinkston, a black friend I've known since my Detroit days, tells me, "When I go to CBGB's I feel like I'm in East Berlin. It's like, I don't mind liberal guilt if it gets me in the restaurant, even if I know the guy still hates me in his mind. But it's like down there they're *striving* to be offensive however they can, so it's more vocal and they're freer. It's semi-mob thinking."

Richard Hell and the Voidoids are one of the few integrated bands on the scene ("integrated"—what a stupid word). I heard that when he first formed the band, Richard got flak from certain quarters about Ivan Julian, a black rhythm guitarist from Washington, D.C., who once played with the Foundations of "Build Me Up Buttercup" fame. I think it says something about what sort of person Richard is that he told all those people to get fucked then and doesn't much want to talk about it now. ...

"Race hate?" says Voidoids lead guitarist Bob Quine. "Sure, it gives me 'n' Ivan something to do onstage: *The Defiant Ones.*"

But the ease and insight of the Voidoids are somewhat anomalous on the New York scene. This scene and the punk stance in general are riddled with self-hate, which is always reflexive, and anytime you conclude that life stinks and the human race mostly amounts to a pile of shit, you've got the perfect breeding ground for fascism. A lot of outsiders, in fact, think punk *is* fascist, but that's only because they can't see beyond certain buzzwords, symbols, and pieces of regalia that (I *think*) really aren't that significant: Ron Asheton of the Stooges used to wear swastikas, Iron Crosses, and jackboots onstage, but I don't remember any right-wing rants ever popping up in the music he did with Iggy or his own later band, which many people were not exactly thrilled to hear was called the New Order.

In the past three years Ron's sartorial legacy has given us an international subculture whose members might easily be mistaken at first glance for little brownshirts. They aren't, for the most part. Only someone as dumb as the Ramones are always accused of being could be offended when they sing "I'm a Nazi schatze," or tell us that the first rule is to obey the laws of Germany and then follow it with "Eat kosher salami." I've hung out with the Ramones, and they treat everybody of any race or sex the same—who *they* hate isn't Jews or blacks or gays or anybody but certain spike-conk assholes who just last week graduated from *The Rocky Horror Picture Show* lines to skag-dabblings and now stumble around Max's busting their nuts trying to be decadent.

Whereas you don't have to try at all to be a racist. It's a little coiled clot of venom lurking there in all of us, white and black, goy and Jew, ready to strike out when we feel embattled, belittled, brutalized. Which is why it has to be monitored, made taboo and restrained, by society and the individual. But there's a difference between hate and a little of the old *épater* gob at authority: swastikas in punk are basically another way for kids to get a rise out of their parents and maybe the press, both of whom deserve the irritation. To the extent that most of these spikedomes ever had a clue on what that stuff originally meant, it only went so far as their intent to shock. "It's like a stance," as Ivan says. "A real immature way of being dangerous."

Maybe. Except that after a while this casual, even ironic embrace of the totems of bigotry crosses over into the real poison. Around 1970 there was a carbuncle named Wayne McGuire who kept contributing install-ments of something he called "An Aquarian Journal" to *Fusion* magazines, wherein he suggested between burblings of regurgitated Nietzsche and bad Céline ellipses that the Velvet Underground represented some kind of mystical milestone in the destiny of the Aryan race, and even tried to link their music with the ideas of Mel Lyman, who was one of the prototypes for the current crop of mindnapping cult-daddies.

On a less systematic level, we had little outcroppings like Iggy hollering, "Our next selection tonight for all you Hebrew ladies in the audience is entitled 'Rich Bitch'!" on the 1974 recorded-live bootleg *Metallic K.O.*, and my old home turf *Creem* magazine, where around the same time I was actually rather proud of myself for writing things like (in an article on David Bowie's "soul" phase): "Now, as we all know, white hippies and beatniks before them would never have existed had there not been a whole generational subculture with a gnawing yearning to be nothing less than the downest baddest *niggers* ... Everybody has been walking around for the last year or so acting like faggots ruled the world, when in actuality it's the *niggers* who control and direct everything just as it always has been and properly should be."

I figured all this was in the Lenny Bruce spirit of let's-defuse-them-epithets-by-slinging-'em-out—in Detroit I thought absolutely nothing of going to parties with people like David Ruffin and Bobby Womack where I'd get drunk, maul the women, and improvise blues songs along the lines of "Sho' wish ah wuz a nigger / Then mah dick'd be bigger," and of course they all laughed. It took years before I realized what an asshole I'd been, not to mention how lucky I was to get out of there with my white hide intact.

I'm sure a lot of those guys were very happy to see this white kid drunk on his ass making a complete fool if not a human TV set out of himself, but to this day I wonder how many of them hated my guts right then. Because Lenny Bruce was wrong—maybe in a better world than this such parlor games would amount to cleansing jet offtakes, and between friends, where a certain bond of mutual trust has been firmly established, good natured racial tradeoffs can be part of the vocabulary of understood affections. But beyond that trouble begins—when you fail to realize that no matter how harmless your intentions are, there is no reason to think that any shit that comes out of your mouth is going to be understood or happily received. ...

Another reason for getting rid of all those little verbal barbs is that no matter how *you* intend them, you can't say them without risking misinterpretation by some other bigoted asshole; your irony just might be his cup of hate. Things like the *Creem* articles and partydown exhibitionism represented a reaction against the hippie counterculture and what a lot of us regarded as its pious pussyfooting around questions of racial and sexual identity, questions we were quite prepared to drive over with bulldozers. We believed nothing could be worse, more pretentious and hypocritical, than the hippies and the liberal masochism in whose sidecar they toked along, so we embraced an indiscriminate, half-joking and half-hostile mindlessness which seemed to represent, as Mark Jacobson pointed out in his *Voice* piece on Legs McNeil, a new kind of cool. "I don't discriminate," I used to laugh, "I'm prejudiced against *everybody!*" I thought it made for a nicely charismatic mix of Lenny Bruce freespleen and W. C. Fields misanthropy, conveniently ignoring Lenny's delirious, nigh-psychopathic inability to resolve the contradictions between his idealism and his infantile, scatological exhibitionism, as well as the fact that W. C. Fields's racism was as real and vile as—or more real and vile than—anybody else's. But when I got to New York in 1976 I discovered that some kind of bridge had been crossed by a lot of the people I thought were my peers in this emergent Cretins' Lib generation.

This was stuff even I had to recognize as utterly repellent. I first noticed it the first time I threw a party. The staff of *Punk* magazine came, as well as members of several of the hottest CBGB's bands, and when I did what we always used to do at parties in Detroit—put on soul records so everybody could dance—I began to hear this: "What're you playing all that nigger disco shit for, Lester?"

"That's not nigger disco shit," I snarled, "that's *Otis Redding*, you assholes!" But they didn't want to hear about it, and now I wonder if in any way I hadn't dug my own grave, or at least helped contribute to their ugliness and the new schism between us. The music editor of this paper has theorized that one of the most important things about New Wave is how much of it is almost purely white music, and what a massive departure that represents from the almost universally blues-derived rock of the past. I don't necessarily agree with that—it ignores the reggae influence running through music as diverse as that of the Clash, Pere Ubu, Public Image Ltd., and the Police, not to mention the Chuck Berry licks at the core of Steve Jones's attack. But there is at least a grain of truth there—the Contortions' James Brown/Albert Ayler spasms aside, most of the SoHo bands are as white as John Cage, and there's an evolution of sound, rhythm, and stance running from the Velvets through the Stooges to the Ramones and their children that takes us farther and farther from the black-stud postures of Mick Jagger that Lou Reed and Iggy partake in but that Joey Ramone certainly doesn't. I respect Joey for that, for having the courage to be himself, especially at the sacrifice of a whole passel of macho defenses. Joey is a white American kid from Forest Hills, and as such his cultural inputs have been white, from *The Jetsons* through Alice Cooper. But none of this cancels out the fact that most of the greatest, deepest music America has produced has been, when not entirely black, the product of miscegenation. "You can't appreciate rock 'n' roll without appreciating where it comes from," as Pinkston put it.

Musical questions, however, can be passed off as matters of taste. Something harder to pass off entered the air in 1977, when I started encountering little zaps like this: I opened up a copy of a Florida punk fanzine called *New Order* and read an article by Miriam Linna of the Cramps, Nervus Rex, and now Zantees: "I love the Ramones [because] this is the celebration of everything American—everything teenaged and wonderful and white and urban. ..." You could say the "white" jumping out of that sentence was just like Ornette Coleman declared *This Is Our Music*, except that the same issue featured a full-page shot of Miriam and one of her little friends posing proudly with their leathers and shades and a pistol in front of the headquarters of the United White People's Party, under a sign bearing three flags: "GOD" (cross), "COUNTRY" (stars and stripes), "RACE" (swastika).

Sorry, Miriam, I can go just so far with affectations of kneejerk cretinism before I puke. ...

[M]y old pal Legs McNeil has this band called Shrapnel, who are busy refighting World War II onstage in dogtags, army surplus clothes, and helmets that fall over their eyes like cowlicks, while they sing songs with titles like "Combat Love." Personally I think it's not offensive (well, about as offensive as *Hogan's Heroes*) that they're too young to remember Vietnam—it's funny. The whole show is a cartoon (it's no accident that they open their set with the "Underdog" theme) and a damn good one. Musically they're up there too—tight dragstrip guitar wranglings that could put them on a par with the MC5 someday, combined with a stage act that could make them as popular as Kiss. The only problem, which has left me with such mixed feelings I hardly know what to say to them, is that the lyrics of some of the songs are nothing but racist swill. The other night I sat in the front row at CBGB's and watched them deliver one of the hottest sets I've seen from any band this year while a kid in the seat right next to me kept yelling out requests for " 'Hey Little Gook!' 'Hey Little Gook!'" the whole time. Christgau, who considers them "proto-fascist" and hates them, told me they also had lyrics on the order of "Send all the spics back to Cuba." I mentioned this to Legs and he seemed genuinely upset: "No," he swore, "it's 'Send all the *spies* back to Cuba.'"

"Okay," I said (Christgau still doesn't believe him), "what about 'Hey Little Gook'?"

"Aw c'mon," he said, "that's just like in a World War II movie where they say 'krauts' and 'slants' and stuff like that!"

I told him I thought there was a difference between using words in dramatic context and just to draw a cheap laugh in a song. But the truth is that by now I was becoming more confused than ever. All I knew was that when you added all this sort of stuff up you realized a line had been crossed by certain people we thought we knew, even believed in, while we weren't looking. Either that or they were always across that line and we never bothered to look until we tripped over it. And sometimes you even find that you yourself have drifted across that line. I was in Bleecker Bob's the other night, drunk and stoned, when a black couple walked in. They asked for some disco record, Bob didn't have it of course, a few minutes went by, and reverting in the haze of my Detroit days I said something about such and such band or music having to do with "niggers." A couple more minutes went by. Then Bob said, "You know what, Lester? When you said that, those two people were standing right behind you."

I looked around and they were out on the sidewalk, looking at the display in his front window. Stricken, I rushed out and began to burble: "Listen ... somebody just told me what I said in there ... and I know it doesn't mean anything to you, I'm not asking for some kind of absolution, but I just want you to know that ... I have some idea ... how utterly, utterly *awful* it was. ..."

I stared at them helplessly. The guy just smiled, dripping contempt. "Oh, that's okay man ... it's just your head. ..." *I've run up against a million assholes like you before, and I'll meet a million after you—so fucking what?*

I stumbled back into the store, feeling like total garbage, like the complete hypocrite, like I had suddenly glimpsed myself as everything I claimed to despise. Bob said, "Look, Lester, don't worry about it, forget it, it happens to everybody," and, the final irony, sold me a reggae album I wondered how I was going to listen to.

If there's nothing more poisonous than bigotry, there's nothing more pathetic than liberal guilt. I feel like an asshole even retelling the story here, as if I expected some sort of expiation for what cannot be undone, or as if such a tale would be news to anybody. In a way Bob was right: I put a dollop more pain in the world, and that was that. There is certainly something almost emetically self-serving about the unreeling of such confessions in the pages of papers like the *Voice*—it's the sort of thing that contributed to the punk reaction in the first place. But it illustrates one primal fact: how easily and suddenly you may find yourself imprisoned and suffocated by the very liberation from cant, dogma, and hypocrisy you thought you'd achieved. That sometimes—usually?—you'll find that you don't know where to draw the line until you're miles across it in a field of land mines. ...

There is something called Rock Against Racism (and now Rock Against Sexism) in England, an attempt at simple decency by a lot of people whom one would think too young and naïve to begin to appreciate the contradictions. Yippie bullshit aside, it could never happen in New York, which is deeply saddening, not because you want to think that rock 'n' roll can save the world but because since rock 'n' roll is bound to stay in your life you would hope to see it reach some point where it might not add to the cruelty and exploitation already in the world. In a place where people are as walled off from one another as we are in America now, all you can do is try to make some sort of simple, humble, and finally private beginning. You feel like things like this should not need to be said, articles like this should perhaps not even be written. You may think, as I do, of the sexism in the Stranglers' and Dead Boys' lyrics, that the people and things I've talked about here are so stupid as to be beneath serious consideration. But would you say the same thing to the black disco artist who was refused admittance to Studio 54 even though he had a Top Ten crossover hit which they were probably playing inside the damn place at the time, the doorman/bouncer explaining to a white friend of the artist, "I'm not letting this guy in—he just looks like another street nigger to me"? Or would you rather argue the difference between Racist Chic and Racist Cool? If you would, just make sure you do it in the nearest factory. Or jail.

Lester Bangs, from "The White Noise Supremacists," *Village Voice*, April 30, 1979.

FOUR

WHITE POWER

Are we gonna sit and let them come?
Have they got the White man on the run?
Multiracial society is a mess
We ain't gonna take much more of this
What do we need?
White Power! For England
White Power! Today
White Power! For Britain
Before it gets too late
            —"White Power," Skrewdriver

"We ain't gonna take much more of this," the British band Skrewdriver sings. Who are the "we" here? Listening to the rest of the lyrics of this, or any, of their songs it's not too hard to figure out. "We" are the white race (minus the Jews, of course), "they" are everybody else. And within the world of Skrewdriver and their fans, "what 'we' need" is equally self evident: White Power. In the previous section, there was a certain indeterminate quality to punk whiteness, that is: a sense that in a multiracial society race needed to be noted yet, other than "in opposition," it was left largely undefined. In this section we witness minds made up and designations demarcated. Whiteness is clearly defined as against racial, ethnic, and sexual Others. We have arrived at a kind of tipping point from the inchoate, oppositional rage of the "white minority." While those punks allowed their rage against the status quo to slip between those in power and those without it, the White Power punk tips primarily into hatred of the powerless. If power is the target, it is in the form of some paranoid fantasy or another (ZOG, Zionist Occupation

Government, for instance) as familiar punk rock discourse takes on horrific new content.

Centered primarily around skinhead music and culture, white supremacists recast punk rock as a medium of intolerance. White Power becomes a rallying cry for disenfranchised, often working-class, white youth who create an imagined community of racial purity through their music and their scene. For those on the political Right, punk offers—illusory—pure white people's music. Through songs like "White Power," bands like Skrewdriver use punk rock to express their rage and spread their fantasy of a world where the only ethnicity is whiteness and all culture is white culture.

It's easy to condemn this music and culture, along with its violence and bigotry, and simply turn away, dismissing it as some sort of aberrant strain of an otherwise healthy organism; it's (self-) satisfying to chant "Nazi Punks, Fuck Off!" along with the Dead Kennedys. But White Power punk's sense of victimization, its valorization of oppositional solidarity, its creation and mobilization of DIY cultural networks, its understanding of the desire of the forbidden and the shocking, and the simple raw emotionality and anger of its expression are characteristics that *all* punk shares. Acknowledging this means accepting that there is no one, clear racial politics to punk and no simple "we." Indeed, this "we" is complicated by some skinheads themselves who draw upon the black roots of skin music and culture as justification and motivation for their own *anti*–White Power activism, reasserting the claim that skinhead culture is not just incidentally but *constitutively* antiracist, and giving rise to some of the most interesting antiracist organizing in punk rock.

JOHN CLARKE, "THE SKINHEADS AND THE MAGICAL RECOVERY OF COMMUNITY"

Coming out of the (now-shuttered) Centre for Contemporary Cultural Studies at the University of Birmingham that also nurtured Dick Hebdige, John Clarke provides an important contribution to the understanding of the origins of the skinhead movement. We have already seen, in the interview with Jimmy Pursey of Sham 69, the importance of working-class solidarity for certain punks in making explicit a distance from their art-school peers, and how such solidarity occasionally tolerates a degree of conservatism—

and racism—in its name. Here, Clarke delineates a similar dynamic, but sets it in the context of the postwar decline of the white working-class community, and posits that what the skinhead movement shows is precisely how culture allows a group to build in fantasy what it feels is challenged or absent in the real world. In what Clarke calls a "magical" community, "solidarity" takes the form of mob mentality, a last resort in an economic field of dwindling options, exemplified by the links maintained between skinheads and football hooliganism. The coherence of the group comes at the expense of racial and sexual minorities. While the "solutions" racist skins arrive at are pure fantasy, and their aims misguided, it's nonetheless important to acknowledge that the problems of poverty, unemployment, and a palpable loss in political and cultural power faced by working-class whites in the deindustrializing West, are real, and the insularity of their "magical community" is not too different from punk's standard operating procedure.

Our basic thesis about the skinheads centers around the notion of community. We would argue that the skinhead style represents an attempt to re-create through the "mob" the traditional working-class community, as a substitution for the *real* decline of the latter. The underlying social dynamic for the style, in this light, is the relative worsening of the situation of the working class, through the second half of the sixties, and especially the more rapidly worsening situation of the lower working class (and of the young within that). This, allied to the young's sense of exclusion from the existing "youth subculture" (dominated in the public arena by the music and styles derived from the "underground") produced a return to an intensified "Us/Them" consciousness among the lower-working-class young, a sense of being excluded and under attack from a variety of points. The resources to deal with this sense of exclusion were not to be found within either the emergent or incorporated elements of youth subcultures, but only in those images and behaviors which stressed a more traditional form of collective solidarity. Material from *The Paint House* illustrates this sense of oppression:

> Everywhere there are fucking bosses, they're always trying to tell you what to do … don't matter what you do, where you go, they're always there. People in authority, the people who tell you what to do and make sure you do it. It's the system we live in, it's the governor system.
>   Schools, you 'ave to go, doncha? The teachers and the headmaster, they're the authority, ain't they? They're telling you what to do and you're glad to get

out and leave and that, aren't ya? They think because you're young and they pay you and that, that they can treat you how they like and say what they want. Then there's the "old bill" and courts … they're all part of authority. Official and all kinds of people in uniforms. Anyone with a badge on, traffic wardens and council and all that … yeah, even the caretaker at the flats, they even 'as goes at you. Then when you finish at work or at school, you go to the clubs and the youth leaders are all just a part of it.[1]

But the skinheads felt oppressed by more than just the obvious authority structure; they resented those who tried to get on and "give themselves false airs," people from within the neighbourhood who had pretensions to social superiority; they resented the "people on our backs":

All these dummoes at school, who always do what they're told … they're the ones who end up being coppers and that. I hate them do-gooders who come to 'elp the poor in them slums … They're all nice and sweet and kind, they pretend to be on your side and by talking nicely find out about you but social workers and people like that, they ain't on your side. They think they know how you should live. They're really authority pretending to be your friends. They try to get you to do things and if you don't do them, they've got the law on their side. With all this lot against us, we've still got the yids, Pakis, wogs, 'ippies on our backs.[2]

The sense of being "in the middle" of this variety of oppressive and exploitative forces produces a need for group solidarity, which though essentially defensive, in the skinheads was coupled with an aggressive content, the expression of frustration and discontent through the attacking of scapegoated outsiders. The content of this solidarity, as we shall see in our consideration of the elements of the skinhead style, derived from the traditional content of the working-class community—the example, *par excellence*, of the defensively organized collective.

However, the skinhead style does not revive the community in a real sense; the postwar decline of the bases of that community had removed it as a real source of solidarity; the skinheads had to use an *image* of what that community was as the basis of their style. They were the "dispossessed inheritors"; they received a tradition which had been deprived of its real social bases. The themes and imagery still persisted, but the reality was in a state of decline and disappearance. We would suggest that this dislocated relation to the traditional community accounts for the exaggerated and intensified form which the values and concerns of that community received in the form of the skinhead style. Daniel and McGuire claim that:

Rather than a community spirit, the Collinwood gang tends to have an affinity with an image of the East Enders, as being tough, humorous and a subculture of their own … The gang sees itself as a natural continuation of the working class tradition of the area, with the same attitudes and behaviour as their parents and grandparents before them. They believe that they have the same stereotyped prejudices against immigrants and aliens as they believe their parents have had, *but they play these roles outside of the context of the community experienced by their parents* …[3]

These observations are reinforced by comments from the skinheads themselves about the gang and its relation to the locality:

When people kept saying skinheads, when they're talking about the story of us coming up from the East End, this has happened for generations before, past … I mean where does skinhead come into it?

It's a community, a gang, isn't it, it's only another word for community; kids, thugs, whatever …[4]

The kids inherit the oral tradition of the area from the parent culture, especially that part which refers to the community's self-image, its collective solidarity, its conception of masculinity, its orientation to "outsiders" and so on. It is perhaps not surprising that the area with which the skinheads are most associated should be the East End, which from a sociological standpoint has been seen as the archetypal working-class community. Its internal self-image has always been a particularly strong one, and has been strengthened by its public reputation as a "hard" area, a reputation which in the mid-sixties was further intensified by the glamorous careers of the Krays.

Finally, we would like to exemplify this relation between the skinheads and the image of the community through some of the central elements of the skinhead style. One of the most crucial aspects is the emphasis on territorial connections for the skinheads—the "mobs" were organized on a territorial basis, identifying themselves with and through a particular locality (e.g., the "Smethwick Mob," etc.). This involved the mobs in the demarcation and defence of their particular "patch," marking boundaries with painted slogans ("Quinton Mob rules here," etc.), and maintaining those boundaries against infractions by other groups. This territoriality, like the community, has its own focal points around which interaction articulates—the street corner meeting place, the pub, and the football ground. Although the football ground did not necessarily coincide with the mobs' patches, its own local identification and the already existent activities of the Ends⁵ provided a particular focal point for the mobs to organise around.

Football, and especially the violence articulated around it, also provided one arena for the expression of the skinheads' concern with a particular, collective, masculine self-conception, involving an identification of masculinity with physical toughness, and an unwillingness to back down in the face of "trouble." The violence also involved the mobs' stress on collective solidarity and mutual support in times of "need." This concern with toughness was also involved in the two other most publicized skinhead activities—"Paki-Bashing" and "Queer-Bashing." Paki-bashing involved the ritual and aggressive defence of the social and cultural homogeneity of the community against its most obviously scapegoated outsiders—partly because of their particular visibility within the neighbourhood (in terms of shop ownership patterns, etc.) by comparison with West Indians, and also because of their different cultural patterns (especially in terms of their unwillingness to defend themselves and so on)—again by comparison with West Indian youth.

"Queer-Bashing" may be read as a reaction against the erosion of traditionally available stereotypes of masculinity, especially by the hippies. The skinheads' operational definition of "queer" seems to have extended to all those males who by their standards looked "odd," as this statement from a Smethwick skinhead may indicate:

> Usually it'd be just a bunch of us who'd find somebody they thought looked odd—like this one night we were up by Warley Woods and we saw this bloke who looked odd—he'd got long hair and frills on his trousers.

We may see these three interrelated elements of territoriality, collective solidarity and "masculinity" as being the way in which the skinheads attempted to re-create the inherited imagery of the community in a period in which the experiences of increasing oppression demanded forms of mutual organisation and defence. And we might finally see the intensive violence connected with the style as evidence of the "re-creation of the community" being indeed a "magical" or "imaginary" one, in that it was created without the material and organizational basis of that community and consequently was less subject to the informal mechanisms of social control characteristic of such communities. In the skinhead style, we can see both the elements of continuity (in terms of the style's content), and discontinuity (in terms of its form), between parent culture and youth subculture.

John Clarke, "The Skinheads and the Magical Recovery of Community,"
Resistance Through Rituals: Youth Subcultures in Post-War Britain, ed. Stuart
Hall and Tony Jefferson (New York: Routledge, 1990).

TIMOTHY S. BROWN, "SUBCULTURES, POP MUSIC AND POLITICS: SKINHEADS AND 'NAZI ROCK' IN ENGLAND AND GERMANY"

In this scholarly essay, Timothy Brown traces the development of punk rock's odd marriage with skinheadism and White supremacy through Oi! music, a genre that combined Sham 69–style punk with pub rock and the chant-along choruses reminiscent of what you might hear at a football match. It is important to note that not all Oi! bands advocate White Power (some are even vehemently antiracist), but that White Power bands are overwhelmingly Oi!-influenced. Through Oi!, skinhead culture establishes itself as an explicitly White identity position by repudiating the first wave skinheads' black/Mod roots. Both White identity and the Black roots take interesting turns in Brown's analysis, as the assertion of whiteness requires reinforcement in the performance of its English variety by laying claim to a profoundly German/Aryan/Norse tradition, rooted in Nazi mythology. This Nazi identification then makes for easy adoption of skinhead culture by disenfranchised youth in Germany itself. Important to notice here, though it goes mostly unaddressed in the essay itself, is the power and reach of punk's communication infrastructure: through zines, music exchanges, and now the Web, it is possible to construct international networks of punk fans. And as Brown shows here, this communications network also opens up spaces for the articulation and spread of a transnational White racism.

Right-wing extremist rock music—so-called "Nazi rock"—is one of the most problematic of popular musical genres. Emerging from the skinhead youth subculture in Britain at the end of the 1970s, and spreading to the continent and across the Atlantic in the following decade, it has served as accompaniment to a rising tide of racist and anti-immigrant violence in Germany, and become a focus of recruiting for the radical right world-wide. Yet as a generic category, "Nazi rock" is inherently unstable.

A phenomenon that is at once artistic and political, it sits uneasily across analytical boundaries. The area of overlap between music genre and political content is, for one thing, far from complete. Right-wing extremist ideas are not strictly confined to skinhead rock music, but have found their way into a variety of other musical genres and youth subcultures.[1] The spread of Nazi rock beyond its original social boundaries—it is no longer simply "skinhead music"—means that the genre and the skinhead subculture are, if still intimately linked, by no means synonymous. Conversely, the various genres that make up "skinhead music" are by no means exclusively right-wing. Although Nazi rock arose out of the skinhead subculture, the subculture is—as will be seen—heavily divided about the meaning and value of the genre.[2]

The original skinhead movement of the late-1960s was a multicultural synthesis organized around fashion and music. The first skinheads were offshoots of the British "mod" subculture of the early 1960s. The mod was stylish, dedicated to cultivating the right look; upwardly mobile, very likely the son or daughter of a worker moving up into the white-collar realm of the bank or advertising firm. Above all, the mod was a music fan, obsessed with dancing to American soul music at all-night parties.[3] From the 1960s, the split implicit in the mod scene—between its working-class origins and its upper-class pretensions; between its subcultural subversiveness and its obvious appeal for boutique-owners and advertisers—began to widen. With the mod subculture swerving ever closer to the commodified, Carnaby Street hippie style of "Swinging London," certain mods began to emphasize the more proletarian aspects of the look, cutting their hair shorter and replacing dandified suits and expensive shoes with jeans and heavy boots. These no-frills "hard mods" prefigured the arrival of the first skinheads.[4] Whereas appreciation for black culture—above all American soul music but also Jamaican ska—had stood at the center of the mod way of life, the skinheads took the connection a step further; their reference point was a local symbol of cool, young Jamaican immigrants who modeled themselves on the authority-defying "rude boy" of the Kingston ghettos. The clean, hard look of these transplanted "rude boys" fit nicely with the stripped-down elements of the hard mod style, and their evening wear echoed the earlier mod emphasis on expensive suits and nice shoes. But by far the most critical element in the symbiotic relationship between skinheads and black immigrants was music. Skinheads embraced the reggae music of Jamaican performers like Desmond Dekker as their own. Reggae artists and labels, in turn, actively courted the skinheads, producing songs and albums aimed at this young white audience. The resulting genre—"skinhead reggae"—fueled the rise of the skinhead subculture while jump-starting the careers of many Jamaican performers in Britain. The identity of the original skinhead was thus constructed in dialogue with black immigrants and organized around music created by black performers.[5]

The decline of the original skinhead subculture by the early 1970s, and its rebirth later in the decade under the influence of punk rock, opened the way for new influences. Not only did fresh musical genres arise around which skinhead identity could coalesce—above all so-called "street punk," or "Oi!" music—but, for reasons to be discussed below, right-wing politics became fashionable and were embraced by increasing numbers of skinheads. This politicization—which became prominent at the end of the 1970s and reached a peak in the early 1980s—produced a crisis of identity in the skinhead scene. A schism developed between—on the one hand—right-wing skins ambivalent toward, or dismissive of, the subculture's black roots, and—on the other—left-wing or "unpolitical" skins who upheld these roots as being central to skinhead identity. The conflict between the two sides in this debate became a struggle to define the essence of the subculture, a fight over authenticity.[6]

Music played a crucial role in this process in two ways. First, music appreciation—specifically, knowledge of the reggae classics around which the skinhead subculture was originally organized—became, for one group of skinheads, a litmus test for authenticity. Second, genre itself became a contested site. On the one hand, the skinhead revival of the late 1970s crystallized around a punk-infused revival of the Jamaican sounds of ska (a precursor to reggae) centered on the Two Tone label and bands like the Specials and Madness. These multiracial bands were explicitly political in their support for racial unity centered on appreciation for music. Yet their fortunes were inextricably linked with the skinheads who embraced them, yet all-too-frequently wrecked gigs with politically inspired violence. On the other hand, the skinhead version of punk rock—Oi!—arose to supply the basis for the creation of an explicitly political style of skinhead music. Although the majority of the Oi! bands considered themselves "unpolitical," by providing an artistic forum for skinheads to express their own ideas, Oi! became a mirror of the left-right divide within the skinhead scene. It was out of this polarization that the genre of "Nazi rock" developed, and through it that successive iterations of the struggle for skinhead identity were played out.

A second site in the struggle over authenticity was personal style. The original skinhead subculture was created out of distinctive elements of clothing organized around the cropped hair: tight Levi's jeans or StaPrest pants, Ben Sherman button-down and Fred Perry tennis shirts, work boots, suspenders (braces), and Levi's or Harrington jackets. Suits modeled on those of the Jamaican rude boys were often worn in the evening, but day or night, the skinhead look was hard, masculine, and working-class. With his boots, sturdy clothing, and cropped hair, the skinhead became, in the words of Phil Cohen, a "caricature of the model worker."[7] Like the "right" music, the "right" clothing signified taste and authenticity. But as new influences crept into the skinhead subculture during the revival of the late-1970s, style, like music, became a source of conflict as well as unity. In order to match the shock valued of punk, these second-generation skins—many of them themselves ex-punks—took the style to new extremes, emphasizing the threatening aspects of the look at the expense of the sharp stylishness prized by the original skins. Boots became taller, military surplus MA-1 jackets replaced earlier, more "civilian" looks, tattoos—previously confined to the arms or torso—began to crop up above the neckline, and hair became shorter to the point of baldness. These changes in style mirrored, to an extent, changes in the content of the subculture, with the more extreme looks coming to signify affiliation with the radical right.[8]

Reacting against this trend—which they considered a bastardization of the original skinhead style—numbers of skins began to stress the cultivation of the "original" look, making fashion, like music, a litmus test for authenticity. Violators of the proper codes were not skinheads, but "bald punks," a category to which racists—who, in the eyes of purists, failed completely to understand what the subculture was about—were likely to belong. The connection between right-wing politics and "inauthentic" modes of dress was personified in the figure of the "bonehead," a glue-sniffing, bald-headed supporter of the extreme right, sporting facial tattoos, a Union Jack T-shirt, and "the highest boots possible."[9] Although the emphasis on correct style was not explicitly political, it grew—like insistence on the subculture's black musical roots—out of a concern with the authentic sources of skinhead identity. As such, it was heavily associated with the attempts of left-wing and so-called "unpolitical" skins to "take back" the subculture from the radical right in the early 1980s.

Hard-and-fast political divisions were, however, never fully encoded in style; outward appearance never corresponded 100 percent to political viewpoint. To understand why, it is necessary to think about the factors around which the cohesion of the subculture was based. Queried about what belonging to the subculture means to them, skinheads inevitably

cite things like drinking, hanging out with their friends, and—more omi-
nously—"aggro" (violence). Less frequently cited, because so obvious, is
the fact that they like the skinhead "look"; that is, they choose to belong
to a community organized around a shared personal style. The style is, to
be sure, connected with meaning(s). During the original wave of the late
1960s, the short hair of the skinhead represented a working-class reaction
against changes in class and gender roles, especially the feminization of
men represented by the hippie movement. The adoption of traditionally
proletarian clothing, attitudes, and behaviors, at precisely the moment
when these were beginning to disappear, was, according to Dick Hebdige,
"a symbolic recovery of working class identity" that sought to preserve
the boundaries of class through culture.[10] This maneuver was a type of
resistance: against the "coming man" of the late-1960s (the middle-class,
peace-loving, long-haired student) the skinhead (short-haired, violent,
and working-class) became the rebel par excellence.

But whatever the semiotic content of the skinhead "look"—and
however subjectively important notions of skinhead as "a way of life" may
be to its adherents—being a skinhead is, at the most basic level, a matter
of adopting a certain outward appearance. The author of a work on gay
skinheads, noting the irony represented by the presence of significance
numbers of homosexuals in a scene based on an image of traditional masculinity, and citing the appropriation of the skinhead look as another in a
series of urban gay stereotypes—i.e., a uniform for "clubbing" rather than
part of a "way of life"—argues that being a "real" skinhead was, in the final
analysis, little more than a matter of "looking the part."[11] While this view
is, I believe, mistaken—gender is, after all, only one element in the skinhead's system of meaning, and the complex relationship among music,
politics, and notions of "authentic identity" in the skinhead subculture
suggest that much more than fashion is at work—it brings up an important point: skinhead is, above all else, a style community. That is to say, it
is a community in which the primary site of identity is personal style.

This appearance, this outward form, is, to be sure, linked with certain
types of content. But the relationship between form and content is highly
unstable. In a specific time and place—say, London in 1969—the relationship between the two is, relatively speaking, fixed.[12] But as the subculture
moves along the temporal plane, going through successive stages—as, for
example, in the skinhead "revival" of the late 1970s—the original form
and content can be pulled apart, giving rise to new configurations. Similarly, as the subculture moves through space, occupying new geographic
and cultural locations, form and content are reoriented yet again under

the influence of new social, cultural, and historical factors. In exploring the development of "Nazi rock"—a hybrid creation that was decisively influenced by transnational contacts between England and Germany—it is important to keep in mind the constantly-shifting relationship between form and content in subculture.

A useful way of thinking about this process is represented by the idea of "articulation." Keith Negus—who has proposed the use of the concept as a means of understanding the relationship between music production and music audiences—follows Stuart Hall in outlining two meanings of the term. On the one hand, articulation is communication, a form of self-expression that has, necessarily, to take place in relationship to an audience. "An artist," in this sense, "is always articulating, via various intermediaries, to audiences who are always part of the process of 'articulating' cultural meanings."[13] Meaning, in this context, is not a pure product of the artist's intention, but is created out of the process of transmission to the audience. On the other hand, articulation represents a process of linkage, of joining together. Just as (to use Negus's example) the cab and trailer of an "articulated lorry" are discrete and contingently linked elements of a single vehicle, so elements in the chain of musical production and consumption can be seen to "articulate" with each other, thereby existing not "as discrete, fixed and bounded moments," but as "a web of mediated connections."[14] Understood in this dual sense of communication and linkage, the concept of "articulation" can serve as a tool for conceptualizing how "particular cultural forms become connected to specific political agendas and social identities."[15]

In exploring the relationship between the skinhead subculture and the development of the "Nazi rock" genre, we can use the concept of "articulation" as a means of approaching two key questions: 1) what accounts for the seemingly paradoxical transformation of the skinhead subculture from one organized around appreciation for black cultural forms to one organized around white and frequently racist forms?; and 2) how and why is a movement based on a specifically "English" working-class identity meaningful in Germany? In approaching these questions, we will focus on three themes. The first is movement. As the subculture is communicated over time and through space—going through successive iterations with differing personnel and external circumstances—it articulates with new influences, musical and otherwise. It is out of these "communicative links" that sense is generated. We will try to understand how movement creates meaning. The second is displacement. We will explore how identities are developed less in relationship to the here-and-now, than in relationship to other times and places, to real and imagined pasts and geographic loca-tions. We will seek to understand how absence becomes presence. The third is conflict. We will explore how identity is created through a series of constantly shifting oppositions played out around a struggle to estab-lish "authenticity." The development of "Nazi rock" is a product of this struggle.

From England with Hate: Skinhead Goes to Germany

The skinhead subculture that was transmitted to Germany was not the original, but the revival. The style was first brought to West Germany by British soldiers during the punk era of the late 1970s, but it was only during 1980–81 that a real skinhead scene began to develop. As noted above, the skinhead revival that grew out of the punk movement in England developed in association with new musical genres, the most important being "street-punk" or Oi! music. Rejecting the alleged art-school preten-sions and commercialization of Punk Rock, street-punk bands like Sham 69, Cocksparrer, and the Cockney Rejects played a raw, stripped-down version of rock 'n' roll that attracted a huge skinhead following. In their use of shouted refrains and audience participation, these bands drew on elements of the traditional "pub sing-along," and it was from the most common of these refrains—"Oi!" (a cockney greeting)—that the new movement received its name. Coined as a moniker for the new move-ment by *Sounds* magazine journalist Gary Bushell in 1980, the term "Oi!" quickly became synonymous with "skinhead."

By 1980, this also meant synonymous with "right-wing." The reasons for this are complex. The skinhead movement of the 1960s was not explic-itly political, but it foreshadowed, in a number of areas, the politicization of the late-seventies revival. As is well known, skinheads were accus-tomed to victimizing Asian immigrants, and as Roger Sabin has shown, they received little discouragement from adult society.[16] So-called "Paki-bashing" was merely a physical expression of the racist animosity of the larger society.[17] The sixties were a period of what might be called a racist consensus in Britain, with repeated legislation to curb immigration and increasing attempts by the conservative and radical right to turn immigra-tion into an election-winning issue.[18] The leading politician Enoch Powell lent respectability to racist views when, in April 1968, he spoke of the pos-sibility of a race war if immigration was not curbed.[19] Powell's warnings gave voice to a widespread anxiety about immigration, an anxiety that was being exacerbated at the time by a media frenzy over the "threat" posed by the immigration of Asians being expelled from the former colony of Kenya.[20] Powell's speech also gave aid and comfort to neo-Fascists and helped to fuel the rise of the newly founded National Front.[21]

In this atmosphere, the relationship between black and white youth began to turn sour as well, and the loss of the relatively short-lived symbiosis between the reggae genre and the skinhead subculture was a factor in the latter's decline. By 1970, as reggae increasingly moved outside of the West Indian community, the honeymoon occasioned by the skinheads' infatuation with the music was giving way to turf battles between black and white kids over the control of key clubs. More important, by 1971, reggae was changing, slowing down, and adopting new themes. Under the influence of Rastafarianism, the music increasingly began to deal with mystical notions of Africa and black liberation that had little to do with the "party music" that reggae had been. Combined with a rising spirit of black pride—exemplified by Bob and Marcia's "Young, Gifted and Black"—the shift in focus began to make the music less congenial to young white aficionados of "skinhead reggae." In one emblematic instance, young skinheads responded to the playing of "Young, Gifted and Black" by cutting the club's speaker wires and launching a violent melee to chants of "young, gifted, and white."[22]

As an attempt to establish a "defensively organized collective" around a mythic image of proletarian masculinity, skinhead involved an embracing, and even an amplification of, the prejudices of the parent society. It was very easy for this stance to "dissolve," in the words of Dick Hebdige, "… into a concern with race, with the myth of white ethnicity, the myth, that is, that you've got to be white to be British."[23] The skinhead subculture thus possessed a right-wing potential, a potential that came to the fore during the revival of the late 1970s–early 1980s. Economic decline, scarcity of jobs, and increased immigration intensified latent racist and right-wing attitudes in British society during the seventies and eighties, and the skinheads reflected these prejudices in exaggerated form. With their reputation for violence and patriotic-nationalist views, skinheads were seen as a particularly attractive target for recruitment by the radical right. The National Front renewed its efforts to win the support of working-class youth, founding the Young National Front in late 1977. The openly Nazi British Movement did the same, and with its emphasis on street combat, was particularly attractive to skinheads.[24] Right-wing skins probably never made up a majority, but by 1980, the sight of bomber-jacketed "boneheads" giving the "Sieg Heil!" salute at Oi! gigs was common, and by 1982, the skinhead subculture was firmly cemented in the public mind as right-wing.

A key event in establishing the notoriety of the skinhead scene, and one which represented the symbolic dovetailing of music genre and subculture, violence and racism, was the so-called "Southall riot" of July, 1981. The riot took place at an Oi! gig at the Hambrough Tavern in the predominantly Asian Southall suburb of West London. Southall was a main area of Asian immigration and therefore a prime target for provocations by the National Front. Southall had previously (April 1979) been the scene of a days-long confrontation between police and Asian youth after the anti-racism activist Blair Peach was killed during a demonstration against a National Front march.[25] The alleged failure of the authorities to adequately investigate Peach's murder left a legacy of resentment that was exacerbated by frequent incidents of "Paki-bashing." Featuring performances by three well-known Oi! bands, the Business, the Last Resort, and the 4 Skins, the gig was seen as the last straw by young Asian locals, who put a stop to the performance by burning the venue to the ground. Large numbers of skinheads were arrested in the ensuing melee, and the press moved quickly to brand the entire skinhead scene as a stronghold of the extreme right, despite the fact that the National Front had no direct involvement with the gig.[26] The resulting "moral panic" was fueled by public dismay over the second of two Oi! compilation albums released by *Sounds* magazine at the urging of journalist Gary Bushell. The first, *Oi! The Album*, had helped to launch the Oi! movement in November 1980. The second album, released only a couple of months before the Southall riot, carried as its title the unfortunate pun *Strength Through Oi!* (a play on the name of the Nazi-era leisure-time organization Strength Through Joy). The album also featured on its cover a photograph of Nicky Crane, a well-known skinhead who also happened to be the organizer for the British Movement in Kent. The album was not financed by the extreme right, nor were the bands represented on it necessarily right-wing, but the right-wing connotations of the title and cover art, taken in conjunction with the violence at Southall and the resulting charges of skinhead fascism in the press, solidified the right-wing reputation of the skinhead scene and Oi! music.

Whatever the political outlook of Oi!—most of the band members protested vigorously against being tarred with the fascist brush, and Gary Bushell went to great lengths to clear the Oi! name in the pages of *Sounds*—the music played an important symbolic role in the politicization of the skinhead subculture. By providing, for the first time, a musical focus for skinhead identity that was "white"—that is, that had nothing to do with the West Indian immigrant presence and little obvious connection with black musical roots—Oi! provided a musical focus for new visions of skinhead identity.[27] With the emergence of Oi!, a skinhead, could, in theory, completely avoid or negate the question of the subculture's black roots. In practice, few did so, on the one hand recognizing that ska—like boots and shaved heads—was a fetish item of skinhead identity, and on the other, seeing no reason to deprive themselves of the enjoyment of the music and social scene around ska gigs. Nor was the lyrical content of Oi! without potentially right-wing implications. Although some of its themes—working-class pride, repression, and the bad luck of the down-and-out—gave it much in common with other genres like country and the blues, others—like violence ("aggro") and soccer hooliganism—could easily be interpreted in extreme right-wing terms. In providing a musical expression of skinhead identity that was exclusively white (and, unlike punk and ska, almost exclusively male), and in foregrounding violence as a pillar of the working-class lifestyle, Oi! provided a point of entry for a new brand of right-wing rock music.

As Oi! came to signify "white music," the relationship between cause and effect was reversed: rather than skinheads adopting right-wing beliefs and expressing them in music, musicians with right-wing beliefs began to adopt the skinhead scene—white, male, violent and patriotic—as a field for their self-expression. These musicians brought new musical influences to bear on Oi!, creating a hybrid form of "skinhead rock" that would maintain its affiliation with the scene long after it ceased to bear any resemblance to the "street punk" sound out of which Oi! developed. Two key bands—Skrewdriver from England, and the Böhse Onkelz ("Evil Uncles") from Germany—exemplify this process. Although different from each other in crucial ways, the two bands represent critical points of articulation between the Nazi rock genre and the skinhead Oi! scene out of which it developed, and illustrate the process by which new identities were created through the process of cultural transmission. London's Skrewdriver was the earliest and most influential of the "Nazi rock" bands. Its leader, Ian Stuart Donaldson, did more than anyone else to forge connections between right-wing rock music and the skinhead scene, and between the skinhead scene and the radical right. An ardent admirer of Adolf Hitler, Donaldson's understanding of the skinhead subculture had little to do with skinhead reggae or the black-white connections from which it sprang, a fact that is hardly surprising given that Donaldson was a musician with right-wing views long before becoming a skinhead.[28]

Donaldson set up vital links for the burgeoning right-wing rock scene in two directions. First, he single-handedly forged a connection between the skinhead scene and the extreme right in Britain, forming the National Front–financed White Noise Club (WNC) to release right-wing bands, and releasing his own "White Power" single on the label. Second, he signed a contract with a German label, Rock-O-Rama, to release WNC bands in Germany, and when a split in the National Front led to a souring of relations between the NF and the White Noise Club, he continued his association with Rock-O-Rama by founding Blood and Honor, an umbrella organization and magazine for right-wing skinhead bands. Skrewdriver released a string of albums on Rock-O-Rama, bringing the right-wing skinhead sound directly into Germany from 1982. Skrewdriver helped build the English-German connection in other ways, touring with one of the best-known German bands, Düsseldorf's Störkraft. Further, the organization founded by Donaldson opened a German chapter—Blood and Honor/Division Deutschland—which came to play an increasingly important role in promoting right-wing skinhead concerts in Germany in the 1990s. Aside from these practical links, the brand of music Ian Stuart Donaldson helped pioneer looked to Germany as a spiritual home. Not only did Skrewdriver gigs resemble Nazi rallies, with hundreds of shaved-head skins shouting "Sieg Heil" as Donaldson held forth from the stage, but White Noise Club and Blood and Honor bands reveled in historical and mythical imagery associated with Nazi Germany, WWII, and Norse mythology. A close friend of Donaldson's, Kev Turner of the band Skull-head, dabbled in Odinism. As much as Donaldson and others like him considered themselves "English patriots," the vision of white identity they championed was constructed in relationship to a mythic-historic past that was less English than German. ...

Timothy S. Brown, from "Subcultures, Pop Music and Politics: Skinheads and 'Nazi Rock' in England and Germany," *Journal of Social History* 38:1 (2004).

IAN STUART OF SKREWDRIVER, INTERVIEW IN *TERMINAL*

No analysis of punk and the politics of race would be complete without Skrewdriver, the standard-bearer of White Power punk. The band's first incarnation came at the height of punk in Britain,

but quickly folded after releasing a few singles. At the time, Skrewdriver had no explicit political affiliation, though they had begun to identify as skinheads. This interview, conducted by mail with the lead singer and sole original member, Ian Stuart Donaldson, around 1982, follows directly after Stuart's decision to reform the band as explicitly White Power and National Front identified. Stuart describes this transition in his first reply: Black kids are beaten up by skinheads at a show, and Skrewdriver—unlike, say, Sham 69—refuse to denounce their fans' racist violence. What remains so remarkable about this text is the degree to which it relies precisely on the rhetoric of victimization often articulated more apolitically by White punks. Finding himself in that slippage between rage at those in power (the police, the music business, "anti-British traitors") and simultaneously those who live the reality of racial oppression ("big mouthed Blacks"), Stuart then doubles back and shores up the impermeable boundaries of whiteness itself. The "magical community" of the skinheads becomes less about a vision of working-class solidarity and more about transnational White pride, while still founded upon those initial gestures of punk rock dejection and rejection.

TERMINAL: Can you give a brief history of Skrewdriver for those who may be hearing of you for the first time?

IAN STUART: Skrewdriver formed in 1977 at the start of the punk explosion. We, however, did not put down the superstar bands like most bands did. We counted the Rolling Stones as well as the Sex Pistols amongst our early influences. In early 1978 Skrewdriver adopted the Skinhead image due to a large amount of posing lefties infiltrating the punk scene. At a concert in 1978 several Blacks were beaten up by skinheads after a Skrewdriver concert in London. We refused to slag off our own fans to the Marxist music press and were therefore labeled "nazis." The music press then mounted a largely successful campaign to get Skrewdriver banned from playing. However, we managed to release a couple of more records. ...

TERMINAL: Why did you decide to reform the band? And what happened to the other original members?

STUART: I decided to reform Skrewdriver because not a lot of bands were playing for the nationalist skinheads, punks and straights. I decided that it would be good to play for a nationalist audience instead of the usual anti-British favored by the music industry. Also, two good friends of mine, Mickey and Margaret from the LAST RESORT shop in East London, said that they would form a record company to release "Back with a Bang/United Skins" for us. This was because of the Capitalist and Communist run record companies—both have a vested interest in suppressing the Nationalists. Of the original members, I am the only one left. Ron Hartley, the guitarist, is now working on a building site. Grinny, the drummer is also a building site worker. Kev McKay, the bassist, owns a glass blowing business and I am still fighting the establishment trying to get gigs.

TERMINAL: Are you what the media would term an Oi! Band?

STUART: I consider the rubbish that the controlled media comes out with is almost 100% lies. We had formed three years before Garry Bushell, the left wing idiot from *Sounds*, even invented the word "Oi!" However, I have heard us *referred* to as an Oi! band …

TERMINAL: Is White Noise your own label?

STUART: White Noise Records is a label set up by a member of the NATIONAL FRONT for the nationalist bands who cannot get a record deal due to the fact that the music business is being run by anti-British traitors. Although an NF financed business, White Noise is not an NF business.

TERMINAL: Are you affiliated with any political organizations?

STUART: I am a member of the NF. I am the youth organizer of the London NF. I used to be the youth organizer of the Blackpool NF whilst I was living there.

TERMINAL: Are you aware that Skrewdriver has had what some would call a "cult" following here in the US and have you received any mail from outside the UK?

STUART: I have had several letters from the USA over the years and have met several Americans on holiday in England. One American I met took 110 copies of "White Power" back with him. Also I have received mail from Holland, Germany, Sweden, Denmark, N. Ireland, Scotland, New Zealand, Australia, and Poland.

TERMINAL: How has the music press responded to your last EP?

STUART: The British music press has largely ignored our latest EP. The music press is very similar to PRAVDA, They lie about people they don't like and ignore anybody that does not agree with their senile policies.

TERMINAL: What do you think of the NF and the KKK's efforts to combine racism with patriotism?

STUART: I am a member of the NF, so I have a lot of feeling for them. I also think the KKK and the National States Rights Party in the US do a very good job. I think that if you love your country, you are a Nationalist. If you love your people, then you are a socialist. So if you love both, you are a National Socialist. Which is the only way to defeat the destructive alliance of Capitalism and Communism.

TERMINAL: Are accounts of violence at Skrewdriver shows true? Do you have a loyal following?

STUART: There has never been any violence at a Skrewdriver gig. The only time there is trouble is when the police come barging into our gigs and try to stop them. Or when supporters are going home after the gigs and they bump into large gangs of big mouthed Blacks. Our support is extremely loyal. We have a regular crowd of 500 people who are loyal White Nationalists.

TERMINAL: Do you have any desire to come to America to tour?

STUART: I would love to play America so long as our gigs did not make any money for Black or Jewish promoters. Also I do not know about touring because we find it difficult to find gigs, never mind tours in Great Britain due to establishment and left wing pressure. The music press even refuse to advertise our concerts. We have to rely on leafleting to let people know when we play. So much for democracy ...

Tesco Vee, from "Interview: Ian Stuart," *Terminal* no. 14 (1982/1983), reprinted in *Colorblind: An Anti-Racist Zine from ARA/Syndicate-Chicago* no. 1 (1989).

MAJORITY OF ONE,
REVIEW AND LETTER EXCHANGE IN
MAXIMUMROCKNROLL

How much hate can you take? This is the fundamental question at issue in this exchange, which begins with a record review from the Mr. T Experience lead singer and currently best-selling young adult novelist Frank Portman. Portman (referred to here by his alias "Dr. Frank") gives a relatively positive take on a 7-inch EP by the band Majority of One, but then, characteristic of *MRR*'s thirst for political context beyond music, remarks upon the fact that, in the band photo, one of the members sports a shirt from the notorious racist band Skrewdriver. A response from the band offers up a standard punk defense: tolerance for the politically reprehensible (e.g., racism, fascism) in deference to aesthetic, or shock appeal. That is, the "it's-abhorrent-but-it-fucking-rips!" trope. Lookout Records

founder and *MRR* contributor Larry Livermore nails the band in his rejoinder, giving us our first look at how such issues get hashed out in the punk scene: a claim is made, often in the name of being truly "punk," another punk weighs in with their criticism, the original interlocutor replies, and so do a myriad of other punks, each with their own, often highly personalized, opinion. The result of these letter exchanges, which figure prominently in the larger punk zines like *MRR*, is a multivocal argument about what it means to be punk, and in this case what it means to be racist, and what might be the limits of punk rock tolerance.

Original review:
Four strong songs from this Toledo band, proof of how good non-metal HC can be. Lots of attention to dynamics and unexpected tempo changes to keep you on your toes. Lyrics are of the "personal trauma" type. Real good. But how come the guy on the cover is wearing a "Skrewdriver" shirt?
—Dr. Frank

From Majority of One's response:
I am going to answer Doctor Frank's question about [Majority of One band member] Ali's Skrewdriver shirt on the cover of our EP, "Decisions Made." That's a good question. First of all, the name "Majority of One" was derived from a passage in Henry David Thoreau's *Civil Disobedience*, meaning power in one's self. We also define it as importance in the individual, each person is a majority and should be treated as such whether they're black, white, red, or green. This shows that we are obviously against racism, white power, and all that Nazi skinhead bullshit … which we are. Ali likes the Skrewdriver sound, not their morals or beliefs. He is not influenced lyrically by every band that preaches their beliefs. Why support a band that is for everything you're against, you might ask? He supports them musically or as people. Why discriminate against a good-sounding band because they are ignorant fools? That's the same as their discriminating against someone because they are black. Maybe Ali's too open-minded—I don't know. Enough said. It's not that big of a deal anyway. Ali's shirt just means that he loves music (hardcore, punk) not Skrewdriver views and to each his own, I guess. I only wrote this to prevent vicious untrue rumors about Majority of One being a "white power" band because of a lousy T-shirt on our EP cover.
—Eric Lemie, Majority of One

MRR's response:
On the Skrewdriver issue, sorry, I don't buy your explanation. It might make some sense in the case of non-English speakers who don't understand what the words mean, but no matter how much you like the "punk, hardcore sound," I'd say you'd have to have a moral blind spot a mile wide to be happily moshing away to lyrics like "Nigger Out." Furthermore, buying Skrewdriver records or T-shirts funnels money into the hands of vicious Nazi racists to use in their hate campaigns which are unfortunately attracting too many impressionable people already. And no matter what your rationalization, most people who see a Skrewdriver T-shirt on your cover will assume, rightly or wrongly, that you support what that band stands for. It is that big of a deal. Is Ali too open minded? As someone once said, "I keep an open mind, but not so open that any old crap falls in."
—Lawrence Livermore

Frank Portman, Eric Lemie, Lawrence Livermore, *Maximumrocknroll*, nos. 59 and 62 (April 1988/July 1988).

GEORGE ERIC HAWTHORNE OF RaHoWa, "MUSIC OF THE WHITE RESISTANCE"

This transcribed radio interview features George Hawthorne of the Canadian white-supremacist band RaHoWa, short for Racial Holy War, who put out two—not very punk—albums between 1993 and 1995. With a candor and transparency oddly characteristic of White Power literature—and often unfortunately lacking in their left-punk counterparts—Hawthorne makes explicit the attraction of White supremacists to punk rock and its forbidden, outsider status. Some of Hawthorne's interview could have come straight from any punk zine: DIY cultural production is celebrated and MTV and the corporate media are condemned. But then there's the break: the music business is not condemned for being controlled by profit-hungry multinationals, but because they are owned and operated by people of the "Jewish persuasion." Hawthorne also provides a rather deliberate articulation of his reasons for choosing music as a form of expression: to reach as many sectors of the youth as possible, by exploiting the attraction that comes with movements that might have "the image of being forbidden." It is

a similar logic—albeit better thought out—to that of the tactics of "shock value" extolled by many punks, and represents exactly the risk Livermore identified in the previous selection: of aesthetic appreciation tipping into political identification. And, as Hawthorne sees it, what's more shocking in this day and age than being a Nazi? It is worth noting that Hawthorne later renounced racism, forming a multiracial group called Novacosm.

Today, we are going to explore one of the most promising developments in Western culture today. It is the flowering of a whole new branch of music, which I call music of the White resistance. The following lyrics are from a song which is a part of that flowering. It is entitled "The Snow Fell." It is about the heroes of many nations who fought against Stalin—here called the Beast—on the Eastern Front in World War II.

> He sat in a room with a square the color of blood
> He'd rule the whole world if there was a way that he could
> He'd sit and he'd stare at the minarets on top of the towers
> For he was the Beast
> As he hatched his new plans to gain power
> And the snow fell, covering the dreams and ideals
> And the snow fell, freezing the blood and the wheels
> And the snow fell, they had to keep warm for survival
> And the snow fell, and defeated the Beast's only rivals ...
> Then came the deadly road back from the steppes, of their retreat.
> The cold wracked the bodies but worse was the pain of defeat.
> Many people who had hailed them once now turned and looked away,
> These people now knew that the Beast was on his way.
> And the snow fell, covering the dreams and ideals,
> And the snow fell, freezing the blood and the wheels.
> And the snow fell, they had to keep warm for survival.
> And the snow fell, and defeated the Beast's only rivals.

AMERICAN DISSIDENT VOICES: Welcome to American Dissident Voices, George Eric Hawthorne. We're delighted to have you here. Please call me Kevin.

GEORGE ERIC HAWTHORNE: Thank you, Kevin.

ADV: The song we just heard, "The Snow Fell," is about the soldiers of Western Civilization on the Eastern Front fighting Communism. Is that right?

HAWTHORNE: Yes, that's right. That whole chapter in human history is one of such immense tragedy when you begin to realize the importance of a victory having been won by the Axis forces during World War II. You realize what a tragic event it was: the soldiers who froze to death out on the Russian front.

ADV: It wasn't only Germans who were fighting against Communism, was it?

HAWTHORNE: Absolutely not. There were many other nations which had bonded together in the Axis forces that were trying to halt the advance of Communism. Even to this day there are remnants of these forces, and the memory of these forces has been kept alive in countries such as Latvia and Lithuania and Ukraine and many more I could mention.

ADV: Are you the author and performer of "The Snow Fell"?

HAWTHORNE: Actually, that is a cover song of an original song by a band by the name of Skrewdriver, which was led by the late Ian Stuart. We rearranged the song, added cello and piano and some vocal harmonies, went into the studio and rerecorded it for a tribute album that is being done for this individual.

ADV: And you are the leader of the band which performed this new version?

HAWTHORNE: I am the vocalist. Our band is called RaHoWa.

ADV: What does that mean?

HAWTHORNE: RaHoWa stands for Racial Holy War. It's an acronym using the first two letters of each word.

ADV: You are also the editor of a very interesting and professionally produced magazine called *Resistance*. You are listed as the editor of *Resistance* and also as the president of Resistance Records. What are you and your colleagues trying to do with your music and your magazine?

HAWTHORNE: My colleagues and I became very concerned with the propaganda that was literally being shoved down the throats of White youth in America and beyond. When we really studied this problem— when we looked at it as objectively as possible, we began to realize that they were not stealing our youth away from our culture and from our past by using written words—using text on paper and handing them books and saying "Here, forget about your past and learn how to commit racial suicide." No, that wasn't what was happening—instead, they were using cultural attrition. They were stealing our youth away using MTV and a whole network, a well-rooted network, promoting decadent values to the young people. And the main tool that they were using was music. Resistance Records was formed to counteract this whole process—so that we would start having our own voice, and we would start being able to express all of our own cultural imperatives and our desire to have a piece of land for ourselves; and to use music as a way of reaching the young people.

ADV: What kind of success have you seen?

HAWTHORNE: In a very short period of time, we have seen our magazine nearly triple in its circulation, from an initial printing of 5,000 copies of issue one just ten months ago; and here we are ready to publish issue four, which will be 15,000 copies, or an increase of 10,000 in just ten months. We have been in touch with several mainstream bands who have told us We would like to come out and support you, but it would probably ruin our careers. So what we'd like to do is help you behind the scenes. These people have put us in contact with an entire renegade network in the music industry, people who know who controls the music industry, who've wanted to do something about it all along, yet have never had the glue to bring these people together and unite them, at least behind the scenes.

ADV: So you're saying that Jewish control is present in the music industry just as it is in the print media, etc.?

HAWTHORNE: Exactly. It should come as no surprise to anybody that is studying what is happening in the United States with the mainstream media, with the entire entertainment industry, that the music industry also falls under the exact same control by a very tight-knit group of people—and they are almost exclusively of the Jewish persuasion.

ADV: So there are certain aspects of youth culture that have naturally developed certain pro-White characteristics. But the people who control what goes on the radio stations, what goes on the major record labels, what goes on the television, have tried to squelch this and prevent it from reaching most of our youth.

HAWTHORNE: Exactly. As a matter of fact, they are very very scared about what we are doing. And they are making every effort imaginable to keep our music off the record store shelves, to keep it out of the big distributors' catalogs, and for the most part they have been successful in the past. However, with the emergence of Resistance Records, we are organized and funded well enough so that we are starting to be able to compete on a similar level. We now have a professionally published magazine you made mention of earlier. We also are publishing music videos; and since MTV probably won't play them, since they are a controlled entity, we are publishing a home video tape, which interested persons can purchase through mail order, which contains music videos and concert footage and interviews with our bands. This is a way that the system cannot control what we are doing.

ADV: People could even take that video and get it on public access television if that is available in their areas.

HAWTHORNE: Exactly. What we have found is that, more often than not, people—especially young people—are attracted to things that are off the beaten path. If something has an "underground" flavor, or the image of being forbidden, the youth are naturally attracted to it. Now, in the past this is something that harmed our youth because they were attracted to things which were forbidden or at least discouraged for very good reasons. Examples would be race mixing or the use of drugs. However, in 1995, the mainstream media have made everything O.K. except being proud of your race and culture, and this tendency of youth is now having a very undesired effect from the perspective of the mainstream media giants because these young people are now interested in the new forbidden thing; and that is being proud to be White.

ADV: Right. Now that the neo-Communists and the New World Order types have things more or less the way they want them, now it is rebellion to be proud of your race. Obviously that's why you chose the name Resistance.

HAWTHORNE: Exactly. The people who run this company are all young ourselves; we're in our early twenties. We see ourselves as being in touch, culturally, with the young people of our generation and the people who are between the ages of fifteen and twenty right now. We know what makes them tick. We know what they listen to and what they are interested in. And we are providing it to them. And they are responding with such enthusiasm, it is just unbelievable. We get hundreds of letters every single day. These young people are writing to us: "Thank you, you've helped me get away from the drugs; you've given me a purpose in my life." They give us such support and thanks for what we are doing; it is really reaffirming our position as having done the right thing from the beginning.

ADV: In the whole pro-White music scene, how many different bands, roughly, are we talking about?

HAWTHORNE: When one starts to investigate the underground pro-White music movement, one discovers that it is absolutely enormous; and it is so underground and kept out of the attention of the mainstream viewer, that you would never realize that there are probably 40 or 50 White Power bands in the United States alone. In Canada there's another dozen. Across Europe it seems like every small locality, every small town and city, and definitely at least every country has a White Power band. A lot of them have published demos themselves that they distribute through a network of fanzines, which are small music magazines in which they print interviews and photographs and lyrics of these bands. There must be about 150 to 200 White Power bands in the world right now—and how many of them can the average American mention?

ADV: How long has this been happening and was it planned by anyone?

HAWTHORNE: I think that one of the most beautiful things about the White Power music movement is the fact that it is a spontaneous development. This was not a development where a bunch of businessmen sat down at a drawing table and said, We're going to come up with the next youth culture. Much to the contrary, what happened with the White Power music movement is that it came out of the racial soul of the young people. They desired to have a voice. They were feeling things that they were told they weren't allowed to express. And music became the medium through which they expressed these things. It all began back in around 1975 or 1976. An individual by the name of Ian Stuart formed a band called Skrewdriver. The inspiration that he provided to a whole generation of young people in England at the time eventually started branching off, and it finally reached the United States in 1984. From that point it started rapidly expanding around the world until now, wherever you find White youth today there is a skinhead movement—developing pro-White music, pro-White bands, holding concerts. I believe this is going to be the real wave of the future for the music industry. I don't think they can keep this down anymore.

ADV: So the larger culture, by design, wasn't providing what these young people felt they needed. And it's been growing for nearly twenty years!

HAWTHORNE: Absolutely. The media like to paint everything with the same brush. They like to put a label on something: Oh, this is Nazi. This is what skinheads are about. It's just about violence and that's it. They just like to put their stamp of disapproval on things, and they think that that's going to make people turn away and not investigate any further. But the reality is that for the last twenty years there have been very real issues of concern to White youth: ways that they do not feel satisfied, things that they feel they have to express, and they turned to the music as a way of doing that. It came out of their hearts. It came out of feeling neglected. White youth today are abandoned before they are even born. So many millions of them are abandoned while they are still in the womb. By the time they're born judgement has been passed on them. They are guilty of the "crimes" of their ancestors. They've held the world back. They've enslaved the planet. They are the evil people. That is what they are being taught, and it has a very damaging effect on the psyche of a young person who is really just trying to grow up. ...

ADV: ... I know that in some racially mixed schools—I recall one news story from Canada—the authorities are so afraid of the rise of the White subculture, they have outlawed suspenders, and certain types of boots and shoelaces that are associated with skinheads, even though many of the kids that were wearing them weren't necessarily skinheads and were just trying to find some kind of common White identity.

HAWTHORNE: Right. I really believe that this is going to backfire on them. Because a lot of these young people that are wearing these symbols are not people that want to cause trouble or cause harm to anyone. They are just young people that are expressing themselves and trying to be fashion-conscious. When they are told that they can't wear these symbols, they say, "Well, why can't I?" And then the principals of these schools say "It's because those are pro-White symbols, and that stands for hatred." And then the students ask "What's wrong with me being proud of being White?" It makes these young people start asking questions that the principals can't answer. And it's having an adverse effect. We had one school here, where we had some young people who were distributing our music in the school. They were selling our music in the cafeteria at lunch time to their friends, who were buying it up as if it would disappear if they didn't get their hands on it as quick as they could. Then the principal suddenly tried to ban this music in his school. What these principals forget is that the young people never asked them for permission to listen to what they wanted to listen to. Stating this has been banned means nothing to these young people.

ADV: Let's hope that it makes your music even more popular.

HAWTHORNE: I think it will.

From "Music of the White Resistance," broadcast on American Dissident Voices, transcribed in *Free Speech* 1:4 (April 1995).

ANONYMOUS,
"ROCK 'N' ROLL: WHITE OR BLACK?"

If you stare into the abyss of White Power punk long enough, the abyss stares back at you. Here, from a 1987 Southern California zine called *Skinned Alive*, we find an anonymous editorial arguing for the exclusively White origins of not just punk but rock 'n' roll itself. While the temptation to dismiss such revisionism as laughable is, admittedly, strong, the article's importance comes in providing us an unspoken-for piece of the puzzle. Previous essays have explained Nazi rock's repudiation of the Black origins of skinhead music and style, but we've yet to see, until now, that culture's own attempt to actually *rewrite* that origin story. Punk rock, according to the logic of the author, is not a White people's offshoot of a Black tradition, but is rather the continuation of a long history of "white people's music." The author, interestingly, resexualizes whiteness in a way analogous to what we saw with the White Negro's appropriation of the fantasy of Black male potency. The fantasy remains, but here Black sexuality is a weak derivative of the primary White male potency. Blackness, to the author, is a "2nd-rate imitation of the Olympian prowess and aristocratic power of the likes of Elvis and Jerry Lee." (In a photo caption accompanying the original article, Jerry Lee Lewis is referred to imaginatively as an "Aryan Wild Man whose prodigious energies are repressed by the consumer police.") The essay also uses unsettlingly familiar punk language to make the case for White Power music. When the author writes that the "music which reflects our rage and which empowers us to unite and repel the alien invasion is rough, rocky, gut-wrenching and we make no apologies to anyone for it," the rhetoric should be immediately and uncomfortably recognizable to any punk or reader of this anthology, making one question the political mutability of punk's "rough, rocky, [and] gut-wrenching" opposition.

The White Race invents and creates the originals which everyone else Xeroxes on those tinny little copy-machines from Japan. They copy, we invent. The secret of the successful (so far) mental genocide campaign launched against the White Race by the envious copycat races is to claim that what they ripped off from us was actually theirs in the first place. That's the ultimate logic of a black mugger: what's yours is mine. The Orientals and other Asians assume the same arrogant claims on Europe and the U.S.: they're not ancestral White homelands or former frontiers built from the brush and wilderness into gleaming White cities beckoning filthy colored hordes, they're the Oriental's by right (but just go to the Orient or Pakistan and see how many rights American Whites or Europeans have there). The race masquerading under the title "Jews" are the masters at this usurpation process: they've stolen God, the Bible & history itself and claim it's the copyright of Pharisee-Khazaria.

This thieving process has always been in operation throughout our history. Only in the old days, our Aryan forefathers knew it for what it was: a scam, a con, a way to nick. But now thanks to a psychological warfare campaign launched by liars in the media and schools we no longer recognize it for what it is. Instead we actually believe that the Aryan Race of original thought and invention really owes the so-called "Jews" and colored races for everything we've got and especially so in the arena of Pop-music where it is repeatedly claimed that the infectious joy and marching power of rock and roll comes out of negro tom-tom banging in Africa (wonder how they plugged them in?).

This claim is also used by the boring old Losers among Whites who are responsible for letting "Jews" and Third Worlders take over in the first place. These old farts claim rock hurts their ears or they say it is just "nigger music." Well, we say, the music of warriors ought to hurt your ears: The sounds of the march into battle were not meant to evoke the charms of a swank drawing room in Mayfair or Beverly Hills. We're in a rage: You're damn right we've gone Berserk—just like our Viking ancestors. Unlike our critics, we simply can't sit still and watch apes steal our women, rape our old women, take our jobs and turn our nations into the same black pits of filth and ugliness as the lands the minorities are descended from. The music which reflects our rage and which empowers us to unite and repel the alien invasion is rough, rocky, gut-wrenching and we make no apologies to anyone for it.

Scotland Comes to America

The roots of rock and roll are electrical. Without electricity and the electrical guitar there would be no rock and roll. And as White Power Rock Music pioneers Ian Stuart told us in a recent interview, "Who invented the electric guitar? It wasn't a nigger."

The roots of the current music scene before Oi, that lay the groundwork for the White rock sound comes from 50's rock and roll. The two undisputed, towering geniuses of that sound are JERRY LEE LEWIS (the Killer) and the King Himself, ELVIS PRESLEY. No other White artists, to say nothing of some black, can hold a candle to these two. They've influenced, directly or indirectly, everyone playing rock music today. They are incomparable and their influence will never be equaled. PRESLEY and LEWIS got their sound, their genius and their power from the heritage of Scottish and Anglo-Saxon folk and church music traditions out of which they sprung. The Scottish Highlanders of the American South were dirt-poor and oppressed working class Whites. Their "mountain music" on banjo, fiddle, harp, guitar and piano is arguably one of the greatest and most potent folk formats on earth. Just have someone pick out "Orange Blossom Special" on a fiddle and see if there's a still foot in the house. There won't be because there can't be: White folk musical genius is too overwhelming to be resisted and that is the root of the appeal of modern Rock.

Besides this influence on 50's White rockers, there is also the influence of the People's Protestant churches in the American South. The Bible heritage of Oliver Cromwell, the Protestant Reformation and most of our ancestors is something most of us disparage today because of the lying words of the pro-Zionist TV preaching crooks. But the truth is, Jesus was not a "Jew." The Israelite-Hebrew people of the Old Testament were White Aryans. It's a fact you've never heard before because the System doesn't want you to know it. They don't want you to read the book THE THIRTEENTH TRIBE to find out the real origin of the Khazar-Pharisees who masquerade as part of the Tribe of Judah (Jews) today.

Why mention this? Because you need to know what your White ancestors knew. And out of their knowledge came hymns of power and joy and from this combination of White Aryan Church music and White Aryan folk music, both finding a home in the American South, having been born in Great Britain, arose the twin comets of Elvis Presley and Jerry Lee Lewis. Elvis was so anti-"Jew" and anti-homosexual when he first began his career that his manager, Colonel Parker had to warn him against speaking out against these groups in Hollywood. "You never know when you're gonna be talking to one," he told Elvis.

Jerry Lee Lewis, when asked who he though the four greatest Popular Music Stylists of all time were, replied, "Al Jolson, Jimmie Rodgers, Hank Williams and Jerry Lee Lewis." Four White men: The Killer may not be modest but he's right. Jerry Lee and Elvis came from poor White working class roots. Both Elvis' Dad Vernon, and Jerry's Dad Elmo had been in jail for moonshining. Yet their sons would shake the world to its core with their unique White sound. In fact the first music every played by the astronauts on the Moon was a cassette by Jerry Lee Lewis. White music for White heroes and explorers. In spite of his achievements Jerry Lee Lewis is almost NEVER given credit for the tremendous influence he has had on the Pop music of the world.

Power and Potency

These two Southern White Males, Elvis and Jerry Lee were possessed of a potency and a power akin to the great orators and generals of our race. Lewis with his trademark "pumping piano" milked the Southern gothic folk tradition for all it was worth as this blond-haired (before it faded) Baptist Dionysus reveled with power and life before audiences inflamed with ecstasy and joy. Jerry Lee and Elvis were paradigms of the American tradition of individualism: each was and is fond of guns and believed in the right to self-defense. Each broke the conventions of society as their youthful vigor outshined any negro bump and grind by a mile. Supposed black masculinity is nothing more than an animalistic, 2nd-rate imitation of the Olympian prowess and aristocratic power of the likes of Elvis and Jerry Lee.

Few if any blacks have ever made up an audience at a Jerry Lee or Elvis concert. They can't stand to see the image of the White Man excelling at singing, musicianship and the calling forth of erotic powers.

Because Jerry and Elvis were products of happier times when White unity was strong and the dividing lines between White and Black were clearly demarcated, their music was naturally pre-occupied with fun, love-making and reveling (although Jerry Lee is constantly harassed by the police and government and some of his music reflects the White Country blues-laments and darker side of his complex personality). In our time, in which there are battles to be fought and invasion to repel our White rock cannot always reflect themes of love and joy. But there can be no question that we are heirs to a White-invented sound pioneered by the White working classes and reflective of our hopes and aspirations. Rock 'n' Roll: White or Black? Our music is overwhelmingly White in origin, style and evolution. 50s Rock was White. Rockabilly was White. Punk's a White invention. Heavy-metal is White. The original Stones and Who sounds were White. SO STAND WITH PRIDE BY YOUR MUSIC SWEET GENIUS WHITE YOUTH. NO ONE CAN COMPARE WITH YOU!

Anonymous, "Rock 'n' Roll: White or Black?," *Skinned Alive* no. 1 (Murrieta, CA, 1987).

KIERAN KNUTSON OF ANTI-RACIST ACTION, INTERVIEW IN *MAXIMUMROCKNROLL*

As it is with any cultural form worth its salt—that is, any form that has taken enough of a hold in culture to inspire fervent communal identification—there is a struggle over the meaning of "skinhead." Refusing to deed ownership to the virulent racists from whom we've heard quite loudly, other skins did everything in their power to reassert the legacy and primacy of Black influence on skinhead music and style, and remake skinhead identity as multiracial and antiracist. Anti-Racist Action, founded by Kieran Knutson, is perhaps this movement's most enduring consequence. Still going strong, though now less explicitly tied to skinheadism, ARA arose in 1987 out of a group of multiracial Minneapolis skinheads called the Baldies. Far from the more emotional registers of, say, the Clash's attempts at "radical whiteness," ARA exhibits a much more subtle and sensitive approach to antiracist politics, seeing not only the allegiances that must be built with other subcultures (extra-bald solidarity!) and around other issues (feminist concerns, antihomophobia, etc.), but also understanding the spectacular aspect of politics and the importance of gaining visibility through zines like *MRR* for organizing purposes. However, the primary tactic of ARA seems to be physical confrontation, that is, beating the shit out of Nazis, and this distinguishes—and separates—ARA from most other antiracist groups and, indeed, many other punks who might otherwise share their politics. But Knutson distinguishes between different kinds of violence, and argues that such violence has to occur within a meaningful context: your actions won't bear any political weight to your average punk if they're not on your side.

MAXIMUMROCKNROLL: Let's start with you explaining your version of "skinhead culture" because what most people hear comes from the mouths of the Nazis.

KIERAN KNUTSON: For me, the Nazis' version is on thin ice. The origins of the movement came from black Jamaican music—the music which came in the form of reggae and soul and later in ska, and was exported to England and shared with white working class people. It was always a multi-racial thing and always embedded with working class politics which are very much against racism.

MRR: The ironic thing is that the Nazi skinheads say that skinheads have always been white.

KNUTSON: That's just not true; it's a lie. You can look at pictures from the English dance halls in the 60's and see that it isn't true. There have always been black skinheads and black music has always been the basis of it. Even Ian Stuart (vocalist for Skrewdriver) rips off the early Rolling Stones who ripped off black R&B artists.

MRR: Let's move onto some of the groups that you're involved with by giving the history of them.

KNUTSON: The group I'm involved with is an anti-racist skinhead group called The Baldies who formed Anti-Racist Action (ARA) in 1987. The Baldies were a multi-racial group of skinheads in Minneapolis who for the most part were apolitical until the Nazi skinheads came on the scene which immediately politicized them. At first there wasn't an open conflict with the White Knights (Nazi skin group in Minneapolis) and the Baldies. We would be at the same shows together but there wouldn't be a big hassle—just bad looks at each other. But this exchange grew and grew until we decided that we weren't going to put up with it. From then on every time we saw a White Knight or a group of White Knights they were physically confronted. These confrontations took place at the major hangouts in town as well as where most of the shows took place. After a while every time we saw them we confronted them and told them that this was their last chance to quit and that next time we saw them they would get it. That's how we beat the Nazis in Minneapolis. After the Nazis had been kicked out of Minneapolis we had won a big victory because it would be hard for them to try and reorganize in the area, but in the meantime we weren't aware of their activities outside of the city. The few Nazis that remained went to St. Paul (right next to Minneapolis) and there they jumped a black kid which started a mini race war at a St. Paul high school. So we decided that we first needed to branch out and let people know that there are anti-racist skinheads and make contact with different communities because it shouldn't be just a battle between bald head kids. This is when Anti-Racist Action was formed. The idea for ARA was not just to be a group of anti-racist skins but to involve all types of young people. Sometimes we were able to mobilize a lot of people from different cultural backgrounds to go confront Nazis, which was pretty successful. Another group that The

Baldies and ARA are affiliated with is the Syndicate, which is a network of anti-racist skinheads mainly from the Midwest. The Syndicate came to be because a lot of The Baldies went on tour with the local band Blind Approach (anti-racist skinhead band). In Chicago they met people who were involved with S.H.O.C. (Skinheads On Chicago) and talked with them about forming ARA, which they later did and now is the leading chapter of the organization because they do the most work and are the largest group. Getting ARA mentioned in the MRR scene reports created a big response because people wanted to do something and we were the first thing that came out that involved kids organizing against Nazis. We had letters pouring in, you could see the sentiment out there and a lot of it was from anti-racist skinheads. We got a few groups together like the Brew City Skins from Milwaukee, S.H.O.C. and the North Side Crew from Chicago, groups in Cincinnati, Indianapolis, Lawrence, and a few individuals in Des Moines and Winnipeg. So that's a brief history.

MRR: What are some of the different approaches that these groups have used?

KNUTSON: There's been a lot of half-assed attempts at newsletters but the Chicago people have done much better at it. The project we worked on was fighting Nazi skinheads and making people aware of this through press conferences and demonstrations. We had one demonstration in coalition with a black student group and a progressive white student group from the university where we painted over Nazi graffiti. We've also been involved in an anti-police brutality demonstration when the Minneapolis police involved in a crack bust in a black neighborhood supposedly accidentally burnt down a house killing an elderly couple, which resulted in an outpouring of rage from the community and many others as well. ARA were involved in the planning of the demonstration, provided security, and provided some speakers. Individuals from ARA are involved in several political demonstrations. The women that are involved in ARA have done a lot of anti-rape and anti-pornography work.

MRR: Are a lot of women involved?

KNUTSON: There are more involved in Minneapolis than other cities but unfortunately it's a macho male dominated scene. There are women in Minneapolis and Chicago that might be forming a women's caucus within ARA which I see as a positive step.

MRR: Let's talk about the one tactic that stands out as dealing with Nazi skins, which is physically confronting them.

KNUTSON: From our experience the tactic that has worked in Minneapolis includes physical confrontation, which is fighting them and kicking the shit out of them. I don't see this means as an end because it's important to talk to people in the scene about racism and not letting it be acceptable. If you are going out there and fighting and the scene isn't going to be behind you then it's not very effective. We started by talking with some of the younger people involved with the Nazis, making sure they know what they will be defending if there is a fight. We made it clear to the Nazi skinheads that they will not organize at shows, they will not organize at hangouts, we will not be friends with these people. Like the Specials song goes, "If you have racist friends then you're supporting racist people." So we kicked their ass, moved them out and wouldn't let them hang out and that has worked. There are no Nazis in Minneapolis because of this tactic being used and same is true for Chicago.

MRR: You make it sound so easy, so can you go into some details as to your approach.

KNUTSON: Some people get this fear that skinheads are these supermen that can't be beat but the fact is that any two people should be able to beat any one person if it comes down to that. One of the reasons why The Baldies won so much isn't because we're on some macho trip or that we're all huge people but because we've been able to get the numbers to support us and that's what's most important. For the most part Nazis are not the majority of the scene and if the majority of the people in some way resist them either by not speaking to them, not letting them into shows, or fighting them they're going to be gone. I think all of those approaches are useful but I think fighting does it best for us.

MRR: Among the baldies, is there a general level of consciousness? How much of your action is political awareness and how much of it is a matter of being in the gang that is going to win?

KNUTSON: I think this is worth talking about because a lot of people accuse us of this. A lot of them are my friends so I won't pretend that I have an unbiased view of it all. I talk a lot about it, other people talk a lot about politics, people have some basic ideas why there are racists out there. They are aware of some basic class politics to understand that by splitting black people and white people up then it makes regular people weaker as a class. People also have moral outrage because they have friends who are black, Latin, and Asian. So those are the main driving forces. Other people are more political and identify themselves as black nationalist, anarchist, socialist, or various different stripes of the left.

Some identify themselves as anti-racist U.S. patriots. But everyone is clear on the fact that racism divides people that should be united. That is our base level of understanding. I wouldn't say that people aren't attracted to us because we won the battle with the local Nazis. Obviously people aren't going to join a gang that is losing all the time. But we're not out looking for a fight every night; people who are looking for that are going to get bored.

MRR: One interesting aspect that we were talking about earlier is the aspects of other consciousness including macho attitudes, homophobia, and sexism.

KNUTSON: I think it's growing. A lot of the women involved are constantly confronting people who make derogatory comments towards them or sexualize women. That's how I learned a lot from women talking to me about it and think this is true for a lot of other men involved. I won't say that it's perfect but it's better than a lot of scenes that I've been a part of. People are struggling with these issues. As for homophobia, there aren't any openly gay members of The Baldies. Gay people have come to our ARA meetings and we've had discussions on how to deal with homophobia. No one is outright anti-gay, there's no gay bashing because that is seen as something the Nazis do, but then again people still at times use the word fag to describe someone's sexual preference but they are usually confronted when this happens. I can't speak for other cities on this topic but this is what it is like in Minneapolis.

MRR: Do you want to talk about some of the other skinhead groups you work with and some of the differences that you have?

KNUTSON: I'm willing to work with people who are willing to fight Nazis because I think it's important to have some type of unity in fighting them. But I'm also going to be honest as to what my politics are. If I see shit that I don't like I'm going to criticize it and I'm not going to apologize for my politics. I think there is a tendency among some sections of anti-racist skinheads to dive into nationalism but to me that's what Skrewdriver does. Nationalism isn't appealing to me and it's as divisive as racism. People talk about how they want the United States to be a melting pot and they think the ideas of the U.S. are good, I think that's a little naïve of them. But if those people are going to put themselves on the line and fight Nazis without pushing their nationalist view on others then I'll work with them.

MRR: A lot of middle class kids who mainly constitute the hardcore scene are not used to violence or they're afraid of violence and when they see it they're put off by it. Do you have any thoughts about that?

KNUTSON: If people feel that they can't fight then that's their decision. Maybe they could do something else to support anti-racist activities. I think we should do what works to fight Nazis and that's what convinces me.

MRR: What about people who say that you employ violence so you're as bad as them or sinking to their level?

KNUTSON: I think that's really fucked up and I think there's some racist attitudes to that.

MRR: How do you distinguish what's OK violence and what's not OK violence?

KNUTSON: I think it's a matter of violence that tries to oppress people and violence that is used to defend a scene or community. We're not fighting so we can have power over everyone (and I don't think we could if we wanted to). I think people just got fed up with Nazism and are willing to do whatever it takes to kick them out. ...

Martin Sprouse and Tim Yohannan, from "Interview: Anti-Racist Action," *Maximumrocknroll* no. 78 (Berkeley, November 1989).

LILI THE SKINBIRD, "ASSOCIATING WITH RACISTS: A WAY TO PROMOTE ANTI-RACISM?"

Coming from *Crossbreed*, an early 1990s antiracist skin zine out of Ontario, Canada, this brief editorial rant argues persuasively for the power of "positive peer pressure" as opposed to physical confrontation in the attempt to reach racist skins. This self-identified "skinbird" makes the important point that mob mentality or macho posturing in certain antiracist skin circles may do more to harden the inchoate racism of punk kids into overt racism than anything else. But something else is questioned here: Does the racist deserve empathy? Both Lili the Skinbird and, thinking back a section, Jimmy Pursey of Sham 69 describe kids victimized and influenced by their parents and social upbringing; and yet both also appeal to the notion (Pursey much more problematically) that such racist attitudes are a reaction to upsurges in minority populations. As Lili points out, ass kicking is hardly a great

conversion strategy, and trying to understand where someone is coming from is a much better means to persuade, but at what point does empathy cross over into excuse? And when is a little ass kicking appropriate?

The question of whether or not it is "cool" to associate with alleged racists, or even those who associate with racists, while claiming to be anti-racist, has long been a relatively controversial question in my mind. It actually has its roots in the eternal question of how to go about ending the entire racist situation itself—racists are the root of the problem, aren't they? I mean, take your average Joe racist: He himself has really no rational reason to be racist in the first place. It's usually the fault of his background, childhood, and position in society. As a kid his parents worked in a factory in which people from other ethnic backgrounds were hired in greater numbers, due to fluctuations in the population at certain times. His family's pride in its heritage was being "threatened" by the others of different origins (be it Black, White, Hispanic, Italian, etc.) and they began to complain about "prejudice" at the workplace, whether it was happening or not in reality. So Joe grows up believing in his parents' views as a very young boy, before he can really decide for himself and by the time he can, these ideas are so instilled in his head that he finds no reason to change them at all. Then Joe has problems at the homestead, and finding nowhere else to turn, he joins his local neighbourhood racist organization, who promise him security and friendship. Joe himself is really not a bad person at heart, just misguided and naïve. One day Joe and his pals are harassed by a group of anti-racists, of whom he has been warned, although totally unaware of what they really stand for. The anti-racists beat them to a pulp, and now Joe begins to despise anything to do with anti-racists. Yet, Joe starts hanging out with a few kids from other ethnic backgrounds, who he is supposed to hate. They don't really understand Joe's ideology, and probably don't even care. Joe has new pals, his racist buddies say "all your ethnic backgrounds are fucked, but you guys are OK," and everyone's just as happy as can be. Until our oh-so-kind anti-racist buddies come along and fuck with Joe's new friends for associating with racists. The new guys go back to Joe's racist pals, who help them out, and eventually these recently harassed friends of Joe become avid anti-racist haters. But what if the anti-racists had helped Joe's new pals realize the whole mess behind Joe's racist mates' organization, and thus change them over to the anti-racist cause? And then they, in turn would inform Joe, educating him about the whole issue of racism, and prejudice in general. He would realize his own faults, and maybe even teach it to his pals—almost all youths growing up in the same environment as himself, until all that is left of the friendly neighbourhood racist organization is a couple of hard-line bigots, who go through major identity crises after being dissed by all their followers! Many people, like Joe, are rarely prejudiced on a personal level. This is the level at which positive peer pressure is the most effective. Preaching and violence is not the way to go about ending prejudice—trying to persuade a friend or an acquaintance you believe to be involved with such attitudes to abandon them is one good approach to it though! Therefore, if you associate with racists, sexists, homophobes, etc. (and don't bother trying to deny the fact that you do!), this relationship could potentially be a good means of promoting anti-racism. If all attempts fail, diss him or her HARD, in the best way you know how!

Lili the Skinbird, from "Associating with Racists: A Way to Promote Anti-Racism?" *Crossbreed* no. 4, ed. Kliphph L@M (Ontario, CA, January 1991).

FIVE

PUNKY REGGAE PARTY

Rejected by society
Treated with impunity
Protected by their dignity
I face reality

Wailers still be there
The Jam, the Dammed, the Clash
Wailers still be there
Dr. Feelgood too, ooh
Yeah, it's the punky reggae party
And it's tonight
            —"Punky Reggae Party," Bob Marley and the Wailers

What was the Punky Reggae Party? The story is that Bob Marley and the Wailers recorded "Punky Reggae Party" in 1977 as a response to the Clash's cover of the classic Junior Murvin reggae song "Police and Thieves." But the party represented more than merely mutual appreciation between musicians; it symbolized a dream: the ideal of *solidarity* across race by those "rejected by society."

While punk rock offered some Whites the means to create an identity in opposition to racial Others, other punks used the music and its oppositional stance to align themselves with nonwhites. When the Clash sang "White Riot" it was a call to arms for White punks ... but to build alliances with Blacks and other oppressed minorities, who had something to teach young Whites about rising up and resisting the powers-that-be. Sometimes the attempts at political partnership channeled the romantic exoticism of Norman Mailer's "White Negro," ("Black people ... don't mind throwing a brick") but elsewhere it offered glimpses of what the music critic Jeff Chang, eulogizing Joe Strummer, called a "radical white-ness," that is, a whiteness which openly identifies itself within the context of a multicultural society and against white privilege.[1]

The identification was by turns musical—all stages of punk, whether directly or indirectly, have borrowed heavily from reggae and other black musical forms—and political, as shared histories of oppression and resist-ance were underscored, and sometimes both. On their first album Stiff Little Fingers covered Marley's "Johnny Was," translating the story of vio-lence in Jamaica to their Belfast home (the same album included "White Noise," a track that equated the racism experienced by Caribbeans, South Asians, *and* Irish in Britain). Helping the party find its political voice and footing were formations like Rock Against Racism, the Anti-Nazi League, and, as we saw in the previous section, Anti-Racist Action, all of whom tried to channel the anger and energy of punk into on-the-ground organ-izing and advocacy.

But not all oppression is equitable, and there are limits to solidarity. Being "rejected by society" because you sport a mohawk is different than being rejected because of your skin color. The slide from inter-race soli-darity to an assumption of shared "freakishness"—à la "Rock 'N' Roll Nigger"—is all too easy to make. Being punk is understood by some Whites as a way to disown their whiteness, to become a "race traitor." But because punk is conceived as a predominately White practice, is it actually a reassertion of whiteness ... but as a radical otherness? Or, to be cynical for a moment: Is punk a way for radical Whites to have their cake and eat it too? In fact, punk rejection can inadvertently lead to further margin-alization of racial minorities as White punks (and the artists and hipsters who closely follow) gentrify minority neighborhoods, and the experiences and concerns of White punks dominate the political agenda of rebellion. Radical whiteness is an inspiring ideal, but it's shot through with contra-dictions, and, unless one is careful, the party can end up looking primarily punky—and mighty White.

JON SAVAGE, *ENGLAND'S DREAMING*

The journalist and cultural historian Jon Savage's account of the British punk explosion and the genesis of the Clash's song "White Riot" is, and we say this with a good punk suspicion of such

assignations, seminal. **Bringing a keen analytical eye to a moment he participated in and chronicled for music magazines like *Sounds*, Savage captures the sense of decline and the unfocused rage that saturated punk at the time. But he also points out that the flipside of punk's nihilist tendencies is a fruitful political idealism, and that the dialectic between these two poles corresponds with punk rock's dueling views on race: either a love for reggae and solidarity with Britain's poor black population or the purposefully provocative appropriation of Nazi imagery, roughly represented by the relation-ship between the Clash and the Sex Pistols, respectively. While this equation is far too simplistic—indeed, the Clash were dealing with symbols designed to shock, and Johnny Rotten, once again Lydon, would later sign reggae acts as an A&R rep—it does prove helpful for understanding the complexity and occasional contradictions of the racial politics residing within the oppositional stance of punk rock.**

It was a time of portents. England's crisis had become what Stuart Hall calls the "articulation of a fully fledged capitalist recession, with extremely high rates of inflation, a toppling currency, a savaging of living standards, and a sacrificing of the working class to capital." In June, unemployment reached 1,501,967, 6.4 percent of the workforce, and the worst figure since 1940. The pound dropped below $2 to reach a figure of $1.70. By July, the Chancellor, Denis Healy, was told by the Treasury that he had to cut public expenditure to regain the confidence of the markets.

"The real state of the British economy," states Philip Whitehead in *The Writing on the Wall*, "was now less important than the impression of it held by those from whom Britain had to borrow." After failing to stem the slide with a package of £1 billion cuts announced for 1977–78 in July, the British government were forced to apply to the International Monetary Fund at the end of September. Although this was a world banking body, the balance of power was held by conservative Americans, inimical to a socialist government.

When the IMF team arrived in England on 1 November, American monetarists came to dictate the policy of a centrist Labour government. Even the avuncular James Callaghan could not disguise the fact that the consensus that had governed postwar politics and social life was cracking up. This consensus, partly inspired by the century-long democratic ideal of American consumerism, was not only inadequate against the recession of the mid-1970s but also patently untrue: one had only to look at the decaying inner cities to realize that poverty and inequality, far from being eradicated, were visible as never before.

It is difficult to remember, after more than ten years of divisive, radical Conservative government, how prison-like that consensus view had become in 1976. Under economic attack, the "social contract" was beset from all sides by a multitude of conspiracies against the English way of life, in which letter-bombs, the Angry Brigade, public-sector strikes and muggings were all seen as a concerted, even orchestrated assault by a multitude of minorities that threatened to swamp the majority. This was a society wallowing in a not entirely unpleasurable masochism and lashing out at scapegoats.

Political and social (even behavioural) extremism seemed very attractive as a way out of this *impasse*: one of the first shibboleths to be overcome was the upper-middle-class liberalism which had been nourished by the 1960s and was now entrenched in parts of the government, the public sector and in some sections of the media, which failed to reflect the new, harsh, urban reality. "Liberal-baiting," wrote Peter York in *Style Wars*, "Doctor Martens ... punk Swastikas ... the Thatcher Government: might work, *try it. Try it. Try it.*"

4.10.76: In fashion at the moment: 50s SF/Sub SF illustration; Razor-blade pendants; 'Sex' gear: T-shirts: Brian Epstein S&M/Gay stud/Cambridge Rapist Hood/Collage Marxist/Mao/Plain with tear/bloodstain/safety-pin; legends: 'I hate true love'/'Chaotic Bass Is Here'; leather trousers; dyed hair; Basic look (if affordable): terminal decadence, up to the wearing of Nazi armbands; Worry: when they start living what they dress. How soon?

Punk announced itself as a portent with its polysemy of elements drawn from the history of youth culture, sexual fetish wear, urban decay and extremist politics. Taken together, these elements had no conscious meaning but they spoke of many things: urban primitivism; the breakdown of confidence in a common language; the availability of cheap, second-hand clothes; the fractured nature of perception in an accelerating, media-saturated society; the wish to offer up the body as a jumble of meanings.

The Punk festival and the Sex Pistols' signing to EMI were big enough events to increase the media coverage. In the first week of October, both *Melody Maker* and *Sounds* ran extensive features on the festival which propagandised the new generation. Caroline Coon uttered for the first time the incantation "Do it Yourself." *Sounds* ran a six-page feature, not only giving the first "history" of the Sex Pistols, but rounding up seven new groups and selecting various individuals—Mark P., Siouxsie and Sid Vicious—as exemplars of the new age.

Ingham's disquisitions on what the movement should be called— "Welcome to the (?) Rock Special," ran the headline—were in vain as, with the name "Punk" firmly in place, it hit first the music press, then the evening London papers, then the tabloids. These initial reports were not unfriendly: a mixture of fashion notes and mild titillation. On 3 October, *People* featured the Newport Punk rocker Mark Taylor with swept-back hairdo and a chain through his nose. On the 15th, the *Sun* gave Punk a double-page spread.

Again, polysemy predominates: safety-pins, a handcuff, leather, rips and swastikas. "The result looks like Hell's Angels in a Clockwork Orange nightmare," runs the copy. At the center of the piece are the Sex Pistols: "Thousands of punks gather wherever they play," claims Judy Wade with a piece of hyperbole that might have come from the lips of McLaren. "We want chaos to come," Lydon is quoted as saying, "life's not going to get any better for kids on the dole until it gets worse first." Whether or not Lydon actually said these words is irrelevant: they show exactly on what terms Punk would enter the world outside the music press playpen. The "movement" had now developed, within six months, into a complex, ironic phenomenon containing a rich mixture of truth and hype. Most of those involved had always wanted to engage with the mass media, indeed sought self-justification by so doing, and they now had their wish. The movement's growth was accelerated by this free publicity, but it was a Faustian contract.

"I hadn't expected to see the idealism of my generation denigrated with such aggressive negativity," says Caroline Coon. "When these boys were slagging off hippies, I realized that they had grown up reading about hippies in the tabloid press, and what they were doing was spouting 'the shock and the filth' of the hippies. So I said: 'The gutter press did to hippies what they're going to do to you.'"

Punk's idea was to play the media's accelerated jumble of signals back at them, like one of William Burroughs' tape-recorder experiments in *Electronic Revolution*. This involved not only contempt for the media, but enough engagement so that there could be some common ground. The media were already encoded in the heart of Punk graphics, songs, clothes and attitudes: they would now dictate the way in which Punk developed.

Punk began to develop a sociology of its own. The most visible examples of this process were the Clash. The Sex Pistols were located in Soho with a dash of Chelsea, but the Clash were rooted in North Kensington. The Sex Pistols uncompromisingly set themselves apart, while the Clash were warmer and more of the people; if the Sex Pistols implicitly and then explicitly advocated the destruction of all values, the Clash were more human, closer to the dialogue of social concern and social realism—more in the world.

> I've been trying to go out recently, but I've had to stay in. And the only thing I've got at home is a TV that hasn't got any sound on it. So I'm staying in, right, and I just want to hear sounds, I don't want to see no visuals, I want to go out and see some groups. But there ain't anything to go out and see. I've seen it all before. So I have to stay at home and watch TV without sound and lip-read my way through it. I'd just like to protest about this state of affairs. So if there's any of you people in the audience who aren't past it yet, and if you can do anything, why don't you get up and do it, instead of, like, lying around?
> —Joe Strummer; stage rap, the Roundhouse (August 1976)

While the Sex Pistols had been put together the previous year—and reflected their time with a sound that was often muddy and sliding—the Clash were brand new that autumn, pin-sharp, straight off the product development line. "We had group discussions," says Strummer, "Bernie would say, 'An issue, an issue. Don't write about love, write about what's affecting you, what's important.' We were strict. We'd look at everything and think: 'Is this retro?' I painted this shirt which said 'Chuck Berry Is Dead.' If it was old, it was out."

The Clash began as a classic Mod group: angry, smart, mediated, pop. They speeded up the heavily chorded, stuttering sound of the Who and the Kinks and added new variations: the massive, galloping beat of Terry Chimes, a minimum of guitar solos, and the plentiful use of "drop-out"— where all the instruments drop away, just leaving the beat—borrowed from the dub Reggae that you could hear in Shepherd's Bush or Porto-bello Road markets. And with Joe Strummer they had a great front man: energetic, tough, humorous yet compassionate.

Early material included songs about love, school, the heat: "How Can I Understand the Flies," "Mark Me Absent," "I've Got a Crush on You." But "London's Burning," "48 Thrills" and "Protex Blue" were ambiguous celebrations of a new urbanism, as up against the wall of Monday morning, the Clash sped "up and down the Westway, in and out the lights." Here was a new map of London, drawn with an innocence and a relish that the Sex Pistols never had.

The big book that autumn was J. G. Ballard's *High Rise*. Set in the near future which is also the shadow of the present, it describes a closed world of techno-barbarism simultaneously recorded and replayed on video. The sheer physical presence of the tower blocks "had a second life of their own"; the blocks themselves are vandalized in the pleasurable exercise of forbidden impulses. High rises were both graphically interesting—for their stark, grid-like shapes which feature in McLaren's Croydon Art School portfolio—and convenient as emblems of harsh urbanism: they had already appeared, rising out of slum clearance, on the cover of Led Zeppelin's fourth album, unfavorably contrasted with the rural landscape. After Ballard's *High Rise* and *Crash*, it was possible to see high rises as both appalling and vertiginously exciting: for now their clean, brutal lines were a perfect site for the Clash's frantic hypermodernism.

From his grandmother's nineteenth-floor flat on the Warwick and Brindley Estate, Clash guitarist Mick Jones had an eagle's-eye view of a whole stretch of inner London: Harrow Road, North Kensington and Paddington, dominated by the elevated Westway; and blocks like the massive Trellick Tower that looms over the whole of Portobello Road and Ladbroke Grove. This was their stretch, marked where the Westway passes over the Harrow Road, by a graffito, "THE CLASH," that remained there, fading slowly, for years after the group's vigorous life was over.

The Clash's urban hyperrealism was quickly overlaid by a more conventional sense of social relevance. The group poached a Subway Sect song, "USA," to spice up their own "I'm So Bored with You." "I'm So Bored with the USA" was a brilliant rant against the popular culture of the day. "*Kojak* and *Columbo* were big at the time," says Strummer. "That lyric's not bad even now, although it's caveman primitive: it says a lot of truth about dictators, 'Yankee dollar talk to the dictators of the world.'"

By the time of the Punk Rock Festival, the Clash were still playing "Flies," with its sheet-metal drumming, but the songs about school and love went out and in came "Career Opportunities," based on Mick Jones's experience at the Post Office during the letter-bomb scare, "Janie Jones," and "I'm So Bored with the USA." Their set was framed by two brand new songs, "1977" and "White Riot," written after the events of the Notting Hill Carnival.

Traditionally held on the Bank Holiday which falls on the last weekend of August, the carnival is one of the few places where England's blacks can relax on their own terms in an otherwise cold, often hostile climate. By 1975, the carnival had been marked by the worsening relations between young blacks and the police. But this year, the police changed their tactics, increasing their presence from just under 200 the previous year to nearly 1,600: the result was a mood of anger and resentment which grew over the two-day event.

"Coming down, coming down," the crowd chanted spontaneously on the Sunday, repeating the phrase over and over again as they passed through Notting Hill's crumbling, narrow stucco terraces. The next day, it did. After 5 pm on Monday 30th, most of the visitors had gone, leaving a hard core of black youth. When the police moved in to make an arrest, all hell broke loose, in the first major riot mainland Britain had seen since the riots there in 1958: 456 injured and 60 arrests.

"It was a lovely day," says Strummer, "me and Bernie and Paul were under the Westway and we were grooving to the Reggae. About twenty coppers came through in a line and I saw this coke can go over and hit one of them in the head. Immediately, twenty more were in the air: then the crowd parted to get away from the targets and the women began to scream. The three of us were thrown back against the wire netting as the crowd surged back. I thought we were all going to fall in this bay underneath the Westway, but the wire held.

"I lost Paul and Bernie for a minute. Chaos was breaking out all over the Grove: Ladbroke Road was lined with rebels, and cop cars were speeding through, these Rover 2000s, and they were being pelted with rocks and cobble stones and cans as they came through, it was like a bowling alley. I ducked in the Elgin and said, 'Gimme a couple of drinks here!' I downed one and took the second outside, and I saw Paul throw a plastic cone at a police motorcycle. He hit the front wheel of the bike but the guy managed to carry on.

"Then Paul and I were standing in Lancaster Road: we hadn't noticed that all the white faces had gone. Suddenly this young posse came up: 'Hey man, what you got in that pocket there?' I had this transistor radio, but I had this brick in the other pocket, and I said 'Don't say that shit to me.' They shrunk back because I was shouting really loud. That was when I realized I had to write a song called 'White Riot' because it wasn't our fight. It was the one day of the year when the blacks were going to get their own back against the really atrocious way that the police behaved."

30.10.76: I go to see my first proper punk group. I know what it's going to be like: I've been waiting for years, and this year most of all: something to match the explosions in my head. The group are called the Clash; everybody I talk to says they're the best.

Into a Victorian Hall, half empty with people standing in bunches. Hostile, insecure. Suddenly four men with brutally cut hair come on stage, bark into a microphone, start making an industrial noise. The noise coalesces with the speed into a perfect chaos. One song: a genuine cry, a child screaming in fear: 'Waa waa wanna waa waa.' Within ten seconds I'm transfixed, within thirty, changed forever.

With its wailing chorus, "White Riot" expressed a desperate longing that a voice and a face should be given to the white dispossessed. "Black men gotta lot of problems, but they don't mind throwing a brick," sang Joe Strummer. "White people go to school, where they teach you how to be thick." And if "White Riot" was a call for whites to organize in a riot of their own, "What's My Name" cast the pop theme of adolescent identity into explicit class terms, in a short burst of loser rage.

This was an uneasy juggling act from a group of three art-school students, one of whom had even been to a minor public school. The Clash's first ever interview, in the fourth *Sniffin' Glue*, set them in their state-of-the-art pink and black studio, with an art-school interviewer, Steve Walsh: they talk about first consuming society in order to change it. "We deal in junk, you know," said Joe Strummer, "what we've got is what other people put in the rubbish bin."

"They were really over the top that day," says Mark Perry. "I went along with Steve and they were complete prats. Paul had a gun, I don't know whether it was real, but they were trying to be heavy. And they had a go at me for liking Eddie and the Hot Rods. Those guys wear flares, all of this. To me that was bollocks. Mick Jones spent three years before Punk learning how to be a Rock'n'Roll star: he wasn't a hooligan. In that sense the early New York groups were more honest."

"Like trousers like brain," Strummer concluded. Despite the posing, the Clash saw it through: their Pollock spatters were at once very arty and very accessible. As much as Vivienne's designs for Sex, the clothes mirrored the group's ideology: not only could the clothes, in theory, be made by anybody, but they could be used to broadcast codes and slogans within the cultural resistance that was Punk. They dramatized the polarization that was the wish fulfillment of their name, yet couched it in fashion.

"After the Pollock look we got into stencils and stuff," says Joe Strummer. "Bernie Rhodes was guiding and packaging. He used to watch us rehearse and say, 'This is good, this is bad.' He was very creative, his input was everything. He'd read all the books, knew all the trends. He probably suggested that we write words on our clothing: I never knew much about that Situationist stuff, still don't today, but that's where it came from."

As autumn deepened, the Clash's clothes announced apocalypse. The custom-painted look was replaced by prison numbers, stenciled group slogans like "Hate and War" or phrases taken from Tapper Zukie's "Rockers": "Heavy Manners," "Heavy Duty Discipline." Another new song counted down the magical year: "In 1977 / Knives in West 11 / Ain't so lucky to be rich / Sten Guns in Knightsbridge." "Knives in W11" and "Sten Guns in Knightsbridge" made it onto the shirts: the nightmare of the middle classes finally came amongst them.

The Clash had learned about more than instrument drop-out from West Indians: anybody looking for a music that reflected a society in crisis had to look no further than Jamaica and its latest rhythm. By 1975, Chris Blackwell's decision to market Bob Marley and the Wailers as Rock stars was finally paying off: not only were they having hits, but they brought Reggae into the open. Stimulated by dreams of crossover success and an expanding English black market, Reggae poured out of Jamaica.

Reggae had an authenticity and a spirituality lacking in the dominant white culture. The Wailers were all Rastafarians, an apocalyptic sect formed by Marcus Garvey in the 1920s. As Henderson Dalrymple says in *Music, Myth and the Rastas*, "Rastas hold the view that black people are the true Israelites and they can trace their lineage beyond Solomon and Sheba. Most of their principles of living have much in common with the ten commandments, Genesis, Revelation."

By 1976, Reggae had its own network of independent labels, such as Atra, while English record companies such as Virgin started their own labels like Front Line. At the same time as the music of dub became more enveloping, so the lyrics delivered apocalyptic visions. Most influential during this period were the productions of Joe Gibbs, not only the "Africa Dub" instrumental series, but also remarkable albums by Prince Far-I and Culture, which set dense rants against minimal music.

Prince Far-I's *Under Heavy Manners* called for a strictness on the part of Rasta—"heavy-duty discipline"—in the face of social disorder: "Under Heavy Manners" was the phrase used by Jamaican premier Michael Manley when security measures were introduced in 1976, after a spate of politically inspired shootings. As Far-I chanted, a synthesizer made otherworldly sounds that resolved into the wail of a police-car siren. "I can see with my own eyes, that it's only a housing scheme that divides," sang Culture in the song that spelt out the deadline: "When the Two Sevens Clash." According to the prophecy, 1977 was the year that Rasta would be free, and Culture sang in the full belief that the world would be transformed.

Reggae transmitted the experience of England's most visible outsiders: those Rastas who, confronted with prejudice, totally refused to enter England's dream. The Clash had seen how Reggae had acted as a soundtrack for social resistance at the Notting Hill Carnival and, with their use of drop-out and stenciled slogans, they were attempting to create their own white Rasta in Punk—a new cultural resistance. The more thoughtful participants, like Mark Perry, believed in this resistance: "I was very much into a working-class revolution, through music, through media, a general take-over of Punk sort of people."

The Clash had picked up their own Punk "everykid," their celebrity follower just like Siouxsie or Sid. Steve Connolly [a.k.a. "Roadent"] had just spent two weeks in prison for an outstanding fine: "I got my travel warrant to London, came down and the Clash were playing at the ICA.

The Clash were the first band to steal fans from the Pistols: they were the construction to the Sex Pistols' nihilism. The two go hand in hand to a certain extent, and John and the Pistols decried the fact, but amongst the punters you couldn't just bang your head against the wall, you had to have some reason why you were banging your head against the wall. I'd already read bits about anarchy and I realised that destruction could be a creative urge. But that was the attraction, wasn't it, that you had to have a generation of destruction before a generation of creation."

"Demand the Impossible" ran the Situationist slogan on the Sex shirt: like other pop movements before it, Punk made impossible demands. Yet by accepting them you made a leap of faith that suddenly made those demands seem possible. At this point, it was by no means certain that Punk would succeed. As the Clash played in London during October and November, they attracted a violence and a hostility that were as much symptoms of the force with which they were trying to make a breakthrough as they were of their rhetoric.

5.11.76: Out of bed with the flu to see the Clash again. I know now that that song is called "White Riot" and that it's "about" the carnival riot. I understand. They play it two or three times to an abusive audience, a few fans and my tape recorder. At the end, not of a set but a set-to, the singer jumps off stage with a helper, who has been lurching with speed-brimmed eyes just a bit too close, and runs through the dispersing crowd to hurl himself at two long-hairs responsible for the heckling and the flying glasses. The crowd clears and circles. A messy and inconclusive fight starts among the beer-slops on the floor.

People watch, hollow eyes: the PA plays the Stooges' vicious, vacant, "No Fun."
Everything fuses together.

At the ICA on 23 October, the Clash had played well, but an incident at the side of the stage got all the press attention, as Shane MacGowan bit the ear of fellow fan Jane Crockford. Great copy, great pictures, delicious mutilation fantasies. Two weeks later, the Clash played in the sixties brutalist surroundings of the Royal College of Art: this time, the violence was directed at the group and resulted in a scuffle—involving Strummer, Simonon, and Sid Vicious—that was not only an expression of genuine anger but a logical conclusion to the Clash's theatre of provocation.

These incidents occurred within the relative security of art colleges and art houses, playpens compared with the council estates which were Punk's desired locations. As Punk entered the real world during that autumn and winter, it was very possible to surrender to the rhetoric. And it was perversely pleasurable: any apocalypse seemed preferable to the slow death by suffocation that is all too often the emotional experience of living in England. It was a way of feeling something, perhaps the only way of feeling left.

"You could tell it was a different world," says Mary Harron, who interviewed the Sex Pistols for *Punk* that autumn. "There was violence in the air. There was violence in the streets. I'd come from a place where it was dangerous, and therefore in your club, you don't want aggression and violence. Your club was an absolute sanctuary and haven where there was friendliness. Backstage at the 100 Club, I saw these little teenage girls with swastikas, and my reaction was, 'to us it's a cartoon, here this is being done for real.'

"There was something electrifying about the mythology which the Sex Pistols had brought with them. They were chaotic. It was wild, whereas everything had been more proficient in New York. There was a sense of chaos, and the New York scene was not about chaos. But the Sex Pistols created a sense of, 'What the fuck is happening?' It had politics. American Punk had no politics at that stage. America at that point couldn't decide what was going to happen next: they had a liberal-ish government. The best thing to do was to disengage. In England, there was a nightmare coming to life, it was overpowering and disturbing. Something had been given permission to show itself, it was exploding out."

If there was one symbol of this nightmare, it was the Punk use of the swastika. "It was always very much an anti-mums and anti-dads thing," said Siouxsie. "We hated older people—not across the board but particularly in suburbia—always harping on about Hitler, 'We showed him,' and that smug pride. It was a way of saying, 'Well I think Hitler was very good, actually': a way of watching someone like that go completely red-faced."

After the thirties retro fad of the early 1970s, the Weimar period of *Cabaret* and Visconti's *The Damned* became an accepted metaphor for Britain's decline. One of the sensations of 1976 was a biography of Unity, the doomed Mitford, the headstrong rebel with her pet rat. During the late 1930s, Unity appeared at major Nazi rallies and penetrated Hitler's inner sanctum. The onset of war put paid to her dreams of uniting Germany and England: the day war was declared, Unity shot herself.

Unity's appearance in the media made it clear that much had been left out of the accepted history of the thirties: for a while, the British had shown a distinct penchant for fascism, whether through Oswald Mosley's British Union of Fascists or the policy of appeasement run by Lords Rothermere or Astor of Cliveden. Fascism seemed a possible British archetype, an inversion of the image that had been rammed down everybody's throats in hundred's of lying war movies: history could have gone another way, like in Philip K. Dick's *The Man in the High Castle*, where the Japanese and the Germans, winners of the Second World War, preside over a defeated USA.

The wearing of the swastika served notice on the threadbare fantasy of Victory, the lie of which could be seen on most urban street corners. That this fantasy was now obsolete was obvious to a generation born after the war and witness to England's decline: "It was a joke," says Sophie Richmond, "like *Oh, what a Lovely War*. But when it came to people buying T-shirts with swastikas on, everybody got very alarmed. I was completely ambivalent about it: I defended it on some occasions, attacked it on others."

"I thought Siouxsie and Sid were quite foolish," says John Lydon, "although I know the idea behind it was to debunk all this crap from the past, wipe history clean and have a fresh approach, it doesn't really work that way." There was one final point to the swastika that goes to the heart of punk polysemy: the erosion of meaning itself. "The political inhumanity of the twentieth century and certain elements in its technological mass-society have done injury to language," writes George Steiner. What better way to display this lack of meaning by detourning a once loaded symbol?

Outside Punk's playpen, unpleasant forces were stirring, to which Punks themselves were not immune. "The mid-seventies was the time of the National Front and International Socialist confrontations so one didn't want to be encouraging those thugs," says Sophie Richmond. "Malcolm always said of the 'Destroy' T-shirt that he was making a general point about leaders, which was a bit too subtle for the average NF or even the average Punk. It was a pipe dream."

As the economic crisis deepened, the scapegoat tactics used by British racists won a certain sympathy. After Enoch Powell's 1968 speech, immigration was a hot issue, exacerbated by successive waves of refugees: the influx of Ugandan and Malawi Asians was exploited by the National Front, which managed to present itself as an orthodox party of the far right. In the summer of 1976, at the height of the tabloid furor about the Malawi Asians, the National Front polled 18.5 percent in the Leicester by-election.

Such extremist activity had already generated a response from the left, as an International Marxist Group (IMG) counter-march led to a pitched battle in Red Lion Square early in 1974, which resulted in the death of a student. The scene was set for public disorder: as Stuart Hall wrote, the National Front "plugs itself into the territorial loyalties of those kids who are clustering on the football terraces. It begins to latch into working-class neighborhood culture and it affirms the kids' feelings about their locality, their whiteness. It put Britain and British into the vocabulary of youth culture."

This was the sort of imagery with which Punk was toying during the autumn of 1976. Pop culture itself was not immune to fascist flirtations: "I think I might have been a bloody good Hitler," David Bowie had said that February; in May, he announced his return to England with what looked like a Nazi salute at Victoria Station. In August, a drunken Eric Clapton made a speech in favor of Enoch Powell at a concert in Birmingham, his debt to black Blues guitarists or Reggae artists forgotten. The next month, a letter signed "Rock Against Racism," calling for action against this "racist poison," was published in the national music weeklies. In this climate, a song like "White Riot" could be taken a different way: not as an admiring shout of solidarity in sympathy with the blacks of Notting Hill Gate, but as a racist rallying call. To those without a key to Punk's bewildering jumble of signals, its combination of cropped hair, emotive symbols and brutal, harsh music that seemed to eradicate almost every trace of pop's black origins, pointed one way.

"I first worked for the Clash at Lanchester Polytechnic in Coventry, on 29 November," says Roadent (who had indulged in some Nazi posturing himself). "The Clash supported the Pistols and they refused to pay us because they thought 'White Riot' was fascist. Then the Pistols did 'God Save the Queen,' which was called 'No Future' then, it was only the second time it had been played. The students called an emergency general meeting of the union and by order of the committee they decided not to pay these fascists."

Punk was trafficking in taboos at the same time as it sought to illuminate and dramatize deep-seated contradictions with a sophisticated, ironic rhetoric. Unlike many historical avant-garde movements, it had the potential to enter the mass market and in November 1976, was posed to do so. But the mass market is notorious for simplifying complexities and steam-rollering irony and the idea of a youth movement with swastikas hitting "the kids" was simply terrifying. Punk's countdown to apocalypse suddenly seemed very dangerous.

Jon Savage, from *England's Dreaming: Anarchy, Sex Pistols, Punk Rock, and Beyond* (New York: St. Martin's Griffin, 2001).

PAUL SIMONON OF THE CLASH, INTERVIEW IN *SEARCH & DESTROY*

In this short excerpt from an interview with the San Francisco punk zine *Search and Destroy*, the Clash bassist, Paul Simonon, gets right to the heart of what the band set out to do, without any of Strummer's rebel troubadour rhetorical flourishes. That is, in one piercing paragraph he articulates the intention and hope that playing reggae music to audiences containing racist National Front members may cause them to rethink their racial assumptions. This doesn't always work out like it should, and one has to wonder how well even the Clash fit into the tradition of racial appropriation of black culture. But they were groping for something more. The critic Greil Marcus once described how Strummer, in introducing the tune "Police and Thieves," characterized the song as "punk *and* reggae" as opposed to "*white* reggae." "There's a *difference*," Strummer continued. "There's a difference between a ripoff and bringing some of *our* culture to *another* culture. You hear that, Sting?"[1] This quotation is worth examining, not merely because perhaps Sting deserves it, but because it illustrates what differentiates this stage of punk's countercultural

articulation of whiteness from the "White Negro" thread: rather than mining Black cultural forms for its authenticity, White punk has to somehow be authentic in order to enact the kind of exchange Strummer is after. Now, whether or not punk actually *in and of itself* untethers itself from such a lineage is questionable, but the Clash were trying.

SEARCH & DESTROY: Were you interested in Rock & Roll before joining the CLASH?

PAUL SIMONON: Not really. There wasn't really much going on that I liked except reggae, which I heard from the people I was around with. The schools I went to—most of the kids there are black. So all I heard was basically just reggae. I used to live in Brixton and then Ladbroke Grove, which are quite heavily populated with blacks. The last school I went to, there were only about five white kids—the rest were black. You just sort of hear their music all the time. ...

S&D: What's your main interest in the CLASH?

SIMONON: There's so many things I'm interested in and that center around the group: the music, the words, everything. I sort of basically design the clothes. I'm very much a visual person.

S&D: Are you into the (political) aspect of the band?

SIMONON: Yeah, definitely. Otherwise I wouldn't be in the group—if I didn't agree with it. What happens in learning a new song is like—well, CAREER OPPORTUNITIES, for example: there was gonna be a line which I sang on the song which was something to do with pensions. And I said, "Oh, I'm not singing that, I don't wanna sing about pensions." And Mick got angry but Joe, he sort of sussed my point and agreed with me—I couldn't relate to it.

S&D: Did you write any of the songs for the new album?

SIMONON: No. I do write, but it's very difficult; I get put off in a way that—I'm always being told that I've gotta learn my bass!

S&D: Has the band started making any money?

SIMONON: ... before we'd always be worrying about where we'd get our next meal. Whereas now we don't have to worry about that so much.

S&D: Can that change the nature of the group?

SIMONON: Don't think so. I mean, we know what we're doing, we know what we want to do.

S&D: What's that?

SIMONON: Well—be a top-selling band which has got something to contribute, which people actually get off on, and which can actually help change people's attitudes. I mean, like, we play reggae in our sets and kids come along to our concerts—and some of them are National Front kids—and they like the CLASH, and when we play reggae, it's sort of like turning them on to black music—which sort of helps lead them away from that racist feeling they might have. Which is like changing them. Also, from what we've done, it's made loads of kids that would normally go around wrecking up streets and fucking up cars, form groups. They're doing something creative, which I think is really important—and they're doing it and they're enjoying it. ...

Howie Klein, from "The Clash," *Search & Destroy* no. 7 (San Francisco: 1978).

DAVID WIDGERY,
BEATING TIME

A physician by training, David Widgery was instrumental in the efforts of the Socialist Workers Party to get Rock Against Racism and its accompanying zine *Temporary Hoarding* off the ground. Widgery, and RAR in general, approached punk rock with equal parts sincerity and opportunism—which represents, one might argue, the key to any successful or effective politics. The sincerity came from the fact that Widgery glimpsed in punk rock the possibility of Black-White cultural solidarity he yearned for; the opportunism, from a keen awareness that the old Marxism was losing ground and needed a radical injection of excitement and youth appeal. Widgery is explicit about punk needing a little help in finding its political footing, calling it "another response to the same social crisis which produced the NF's successes" which "could go in any direction." While the marriage RAR represented between antiracist Marxism and punk rock was always tense and suspicious —and may have reinforced certain ideas each had about its own predominate whiteness, it at least allowed punk to make its own politics explicit in a way that would prevent its audience from mis-interpreting some of its more ambiguous statements and slogans. While the earnestness of Widgery's attempts may oversimplify the degree to which solidarity drifts into cultural appropriation, he and RAR represent a crucial moment in punk finding its antiracist voice.

I had been brought up to regard Billie Holiday as possessing one of the most expressive and affecting voices in music, my skin has been burnt by the dry ice of James Baldwin's prose, my map of the world turned upside down by *The Black Jacobins*, my pulse set racing by Charlie Parker's assault on the Winter Palace of jazz, tears brought to my boyish eyes by Miriam Makeba singing in the musical *King Kong*, my Marxism shaped by encounters with the views of C. L. R. James and W. E. B. DuBois, and my Dalston Sundays slipstreamed by yearning, sublimely logical dub floating up from underneath the Cortinas. The black experience is critical to the twentieth century, to modern culture and to me—my pleasure and my understanding.

Tens of thousands of white people with different lists share the same identification. What lent RAR its particular urgency was that it wasn't just fund raising for a good cause out there but we were defending and thereby redefining ourselves and the cultural mix of the inner cities in which we had grown up and in which our children are now finding their feet.

RAR cured the schizophrenia between Marxist politics and modern culture. After the RAR letter, "There was a tremendous relief," Red Saunders remembers. "At last someone had said, be proud of using electric modern music and culture to fight the Nazis and racism, not Hungarian linocuts."

Roger Huddle remembers; "The most staggering thing about RAR was that not only did revolutionaries who were my age also happen to have gone down the mod clubs in Wardour Street in the early sixties, but they never even let on that they were also J. B. Lenoir fans and had obscure Delta blues records tucked away in the back of their collections. With RAR, we could all come out." For Syd Shelton, the photographer and designer, it was: "Like you've come from the working class, you've been a lifelong socialist but you've also secretly loved Jaguar XJ6 saloons. Now RAR suddenly tells you, after the revolution, we're all going to drive XJ6s."

Black music was our catechism, not just something we listened to in our spare time. It was the culture which woke us up, had shaped us and kept us up all night, blocked in the Wardour Street mod clubs, fanatical on the Thames Valley R&B circuit, queueing all down Gerrard Street to see Roland Kirk in Ronnie Scott's old basement. It was how we worked out our geography, learnt our sexuality, and taught ourselves history. There was no question of slumming or inverted snobbery, we went for black music because it was so strong rhythmically, there was a passion in it, it was about life and had some point to it. And if white musicians were as good and as exciting (as Georgie Fame, Alexis Korner, and the early Stones certainly were) we worshipped them, too.

Because of Lenin and Marx we had some analysis of the social contradictions which had produced the music. We also knew how white musicians and the record industry had copied, borrowed and stolen from the black origins, from the Original Dixieland Jazz Band through Elvis's songs by Arthur Crudup and Otis Blackwell, Pat Boone's cleaned-up cover of Little Richard's "Tutti Frutti," Led Zeppelin's Willie Dixon references on "Whole Lotta Love," right down to Clapton's hapless impersonation of Marley's insurrectionary "I Shot the Sheriff" and the Police's preposterous white reggae. Despite all that, we knew from experience that music—good music—of all popular cultures had the potential to be the best sort of race relations going, as Selwyn Baptiste of the Notting Hill Carnival used to say. In some ways the Soho jazz and blues clubs had been pioneering islands of racial equality since the forties.

Our clubland apprenticeship was, of course, a phase. As Roger Huddle now says, "R&B's attraction was the passion, which was as strong as one's political feelings. But then the whole world of music opens up to you, not just jazz, but then you can start listening to John Cage, Steve Reich, and Schoenberg because you've broken out of the pop trap, you're into the universality of sound." Other people and other generations are shaped by different passions, fashions and political movements. But our experience had taught us a golden political rule: how people find their pleasure, entertainment and celebration is also how they find their sexual identity, their political courage and their strength to change.

RAR's first major production was held at the Royal College of Art in December 1976, where the chairman of the student union was in the SWP. Red had been approached by two delightful West Indian hustlers who could see the potential of the idea: "Maaan, you could make a fortune," they told him, plying him with rum. "Give us the deal, maan. Just sign here. What car you want?" They took him to see Matumbi in a rampacked all-black South London blues club. Dennis Bovell, Matumbi's leader, only recently out of prison after a police raid on his sound system, agreed to play the RCA with Carol Grimes, the London Boogie band, and Roger Huddle's immaculate R&B disco, the Night Train.

It was a wonderfully bizarre night with punks in tens, then hundreds. The art schoolies were outdone by the sheer nerve of fifteen-year-old girls with mauve and green hair, string boleros, leotards, and plastic flower wedgies. The kids swanned round as if they owned the college. Freaks from past history and costume-drama cases from the summer of love queued up quite amiably with maximum dreadlocks and members of the Clash and the Slits. The music was extremely loud, the dancing very rowdy and the stalls sold political and anti-racist literature, food and banners. Something was in the air; not just dope, but a serious music-politics-black-white mix-up.

Matumbi were heaven: a springy bass line, urgent near-rock lead guitar, horns playing as if backing Otis Redding but lyrics about London betting shops and boozers. Matumbi and Carol Grimes were somehow manoeuvered together, the punks leapt on stage completely zonked, and seasoned lefties gasped into their mild and bitters. It was as infectious as German measles and melted all the usual show-off super-cool of the RCA, swamping it with bouncing bodies and bass frequencies.

But it was hard going. People would come up and say, "RAR—that's the anti–Eric Clapton group, isn't it?" The Left thought us too punky and the punks feared they would be eaten alive by Communist cannibals.

At the founding conference at the North London Poly in January 1977 it was clear RAR had pulled together a caboodle of oddballs who were going to work together a lot more imaginatively and explosively than the worthies of the conventional anti-racist platforms. There were musicians, theatre workers, punks and politicos who all recognised RAR as something they agreed with and, more important, could be part of. And young SWP organisers in Sheffield, Paisley, and Birmingham were phoning up Red's Soho studio—activists who weren't just keen but who knew how to organise, could get a decent silk-screen poster printed and flyposted, understood the kind of hall to book and how to make the stage look good.

The music press, with the exceptions of Pete Silverton and Miles, were suspicious and cynical about attempts to "*bring politics*" into their precious world of professional attitudinising. But something was happening inside the music and the culture itself. Other inner-city inhabitants were clambering out of the same cultural car crash—the Clash, Johnny Rotten, and thousands like them. All of them were anti-racists from the heart and not afraid to say so. The sound systems were whispering and bumping with mighty dub messages produced in London in an emerging UK style. In 1976 the Notting Hill Carnival had been saturated by uniformed and belligerent policemen. The Clash's "White Riot" was inspired by the courage of the black youth who stood up to them. Soweto was rising, Hull prisoners were on the roof, *Gay News* was on trial for blasphemy, and nearly a quarter of a million workers marched through London against the Labour government's IMF-ordered cuts. After three years' political slumber, things were beginning to stir again. When Johnny Rotten told Bill Grundy to "fuck off" on Granada TV in December 1976, the punk mood that had been brewing up in the clubs finally punched through into national notoriety.[1]

Punk was simple to analyse: complete mad anarchy. It was another response to the same social crisis which produced the NF's successes and it could go in any direction. The musicians who were riding it knew just how precarious the thing was: in his first important interview, Joe Strummer of the Clash said "We are against the NF" because he knew the fascists could have a field day in the nihilism which was punk reality when the music stopped. But the punk musicians and fanzine editors equally loathed the moralism of conventional leftist rhetoric about fascism. Fortunately, so did we.

Yes, punk is violent and sexist, the argument went. It's also subversive and disorienting and highly political and about time too. The people who harp on about the ambiguities and the rip-offs and confusion want a reason to disapprove, want youth to fight the correct battles in the language that we have handed down to them. Punks send up a lot of those categories in an unfooled and honest way. What's happening with the fanzine design and writing DIY clothes and the return of singles and independent record labels is a great wave of new energy just when it seemed everything had run out of steam. Where it ends up, which way it goes, depends in part on what people like us do, whether we can improvise and innovate and break our rules to get through to people. Otherwise the business will take back the initiative, even if it takes a year or two. Wanted: garage politics. ...

RAR's next concert wasn't put on till May 1, 1977, the first May Day to be an official public holiday in Britain. Red was the producer: "For the first time I instigated "Full Propaganda" which meant pulling out all the theatrical, visual, and emotional stops. Advertised on the bill were the young reggae lions Aswad, hard-core punks the Adverts with TV Smith, the African cultural group Steel and Skin, the last incarnation of the Kartoon Klowns, and a host of guests. In the foyer of London's Roundhouse theatre, richly embroidered and lavishly ornamented trade-union banners direct from the May Day parades piled up. Inside, the photographer Gered Mankowitz, who covered the Stones' first tour of America and did their early album covers, was slicing the stage with raking, searing prussic and lemon rock-and-roll lighting.

Robert Galvin, a young art student, had devised an RAR typeface for mass production of banners by which a template alphabet was stencilled onto the self-adhesive plastic fabric Fablon, cut out and stuck down on Day-Glo cloth from the specialist shops in Berwick Street. So the Round-house, melting pot of the countercultural sixties, was riotously decorated with colossal red and green, purple and gold, and black and white banners with RAR slogans. Onstage, members of Aswad, the Adverts, the Carol Grimes band, Ari Up and Tessa from the Slits-to-be, and Mitch Mitch-ell of the Jimi Hendrix Experience–that–was ended the evening with a jam which began slowly (jamming is very much a jazz tradition and, in general, pop musicians loathe it) but built to a tremendous surge of energy between stage and audience as punk iconoclasm, reggae rhythms, blue soul, and good ol' rock and roll managed to merge for a common purpose. Paul Jones, a veteran of the R&B days, sang his heart out and, in one of those moving backstage moments, presented the young drummer of Aswad with a giant spliff and his mouth harp. Carol Grimes summed up the Roundhouse gig: "It showed that music can break down the barri-ers. What you want is the jam on stage to be reflected in the audience—it can't be the property of the musicians."

Then came the Lewisham march. Seven days later, on 21st August, RAR was still high for a joint gig with the Right to Work campaign at Hackney Town Hall. It was packed with post-Lewisham punk pride. Generation X and the Cimarrons were using the mayor's chamber as a dressing room. Along the corridor were the portraits of outstanding leaders of Hackney labour. The two women on the bar were just about concealing their horror at the waves of punks drinking them dry. The lights were useless, the stage was an island, the atmosphere exceptional, everywhere there were faces from New Cross. Security was ten of the largest SWP locals with linked arms between band and pogo front line.

Generation X were surprisingly good, especially on John Lennon's "Gimme Some Truth": the real passion in Billy Idol's voice and Tony James's guitar. The Cims moved straight into their Philadelphia-originated "Ship Ahoy" sequence and it was another world aesthetically, candid, artful, rich in musicianship. Then a momentous jam started with "Gloria," went into Bob Marley's "Johnny Too Bad," and ended with a gaunt white Gen-eration X hand clamped with a black Cimarrons hand held aloft while everyone in the hall chanted "Black and white. Black and white." We felt so strong and so close we didn't need to add *unite*. Billy Idol called it "One of the greatest nights in my life" and the Cimarrons were moved to record a 12-inch tribute called simply "Rock Against Racism." ...

Within a year punk went from the Roxy to the High Street. Reviled, mocked and censored, it was winning the battle for teenage minds. "Punk meant no more bullshit," said Kosmo Vinyl, Ian Dury's aide-de-camp and then Clash minder, "and we were heard around the world." The attempted Anarchy in the UK tour in December 1976 (the Clash, the Sex Pistols, the Damned, and Johnny Thunders's Heartbreakers) had been brought to a swift standstill by county-council moralists and scandalised record companies. And when it played, it was amateurish and off beam. In Leads, the local lefties were still at the "punk, isn't that rather neo-fascist?" stage, the students had Gandalf's Garden tresses, and when the local fascists did beat up a *Socialist Worker* seller in the Poly toilets while the Pistols were on, no one on stage knew about it. Joe Strummer of the Clash was angry and tense. "We've been on the road five days and this is the first time we get to play." But in the Leeds Poly urinal was a gay farm worker with a South Yorkshire accent you could hang your coat on who had nothing but black tights and a T-shirt of safety pins underneath his greatcoat.

When, a week after RAR's 1977 May Day Roundhouse show, the Clash's White Riot tour hit the Rainbow supported by the Jam (with their Union Jack), the Buzzcocks, and a roots-reggae sound system featuring I Roy and dub from the Revolutionaries, punk was clearly a mass movement. The gaunt Gaumont-Egyptian Rainbow (the old Finsbury Park Astoria, which used to house the Beatles' Christmas shows) was filled with marble fountains, scrunched beer beakers, and working-class kids in urban destructo chic: Jackson Pollock boiler suits, school-prefect blazers, Al-Fatah headscarves, blanket pins, aviator goggles, gas masks, studded dog collars, suspender belts, and Pacamacs.

Watching couples hobbling up from Finsbury Park tube, it was clear why bondage garments had become an image of liberation. It was better to make explicit the way we are restricted and fetishised than pretend, as the hippies had, to be free. In anti-hippy polemics in *OZ* magazine I had argued in 1967 that the acid generation's "adoption of oriental plumage and religious bric-a-brac is not an answer to the plunder of Indian and African civilisations by imperialism, just impotence and guilt decked out as romanticism." But, in opposition, I had offered a puritan working-class world of "productivity deals, trades councils, football fighting, women talking in launderettes, and Guinness." Against stylistic revolt was just styleless intransigence. Perhaps the punks were the answer to that dichotomy: subverters of pulp journalism, gutter TV, and brutal policemen, who under their monochrome exteriors were peacocks of proletarian revolt.

The Clash hit the stage with a billboard-size photo blow-up of British coppers under attack at the Notting Hill street festival the previous August, and went straight into "White Riot," a cleverer lyric than the title suggested. Without warning, they had become rock stars, with Mick Jones posturing around the stage like an old-fashioned guitar hero. Strummer had kept his head and announced their wailing punk reworking of Junior Murvin's dreamy "Police and Thieves" like this: "Last week 119,000 people voted National Front in London. Well, this next one's by a wog. And if you don't like wogs, you know where the bog is." The bog was in a very wretched state and being used enthusiastically for all sorts of purposes by both sexes, in an excess of new-wave iconoclasm.

David Widgery, from *Beating Time* (London: Pluto, 1986).

PAUL GILROY,
"TWO SIDES OF ANTI-RACISM"

Also affiliated, like so many scholars writing on punk, with the Centre for Contemporary Cultural Studies, Paul Gilroy is probably best known for his pioneering work on blackness and modernity in *The Black Atlantic.* Here, in an earlier text, *"There Ain't No Black in the Union Jack,"* he situates Rock Against Racism within the history of antiracist activism in twentieth-century Britain. Gilroy praises punk for bringing its do-it-yourself ethos to antiracist organizing and acknowledges how groups like RAR were able to broaden the organizational capabilities of antiracist work. But one of his most important interventions is to contrast the antiracism of RAR, and its affiliate the Anti-Nazi League, with black liberation, a distinction that brings to light some of the failings of the punk-inflected organizations. Gilroy also points up the political problem of the Anti-Nazi League shifting focus away from the more complex problems of race to the oversimplified, almost caricatured, target of fascism. This critique poses a crucial question for contemporary punks as well: To what extent does the focus on bogeymen like "fascism," "the state," and "cops" get in the way of understanding and transforming the far more complex racial (and class and sex) dynamics of punk rock itself?

Anti-racism in the 1970s

Blacks have been actively organizing in defence of their lives and communities ever since they set foot in Britain. Several writers have looked at these patterns of self-organization in greater detail than is possible here.[1] Their histories have also occasionally drawn attention to the anti-racist organizations and struggles created during the 1950s and 1960s, which brought black and white together and formed a significant counterpart to the movements for black liberation in Britain and its colonized countries.

The rise and demise of organizations such as the Co-ordinating Committee Against Racial Discrimination (CCARD) formed to oppose the 1961 Commonwealth Immigrants Bill and the Campaign Against Racial Discrimination (CARD) inaugurated in February 1965 after a visit to London by Dr. Martin Luther King and dedicated to campaigning for the elimination of discrimination in civil society and in the immigration legislation, are important subjects for further research.[2] Yet the anti-racisms of the 1970s are even less well known. That decade contained a series of qualitative shifts in the racial politics of Britain. The 1971 Immigration Act brought an end to primary immigration and instituted a new pattern of internal control and surveillance of black settlers. It was paralleled by a new vocabulary of "race" and crime which grew in the aftermath of the first panic over "mugging." These developments are two of the most important from the point of view of black self-organization. However, the expansion and consolidation of organizations of the extreme, neo-fascist right was also to transform decisively the meaning of anti-racism. Dilip Hiro points to the existence of street level harassment and other activity by extreme racist groups including the British Ku Klux Klan as early as 1965, two years before the National Front (NF) was formed. Threatening letters to the London secretary of CARD had promised "concerted efforts against West Indians, specially those living with white women."[3] It was the entry of these groups into the process of electoral politics which acted as a catalyst for the creation of anti-fascist/anti-racist committees as an outgrowth of the organized labour movement in Britain's major towns and cities during the early and mid 1970s.

The NF had enjoyed its first party political broadcast during the February 1974 election and had fielded fifty-four candidates, a substantial increase from 1970 when only ten had stood. The party's journal, *Spearhead*, told its readers in January 1974 that "It need hardly be said that our election campaign now takes absolute priority over everything else."

In the second election of that year, the Front fielded ninety candidates, who obtained 113,844 votes. In the local government elections of May 1974, the NF averaged nearly 10 percent of the poll in several districts of London,[4] and in a by-election at Newham South, beat the Conservative candidate and took 11.5 percent of the total votes cast.

In June 1974 the anti-fascist forces organized a march and picket of a National Front meeting at Conway Hall in Red Lion Square. The resulting confrontation between demonstrators and the police ended with the death of one protester, Kevin Gately, who had been part of the International Marxist Group's contingent on the demonstration.[5] The fascists had been using the hall for meetings during the four years before 1974, and anti-fascist pickets of these meetings had begun in October 1973. Gately was claimed as something of a martyr to the reborn cause of anti-fascism. His death was seen as proof of the destructive nature of the extreme and anti-democratic forces which had reconstituted on British streets, twenty-nine years after the war which had been fought to free Europe of fascist tyranny.

> Trades Unionists of the older generation were doubly shocked when reaching for their newspapers on the 16th June 1974. Firstly they learnt of the tragic death in a central London street of a young man, Kevin Gately. Then they read deeper to discover the circumstances of his death. They were to find that the ugliest and most brutal of twentieth century movements—fascism—which they had dearly hoped was buried forever in 1945, had returned to plague us anew.[6]

These words begin a pamphlet issued by the Transport and General Workers' Union which set out to alert its members and other trades unionists to the growing danger of British neo-fascism. Jack Jones's introduction to the pamphlet was clear about why the fascist groups should be opposed but the reasons he cites are unconnected with the experience of black settlers, make no mention of Britain's black population and contain no acknowledgement of the problem of racism as something distinct from, though connected to, fascism: "Although they may deny it, the 'National Front' is the modern version of the Fascism of Hitler, Mussolini and Mosley."

This definition of British neo-fascism exclusively in terms of the fascisms of the past against which the British had enjoyed their finest hours in battle, recurs again and again in the politics of anti-racism during the 1970s. Jones's words betray the central tension in the politics of the anti-racist struggle, namely the tendency to conceive of neo-fascism and racism as distinct and unrelated problems and to make the popular memory of the Second World War the dominant source of images with which to mobilize against the dangers of contemporary racism.

It is almost as though the activities of the National Front and similar groups only become a problem when they threaten democracy by their participation in its electoral system and only visible where a sham patriotism is invoked. Their record of racial violence against black individuals and communities remained either unseen or was not thought to have a place in the development of a socialist anti-fascist politics.

An informal and locally-based network of anti-fascist/anti-racist committees grew in the period between 1973 and 1976. It is during this period that the emergent anti-fascist movement began to express itself as a self-conscious political formation and to create its own organs for communication and debate. Though its primary audience lay in the black communities rather than among anti-racists, the journal *Race Today* (hijacked from the Institute of Race Relations and re-oriented by its activist editorial collective) had an important role in these discussions. The magazine's central place in the struggles between blacks and the police, around education and housing in the East End of London and in the attempt to build links between black political organizations in different parts of Britain as well as between British blacks and radical struggles elsewhere in the world, all made considerable input into what anti-racism was to mean.

Race Today posed a consistent challenge to the idea that black liberation was reducible to "anti-racism" and to the related fallacy that the struggle against racism could be contained by the need to oppose the neo-fascist groups. At the opposite pole of the embryonic anti-racist movement was the anti-fascist magazine *Searchlight*. It had been founded in February 1975 with the aim of consolidating the anti-fascist forces so that they could challenge the electoral and popular success of the NF. The magazine's first editorial took its cue from the slogan of the anti-fascist movement of the 1930s, "They Shall Not Pass." This motto was used as a caption for the magazine's front cover, a photograph of a young male neo-fascist with dark glasses, leather jacket and quiff, rather incongruously holding a Union Jack. The mandate for a new anti-fascism announced by the magazine derived from the need to defend democracy from the encroachments of the extreme right. *Searchlight* combined detailed information on the activities and histories of the extreme right groups with coverage of fascist violence and race related stories from mainstream and local press.

Though the network of local groups developed and the need to combat the growth of neo-fascist organizations was more widely accepted as the

Nazi backgrounds of the NF leadership were gradually revealed, anti-fascist organizing remained locally-oriented and essentially small scale. A move towards anti-racist rather than anti-fascist politics was initiated by the conflict between blacks and the police which grew steadily after 1973 and culminated in the "Long Hot Summer" of 1976 when London's young blacks defeated the Metropolitan Police at the Notting Hill Carnival and major confrontations with the police took place in Southall and in Birmingham. The neo-fascists had organized a "March Against Mugging" in September 1975 under the slogan "Stop the Muggers. 80% of Muggers Are Black. 85% of Victims Are white." This was significant not simply for its open defiance of the laws on incitement to racial hatred and the new tactic of provocative marches through black areas but for the convergence it represented between the official respectable politics of race signalled by the authoritative official criminal statistics and the street level appeal of the neo-fascist groups who had seized the issue of black crime and begun to refine it into a populist weapon which could prove the wisdom of their distinctive solution to Britain's race problems—repatriation.

The process in which anti-fascist and anti-racist activism became a movement rather than an aggregate of uneven and disparate local groups significantly had its origins outside the realm of politics. It relied for its development on networks of culture and communication in which the voice of the left was scarcely discernible and it drew its momentum from the informal and organic relationship between black and white youth which sprung up in the shadow of 1970s youth culture.

Rock Against Racism (RAR) was formed by a small group of activists in or around the Socialist Workers' Party (SWP) in August 1976. Its founders wrote to the music press inviting support for an anti-racist stance in answer to the racist pronouncements of rock stars like Eric Clapton,[7] who had expressed his admiration for Enoch Powell on several occasions, and David Bowie,[8] who had not only said that Britain was in need of a right-wing dictatorship but declared Hitler to be "the first superstar." The image of Bowie beside Hitler and Powell was to recur in RAR's visuals. The SWP had made anti-fascist organizing a major priority during the summer of 1976 and the original RAR letter was heavily derivative of their analysis and political style. It called for black and white to unite and fight along the fundamental lines of class. However, it deviated sharply from this traditional leftism in its insistence on the autonomous value of youth culture and on the radical potential of "rock" and its offshoots. This position seems to have been part of a wider argument about the value of populist struggle. "Rock was and still can be a real progressive culture, not a packaged mail-order stick on nightmare of mediocre garbage. Keep the faith, black and white unite and fight."[9] Following this intervention, the RAR group produced the first issue of its fanzine *Temporary Hoarding* for the 1977 May Day celebrations at the Roundhouse in London.[10] The appearance of RAR coincided precisely with the growth of punk and the two developments were very closely intertwined, with punk supplying an oppositional language through which RAR anti-racism could speak a truly populist politics. The first issue of *Temporary Hoarding* made this relationship explicit and asserted the fundamental commitment to music which characterized the early RAR output. "We want Rebel music, Street music. Music that breaks down peoples' fear of one another. Crisis music. Now music. Music that knows who the real enemy is. Rock against Racism. Love Music Hate Racism." This kind of appeal was later to be expressed in slogans which made an even more overt plea for a non-sectarian transcendance of the various subcultural styles and identities and asserted a vision of the musics and the styles they had created in a pluralist coalition: "Reggae Soul Rock and Roll Jazz-Funk and Punk Our Music" read RAR's poster/broadsheet. The first issue coupled practical advice for the organizers of RAR gigs with some powerful photomontages and a short, didactic article, "What Is Racism?" by David Widgery. He coupled an overview of the development of racism in Britain's crisis with an important political argument which showed that from the start RAR was fighting for its corner in an anti-fascist/anti-racist movement which was reluctant to face the novelty of the forms in which racism was expressing itself.

The definition of racism proposed by Widgery and expanded in RAR's practice over the next three years stressed that racism linked the activity of the neo-fascists directly to the actions of state agencies, particularly the courts, police and immigration authorities.

> The problem is not just the new fascists from the old slime a master race whose idea of heroism is ambushing single blacks in darkened streets. These private attacks whose intention, to cow and brutalise, won't work if the community they seek to terrorise instead organises itself. But when the state backs up racialism it's different. Outwardly respectable but inside fired with the same mentality and the same fears, the bigger danger is the racist magistrates with the cold sneering authority, the immigration men who mock an Asian mother as she gives birth to a dead child on their office floor, policemen for whom answering back is a crime and every black kid with pride is a challenge.

The strategic consequences of this position can be spelled out. Racism was there to be smashed, and the activity involved in smashing it was neatly counterposed to the passivity of sitting back and watching it unfold. The central problem perceived by this approach was the absence of adequate organization. The new structure which RAR was creating would fill the gap. Just as *Sniffin' Glue*, the punk fanzine, included a couple of chord diagrams and then told its readers, "Now go and form a band," *Temporary Hoarding* included a blueprint for doing RAR's political work. It would be implemented with the guidance and assistance of experienced and sympathetic SWP members and supporters. Yet the defeat of racism was not to be accomplished in the name of youth or even of a common class position though both were implied. The hatred of racism and its organic counterpart—the love of music—were enough to hold together a dynamic anti-racist movement of young people. RAR's audience, the anti-racist crowd, was conceived not only as consumers of the various youth cultures and styles but as a powerful force for change which, in its diversity, created something more than the simple sum of its constitutive elements.

This anti-racism drew attention to the complex race politics of all white pop music and grasped the importance of the black origins of even the whitest rock as a political contradiction for those who were moving towards racist consciousness and explanations of the crisis. The third issue of *Temporary Hoarding*, published to coincide with the 1977 Notting Hill Carnival, contained an obituary for Elvis which, though seemingly at odds with the punk orientation of the rest of the magazine, made these very points:

> What Presley did in music was stunning. Everyone down in Memphis—which was the heart of the new South—50% black population—stayed on their own side of the tracks or across the airwaves. Presley took the two and hurled them together. Black soul, hillbilly insistence. His fusion changed everything. It accelerated the Civil Rights movement. It jerked a dead generation alive. It changed the future. Sinatra symbolised a generation, Presley created one.[11]

Punk provided the circuitry which enabled these connections to be made, rendering, as Hebdige[12] has argued, the hitherto coded and unacknowledged relationships between black and white styles an open and inescapable fact. Drawing on the language and style of roots culture in general and Rastafari in particular, punks produced not only their own critical and satirical commentary on the meaning and limits of white ethnicity but a conceptual framework for seeing and then analysing the social relations of what *Temporary Hoarding* called "Labour Party Capitalist Britain." The Dread notion of "Babylon System" allowed disparate and apparently contradictory expressions of the national crisis to be seen as a complex, interrelated whole, a coherent structure of which racism was a primary characteristic, exemplifying and symbolizing the unacceptable nature of the entire authoritarian capitalist edifice.

If the language and symbols of black culture provided the melody and harmony from which RAR would imporovise its two-tone tunes, the key of its performances and the register of the movement was influenced by the general political mood of the period. Novel combinations of ethnicity, "race," and national consciousness had emerged in popular celebrations of the Royal Silver Jubilee. This brought festivities—street parties, school holidays—and an explosion of monarchist memorabilia which pushed the icons and symbols of a royalist and patriotic definition of Britishness and the British nation to the fore.

The explosion of popular nationalism provided the punks with images of Britishness from which they could disassociated themselves and against which they could define their own, alternative definitions of the nation: past, present, and future. No less than the upsurge of neo-fascist activity in the 1976–77 period, the Royal Jubilee formed the immediate context in which the relationship between racism and nationalism could be revealed and new forms of anti-racism created which were equally opposed to both.

The punks' assault on the central icons of patrician British nationalism, particularly the Queen's face (transformed by safety pins on the cover of the Sex Pistols' "God Save The Queen," which was the number one record in Jubilee week), was an important symbolic manifestation of this element in their sub-culture. The ultimate talismans of the national culture they were rejecting—the Union Jack and the Royal visage—were used to generate a new political ideology which Hebdige has described as a "white ethnicity."[13] This both paralleled and answered the proscriptive blackness of the dread culture to which it was a cryptic affiliation.

Whether or not these stands within punk warrant the term ethnicity, they signify that the encounter with black culture in general and Rastafari in particular had changed the terms on which black and white young people engaged with each other. From now on, "race" could no longer be dealt with as a matter for private negotiation in the shadows of the ghetto blues dance or the inner-city shebeen where a token white presence might be acceptable. The rise of an articulate British racism, often aimed squarely at the distinct experiences and preoccupations of the young, destroyed the possibility of essentially covert appropriations of black-style music and anger which had been the characteristic feature of the mod and skinhead eras. "Race" had to be dealt with, acknowledged as a primary determinant of social life and, in the same breath, overcome. If contact with black culture was to be maintained, then a disavowal of whiteness was called for, not by the blacks themselves but by punk culture's own political momentum. This drew selectively on the input of RAR activists and supporters.

Some recognition of the persistent slippage between British and white was also required. Rather than constituting a wholly alternative British-ness which could justly be named an ethnic culture, these parts of punk were articulating a satirical commentary on the limits of ethnicity and "race," on the very meaninglessness of whiteness which both neo-fascists (explicitly) and popular nationalism (implicitly) alike sought to endow with a mythic and metaphysical significance.

This was a struggle over the meaning of the nation and over the meaning of punk. It was to continue long after the heyday of the movement. In the March 1981 issue of the National Front journal *Spearhead*, Eddie Mor-rison, an NF activist, argued that "Punk rock and its attendant new wave style" were worthy of support from racial nationalists because they were "totally white in origin" and "carried a message of the frustration of the masses of White working-class youth." He continued, "Electronic music and New Waves Bands is [*sic*] a new style of White Folk music."[14]

There were crucial ambiguities in the punk anthems which dealt directly with "race" and sought to make a connection between the posi-tion of dispossessed whites and the experience of racism. The Stranglers' "I Feel Like a Wog" and the Clash's "(White Man) in Hammersmith Palais" both featured almost continually in the Rock Against Communism chart in *Bulldog*, the paper of the Young National Front. They held the number one and number two positions as late as September 1982.

The attack on the Queen's portrait and on the Union Jack was as much a direct gesture to the neo-fascists as it was a reworking of the ideologi-cal themes and signs which had, in an earlier period, defined "Swinging London" and turned Carnaby Street into a mecca for subculturalists from all over the overdeveloped world. The Sex Pistols' lead singer, John Lydon, pronounced frequently and at length on the subjects of "race," nation, and Britishness. He told one American journalist:

There's no such thing as patriotism any more. I don't care if it blows up ... England never was free. It was always a load of bullshit. I'm surprised we [the Sex Pistols] aren't in jail for treason ... Punks and Niggers are almost the same thing ... when I come to America I'm going straight to the ghetto ... I'm not asking blacks to like us. That's irrelevant. It's just that we're doing something they'd want to do if they had the chance.[15]

Punk's leading musicians cemented their appropriation of black style and their hostility to both racist nationalism and nationalist racism in several records which recast reggae music in their own idiom. The similarities and the differences between punk and black styles were pinpointed. The best example of this is the Clash version of "Police and Thieves," a tune which had been a roots hit in 1976 for Junior Murvin and which had blared out from a speaker dangled from an upstairs window when anti-fascist demonstrators attacked the National Front march in Lewisham during August 1977. It thus acquired a special place in the cultural history of the anti-racist movement of this period, symbolizing in itself the coming together of black and white in opposition to racism.

Another record, similarly created as a dread commentary on the state of Jamaica after Michael Manley's election victory of 1976 but masquerading as a mystical invocation of the apocalypse, was seized by the punks and given a central place in their cultural cosmology. This was "Two Sevens Clash" by the roots vocal trio Culture, and like "Police and Thieves" it became something of a punk anthem.

Though many punk bands refused to play reggae, the music remained a constant point of reference and a potent source of their poetics. It should also be remembered that the genesis of punk coincided with militant action by young blacks in the 1976 Notting Hill Carnival riot. The imagery of black, urban insurgency was particularly visible as the nation reflected on the carnival explosion and the defeat of the Metropolitan Police by mobs of stone-throwing youths. Understanding why black youth had turned on the police was ... now inseparable from reckoning with the cultural context in which the riot had occurred. The cultural backdrop to black combativity was important to punks also, though for rather different reasons. The street carnival, with its bass-heavy sound systems pumping out the new militant "rockers" beat of reggae as the half-bricks and bottles flew overhead, demonstrated to the punks the fundamental continuity of cultural expression with political action. The two were inextricably interwoven into a dense and uncompromising statement of black dissent which was a source of envy and of inspiration to a fledgling punk sensibility. This envy and its creative consequences were spelled out by the Clash in their song "White Riot," described by one writer as the after-effect "of being caught in the racial no-man's land between charging police and angry black youth at the Notting Hill carnival riots of 1976."[16]

> Black men got a lotta problems
> But they don't mind throwing a brick
> But white men have too much school
> Where they teach you to be thick
> We go reading papers and wearing slippers
>
> White riot, I wanna riot
> White riot, a riot of my own
> All the power is in the hands
> Of people rich enough to buy it
> While we walk the streets
> Too chicken to even try it
> And everybody does what they're told to do
> And everybody eats supermarket soul food
>
> White riot, I wanna riot
> White riot, a riot of my own

The intimate political and ideological connections embodied in this musical relationship were given substance by RAR's efforts to put on gigs up and down the country in which black and white bands and their audiences could combine. The organization put on 200 events in just over one year. In these, the emphasis was on the creation of an experience in which the emptiness of "race" could be experienced at first hand and its transcendence celebrated. The Clash were to maintain a link with RAR throughout its early years and were the main attraction of the RAR/ANL Carnival in East London in May 1978.

The effect of punk on RAR's ability to function effectively was not confined to its pronouncements on "race" and nation. Punk style, like its anti-authoritarian ideology, was also borrowed, used and developed by RAR. It became an integral part of the movement's capacity to operate in a truly popular mode, a significant component in its ability to be political without being boring at a time when the NF was identified as being "No Fun." ...

Anti-Nazi or Against Racism?

The fourth issue of *Temporary Hoarding* came out in late 1977. The Anti-Nazi League (ANL) was launched on 19 November that year. It was to change and redirect RAR's politics and orientation. The League was launched as a broad initiative, drawing together sponsors from right across the spectrum of radical politics with a variety of show business personalities, academics, writers and sports people. The League's founding statement drew attention to the electoral threat posed by the NF and their associates. The danger they represented was once again conveyed by reference to the Nazism of Hitler.

> Like Hitler with the Jews, the British Nazis seek to make scapegoats of black people. They exploit the real problems of unemployment, bad housing, cuts in education and in social and welfare services. ... In these months before the General Election the Nazis will seize every opportunity to spread their propaganda. During the election itself, National Front candidates might receive equal TV and radio time to the major parties. The British electorate will be exposed to Nazi propaganda on an unprecedented scale.

The League's sponsors sought to "organise on the widest possible scale" and appealed to "all those who oppose the growth of the Nazis in Britain [to unite] irrespective of other political differences." As the League's name suggests, its aims were simpler and more straightforward than RAR's heterogeneous concerns. It was a single-issue campaign modeled on the Campaign for Nuclear Disarmament (CND) and centred on electoral politics, whereas RAR's critique of Labour had fused with punk's anarchic and cynical analysis of parliamentarism.

What we must examine now is the degree to which the ANL deliberately sought to summon and manipulate a form of nationalism and patriotism as part of its broad anti-fascist drive. The idea that the British Nazis were merely sham patriots who soiled the British flag by their use of it was a strong feature of ANL leaflets. This inauthentic patriotism was exposed and contrasted with the genuine nationalist spirit which had been created in Britain's finest hour—the "anti-fascist" 1939–45 war. The neo-fascists wore the uniforms of Nazism beneath their garb of outward respectability and it is hard to gauge what made them more abhorrent to the ANL, their Nazism or the way they were dragging British patriotism through the mud. The League's leaflets were illustrated with imagery of the war—concentration camps and Nazi troops—and were captioned with the anti-fascist slogan "Never Again." One leaflet, "What Would Life

Be Like under the Nazis?" warned potential NF supporters that "The NF says they are just putting Britons first. But their Britain will be just like Hitler's Germany." Another, "Why You Should Oppose the National Front," made a more direct challenge to the quality of NF patriotism: "They say they are just patriots. Then why does Chairman Tyndall say: 'the Second World War was fought for Jewish, not British, interests. Under the leadership of Adolph Hitler, Germany proved she could be a great power.'"

In the *Guardian*, the ANL spokesperson Peter Hain described the NF brand of patriotism as a "masquerade."[17] Above all, the popular memory of the anti-fascist war was employed by the ANL to alert people to the dangers of neo-fascism in their midst. Pictures of the NF leaders wearing Nazi uniform were produced as the final proof that their Britishness was in doubt. How could those who secretly aped the fascistic antics of Britain's sworn enemies then pose as guardians of national culture and interests? asked the League. Its resources were channeled into materials which could be used in anti-fascist campaigning for local polls and the anticipated general election.

The attempt to impose the elimination of Nazism as a priority on the diverse and complex political consciousness crystallized by RAR was a miscalculation. The narrow definition of the problem of "race"—as a product of fascism—matched by a rapid broadening of the campaign against it drew on RAR's momentum, punk and the residues of anti-Jubilee sentiment. However, this shift imposed a shorter life and more limited aims on the movement. The goals of anti-racism were being redefined. The Rasta-inspired pursuit of "Equal Rights and Justice" was being forsaken, in the ANL if not RAR. It was replaced by the more modest aim of isolating and eliminating the fascist parties at the polls. The exposure of fascist leaders as Nazis was rapidly taken over into Fleet Street, broadening support still further and increasing popular hostility to those who would threaten democracy, but the exclusive identification of racism with Nazis was to create problems for anti-racism in the future. ...

Paul Gilroy, from "Two Sides of Anti-Racism," *"There Ain't No Black in the Union Jack": The Cultural Politics of "Race" and Nation* (London: Hutchinson Education, 1987).

JOEL OLSON,
"A NEW PUNK MANIFESTO"

What happens to radical whiteness after punk's first wave? Exemplifying one trajectory of punk in the 1990s, Joel Olson, a member of the Minneapolis-based anarchist-punk collective *Profane Existence*, and frequent contributor to the journal *Race Traitor*, gives his answer. More than merely rejecting the "the white supremacist, patriarchal, capitalist world order," it remains the task of punk to re-create society according to its ideals. In this way, Olson makes explicit what was always true of punk: its main innovation was not so much its music as it was an alternative cultural infrastructure of bands, zine writers, record labels, venues, and group houses, which, coupled with punk's oppositional stance, can be a potentially powerful political force. Punk needs to mature past its knee-jerk negation and cultivate "positive political activities" proper to it. Punks, Olson goes on to argue, also need to reach past their own and work with "the underprivileged people in our communities." But here's the rub: as we will see, this same entreaty is made again and again. So, what is it about punk rock that produces, at one and the same time, this (a) acknowledgement and rejection of privileged whiteness, (b) desire to join in solidarity with other races struggling for change, and finally, (c) a difficulty in producing anything concrete or lasting from those desires? Perhaps the punk dialectic between wanting to perform society's ugliness and desiring to change it can't be so easily divided.

Punk has done important things in its short history. (It's done some really stupid things, too, but that's for someone else to chronicle.) Out of the waste heap of middle-class values and shopping-mall esthetics, we've built a culture that has allowed us to survive the postindustrial world while at the same time salvaging some semblance of our independence, freedom, creativity, and human integrity. As important as this is, it is now time for punk to enter a new phase. Punk has allowed thousands of youths to survive in this rat heap of a world through its music, zines, and communities; now it's time to change the rat heap itself.

For the most part, punks, have historically been interested in shocking society. In North America, at least, punk's political practice has been to reject the middle-class values shoved down our throat. Being a largely white, middle-class youth movement (again, at least in North America), punk's relations with the outside world have been concentrated on shocking and rejecting that world, from the most political Crass punk to the drunkest Sore Throat punk to the sincerest Minor Threat punk to the most idiotic Exploited mall punk. About the only punk subgroup I would exclude from this generalization would be the wave of upper-middle-class straight-edge and pop-punk fans, although there are significant numbers of people in these groups who also spend most of their political activity (where "political" is defined as one's relations with the social world) rejecting the morals and values of white bread America.

This rejection of our roots, our middle-class backgrounds, is important, for (theoretically, at least) we are the inheritors of the white supremacist, patriarchal, capitalist world order. A prime position as defenders of the capital of the ruling class and the overseers of the underclass has been set aside for us by our parents, our upbringing, our culture, our history, and yet we have the moral gumption to reject it. As punks we reject our inherited race and class positions because we know they are bullshit. We want no part in oppressing others and we certainly want no part of Suburbia, our promised land.

However, as important as it is for us to reject our somewhat privileged backgrounds, it is also not enough. Our goal needs to be not to merely reject society, but to re-create it as well. Punk's effectiveness up to now has primarily been negative in the sense that its primary political activity has been to criticize and reject America and everything it stands for. Now it is time to take positive action. We need to turn our anger and disgust with middle-class America and creatively channel it into mass-based political action.

To say that punk's effectiveness has been entirely negative and reaction-oriented would be dead wrong, and I don't mean to demean the accomplishments of punk by any means. To see the positive influences of punk, we need to look beyond the average mosher at an Agnostic Front gig and examine the smaller, more active community of punks who do zines, write mail, run independent labels and distribution services, organize gigs and/or demos, etc. The people in these communities do an enormous amount of very vital work, work that keeps us from going insane within this fucked up Amerikan society. That work needs to continue.

The positive political activities of punk primarily fall in two categories. One is our work in developing the punk community. This kind of activity includes writing fanzines, putting out records, setting up gigs, having picnics, distributing punk materials, writing mail, traveling, and simply hanging out with our good punk friends. The second kind of positive punk political activity is the focus on changing our individual selves. This includes vegetarianism/veganism, emphasizing recycling, exploring racism, sexism, and homophobia in our punk communities and within ourselves, etc. As I've said, these activities need to continue. They are absolutely necessary in creating change, and in making change fun. After all, without punk, what would the disaffected middle-class youth of Amerika have to listen to, the goddamn Grateful Dead? The Chili Peppers? Yeesh.

However, we need to add a third element in our goal to make positive change: organizing with other revolutionary elements in our society. In case you didn't know, punk is and needs to be revolutionary. The fact that it doesn't seem so indicates not that punk is liberal or reactionary but that we as punx have been selling ourselves short in realizing the potential of punk and our potential to thoroughly fuck up this society. Punk is one of the very few middle-class youth cultures in North America that actually rejects middle-class values. This puts us punks in a unique position, and we need to use this position as rejectors of the inheritance to our advantage and to the advantage of oppressed peoples by working with them: women, blacks, Native Americans, homeless, queers, i.e., the underprivileged. We've abandoned our middle-class backgrounds, now it's time for us to unequivocally side with the oppressed.

Punk rejects America completely. Punk demands something new. Punk is and needs to be revolutionary, and if you don't agree, maybe it's time for you to turn in your 7-inch collection for a Columbia House CD Club membership. Just don't be surprised when we bulldoze through your fucking house someday.

Punks do an excellent job, for the most part, in developing our own community. It's time to take that experience into the larger community and infuse our spirit and creativity with mass-based revolutionary potential. We need to help organize and work towards a mass movement, one that's set on destroying America as it stands and empowering the dispossessed. We need a revolution and it's time for punk to be a part of it!

Further, we need to be more than superficial. We need more than another zine. We need to organize and get established in our local communities. We need to offer our collective strengths to the struggles of oppressed people, which, after all, are our own. I'm talking about expanding our present facilities, I'm talking about developing new ones. We need to continue to put out zines, but we need to get them out beyond the punk community, even if that means giving them away. We need to make better use of our present facilities and open them up to the rest of the community. Epicenter, the punk-run nonprofit record store and community center in San Francisco, is an example of this, like when they opened their doors to the community as a meeting space for the General Strike meetings during the Gulf War and when they open their space for various community groups to hold their meetings. Not every city has an Epicenter, to be sure. It's time to work with the rest of the underprivileged people in our communities and build them.

We need other new resources. We need outreach: punk soup kitchens, community groups, free stores, etc. We need to let people know that we are on the side of people, not privilege. The fascists are organizing in our communities; we need to beat them at their own game. Why do you think the KKK and the racist populist movement enjoys such success in poor farming and lower-middle-class communities? Because they actually go into those communities and work with the people there and help them in their struggles with the rich and powerful who are trying to destroy their lives (e.g., by helping farmers keep their land from the banks, etc.). We need to do the same thing, but we need to offer anti-fascist alternatives to the people who need help in empowering themselves. This will take a mass, broad-based movement, and punks need to take an active part in that.

The fascists are organizing in our communities; we're not. Time to change. Make no mistake, war is coming to Amerika. It's overdue. Look at the economy, look at the deteriorating condition of our cities, look at whatever you want. The New World Order of Bush and his lackeys is heralding in a new age, and it's not going to be pretty. The New Right wants a piece of you, the racist Right wants a piece of you, the upper class want to keep their piece of you. Are you going to let them? War is coming to Amerika, and it's time to prepare, punx. We need to fight if we are to survive, and being punx, we undoubtably can figure out a way to have a good time doing it.

Getting involved in the community does not mean we have to sacrifice our identities. We don't have to "grow up," look nice, act polite, or refrain from drunken binges to be revolutionary or to work with non-punks. We're punks and we will change the world as punks. We need to help out those who need help in our community as punx and let folks know that we're on their side and that we're ready for a revolution, even though we're white and largely middle class and male. ...

It's time to fess up. We're punks, we hate society, and we want a new world. We're revolutionaries. As revolutionaries, it's time to work with the underprivileged and angry elements in our communities and to get organized. It's in our hands, and we should expect nothing less from punk and from ourselves. We will make punk a threat again, together. Let's do it!

Joel Olson, from "A New Punk Manifesto," *Profane Existence* no. 13 (Minneapolis, February 1992).

ANONYMOUS, "NOT JUST POSING FOR THE POSTCARD: A DISCUSSION OF PUNK AND THE NEW ABOLITION"

The following essay touches upon familiar themes: Clash-style dreams of solidarity, a profane existence defined by presumed racial treason, all written in the dominant White-punk register. However, this White punk, writing in the progressive political magazine *Clamor*, pushes the argument one step further: that punk's stylistic subversions (dyed hair, mohawks, back patches, tattoos, piercings) function to destabilize the assumption of White superiority. Furthermore, punk signifiers become markers of racial otherness that can serve as signals to people of color that White punks are potential allies. "In my dream," as the author writes, "people of color will see me and not think how weird I look, but recognize me as a friend." The implication here is that taking on the subject position of punk relieves Whites of some of their whiteness and renders solidarity unproblematic. There remains, however, a difference between a marginality that is self-adopted—even with the best of intentions—and one imposed by a larger racist society.

> I am a poseur and I don't care;
> I like to make people stare.
> —"I Am A Poseur," X-Ray Spex

I fell into a seat on the El with the haziness of a new day suffocating my brain, only really concentrating on the next few tasks ahead of me: picking up my morning coffee, going to class, buying some groceries, cashing my check, and maybe stopping by Ear Wax for a movie for later. Staring at the buildings drifting by, I let my thoughts drift to Catherine Deneuve and Bridget Bardot's hair until I heard near me, "I mean, I would disown my daughter if she came home looking like that … why would you do that to yourself?" The lavender hairs on the back of my head prickled and my ears burned as I fiddled with the cold silver loops rimming the outer edge. My feelings are easily crushed; how many more stops until I could escape? But I needed to stop running from this recurring criticism. The two White women discussing my appearance enjoyed the discomfort they could see I was feeling. "Hmmmph," the larger one grunted as she looked me in the eye and slowly shook her head, her large breasts heaving with her disapproving sigh. "It just looks horrible!" the other one moaned. I swallowed tentatively, tasting the metal protruding from my lips, gathering some strength to confront the seat curmudgeons. I'd been working on my argument and polishing my points, just for this kind of occasion when I would have to defend fishnets and tattoos and even the holey Dicks T-shirt to the close-minded and loud-mouthed Chicagoan. Oh, I was ready.

The words I really wanted stuck in my throat as the women grimaced at each other, then at me, and stood to exit at the State Street stop. "What?" I quietly began, which was meant to be followed with, "… does my appearance signify to you? Am I damaging my inherent privilege of bonding with you as a 'normal White person?' And am I threatening the stability of yours? I fucking hope so." But I was too reserved, and too late.

Before risking taking this idea way too seriously, I have to note that young folks in the punk community often begin to dress outrageously as a form of rebellion only against their parents, their first and most obvious constricts. Also, it is common for young punks to dress a certain way just to fit in with others in the punk community. I am looking more at folks who have been involved for some length of time, and are politically aware and active. I am talking about the people who, like me, decided they were "non-conformists" when they were pre-pubescent, and today still dress in a way that tells the White businessman they pass downtown that they are not cut from the same cloth, and would never choose to be. …

Punks as Potential Race Traitors

In the past decade or so, ideas of race in America have been rapidly changing. More and more, White folks, even in the mainstream, are owning up to the reality of racial privilege, as well as the inherent truth that "race" actually doesn't exist, and was actually a creation to promote domination by those already in power. "Race" itself cannot in any way be nailed down as a genetic of physiological reality, but was an important belief of those who founded this country. When the term "White" is used to describe someone, unfounded associations are made, due to America's race-conscious socialization, just as the term "Black" comes fraught with associations. (This is why I choose to capitalize White and Black: none of those people are actually white or black. The terms are social descriptors, relating to the way the people relate and are treated by society.) To be clear, to abolish race is not to diminish the importance of culture and heritage. To pretend like everyone is the same (to be color-blind) is perhaps one of the greatest mistakes liberals have ever made in the hopes of taming racial tensions in America.

I have mixed feelings about recent attempts of punk bands and zines to articulate their position in understanding race. A few years back, I saw a Minneapolis band try to begin a discussion while onstage with the audience on why the scene was so White. It was a heartfelt attempt: the idea piqued my interest, and I was pleased that these folks were interested in having a diverse audience. However, the crowd was not interested in discussing it, for various reasons. I no longer wish for a multi-cultural audience (and Minneapolis already has a healthy Latino/punk contingent); I hope for the White punks to make alliances and build bridges to other cultures with similar goals. Yeah, punk is pretty White.

Also, there is a hardcore band out of Chicago actually called "Race Traitor." In many of their songs they demonize White culture:

> white empire built on top of a golden pedestal … white kingdom plastic culture on top of the enslaved and colonized … on top of their swollen naked corpses gorging off their blood and slag … kill white culture …
> —H-3030

Despite their faults (the band has been chided for their abrupt and perhaps condemning tone and often dogmatic approach), they were one of the few bands out there willing (more than willing) to discuss whiteness and racial privilege. In fact, it is difficult to find American bands who write songs about racial oppression, the large exception being Latino bands (who are on the receiving end), like Huasipungo and Los Crudos ("we're that Spic band!")

Among zines, the literary arm of punk, the story recently is a bit different. *After the Revolution* #2 contains a thoughtful printed discussion on gentrification, citing how White punks and artists are often the first to cross into lower-income neighborhoods of color, setting off the process of gentrification. *Praxis* #2 includes words, much like those of the Black Panthers, which inform White folks to be allies of people of color by working "on racism for your sake, not for 'their' sake." Also, to be an ally does not mean to organize communities of color or fighting anyone else's battles. The author encourages Whites to look at themselves, and to talk to the White community about those seemingly invisible privileges. The recently-defunct *Primordial Soup Kitchen* #3 includes a quick analysis. Sean says, "White America (or at least those who identify themselves as white) and those who benefit from having white skin, view themselves as morally pure … [under this system] All must conform to whiteness because it is superior." The *Antipathy* zine contains an article rejecting the notion of White skin privilege, arguing that "not all whites are created equal." Although I believe the author here has missed the point, I am pleased that he and so many other zine writers are at least engaging in the discussion.

This discussion of race will hopefully bloom into something much greater, and punk will be widely known as a strong ally of movements for the rights of people of color. In my dream, people of color will see me and not think how weird I look, but recognize me as a friend.

I had that experience once: seated in a room full of mostly White college students in one of the most poverty-stricken Black neighborhoods in the United States, I felt a bit caught. My folding chair squeaked as I turned to take in my surroundings. We were waiting for a speaker in a meeting room of a community center in the heart of Cabrini Green, the notorious public housing project on Chicago's north side. The group I came with were fresh-faced White liberal, artsy-fartsy students, ready to save the world. But, wasn't that me? I was even confused. How was I different? In my mind, I knew my ideas were much more revolutionary and my methods much more daring, but was this apparent to everyone else?

A young Black woman stood at the front to begin her lecture on public housing. With a cheerful grin she said, "Well, just looking at you all, I can tell you're down." She paused and raised her finger to me, leafing through my notebook back in the third row. "Especially her."

Before concluding, there are a few more qualifications I must throw in, for fear of misrepresenting myself. In 1977, punk was scary, new and unpredictable. In 1984, punk was proving it wasn't dead, and bands and writers were finding new and important ways of showing disapproval of mainstream society's practices and attitudes. In 2000, punk is no longer new, the punk look has been co-opted by many apolitical subcultures (ravers, Goths) and DIY can be purchased at a shop at the Mall of America. We must find new ways to grow, prove we are still relevant and, yes, continue to shock people, whether by appearances or by ideas, which brings me to my second qualification. Although punk looks are helpful in showing dissatisfaction and disassociation with force-fed mainstream culture, nothing is as shocking as a well-thought out, rebellious idea, or a well-planned culture jamming act.

To all the punks, one of the most important things that could strengthen the political punk movement and create ways for White punks to understand their place in the way race is constructed, is for punks to form alliances with the hip hop community. As a culture generally made up of people of color, hip hop often espouses similar politics: anti-consumerism, anti-capitalism, DIY, and anti-corporate greed, as well as emphasizing a total lifestyle change with a soundtrack, reading material and art all its own. If you don't believe me when I say the parallels are uncanny, pick up copies of Billy Wimsatt's *Bomb the Suburbs* and *No More Prisons*.

Secondly, use what you know. By actively questioning, which probably got you into punk in the first place, you have acquired the power to move past just being White. Whiteness means to passively accept privileges, oppressing others in the process. Be something else. Be an abolitionist, and don't be afraid to let other people know what you are.

To everyone else, when you see someone like me on the bus or in the grocery store, don't assume that she is "just going through a phase." Many of us understand deeply what it means to give up privileges by choosing to look the way we do, and we're doing it for that exact reason.

Anonymous, "Not Just Posing for the Postcard: A Discussion of Punk and the New Abolition," *Clamor Magazine* no. 2 (Bowling Green, OH: April/May 2000),

DAISY ROOKS,
"SCREAMING, ALWAYS SCREAMING"

If there's one U.S. publication that exemplifies punk's turn in the 1990s to a self-conscious and sober leftism (found in the Profane Existence collective and Olson's "New Punk Manifesto") it is *HeartattaCk*—known affectionately by the odd abbreviation "*HaC*." In this new, politically responsible, phase, punks explore an issue germane to the scene since its inception: the problem of gentrification. With withering sarcasm and legitimate hilarity ("I can't believe they don't have that vegan cereal that they do in the Safeway near my parents' house"), the *HaC* columnist Daisy Rooks articulates the (presumed White) punk position as the first wave of gentrification. At issue here is not merely the articulation of a radical, or

marked White subject position, but rather its effect upon surrounding racial "others," whose preexisting communities one attempts to enter and yet hopefully not dissolve in the process. Compare this with the earlier Fuck-Ups interview, and you can see the trajectory of punk-rock thinking on race between the '80s and '90s. Then: conflict within one's adopted neighborhood was just one more way White punks were oppressed. Now: it may just be punks who are also doing the oppressing. And yet, the fundamental assumption is the same: that punks are White.

Hair nets and fancy 10 speed bicycles riding by you and sneering at you as we come out of your store and onto the street where we won't/can't even condescend to look at you, never mind the talking part because of course you're drunk or gross or a fucking asshole. And we talk all this shit all the time about how maybe eventually we'll get around to volunteering at that church one of these days, but probably we'll just end up sitting outside of it smoking and seeing some band play inside as we sneer at the guy who's sweeping the bathroom floor. Cleaning up after us, as we think that they all should, but just won't say it.

But we're totally on the cutting edge you know, totally living dangerously because we live where our parents would call a "bad" neighborhood and they won't even come to see us after dark and just keep slipping us all those snide comments about needing a little riot to get the streets repaved. But we're not like them we assure ourselves, as we yell at the man across the street who called us baby. Who tried to say hello to us, or who maybe even didn't say anything but just looked. 'Cause they're not allowed to look at us here, they're supposed to sit back as we saunter lazily through the aisles of their stores swinging the Blatz lunchbox so absentmindedly and talking about how oh my god I can't believe they don't have that vegan cereal that they do in the Safeway near my parents' house. That sucks, doesn't it?

As long as you continue to call it a "bad" neighborhood and you are still thinking of someone out here as bad, or maybe perhaps as everyone who lives on your street as "one of those people." As long as we go into the park to yell at people because we don't feel safe walking down the street. Yelling and passing out fliers in a language that they not only don't read, but probably don't even understand.

In the name of convenience, the shorter distance to our favorite smoke filled clubs and white kid restaurants and hang-out spots, we'll come in to live here and probably not leave until we get so fed up with the yuppies who are moving in right on our heels looking for the new/cool hot spot. As we spit on them on our way out of the grocery store and talk about how much it sucks that all these white people are moving into the neighborhood and what changes that'll bring, we don't even realize what our presence has done to (change) the neighborhood. Not only did we make it safe for mr and mrs sweateraroundtheneckshortshortsboatshoesslickedbackhair to move in and feel safe, we set the standard for people here being treated like shit for having the audacity to live in the same neighborhood as us. Neighborhoods that they created and have built over the past 20/30 years. We set the stage for them hating our guts because of (what we are and) how we act and what we are doing/bringing to them and their communities. And because soon the rent will be jacked up so high that they too will have to move out and then we'll follow them again, or maybe by that time the sweaters will be tied so tightly around our necks that we'll have to follow this year's new crop of rebel kids to the hot spots.

But no matter what, the fact remains that we are doing this and we are part of the problem unless we learn to live and function within the communities that are already set up where we decide to (and the fact remains that this is a decision, and that most of us can choose to retreat back into the suburbs at any time) live. Until we no longer think of places as "good" and "bad" or people as clean and dirty, and begin to be able to treat them with the fucking respect that they deserve. And when we realize that we will never be immune, we will not be safe anywhere. Not here, not down the street, not at our parents' house safely locked in with the security system on and all the doors double locked. Nowhere. And it is not until we acknowledge this and learn to incorporate some fucking respect into the ways that we deal with people that we will be able to live here (or wherever) without wrecking havoc wherever we are/live.

Daisy Rooks, from the column "Screaming, Always Screaming," *Heart-attaCk* no. 3 (Goleta, CA, August 1994).

OTTO NOMOUS,
"RACE, ANARCHY AND PUNK ROCK: THE IMPACT
OF CULTURAL BOUNDARIES WITHIN THE
ANARCHIST MOVEMENT"

A large part of punk's political evolution has to do with its affiliation with anarchism. Like the swastika, the Circle A and black flag of anarchy may have been first adopted by punks for their capacity to shock, but as the decades progressed more and more politically minded punks put substance to the symbols and embraced anarchism as a political ideology and practice (just as a minority of punks turned to Nazism and White Power). In light of this development, Otto Nomous, in a widely distributed article, gets down to the business of pointing out what might be going wrong within that alliance, observing that as the anarchist movement in the United States became more and more closely linked with the punk scene, the punk scene's relative racial homogeneity came to be reflected in the movements' political activities. Everyday struggles against racism, sexism, homophobia, and the like take a backseat to "white riots" against the World Trade Organization and like bodies. Otto Nomous also challenges the punk-anarchist movement's core value of "Free Association," for while punk and anarchism's overarching whiteness is often lamented, it is rarely challenged because the scene and its White participants see themselves as open to all comers ... and it just so happens that few black, Asian, or Latino folks show up.

> Yes that's right, punk is dead ... Punk became a fashion just like hippy used to be and it ain't got a thing to do with you or me.
> —Lyrics by Crass, *The Feeding of the Five Thousand* (1978)

Ever since the historic protests against the WTO in Seattle at the close of the last millennium, anarchism as a revolutionary theory has been sought after by an increasing number of people from wider-ranging walks of life than ever before in recent memory. However, the undeniable fact remains that the makeup of the anarchist movement in the U.S. for the last couple of decades has been a largely homogeneous one, i.e., predominantly white and middle class. It also happens to be the case that the vast majority of people who identify themselves as anarchists in the U.S. today are connected to alternative subcultures, such as punk rock, in varying degrees. As a person of color and an anarchist with roots in punk rock, I have become deeply concerned with the lack of diversity within the anarchist movement. As long as we fail to attract significantly diverse participation, thus remaining isolated and politically weakened, and fail to link-up with and support anti-racist struggles, we shouldn't keep our hopes up for any radical social transformation in this country. I began to realize that a significant part of the problem lies in the subcultural lifestyle of many anarchists, including myself. What follows is an attempt to offer insight in finding answers for the ever-pressing quest for diversity within the anarchist community.

From the numerous Situationist slogans that graced the lyrics of early punk bands, to the proliferation of anarcho-punk bands such as Crass and Conflict in the early eighties, punk rock as a subculture has had a unique history of having a strong relationship with explicitly anarchist and anti-capitalist political content over the years. Many anarchists today, including myself, are by-products of punk rock, where most become politicized from being exposed to angry, passionate lyrics of anarcho-punk bands, do-it-yourself zines, and countless other sources of information that are circulated within the underground punk distribution networks. Some are introduced to punk through the introduction to the anarchist social circles. Regardless of which comes first, the correlation between the punk scene and the anarchist scene is hard to miss, especially at most anarchist gatherings and conferences. It is by no coincidence that the punk scene also shares the familiar demographic as its counterpart, of mostly white, male, suburban, middle class youths.

It should be clear then, that the problem of the lack of race/class diversity within the U.S. anarchist movement will exist as long as it remains within the boundaries of any one particular culture, such as punk. To ignore this reality as merely an insignificant annoyance in an otherwise politically correct movement, and pretend that it can be solved as long as we recruit folks of color by being more open, or if one analyzes the connection between global capitalism and white supremacy, would be a short-sighted mistake, albeit a frequently made one. It is critically important to realize how cultural boundaries can alienate other communities, how subtle forms of denial and guilt-complexes prevent real solutions, and why many of our attempts in the past have failed to provide new, effective approaches in achieving a truly diverse anarchist movement.

Looking at the fact that most people who rear their heads at anarchist movement events are roughly between 16-30 years old, with background influences of punk or other "alternative" persuasions, it is easy to understand why such movements tend to alienate most people than interest them. Punk has primarily appealed to middle-class, straight white boys, who, though they are "too smart" for the rock music pushed by the multinational corporations, still want to "rock out." It is also a culture that is associated with alienating oneself from the rest of society, often times in order to rebel against one's privileged background or parents. There's really nothing wrong with any radical counterculture having its own, distinct character, of course. Indeed, it's probably very good for those included. But we have to admit it is exclusive. Plus, the anarchist movement today has determined its issues of importance. Rarely do these include community organizing or working for social change around issues that most people prioritize, such as against the more subtle forms of racism, agism and sexism, for a living wage, health care, and so forth. We are often more interested in promoting anarchism and so-called revolutionary organizations than working to provide real alternatives among everyday people. The current anarchist movement, for this reason, is not very relevant to the actual lives of most oppressed people.

Quite disturbingly, my experiences have shown that instead of acknowledging their impact and actually addressing them, many white anarchists rely on either constant denial of their responsibilities or engage in patronizing, token gestures out of privilege-guilt complexes. For example, I have received quite a few very negative and defensive reactions from white anarchists whenever I would mention the words white and middle class in the same sentence. Some of them defiantly point out that they're actually working class because they grew up poor or have to work. What they fail to realize is that it doesn't change the fact that they are able to blend in and benefit from the current anarchist scene which is predominantly middle class, and from white skin privilege.

It seems as though a fairly extensive arsenal of denial and rationale has been developed within the anarchist scene over the years. One of my favorite examples is from when I approached some members of a group that was organizing the anarchist conference that happened in L.A. during the Democratic National Convention with the fact that the group was almost entirely white punks. Many of them defended it by saying, "I believe in 'Free Association,'" or "I'm not stopping anyone from joining our group. In fact, we'd like other people to join us, but they never do." Such remarks indicate just how little they understand that it is because they operate in comfort zones that suit their subcultural lifestyle or upbringing, which many people cannot relate to. I believe this is one of the most serious and significant obstacles that anarchists face today. Until white anarchists figure out that they actually need to proactively break through race/class/

cultural boundaries, they will only continue to perpetuate the isolated anarchist ghetto. One of the more insulting things I've heard not too long ago from a local anarchist, however, is "C'mon, I work with YOU. And you're not white ... so I can't be racist." The thought of my (or any other person of color's) mere presence somehow legitimizing someone's attitude on race that is implicit in that statement is painfully absurd. But it reflects the reality that a lot of people still think in those ways. I have also encountered a slightly more subtle form of denial from anarchist discussion lists of people who insist that since the concept of race is a social construct, we shouldn't acknowledge racial identities and instead pretend as if such categories do not exist. What's funny is that they almost always identify themselves as being white. It sure must be convenient as a white person to pretend that issues of race didn't exist, which reminds me of the similar line associated with the anti–Affirmative Action campaigns of how we now live in a colorblind society with equal opportunities.

Of course, not all white anarchists are clueless about racial/class relations and their positions of privilege. In the Minneapolis anarcho-punk zine *Profane Existence*, Joel wrote circa '92, "We are the inheritors of the white supremacist, patriarchal, capitalist world order. A prime position as defenders of the capital of the ruling class and the overseers of the underclass has been set aside for us ... as punks we reject our inherited race and class positions because we know they are bullshit." However, no matter how well-intentioned, the anarchist scene has been for the most part so deeply entrenched in the lifestyle of the know-it-all, punker-than-thou, vegan/straight-edge-fascist, fashion victims or young, transient, train-hopping, dreadlocked, dumpster-diving eco-warriors that not only do most people find it hard to relate to them but they themselves are at a loss when they actually try to reach out to other communities. A typical scenario I find when this is attempted usually only amounts to the aforementioned fluffy, token gestures of solidarity, such as visiting a local black revolutionary group's headquarters and staying just long enough to take pictures with a fist in the air or inviting a person of color to an all-white group just to ease one's guilt. But, to be fair, I must acknowledge that I know of a few exceptions of white/punk anarchists that actually attempt to do serious work with people of color and/or are committed to community organizing. The point I'm making basically is that the general tendencies of most white/punk anarchists tend to be to settle for the symbolic, and fail to support the real struggles of people to change the world precisely because they have a choice as opposed to people who have to struggle for their livelihood.

It would be useful to look at anarchist groups and projects such as Anti-Racist Action, Earth First, Food Not Bombs and various other anarchist collectives to find out the extent to which such groups are influenced by subcultural lifestyles and how they deal with the issue of diversity. They tend to be good at politicizing lots of people who may identify or feel comfortable with the distinct counter-culture, but they almost never go beyond the boundaries of their comfort zones. Our closest comrades aren't people chosen because of their politics alone—plenty more share our principles and political beliefs—but we never see them, because they don't share our style or cultural preferences. Furthermore, we have seen numerous infoshops spring up in many cities over the years. They usually stand out like an eyesore by becoming more of a punk activist hangout and turn off the people who live in the neighborhood who may have been interested in the project otherwise. We should also be conscious of the fact that many times these projects contribute directly to gentrification of low-income neighborhoods, as punk and anarchist subsocieties are not well-known for their ability to pay high rents. It will ultimately depend on whether they operate as trendy, social gathering spots for punk/anarchists or a place that is respectful of and actively involves the local community.

Undeniably, there is a strong connection between cultural lifestyles and comfort zones and the extent of diversity within any movement. Groups cannot make their racial nature and composition into side issues, an ongoing "process," or working groups. They've got to be right next to the groups' foremost goals. We can keep our subcultural milieu intact, but our organizing efforts have to step well beyond it. At this point at least, it makes more sense to organize according to neighborhoods and values than according to aesthetic tastes and specific ideologies and develop a culture that draws people together. Anarchism will not solve racism without the people affected by it. And we certainly won't be seeing any kind of a revolution made up of subcultural lifestyle ghettos.

Otto Nomous, "Race, Anarchy, and Punk Rock: The Impact of Cultural Boundaries Within the Anarchist Movement," reprinted in *Turning the Tide* 14:2 (Culver City, CA, Summer 2001).

SIX

WE'RE THAT SPIC BAND

You say you call yourself a punk?
Bullshit!
You just a closet fucking nazi
You are bullshit!
You just no understand us
Bullshit
You just fucking fear us!
Bullshit
We're that SPIC BAND!
　　—"We're That Spic Band," Los Crudos

Just how White is the White Riot? Los Crudos provide an answer. The very existence of an influential Latino hardcore band that sang its songs in Spanish ("Spic Band" being an exception) suggests that punk doesn't merely play to disaffected White middle-class youth. In fact, it *never* did. As we've already seen, Black musical and cultural forms, whether embraced or rejected, have been part of punk since its beginnings. But punk's "color" runs deeper than cultural poaching. Before the quintessential "angrywhiteman" Henry Rollins made his name and garnered fame as the front man for Black Flag there was Ron Reyes, the Puerto Rican singer who belted out one of the band's best-known songs, "White Minority." Further, Greg Ginn and Ian MacKaye would've had a hard time "inventing" hardcore in L.A. and D.C. without spending their nights getting psyched on the Bags (with the Chicana vocalist Alice Bag) and the all-black Bad Brains, respectively. Punk's long first wave in Britain included the mixed-race Poly Styrene, who fronted X-Ray Spex, as well as the Clash-inspired and primarily South Asian Alien Kulture. Indeed, punk's nonwhite lineage extends back to its very roots: playing in proximity to

MC5 and the Stooges in mid-1970s Detroit was the Black proto-punk power trio Death.

While punk has been largely, and largely correctly, defined as a White subculture, there is a vibrant history of punks of color that is often sequestered to the shadows. This history includes headlining acts like the Bad Brains, long-running but often overlooked bands like the "NDN" Navajo group Blackfire (the last band Joey Ramone worked with before he died), and also the scores of local bands and legions of nonwhite punks who make up the crowds in clubs and write for fanzines. Documentaries like James Spooner's *Afro-Punk: The "Rock 'N' Roll Nigger" Experience*, Martín Sorrondeguy's *Beyond the Screams: A U.S. Latino Hardcore Punk Documentary*, and Vivek Bald's *Mutiny: Asians Storm British Music* provide visible evidence that punk is not as White as it might sometimes seem.

So why does punk continue to be thought of as a White Riot? Why does punk's self-image so violently resist this long-overdue decentering? Again, Los Crudos give us an answer: we're *that* spic band. Implicit in the song and its title is the assumption that there's only *one* "spic band" on the scene. As a minority, you're always pushed toward invisibility: Ralph Ellison's *Invisible Man*. Or worse: as the anger in the lyrics of the song suggest, punk, which sets itself in opposition to mainstream society, also reproduces its racism. (Los Crudos wrote the song after a "fan" called them a "spic band.") However, each "spic band," whatever the particular ethnicity of their members, not only provides evidence that the riot is not entirely White, but also provides a claim to visibility directed not so much at White punks, but at other punks of color, who employ punk's infrastructure to build communities of their own.

DARRYL A. JENIFER OF BAD BRAINS, "PLAY LIKE A WHITE BOY: HARD DANCING IN THE CITY OF CHOCOLATE"

In 1977 the artists formerly known as Mind Power changed their name to Bad Brains, ditched their jazz fusion for punk rock, and drafted the blueprint for modern hardcore. In this reflection, the Bad Brains bassist, Darryl Jenifer, addresses the question of "black rock" while indulging in some of the Brains' early history (including the origins of the term "mosh," which he describes as coming from a Jamaican-accented "Mash down Babylon!"). While he acknowledges the complex racial situation of Washington, D.C., where

one is constantly confronted with the White power structure both in the form of the halls of government and the predominantly White composition of your average punk rock audience, he ultimately comes down on the side of, to quote his last phrase, "simply music." For Jenifer, the odd history of rock 'n' roll coming from Black artists to White artists and back again (from Chuck Berry to the Pistols to the Brains ... who then inspired the D.C. teenagers Ian MacKaye of Minor Threat and Henry Rollins of Black Flag) illustrates the power of music to "destroy all that is Babylon ... absent of all this black/white nonsense." That punk is its own kind of neutral universal that transcends race is a familiar claim. However, the fact that it is made by a Black punk like Jenifer makes it no less problematic.

Black rock, blacks performing rock: What does this all mean? Well, being a full-fledged, bona fide "brother" born as the fires engulfed the civil-rights-movement-era Chocolate City. Me and my mom lived on Bruce Place—southeast D.C., to be exact, in a cinder-block, four-story apartment just adjacent to the more projectlike, two-leveled barracks that my ma often referred to as "the projects"—living in these smelly-ass buildings wasn't that bad when you knew better, but after a couple afternoons watching the Brady Bunch livin' it up in their suburban split level, I began to fantasize about living the white life. The "good" life.

Reflecting on back in the day when I was just a kid, I vividly recall listening to Aretha Franklin, the Temptations, and Sly Stone on the ever-crackling WOOK—D.C.'s own black-supported radio station. Music somehow always seemed to be in my life. Strangely enough, neither of my parents played or sang, but my father was nevertheless a very talented artist, thrilling my nana and me at least once a week with a hot buttered sketch.

Living in D.C. on certain levels can be very tribal when you're black, because you are constantly surrounded by all that is Babylon: the government, the monuments, even the alleged so-called leaders of the so-called free world reside there. The White House? Ha, that brings to mind, if the White House is white and the black rock is black. Anyway, one day while being baby-sat by my cousin Jack (who was and still is a brilliant guitarist), I fondly remember him saying, "Darryl, you wanna learn to play guitar, man?" Me being the knucklehead that I was, I smart-assly spit back, "I already know how to play." Then Jack broke into "Light My Fire" on some ol' Wes Montgomery–type shit; I was in awe of the sound and magic of the chords. It was amazing how the sound of his then vintage Bradley Les Paul deluxe filled the air, not to mention my soul. This, I believe, was the day I fell in love with music and instruments.

Years would pass, my skills would grow, and through some twisted, bizarre turns of fate, I have become the self-elected "dropper of jewels" on matters of "black rock." I have come to recognize just exactly how this black rock term evolved (peep this): As we all should know by now, rock and roll has its roots in blues—the original swamp-bucket styles that were (unfortunately) rooted in slave field hymns, which I'm sure came across the sea from Africa. Okay, I'm not gonna leave out the styles rooted in bluegrass and hillbilly-type shit, which I'm sure were imported across the seas by the Irish and other assorted Euro types (kids: learn your American history).

But how about the first time Little Richard stomped on his piano in them pointed-toe, hurtin'-ass shoes? Or when Mr. Berry duck-walked across stage while shredding some mangled guitar solo? It seems to me that rock and roll has been on the "take"—raided by bands of British invaders, who wound up biting and pillaging all that is rock, to the degree that now the passionate primal screams of musical abandonment have been deemed, um, "white music." How is this so? Is it because blacks like to dance, like to "get dey groove on," and the abrasive, often awkward rhythms of today's rock ain't cutting it (the rug, that is)? As we all know, dancing is essential to African culture, so trying to Harlem shake to some Hendrix might get kind of crazy (unless you're tripping on acid).

Have you ever noticed the dance that the Anglos created for their own punk rock music, a.k.a. the pogo? Yes, the pogo is a dance rooted in white culture; when early punk forerunners the Buzzcocks would rip into their power-punk-driven joints, the crowd had no choice but to bounce up and down like a gang of deranged lemmings, creating the perfect dance for punk rock: jumping up and fucking down (big up to Eater). Now (y'all still wit me?) who, what, and how did this mosh thing come along? And what does it mean to mosh? Well, I'm going to drop some original, hardcore history on you about the origins of mosh. Check it: Once there was a group of black teens from the Washington, D.C., metro area. These teens were always on the lookout for different and new horizons in life—especially when it came to music. They loved all sorts of sounds—from the smooth psychedelic jazz flavors of Lonnie Liston Smith to the complex musical corridors of Return to Forever. These guys were young, black, and eclectic with their ears wide open.

And don't mistake them for just a band, for they were a clan, always living their daily lives under the premise of PMA (positive mental attitude); concepts derived and practiced by cats like Andrew Carnegie and the Rockefellers during the industrial age. These concepts that promoted the power of positive thinking would go on to fuel the fires of musical exploration and inventiveness in each one of the Brains for years to come/years to cum.

"Go-Go" was the music of their youth, but these cats were just straight tired of it, and found it to be not so much boring, but *normal*. Then one day, thanks to Channel 13, a special on "British rock" came across the airwaves. The uninhibited sounds and fashion of the wild punk rock seemed to be the perfect deflection from their everyday D.C. existence, which in turn inspired the four young brothers who were the band Mind Power to change their musical approach (abandoning jazz fusion) and name (to the undisputed Bad Brains); their poster for their first gig billed them as "the greatest punk rock band in the world." The powers of positive suggestion came in handy when it was time to capture the attention of the sparsely cool alt-rock crowd of the era; these scene players are cats who would go on to become "extreme" show hosts on cable television and green punk rock icons.

Anywaze, one day the Brains were performing at the famed 9:30 Club in D.C. (the venue's load-in area was the same alleyway John Wilkes Booth fled down after poppin' the prez in the back of the head—Honest Abe, that is; it was the same alley dudes would puke in after running offstage). This was during the time when the Brains were discovering that their beloved PMA was really Rastafari: a way of life, not a religion, not a philosophy, but a way of life. With this divine discovery came the ever-colorful, widely imitated, never underrated Jamaicanisms.

Jamaica is the birthplace of Rastafari essentially because her people were the first to find a link between "the gods must be crazyish" coronation of Ethiopia's emperor Haile Selassie and the second coming of Christ; thus we have Rastafari. It has been written in the Christian text that a king will be crowned—king of kings, lord of lords, the conquering lion of the tribe of Judah. Lo and behold, the Jamaican daily gleaner ran this very prophesy on its front page, divinely hailing Haile Selassie's coronation and launching the Rastafarian faith.

Now let me return to clearing up this "mosh" crap. The very second the relationship between PMA and Rastafari was overstood, the Brains would introduce its all-white, black dot-spec'd crowd to the true and living jungle (not that French synth-wank sound of yesteryear, but the original kings music: roots rock reggae). Reggae music opened the eyes and spirits of the

Brains as they spent months to years living the Rastaman vibration. One of the early songs to be dropped on the pre-straight-edgers was "I Love I Jah," a tune penned by H.R., inspired by a clash he had with a gang of our sisters—D.C.'s own—at a Salvation Army. Them sisters didn't understand the rip tear Rasta, and the Brains were not trying to hear about their "neck poppin,'" hence the song's lyrics: "My lovely sister judge me by my cloth / only to learn to her mistake—not everyone's alike." "I Love I Jah" was the first reggae song ever to bring hope and humility to our lives, and we would perform it every show like some special request sent down from the king himself. But I digress.

I remember one particular show at the 9:30 Club in which the four black rebel teens from the District arrived in full Rasta spec khakis and Clark's, with a vast adornment of pins and medals that celebrated the glory of their newly found father H.I.M. (His Imperial Majesty) Haile Selassie. The crowd was used to the Brains' way-out fashion sense (inspired, of course, by the Sex Pistols), but this new rebel Jah soldier look was something to behold. And to top that all off, the Brains would find it hard to slide all of two weeks' worth of dreadlockage into those knit crowns of Rasta recognition (which created a sort of elfish, Papa Smurf sleeping hat appearance; Ian "Minor Threat/Fugazi" McKaye and Henry "S.O.A./ Black Flag" Rollins would come to imitate this steelo).

But back to the mosh. The early D.C. crowd would severely slow down their pre-slam dance routine while jockeying along to our reggae songs; their movements came off sorta like a goofy, satirical interpretation of the ska skank. I remember laughing as I watched my friends skanking in a circle with their knit ski caps flailing, as if to say "we are down with y'all Brains. Do it Jah!"

Then there was the song "Banned in D.C."—at the end of which the Brains would switch the gears of their revolutionary sound, causing the whole house to drastically change their slam tempo. Well, it was at some point in either late 1979 or early 1980 that H.R. of the Bad Brains yelled a Rasta/reggae inspired "mash it—mash down Babylon!" Add a little Jamaican accent to the mix and the untrained ear hears "*mosh* it—mosh down Babylon."

There you have it, from the lion's mouth. It was during this time that the pogo grew into slam dancing and slamming morphed into moshing; the front row begat the pit and the pit begat the mosh pit. So the next time some tribal band tattoo-wearing knucklehead tells you Metallica or some other ass-biting hair band invented mosh, you tell 'em to go look up the Brains.

Black rock? A few quick thoughts: Was Jimi Hendrix black rock, or was he an ill-ass blues guitarist who happened to dig altered states? (Yell at me about that when you see me.) Being a so-called black rock brother, I always had reservations about brothers attempting to appear white when performing rock. It seems to me that unless a brother breaks with the spandex, extensions, and wrestling boots, the wide white world of rock won't really have it. I've come to this conclusion based on the black folk who appear in the media reppin' rock. So I've got to say to the new school of rock and rollers, be yourself, invent and expand the music, expand the *art* form; you don't have to dress like Motley Crüe or play like Hendrix to be rock, all you have to do is rock the fuck out from your heart.

Rock and roll is about the liberation of the spirit, about one's musical soul—and rock has no rules. Actually, the only true rule to rock is really to mean what you are exalting—whether you're kickin' it about girls, cars, parties, whatever. I'm personally a fan of conscious rock—word sound, power (except for when I moonlight wit the White Mandingos. Look out, world); a sound with a purpose, not just loud amps and a party. Then again, all music has its purpose.

Man, the next time someone says "black rock," you should say "white rock," or how 'bout "just rock"? The youth of today should continue to destroy all that is Babylon and thrive for a new way; a way absent of all this black/white nonsense. Just like H.I.M. said to the League of Nations many moons ago: "Until the color of a man's skin is no more significant than the color of his eyes, there will be war." And I say until the sounds that soothe our very souls and nourish our beings are absent from issues of color, there will be wack-ass bands, concepts, and organizations out to taint the blessed magic that is music.

Simply music.

Darryl A. Jenifer, "Play Like a White Boy: Hard Dancing in the City of Chocolate," in *Rip It Up: The Black Experience in Rock 'n' Roll*, ed. Kandia Crazy Horse (New York: Palgrave Macmillan, 2004).

GREG TATE,
"HARDCORE OF DARKNESS: BAD BRAINS"

By 1982, Bad Brains had released their first album and were attracting interest and appraisal outside the punk scene (including that of the Cars' front man, Ric Ocasek, who produced their next

LP). We find one such "outsider" assessment in this piece by the longtime *Village Voice* writer Greg Tate. For Tate, Jenifer's call for "simply music" proves more than a little untenable. Tate's fascination with Bad Brains derives from the fact that they are Black kids playing White kids' music: "just like the white boy—only harder." With his trademark laid-back brilliance, Tate develops his thinking on the Brains in two main directions. First he identifies a conviction that pushes punk rock to parts previously unknown. Bad Brains play punk rock not just to the tune of nihilism, but, as a result of their commitment to Rastafarianism, with a quasi-religious effort to communicate ideas. In other words, with Bad Brains, punk rock looks more and more like it could evolve into a tenable politics—the sort of "committed punk" that ended up being articulated decades later in zines like *Profane Existence* and *HeartattaCk*.[1] Yet Tate also writes that for all their conviction, "their reggae ain't shit," and that in their zeal to be the best, hardest, fastest punk band yet in existence, Bad Brains put themselves at a remove from the Black community. So in the end Tate, too, seems to accept the dubious claim that punk is just a White Riot.

Hardcore? I can't use it. Not even if we talking Sex Pistols. 'Cause inner city blues make me wanna holler open up the window it's too funky in here. And shit like that. Or rhythms to that effect. But listening to the Sex Pistols is like listening to a threat against your child, your wife, your whole way of life: You either take it very seriously or you don't take it at all. Depends on whether or not you're truly black or white I guess. Or so I thought. Because never mind the Sex Pistols, here come something for the ass. Namely, the Bad Brains. Baddest hardcore band in the land, living or dead. So bad bro that even if you ain't got no use for hardcore on the blackhand side, you'll admit the Brains kick too much ass to be denied for the form. Whether you dig it or you don't. Besides which, sis, sooner or later you got to deal with this: The Brains are bloods. That's right, I'm talking a *black* punk band, can y'all get to that? Because in the beginning, the kid couldn't hang—I mean when I was coming up, you could get your ass kicked for calling another brother a *punk*. Besides which, very few black people I know mourned the fact that Sid Vicious fulfilled his early promise. But, then, being of black radical-professional parentage, the kid has always had the luxury of cultural ambivalence coupled with black nationalist consciousness. That's why my party affiliation reads: Greg Tate, Black Bohemian Nationalist. Give me art or give me blood. Preferably on the One, but everything I do ain't got to be funky. So, a black *punk* band? Okay, I'm game.

Dig: Formed in District Heights, Maryland (a black low-moderate-income D.C. suburb), around 1977, the Brains turned to hardcore from fusionoid-funk after getting sick of the AM/FM band and hearing a Dead Boys LP. Or so the story goes. Less apocryphally, virtually anybody who cares will tell you that Chocolate City's hardcore scene begins with the Brains. Which means that to this day defunct punkateers like Minor Threat, Teen Idles, S.O.A., and the Untouchables still owe the Brains some play for being the first to say, "Let's take it to the stage, sucker!" Or however one punks out to that effect.

Now when spike-headed hordes of mild-mannered caucasoids came back from the Brains' first gigs raving that these brothers were ferocious, I took the brouhaha for okey-doke. Easily intimidated, easily titillated white primitivism is how I interpreted that mess. Just some freak-whiteys tripping behind seeing some wild youngbloods tear up white boy's turf. No more, no less. But when my own damn brother—Tinman we call him—came back raving the same shit, I had to stop and say, well, goddamn, these furthermuckers must not be bullshitting. And now that the Brains got this 14-song cassette out on ROIR, it's for the world to know they ain't never been about no bullshitting. *Hardcore?* They take it very seriously. *You say you want hardcore?* I say the Brains'll give you hardcore coming straight up the ass, buddy. I'm talking about like lobotomy by jackhammer, like a whirlpool bath in a cement mixer, like orthodontic surgery by Black & Decker, like making love to a buzzsaw baby. Meaning that coming from a black perspective, jazz it ain't, funk it ain't hardly, and they'll probably never open for Dick Dames or Primps. Even though three white acts they did open for, Butch Tarantulas, Hang All Four, and the Cash, is all knee-deeper into black street ridims than the Brains ever been and ain't that a bitch? Especially considering that sound unseen some y'all could easily mistake these brothers for soulless white devils. Because unlike Hendrix or Funkadelic, the Brains don't transmute their white rock shit into a ridimically sensuous black rock idiom: When I say they play hardcore, I mean they play it just like the white boy—only harder. Which is just what I'd expect some brothers to do, only maybe a little more *soulfully*. Complicating this process in the Brains' case is that while 95 percent of their audience is white, they're also Jah-praising Rastafari who perform hardcore *and* reggae (albeit discretely). Making them two steps removed from the Funk, say, and a half-step forward to Mother Africa by way of Jah thanx to the Dead Boys. Or more specifically the British Rasta/punk connexion.

While only three tunes on the Brains' cassette are Ital—if mediocre—roots musics, Rasta permeates their hardcore via a catchphrase they use liberally: P.M.A., or Positive Mental Attitude. In practice, this means that unlike many of their hardcore contemporaries the Brains don't shit on their audience—which last time they played D.C. was two or three dreads, a whole lotta skinheads, lunatic funkateers, heavy-metal rejects, and some black fashion models—but instead *reason* with them in hardcore dialect, a messianic message of youthful unity, a rebellion, and optimistic nihilism. Which is somewhere not even a "progressive" punk anarchist like Bellow Appalachia of the Daft Kindgarteners has gotten to yet. In *The Meaning of Style*, Dick Hebdige says that the critical difference between Rasta and punk rebellion—one life-embracing, the other death-defying—derives from Rastas holding to the dream of an African utopia and punks seeing themselves as locked into a culture without a future. The Brains' extraordinary synthesis of the two is of course made possible by the fact that they're black. Nobody seems to know how or why they arrived at this synthesis—apparently not even them. But the contradictions such a fusion reconciles are not only profound but very handy: How to be black (not Oreo) punks and how to be punks and look forward to waking up every morning.

And while that may just sound like some seriously schizzy shit to you, sis, I don't think the Brains' mutation into triple-identity Afro-American/Rasta/punk was brought on solely by an identity crisis. It was also encouraged by their convictions. Because when the Brains adopted British punk's formal conventions and "classic" thematic antipathies—toward mindless consumerism, fascistic authority, moral hypocrisy, social rejection—they took to them as if they were religious sacraments. And when the Brains play hardcore it is with a sense of mission and possession more intense than that of any of the sadomasochistic Anglo poseurs who were their models. And yet, though locked into the form by faith and rebellion, the Brains inject it with as much virtuosic ingenuity as manic devotion. Their hardcore juxtaposes ergs of sonic violence against a surprisingly inventive slew of fusion-fast sledge hammer riffs, hysterical stop-time breaks, shrieking declensions, and comic asides (like the surf harmonies and soul arpeggios in "Sailing On" or bassman Darryl's gonzo Segovian intro to "Banned in DC"). And onstage, the band's Scot-screeching frontman H.R. throws down like James Brown gone berserk, with a hyperkinetic repertoire of spins, dives, backflips, splits, and skanks.

Ironically, the Brains' genuine feeling for this music isn't unlike what British rock's first generation felt for the blues. Ironic because the Brains are black; hardcore is white (and no matter how much Hendrix and Berry they ripped, it still ain't nothing but some whiteboy *sounding* shit now) and who would've ever thought that one day some bloods would go to the white boy looking for the spirit? Not to mention the revolution! I mean, if the Brains wasn't so serious I'd think they were trying to revive minstrelsy. Because while they play hardcore as good as any white man ha ha, like it was in fact second nature, their reggae ain't shit. Not only does it have less bottom than their punk, it also sounds half-assed and forced; more an outgrowth, like Dylan's nascent gospel, of sanctimonious intent than of innate religious fervor. Signifying, if nothing else, how far down the river the Brains' missionary work has taken them from the wellspring of most black music's spirituality—namely, the black community. Because where punk's obnoxious energy is an attack on the parent-community, Rasta-influenced reggae draws strength from the ideal of a black community working in harmony. An ethic which isn't foreign to black music not from Yard either: The Funk Mob identified it as one nation under a groove, James Brown called it soul power, and I call it doowop tribalism. The need for which makes even such outré individualists as Jarman-Moye-Favors-Mitchell-Bowie bind into "Great Black Music" ensembles; makes Cecil Taylor work himself into a "Black Code Methodology/Unit Structure"; makes Ornette Coleman improvise a funk-based, democratic system of notation. The need, in other words, for a unified black community respectful of both holy tradition and individual expression. An ideal which leaves me respecting the Brains for their principled punk evangelism and worried for their souls.

Greg Tate, "Hardcore of Darkness: Bad Brains," *Village Voice*, April 27, 1982.

SIMON JONES,
BLACK CULTURE, WHITE YOUTH: THE REGGAE TRADITION FROM JA TO UK

These days, with a few exceptions, most punks wouldn't be caught dead with a Bob Marley record, as reggae as a whole has come to signify a kind of collegiate bohemianism (or worse: frat boys partying on spring break) and is incompatible with punk's serious politics and no-bullshit aesthetic. In this selection Simon Jones revisits the Punky Reggae Party, but his point is not merely that some punks and Rastas saw the potential for solidarity between the musics, but

**rather that reggae as a Black art form actually structured what punk
would become. As Jones argues, it is precisely punks' involvement
with reggae and appropriation of some of its tropes that gave rise
to "the movement's DIY approach to music-making, its directness
of expression and its attempts to close the gaps between artists and
audience." One could even argue that these three elements represent punk distilled to its most basic operating assumptions. If this is
true, then why the subsequent repudiation? Despite claims of "punky
reggae" reciprocal solidarity, another path is open: cooptation and
then *pure disavowal*; or Black culture without Black people. This road,
of course, is well traveled in the history of (White) popular music,
the very culture against which punk is ostensibly in rebellion.**

The fruits of Island [Records]'s campaign with Bob Marley were first sig-
naled by the successful 1975 British tour, during which Marley played to
large, mixed audiences in London, Birmingham and Manchester. However,
it was not until the following year that the mass gravitation towards reggae
by white youth really began. That process must be understood against the
backdrop of an increasingly inert and clichéd rock culture in the mid-
1970s. As one journalist succinctly put it:

> The white kids have lost their heroes; Jagger has become a wealthy socialite,
> Dylan a mellow home-loving man, even Lennon has little to say anymore.
> So along comes this guy with amazing screw top hair, and he's singing about
> "burning and looting" and "brain wash education," loving your brothers and
> smoking your dope. Their dream lives on.[1]

In Marley's music a generation of white rock-fans rediscovered the oppositional values which so much contemporary rock music appeared to have
lost. The marketing campaigns conducted by Island and Virgin caught the
eyes and ears of white fans increasingly dissatisfied with mainstream rock.
For while Marley made compromises in his musical style, by successfully
combining reggae with other international pop forms, his songs maintained a political militancy and a counter-cultural quality which appealed
deeply to young whites. In the universal, egalitarian themes which he
addressed, white youth found meanings with which to make sense of their
own lives and experiences in post-imperial Britain. The live performances
to which Marley regularly attracted large white audiences throughout the
1970s, often witnessed the remarkable spectacle of thousands of young
whites chanting "Rastafari" in unison and singing "stand up for your
rights" along with the band.

The promotion of Marley as "reggae superstar" by sections of the recording industry served to encourage his reception as a "hero figure" amongst thousands of young whites. Indeed, the projection of reggae as a whole as "rebel music" and the imagery by which many other artists were marketed as "protest" figures and counter-cultural heroes, enhanced their political appeal amongst those white youth disillusioned with the complacency and self-indulgence of many rich white rock-stars. It was out of similar concerns and conditions that the punk movement emerged in 1976 as something of a reaction against rock's increasing technological sophistication, the gigantism of its live concerts and widening gap between audience and artists. Punk challenged the musical orthodoxies and aesthetic criteria of rock which had become dependent on recorded rather than live performances and on the primacy of albums over singles.[2] It was no coincidence, therefore, that many punks chose to register their rejection of the "dinosaurs" of rock culture through a strong identification with reggae. Reggae was particularly suited to signify that opposition. It had the political "bite" and the spontaneous, participatory qualities that were absent from so much contemporary pop. Reggae singers, by addressing themselves to the concerns of everyday life, and to themes of poverty, suffering and protest, were felt to have an authenticity that was lacking in rock. In its attempt to "shock" mainstream morality and culture, punk found in reggae and Rastafari a rich source of subversive and forbidding qualities, qualities of "dread," of conviction and rebelliousness.[3]

There were similarities between the discourses of punk ("Crisis," "Anarchy in the UK") and those of Rastafari ("Armaggideon Time," "War inna Babylon"). Punks drew analogies between their position and that of Rastas on the basis that both faced discrimination as a result of their appearance and beliefs. Such connections were immortalised in the Bob Marley song "Punky Reggae Party," which acknowledged the links between the two movements, proclaiming that while "rejected by society" and "treated with impunity," both were "protected by their dignity." Punk and new-wave groups like the Ruts, the Clash and the Slits incorporated reggae and Rasta rhetoric directly into their music. The Clash, for example, played live in front of a large backdrop of the 1976 Notting Hill riots, wearing stage clothes stencilled with phrases like "Dub" and "Heavy Manners." (The riot at Notting Hill was a seminal event in punk culture and had provided the inspiration for the Clash's "White Riot.")

At many punk gigs, reggae was frequently played during the interval between bands, as the only acceptable alternative to punk.[4] Punk artists like the Sex Pistols' John Lydon, moreover, openly declared their enthusiasm for reggae, an enthusiasm which in Lydon's case was pursued further into an experimentation with dub in his subsequent group, Public Image Limited. The Clash also paid homage to the music by recording their own version of popular root songs like Junior Murvin's "Police and Thieves" and Willie Williams's "Armagiddeon Time." (Thousands of copies of the originals, together with cult records like *Two Sevens Clash* and "Uptown Top Ranking," were also bought by punks on import.) Besides the Slits, several other all-female and mixed new-wave bands, such as the Mistakes, the Au Pairs and the Raincoats, also employed reggae rhythms in their music.[5] Some groups began the practice of putting instrumental or dubbed versions of their songs on the B-sides of their singles. This practice, clearly borrowed from the dub mixes on soul and reggae 12-inch records, opened up possibilities for new kinds of experimentation with instruments, sounds and voices, through an appropriation of dub techniques.

Reggae was adopted by the punk movement for its ability to signify, in a particularly graphic way, white youth's own struggles for political and cultural power. In the same way that young white rock-musicians in the 1960s found in the blues a particularly apt means of expressing the collective experience of youth, so the model for punks seeking to recreate rock as a communal music in the mid-to-late 1970s was reggae.[6] Like the organic artists of the reggae tradition, punk musicians insisted on relating musical expression to the mundane concerns and experiences of everyday life. Punk's concern to expose the oppressive nature and boredom of everyday life under capitalism resonated with reggae's antipathy to commodity forms, its emphasis on "roots" and its faithful documentation of topical issues and current events. That resonance was itself partly predicated on white youth's own developing political consciousness of Britain's gathering economic and social crisis, experienced increasingly in the form of unemployment.

It was in punk's challenge to orderly consumption and its deconstruction of reified notions of pleasure that the movement intersected most clearly with reggae's own refusal to distinguish between "leisure" and "politics." Reggae's ability to integrate explicit lyrics with musical intensity, its spontaneity, performance-orientation and commitment to improvisation, all proved profoundly attractive to young whites increasingly alienated by the predictable musical products of mainstream rock and pop culture. Reggae's contribution to punk's demystification of pop ideology and its reaffirmation of young people's creative power was everywhere evident, in the movement's DIY approach to music-making, its directness of expression and its attempts to close the gaps between artists and audience. The fruits of this connection were realised not only in the democratisation of musical performances and band formation, but also in a widening of access to the means of production and distribution themselves. Here the parallels with the reggae industry were striking, in the emergence of an autonomous network of independent labels, distribution organisations and retail outlets. Such connections were made concrete in organisations like Rough Trade, which provided a distribution service and retail outlet for both punk and reggae records.

In these ways the impact of reggae created scope for new kinds of opposition and new ways of being "political" in white youth culture which reflected the continuity of cultural expression with political action in black musical traditions. ...

Simon Jones, from *Black Culture, White Youth: The Reggae Tradition from JA to UK* (London: Macmillan Education, 1998).

SKEETER THOMPSON OF SCREAM, INTERVIEW IN *FLIPSIDE*

Scream is now perhaps better known for being the band Dave Grohl left in order to move to Seattle and join the first stratospherically popular punk rock band: Nirvana. However, for many years prior Scream had been a pillar of the Washington, D.C., punk scene. In this interview, conducted by Donny the Punk for *Flipside*, the bassist Skeeter Thompson is posed a series of questions about the issues raised by being a Black punk kid in a predominantly White scene. The brief exchange is characterized by both sincere affection for, and a deeply hurt suspicion of, the punk scene. "[I]t doesn't really matter if you're black or white," as far as Thompson is concerned, but he then describes the casual racism of his White bandmates, the lip service given anti-racism by the punks, and what it feels like to be racially isolated at shows. Using words like "walls," "blocks," "tension," and "pressure," he reveals something about the seeming impenetrability of punk rock's whiteness. Yet not completely impenetrable, as Thompson also describes the "special kind of relationship" he feels with the other Black punks who come to shows—a sentiment which, we'll see later in Afro-Punk, will turn into a call for the building up of a Black punk community.

FLIPSIDE: Skeeter, how does being black affect your relationship to the scene?

SKEETER THOMPSON: It's different. You notice it every time you walk into a town. There's always some sort of hesitation. I feel a certain pressure, there's a block there, a wall.

FLIPSIDE: I've noticed that the few blacks that come to the shows stand near and watch you. Do you feel a special kind of relationship with the blacks that come to the shows?

THOMPSON: Of course I do. In a club, at a show there's gonna be maybe 3 or 4 blacks. A lot of my friends are white or other minorities.

FLIPSIDE: Why do you think so few blacks come to the shows?

THOMPSON: Because our society teaches you to be tense about certain things, so when you go into a room that's all white, even myself, you feel a certain hesitation like you're holding back, you gotta restrain something, but just have to break through all that.

But it doesn't really matter if you're black or white.

FLIPSIDE: What's it like being in an integrated band?

THOMPSON: No different from being in a segregated band, I guess. It feels like I've known these guys all my life. The issue does come up. When they think I'm pressing a fact, yeah, I'm "being black," ya know. Sometimes they let me know maybe I'm using that too much. In a sense maybe I'm not. I have feelings and they have feelings and we understand each other's feelings. When I look out, I can't see my color, looking straight ahead: I can only see the other people, and the way they act towards me.

FLIPSIDE: Punk rock is notable among white music for having a large number of songs which directly refer to racism, coming from an all white band. How do you feel when you hear songs like "Anti-Klan" or Dee Dee Ramone singing about "discrimination against the blacks"?

THOMPSON: It really makes me wonder if they really mean it sincerely. I've never really talked to those people one-on-one. I've talked to MDC and I give them a lot of respect because they really stick to the issues. I've talked to Kevin Seconds [of 7 Seconds] and I asked him about what was the racial scene out there, 'cause I'm always interested about that. When you're in high school, it's stupid, it's an integrated system, but when they go eat lunch, they go eat in their own separate corners.

FLIPSIDE: Has Scream played to any mostly black audiences?

THOMPSON: Yeah, we played in DC at the Armory with Chuck Brown and the Soul Searchers, Rare Essence, Experience Unlimited and Outrage.

FLIPSIDE: What kind of reaction do you get at a show like that?

THOMPSON: At first they were sitting down, then they moved up and they started heckling us and we started heckling them back. They'd say stuff like, "What the fuck you think you're doing? Get hip!"

FLIPSIDE: That's like a classic punk dialog ...

THOMPSON: Most interviews are: "How long have you guys been together?" This is the only deep interview we ever had. I've changed from the person I was 2 years ago. I'm not afraid to speak my mind anymore. ...

Donny the Punk, from "Interview: Scream," *Flipside* no. 47 (Los Angeles, 1985).

MICHELLE HABELL-PALLÁN,
"¿SOY PUNKERA, Y QUÉ?"

In this piece, the scholar Michelle Habell-Pallan examines the complex status of Chicanas and Chicanos in late-'70s L.A. punk. The Chicana singer Alicia Armendariz Velasquez of the Bags and her contemporary Teresa Covarrubias of the Brat, like their fellow White punks, were attracted to punk rock for the open space for expression that the scene provided. But they also found in punk a way of articulating their own Chicana identity away from the repressive sexual and gender tropes of the traditional Latin family. Additionally, Habell-Pallán situates this attraction in the context of the more direct appeal of punk's DIY ethic and stripped-down aesthetic to Chicana/o subcultures, producing an interesting discussion of exactly where the roots of punk are located. On a final note, the author's interpretation of X's "Los Angeles" is probably the one the band itself would hope for, that is: a fictional account of bigotry through the eyes of a bigot. But, at the same time, Habell-Pallán points up the uncomfortable pleasure experienced by a band of White punk kids when vocally slagging "every nigger and Jew, every Mexican who gave her a lot of shit, every homosexual, and the idle rich." For all its racial complications, however, these Chicana punks made punk work for themselves because, as Habell-Pallán says, it was the only subversive game in town.

Punk allowed people to just get up there, and even if you were not feeling confident—which was not a problem I ever had—but I think for women

who felt like they weren't sure of themselves, it was very easy to get up and do it anyway, because you weren't being judged on how well you played.
—Alicia Armendariz Velasquez, interview with author

Working-class Chicanas such as Alicia Armendariz Velasquez, Teresa Covarrubias, and Angela Vogel shaped independent, noncommercial music communities and subcultures in Los Angeles and responded to the shrinking of the public sphere and the increased privatization of daily life in contemporary U.S. culture through their musical practices. Although these women helped shape the sounds and concerns of the local independent music community, with a few notable exceptions almost no scholarly documentation of their participation exists. Perhaps these women do not register in nonacademic accounts because of the way they disrupt fixed, one-dimensional notions of identity.[1] In other words, Chicanas are not punk; women are not true musicians. Hence, fixed notions of Chicana identity framed by the dominant culture do not allow for recognition of these women in discussions of subcultural musical practices or in discussions focused on countering the shrinking of the public sphere.[2]

These women appropriated, reshaped, and critiqued the imagery from unexpected sources, such as the British youth musical subculture, to invent local cultural practices that allowed them to express their realities in a public context. Chicanas as producers transformed punk and New Wave aesthetics into sites of possibility for transnational conversations concerning violence against women and the effects of the growing corporitization of public space. Given that most youth musical practices and communities are understood to be male-dominated arenas, and rarely as Latino social spaces, these subcultures may seem an unlikely space for the development of a transnational conversation. Yet, it was a site of possibility for the young Chicanas who engaged these subcultures.

As transformative as this music was, however, it was certainly not without some of its own contradictions. The scholar José E. Muñoz illustrates this point in his meditation on some of the lyrics of X, one of the most critically acclaimed punk bands to come out of L.A. in the 1980s. With no small amount of unease, Muñoz relates that the title track of X's album *Los Angeles* "narrates the story of a white female protagonist who had to leave Los Angeles because she had started to hate 'every nigger and Jew, every Mexican who gave her a lot of shit, every homosexual, and the idle rich.'"[3] Although, as a teenager, Muñoz considered X his favorite band, the lyrics like those cited leave him with "a disturbed feeling" today. I, too, remember cringing at those lyrics as a teenager, as I do now, wondering why my favorite band had to write such horrendous words, especially since, at the time, I thought, mistakenly, that the lead singer, Exene, was Mexican American. As a high school student, however, I found it less difficult to digest those lyrics as I existed year after year in a mostly white, conservative, working- to middle-class public school, in which I experienced no small amount of anti-Mexican hostility, despite that fact that I had been born in California. X was my favorite band, and I truly believed that the lead singer of the band was Mexican American because her name was Exene Cervenka (which to my English-dominant ears sounded Spanish) and because she frequently made poetic allusions to Catholic iconography. In addition, to my young eyes, she looked like the Chicanas at the dance clubs in Hollywood, Whittier, and Long Beach that my friends and I frequented. Like them, Exene had dark hair and wore thrift-store chic and dramatic makeup. At the time I made sense of the song "Los Angeles" by imagining it was about one of my bigoted class-mates. Nonetheless, this interpretation did not take away the sting I felt every time I heard the lyrics. Yet, I was able to hear beyond the sting and maintain my identification with punk primarily because, for me, as it did for Muñoz, the music functioned as "the avant-garde that I knew; it was the only cultural critique of normative aesthetics available to me."[4]

Years later, I was to find that my misrecognition of Exene as Chicana was not that off base. She had hand-printed the lyrics for the liner notes for the Brat's extended-play record, or EP, *Attitudes*. X had performed at Self-Help Graphics in East L.A.[5] Photos had been published of Exene hanging outside the Vex, in East Los Angeles.[6] The band members were friends with Los Lobos, the famed East L.A. group. One could argue that Exene's fashion style had been inspired by the young women in East L.A., and vice versa. I also discovered that Exene was not Mexican Ameri-can. Exene had shortened her last name from Cervenkova, a much more Slavic-sounding name. Exene has never denied her connection to East L.A., but it has yet to be fully explored. The following section describes the practices of the young Chicanas who, in part, inspired Exene. ...

In the Bag

Alicia Armendariz Valasquez (who used the stage name Alice Bag, of the Bags) is the daughter of Mexican immigrants. Growing up in East Los Angeles, she came of age in the late 1970s and "began singing profes-sionally at the age of eight."[7] She, like Teresa Covarrubias, described her engagement with punk as a way out of an environment that she found too judgmental in terms of ethnicity and sexuality. She found no recourse in the mythic traditional Mexican family to discuss the domestic violence she witnessed as a child. Her embrace of punk culture occurred in a "period when Chicanas were questioning their traditional roles, increasing their participation within the political arena, and inscribing a budding Chicana feminist discourse and practice."[8] Although Armendariz Valasquez's path diverged from that of most Chicanas of the day, so profound was her influence on the L.A. punk scene that she was a featured artist in the recent photo exhibition and catalog *Forming: The Early Days of L.A. Punk.* Because the Bags "provided a blueprint for the hardcore sound popularized by Black Flag and other punk bands," the punk music chronicler David Jones considers Armendariz Valasquez the inventor of the West Coast hard-core punk sound.[9]

In 1978, Armendariz Velasquez was featured in a *Los Angeles Times* article, "Female Rockers—A New Breed."[10] Armendariz Velasquez, then known as "Alice Bag," along with Diane Chai, of the Alleycats, and Exene, of X, were considered the most groundbreaking women on the punk scene because their performances demolished narrow models of "women in rock": "the wronged blues belter à la Janis Joplin or the coy sex kitten typified by Linda Ronstadt. In tune with a new wave's spirit of change, women punkers are rejecting the confining stereotypes and demanding more."[11] Although no explicit mention of Alice's ethnicity was made, McKenna describes her with code words reserved for ethnic others: "Alice, an exotic beauty whose frenzied vocal seizures generate such chaos that the Bags has earned a reputation for closing clubs."[12] In retrospect, we note that McKenna, perhaps unknowingly, cites two Chicanas, Ronstadt and Armendariz Velasquez, as wildly divergent models of "women in rock."

Often accused of being too aggressive on stage, Armendariz Velasquez performed in pink minidresses and severe makeup. In a clip from Penelope Spheeris's 1981 documentary film, *The Decline of Western Civilization,* we witness Armendariz Velasquez exploding onto the stage and wrestling the boys who jump onstage to join her during the show. The pink of Armendariz Velasquez's dress clashed with her performance and produced a complex statement about women's realities. Armendariz Velasquez did not reject femininity per se but rejected the equation of femininity with victimization and passivity. In fact, McKenna states, "women punkers like Alice Bag and Exene project an oddly incongruous sexuality. While not exactly neuter, their shock-level redifinition of the female role will take a while to be assimilated culturally."[13] Yet, Armendariz Velasquez's assertion that "female performers have always tended to be more reserved but all that is changing" foresaw and provided models for performers like Court- ney Love, often noted, if not entirely correctly, for what has been called her unprecedented feminine rock aesthetic.[14]

Armendariz Velasquez also described the appeal of punk to young women in practical terms. She explains that while she detested the vio- lence that surrounded her at home and public school, she could not help but internalize it. As lead singer of the Bags, she found an outlet: "all the violence that I'd stuffed down inside of me for years came screaming out … all the anger I felt towards people who had treated me like an idiot as a young girl because I was the daughter of Mexican parents and spoke broken English, all the times I'd been picked on by peers because I was overweight and wore glasses, all the impotent rage that I had towards my father for beating my mother just exploded."[15] One of the best preserved and most accessible documents of Armendariz Velasquez's fearless per- formance as Alice Bag is the Bags' song "We Don't Need the English," on the 1979 *Yes L.A.* recording.[16] With characteristic sardonic humor, Alice and the band loudly refute the notion that the only authentic punk scene was found in Great Britain. "We don't need the English, telling us what we should be / We don't need the English, with their boring songs of anarchy, telling us what to wear." The song opens by rejecting "the English, with their boring songs of anarchy," a direct reference to "Anarchy in the U.K.," by the infamous punk band the Sex Pistols. The song concludes by metaphorically barring the English from the "Can- terbury," an infamous run-down apartment complex in Hollywood that served as a breeding ground for Hollywood punks.[17] Though Armendariz Velasquez did not write the song, the lyrics hold a different valence today when we consider that Armendariz Velasquez was bilingual in a city that often denigrated Spanish-speaking ethnic minorities and that she has taught bilingual education for the Los Angeles Unified Public School District.

Although Armendariz Velasquez emerged as a performer in the 1970s Hollywood punk scene (unlike Covarrubias, who grew out of the East Los Angeles punk scene), she came to Chicana consciousness in the early 1990s. After performing as a Lovely El Vette for El Vez and the Memphis Mariachis, forming Cholita with Vaginal Davis, and performing as well as other L.A.-based bands, she fashioned a folk group, Las Tres, with Teresa Covarrubias and Angela Vogel, a former member of the East Los Angeles band the Odd Squad.[18] When Vogel left the band, the two remaining members formed the duo Goddess 13. In 2002, she formed Stay at Home Bomb with another East L.A. feminist rocker, Lysa Flores.[19]

East Los Angeles's the Brat

What fascinated Teresa Covarrubias, who was born to a working-class Mexican American family, about punk musical subculture was its Do-It-Yourself attitude, what she calls the "non-pretentiousness of it."[20]

Covarrubias discovered punk in the mid-1970s, when her older sister went on a backpack trip through Europe and began sending her punk fanzines from Germany and England. She recalls,

> What attracted me to punk was the notion that "Gee, I could do that." 'Zines had all these paste-up things and all these crazy little articles, and these girl bands and guy bands, and it just seemed like so open. It didn't seem like ... you had to play really well. It seemed like a "from your gut" type thing, and I just fell right into it. You know, it was really raw, and it was in your face, and I really liked it, it kind of got me going.[21]

Inspired by this low-tech sensibility, one that she says "emerged" from the gut and seemed open to young men and women, she decided to form a New Wave band with Rudy Medina, called the Brat. The Brat is synonymous with East L.A. punk. In contrast to Armendariz Velasquez's family, which was fully supportive of her musical lifestyle, Covarrubias's family discouraged her. Although she found a place in the band to critique gender norms with song titles like "Misogyny," she found that sexism did exist in the scene, especially among her own bandmates. At times they dismissed her creative opinions because she did not play an instrument. During those times, she explains,

> Because I couldn't get what I wanted, I started acting out in really self-destructive ways ... because I just felt like I had no say ... even now, women don't have a lot of faith in themselves, especially if you are going outside of the norm, when you're treading new ground. Everybody's always telling you what you can't do ... people look at you and you're brown and you're a woman, and they think, "she can't do that." It's like they immediately assume less.[22]

Fortunately, visual documentation exists of Covarrubias's performances of her song "Misogyny." In 1992, the public television program *Life and Times* dedicated an entire segment, "Chicanas in Tune," to Covarrubias and Armendariz Velasquez.[23] "Misogyny" was originally written while Covarrubias was in the Brat. The "Chicanas in Tune" clip captures Covarrubias's 1980 punk/New Wave mode and documents her performance as she swings to the beat in a shimmering early-1960s-style dress. Her voice is forced to compete with the guitar, but she holds the attention of her enthusiastic audience. The lyrics critique the position of women within patriarchal culture:

> A woman is a precious thing / Far beyond a wedding ring / You have kept her under your thumb / Creating the light-haired and dumb / You don't love her / You abuse her / You confuse her / You just use her / A woman's mind is a priceless gift / You talk to her as if it's stripped / Women's beauty is in her mind / All you see is the sexual kind / You don't love her ... / Blatant is misogyny / Scattered in our history / You will find it hard to kill / The strength from within a woman's will / You don't love her ...

The narrator breaks down the elements of misogyny by exposing their practice in everyday life in the following way: "you don't love her, you abuse her, you confuse her, you just use her." She critiques the strictures of matrimony that reduce women to property, to be possessed much like a wedding ring. And the narrator exhorts the listener to understand that a woman's strength lies in her mind and will and that it is a waste to value women *only* for their sexuality. Moreover, the power of the narrator's critique lies in her acknowledgement of the blatancy and frequency of women's abuse. Violence against women is so prevalent that its practices can be tracked throughout history and across geography, though its effects often go unacknowledged.

Though the Brat released a successful EP (extended-play recording), *Attitudes*, in 1980, they eventually broke up and morphed into Act of Faith, which released a self-titled compact disk, in 1991, and then broke up again. Covarrubias has continued to write and perform, in addition to continuing her duties as an elementary school teacher in the Los Angeles Unified School District.

Mex Goddesses

Armendariz Velasquez was part of a group of young singers who in the 1970s "blanch[ed] at being described as women's libbers—a tame, middle-aged scene by their standards [but] ... could accurately be described as nihilistic feminists."[24] Meanwhile, at Hollywood punk shows in the 1980s,

Covarrubias encountered a "punk elite" that was "really particular about what you looked like. If you didn't look right, they could be rude. There were a couple of times that they would tell me, 'you don't belong here,'"[25] In the early 1990s, however, with Angela Vogel, first as two-thirds of Las Tres and later as Goddess 13, she forged a sound that disrupted the exclusivity of white feminism and anti-Mexican punk. This sound, Armendariz Velasquez declares, "speaks to women of color about their experiences as women."[26] "Happy Accident," by Armendariz Velasquez, typifies the ways the group highlighted violence against women in their performance. The song's narrative centers on a battered woman's response to her partner's violent abuse:

> Please believe me / I didn't mean it / All I saw was / the look in his eye / and I feared for my life / once again.
>
> I didn't know / it was coming / all I know / is he done it before / sent me crashing to the floor / but no more.
>
> Oh and / I can't say that / Oh no, no / I regret it / 'cause after all I had tried to leave every other way / And if I had the chance / to do it all again / I don't think it / would have a different end / I'm quite happy with this accident.
>
> I didn't know / it was loaded / Yes, I knew where he kept all his guns / and I just grabbed the one / that was closest / So, if you ask / why I'm smiling / You may think / that a prison cell's tough / but I'm much better off / than before.
>
> Oh and / I can't say that / Oh no, no / I regret it / 'cause after all it be him or me / you'd be talking to.

Though the narrative is bleak, the mid-tempo beat and clave accent create a "Chicana trova sound."[27] The contrast between the rhythmic sound of the music and the lyrics creates a punk-like disruption. The limited options the woman possesses in response to the domestic violence that has "sent [her] crashing to the floor" end up freeing her from one situation but contain her in another. She finds that a "prison cell's tough / but I'm much better off than before." This tragic all-too-real scenario speaks to the alarming rate of incarceration among women of color and to the quadruple bind of race, color, caste, and gender.[28]

Before Las Tres was reconstituted as Goddess 13 after Vogel left, the trio recorded a live performance at the Los Angeles Theater Center in 1993 and had recorded enough material to shop a compact disk to labels. However, the recording never saw the light of day because the two remaining women could not afford to buy the master tapes from the recording engineer. The band had been in hiatus since the mid-1990s but reunited for El Vez's 2002 Quinceañera Show and for the Eastside Review, a reunion of East Los Angeles boogie and rock 'n' roll bands from the 1940s on, at Los Angeles Japanese American Cultural Center, in October 2002.

Vexed

Because "the Vex became a center for artistic activity of all kinds," punk musicians began to interact with visual and performance artists.[29] Teresa Covarrubias remembers that the Brat "did a show there with local artists. ... It was through the Vex that I realized there were a lot of artists and poets in East L.A."[30] This must have been exciting for Covarrubias, considering that she was "an aspiring poet before she formed the Brat."[31] Equally important for young Chicanas gathering at Vex, whatever their artistic medium, themes of sexuality, antiwar protests, and antiracism ran throughout the narratives. In fact, Reyes and Waldman claim that bands like the Brat "produced enough original, exciting material to generate interest in the band throughout the LA punk underground. It was not long before punk fans from the West Side [of Los Angeles], maybe some of those who sneered at Teresa when she traveled to their part of town, came to see the Brat perform at the Vex."[32]

It can be argued that Chicana/o youth, marginalized by the West Side rock scene, enticed West Side youth, who otherwise refused to see Chicano culture as cosmopolitan or as worthy of their interest, and succeeded in creating integrated places in the most unexpected ways. As Sean Carrillo claims, "the punk scene had done the impossible. It accomplished what few cultural movements before had been able to do: it attracted all people from all over town to see Latino bands, and it brought musicians from all over the city to ... deep in the heart of East L.A."[33]

Covarrubias and Armendariz Velasquez found punk to be an alternative oppositional movement to the Chicano movement, from which they felt excluded because of their position on gender issues, but they also felt alienated from white, middle-aged feminism. For these Chicanas from East L.A., punk subculture was not the end of their identity formation, but it was a path to a new way of being in the world and a way to expose the world to their reality.

Michelle Habell-Pallán, from "'¿Soy Punkera, Y Qué?' Sexuality, Trans-locality, and Punk in Los Angeles and Beyond," *Loca Motion: The Travels of Chicana and Latina Popular Culture* (New York: New York University Press, 2005).

ALIEN KULTURE,
INTERVIEW WITH THE BBC

As in society at large, when the issue of race and racism is discussed in punk rock, it is usually in, quite literally, black and white terms. This was especially true of late-1970s Britain, where, as we saw, white punks appropriated elements of Rasta culture and aesthetics in an attempt at artistic solidarity, taking the Notting Hill resistance as their political starting point. What this dialectic overlooks, however, and what its political organizations can allow to fall through the cracks, is the emerging population of Asian immigrant youths coming up in the same era—indeed, for all Rock Against Racism's attempts to get "Black and White" to "Unite and Fight," the National Front was busy forming, pointedly, its own Anti-*Paki* League, and Thatcher was predicting the dissolution of British culture at immigrant hands. As punks of color, how do you disrupt this binary and fight back? If you're the three second-generation Pakistani immigrants: Ausaf Abbas, Azhar Rana, Pervez Bilgrami, and, as they called him, "token white man" Huw Jones of the early-1980s British punk band Alien Kulture, you write ripping Clash-inspired songs chronicling your own experience of the in-between. While they released only one single and played around thirty shows in their short, two-year existence, Alien Kulture, in this profile from the 1980 BBC program *Art Asia,* which intersperses the band's songs with interviews with its members, powerfully illustrates that punk identity could provide a way of directly living a different version of one's race and ethnicity *through* punk, the dominant racist culture, contesting one's own cultural inheritance, and the intransigence of rebellious youth culture itself.

Caught in a culture crossover
1-2-3-4
We're taught how to pray five times a day
But that's not what we're about
We just want to live out our lives
Run and dance and sing and shout
Trapped in a void and
We don't know just which way to turn
This way and that way
But we're still stopped from having fun
First generation, illegal immigrants
Second generation juvenile delinquents
Torn between two cultures
Caught in a culture crossover.

HUW JONES: We're called Alien Kulture after Margaret Thatcher made
a speech about immigration, in which she said that British people were
in danger of being swamped by an alien culture. As we considered ourselves part of the alien culture, we thought it was the best way, to call
ourselves Alien Kulture.

ZAF ABBAS: I feel that everyone who stands for something that's different from what the ruling elite like the Tories—and including the
Labour Party, who are just as bad sometimes—who don't fit in with
their views, their way of thinking, their culture, their morals, then you
are alien. As far as that goes, we don't fit in with the normal bourgeois
culture, we are "alien culture."

AZHAR RANA: You're not only that, but we're alien in a sense that we're
caught up in two cultures—as one of our songs says—and that is sort
of a new thing, not known before. I mean, we're alien in that sense as
well. To have, on the one half, been influenced by the English culture,
and on the other half by the Asian culture, and, hence, a new sort of
situation arises, a new sort of culture, which doesn't exactly fit in with
both.

You want something to belong to
You want something to hold on to
You go to college, you read your books
Buy your white pegs and structureless jackets
At weekends you're on maximum pose
Down at the Disco
Asian Youth
Oh, where you been?

> Asian Youth
> You wanna be seen
> Asian Youth
> You dunno who to turn to
> Oh, Asian Youth

JONES: All we can hope to achieve, as Alien Kulture, is to echo the fears, the hopes, the aspirations of a lot of kids both Asian and white, and hope they can find something to identify with, something to show that someone cares about them and thinks the way they do.

PERVEZ BILGRAMI: What I hope I achieve and what we achieve is to show people that there is an Asian youth in this country. We're here, we've got something to say, and we're here to stay. Basically that is it. That is our message, as far as the Asian theme goes.

ABBAS: ... Asian youth have really taken a backseat in British life. You see a lot about white youth and what they're doing, and also a lot of what black youth are doing, and black youth are obviously very alienated from this society, as sort of shown by things like St. Paul's riots down in Bristol and by things that have happened in Brixton and Notting Hill. Asian youth really haven't figured in anything, they just seem to be non-existent, and the new feeling, the growing feeling is that Asian youth are coming out, shown by things like the Southall youth movement, and the Bradford youth movement, and very recently the Newham youth movement, things like that with Asians coming out and saying what they believe, and they're saying that this is our country, and that we're going to be staying here whether other people like it or not. ...

> Your elders want to control you
> Your elders want to protect you
> They're using their ancient values
> Whilst living in the modern world
> You kids end up wondering just who the hell you are
> Asian Youth

BILGRAMI: You've got people like the National Front, or the British Movement now, who do feel like if they go 'round the streets beating people up, killing people in the East End ... I mean, that bloke who got stabbed in the East End a couple weeks ago, things like that, we're standing up against that: against the National Front, against Thatcher, against people like that. And it's the first time that anyone's done it.

One of the first song's we wrote was "White youth got rock, black youth got reggae, Asian youth got nothing." Now they've got us.

> You come from different countries
> You belong to different religions
> You hate each other, you swear and fight
> But you don't realise that you're the same
> Nothing's achieved by being divided
> Why can't we be united?
> Asian Youth
> Oh, where you been?
> Asian Youth
> You wanna be seen
> Asian Youth
> You dunno know who to turn to
> Oh, Asian Youth
> Asian Youth
> Oh, where you been?
> Asian Youth
> You wanna be seen
> Asian Youth
> You dunno know who to turn to
> Oh, Asian Yeeeeewth!

ABBAS: We're one of the few bands that gets lots of Asian people coming to see us, and almost at the same time a lot of punks and black people as well, skinheads, the whole lot, and they have a good time, and it really is a lot of different people coming together, not just one specific type.

JONES: Any mix of cultures can only be good for the community as a whole. I've always been interested in and followed black culture, and I'm learning about Asian culture, and hopefully these three are learning about white culture. And it can only do good.

BILGRAMI: When we played Birmingham about three months ago, a skinhead came up to one of us and said, "I didn't like Pakis before, but now after I've seen you I think you're the same as us, that you're pretty much the same as us, doing the same things." And that's what we've got to get across: that we're really not any different except for our colour. …

> Start off with clear minds which always end up cluttered
> Parents say what we do and all our dreams

They end up being shattered
Pressure all around us
Without having to fight our elders
All we need is understanding to be happy and content
First generation, illegal immigrants
Second generation juvenile delinquents
Torn between two cultures
Caught in a culture crossover.

"Alien Kulture," *Art Asia*, BBC Birmingham, September 29, 1980.

MICHAEL MUHAMMAD KNIGHT, "MUHAMMAD WAS A PUNK ROCKER"

SIDDHARTHA MITTER, "TAQWACORE: SALAT, ANGST, AND ROCK & ROLL"

Taqwacore began as fiction. In 2003 a young White writer named Michael Muhammad Knight, who had converted to Islam then grew disenchanted with its orthodoxies, self-published *The Taqwacores*, a novel about a group of Muslim punks living together in a group house in Buffalo, New York. The book opens with the poem "Muhammad Was a Punk Rocker." *The Taqwacores* quickly spread underground among young Muslim punks and other misfits caught between the racism and bigotry of the communities in which they now lived and the conservatism of the religion and culture in which they were raised. One of the book's fans was Kourosh Poursalehi, an alienated sixteen-year-old Sufi punk from San Antonio, Texas, who put Knight's poem to music and made Taqwacore music a reality. Drawing upon familiar punk networks and the DIY ethos, Taqwacore has flourished since then, spawning numerous bands, tours, and even two films. Taqwacore punk provides an identity that in equal parts draws from and rebels against White culture and Muslim tradition, in the process expanding punk's very stylistic and aesthetic vocabulary. As the journalist Siddhartha Mitter writes: "If there was any music capacious enough for all of this, it had to be punk—with its embrace of contradiction and its zest for the absurd, the historic and cultural references making energy out of collision like bodies in the mosh pit."

Muhammad Was a Punk Rocker

I see Muhammad
down at the corner store
rocking on Galaga
getting the high score
When he delivers sermons
the kids think he's a bore
but when he smashes idols
everyone cheers for more

Muhammad was a punk rocker
he tore everything down
Muhammad was a punk rocker
and he rocked that town

All the people in Mecca
knew Muhammad's name
They knew him by his fucked-up hair
and dangling wallet chain
They knew him by his spikes
and said he was insane
But Ali knew better
Uncle wouldn't play their game

Muhammad was a punk rocker
you know he tore shit up
Muhammad was a punk rocker
Rancid sticker on his pickup truck

When he was in a dumpster by himself
Allah told him crazy things
for Muhammad to share with all of us
on his six holy strings

Taqwacore: Salat, Angst, and Rock & Roll

On a warm evening last August in Oakland, California, a group of young men—relaxed, casually dressed, not all of them freshly showered—stand barefoot on flattened cardboard boxes in the yard behind a scruffy bar on Telegraph Avenue. They figure out which way is east: Mecca is out there, somewhere across the alley and over the hills. Nearby, friends and early arrivals for the evening's show mill about. Someone has fired up a grill for burgers and dogs. Bottles of Corona circulate. Those who drink, drink; those who don't, abstain. At the proper moment, one of the worshippers steps forward and begins the ritual of maghrib, the evening prayer. "Allahu Akbar ..." drifts out on the California breeze.

The show begins. The Kominas headline. Through their own efforts and a raft of curious media coverage, the Pakistani- and Indian-American foursome has become the flagship band for Taqwacore—the genre, or style, or movement, or *something*, that may or may not be describable as "Muslim punk" (we'll get to that in a bit). The Kominas have driven cross-country from Boston, stopping to perform in various bars, basements, and community centers along the way. A series of opening acts precede them, including their tour-mates Sarmust and Propaganda Anonymous. Sarmust is the stage name of the Pakistani-American Omar Waqar, who plays rock inspired by Sufi poetry. Prop Anon is a white kid from New York who hangs out with the Five Percenters, the esoteric Harlem-based movement whose members call each other Allah or God, because the divine is within each of us. He raps about urban politics, broken communities and empty condos. Some local Bay Area acts play too. One is Micropixie, a tiny South Asian woman whose fragile electronic ballads have nothing to do with Islam or politics. And there's something called the Mujahideen Bernstein Affair, a pierced and tattooed duo who play a kind of modified Indian classical music on odd homemade instruments; during their set, the audience sits, reverential, on the sticky floor.

The Kominas begin; the energy spikes, and a mosh pit forms. The crowd knows the hits: "Suicide Bomb the Gap," which is about, well, suicide-bombing the Gap; "I Need a Handjob," which in addition to the title subject evokes the martyrdom of Imam Hussein at Karbala; "Rumi was a Homo (But Wahhaj Is a Fag)," which eviscerates a conservative Brooklyn imam for his homophobic statements; and of course the rousing "Sharia Law in the U.S.A.," with its Sex Pistol echoes. Silliness ensues. The singer/bassist Basim Usmani, hair ablaze in a glorious purple mohawk, jumps into the crowd and ends up on the floor, under a pile of revelers. People take off their shoes and toss them at the musicians, in the manner of the Iraqi reporter who took a shot at George W. Bush. At some point a few Oakland cops turn up at the bar, supposedly on a routine visit to check liquor licenses. "That never happens," a local comments, suggesting it's the Muslim weirdos who have warranted the visit. A chant greets the cops, using the religious term for unclean: "Pigs are haram! Pigs are haram!" It was pioneered the time the Kominas and friends tried to perform at an open-mic session at the Islamic Society of North America conference, prompting shocked organizers to get security to clear the stage. The Oakland cops aren't so bothered. They scope the scene, find it harmless, then leave.

Amid the raucous party, a blue-eyed white guy in an Alternative Tentacles T-shirt and red Harvard baseball cap is keeping the mosh pit busy and getting extra love from the band. He is Michael Muhammad Knight, cult author of six books including the 2004 novel *The Taqwacores*, which arguably launched this scene and certainly named it. This Oakland show is doubling as Knight's bachelor party; he's getting married the next day to his Indian-American fiancée, and everyone is here to celebrate. Knight and the Kominas are veterans of the original Taqwa Tour, when a bunch of Muslim-American misfits, including key members of most of the bands on the Taqwacore scene, roamed the land in an old school bus, painted green for Islam, that Knight purchased with his books' slender earnings. Knight's novel had imagined a scene of Muslim punk rockers torn between devotion and blasphemous mayhem, living in a group house in depressed Buffalo, N.Y. As the spiral-bound, self-distributed book circulated, actual young Muslim Americans recognized themselves in Knight's characters, and groups like the Kominas and the Chicago-based crust-punk band Al-Thawra surfaced as their real-life embodiments.

In Oakland, the collision of art and life continues: not only are bands like the ones in Knight's novel performing on stage, but in the crowd are actors from the upcoming feature film adaptation. It's a great night for Taqwacore; everything has come full circle.

The next day is the wedding, an Indian-Muslim affair with several hundred guests in a strip-mall function hall in immigrant-heavy Fremont. To the rhythm of drums, the punks and actors ceremonially escort Knight, now bedecked in a lavish turban, into the room, then dissolve in crowd of Desi uncles and aunties. Enthroned on stage with his gorgeous bride, Knight is the lovely new son-in-law, the handsome Western convert now welcomed into family and community. At the proper time, the Kominas guitarist Shahjehan Khan—now clad in a swank sherwani—gives the azaan, the call to prayer. After the meal, Kominas and other male guests engage in lively ceremonial back-and-forth singing with some of the women, before bride and groom disappear into the night. "Just your standard Desi wedding," one guest remarks later, "except most of the groom's side had some kind of colored hair."

What Is Taqwacore?

Taqwacore is a cultural development of our time, meaning that it is at once organic and something of a media-amplified phenomenon. Taqwa bands—the term means religious consciousness, or righteousness—have sprung up across North America; the Kominas and Al-Thawra are the most active, but there's also Sarmust, Vote Hezbollah out of San Antonio, Sagg Taqwacore Syndicate in Oregon, the queer, all-girl Secret Trial Five in Toronto, and a constellation of bands, bedroom producers and MCs in the U.S., Europe, and elsewhere who may or may not call themselves Taqwacore but fit the general spirit. Through word of mouth and MySpace, they have spotted other bands across the Muslim world—apparently there's an all-girl punk group in Saudi—who feel like fellow travelers. ...

The existence of "Muslim punk" is catnip to an editor in search of an offbeat story with possibly large implications, and Taqwacore has made it to CNN, *Newsweek*, the *Guardian*, BBC, and more. The artists aren't upset at being covered, but they're less than thrilled about the lines of questioning they've faced and the resulting stories, many of them trying to shoehorn Taqwacore into some kind of ideological mission—street preachers? Islamic reformers?—instead of the plural, disorderly and sometimes ridiculous reality of their lyrics and behavior.

Part of the pushback is just punk-kid petulance, but most is well-founded annoyance at exotification of a phenomenon that sprang from suburban basements, just kids growing up in America with various migrant backgrounds and flavors of alienation, making music with the materials at hand. That's why lots of Taqwacore songs contain zero Islamic references at all—and why the Kominas guitarist Arjun Ray, the rapper Prop Anon, and any number of other people can identify as Taqwacore without being Muslim nor coming from Muslim families. It's why the musical and lyrical references of Taqwacore mine the range of ethnic, political and pop-culture content that brown youth encounter coming up in post-globalization America (and elsewhere): Arabic and Urdu poetry, bhangra, qawwali, mosque and temple etiquette, pious aunties, airport security, terrorist paranoia, hip-hop, video games, Malcolm X, road trips, sex, prayer, skateboards, everything.

The Warm Embrace of Punk Rock

Still, if "Muslim punk" is too reductive a term to describe Taqwacore, it does get at something important at the heart of this music and emerging community. There's a kind of experiential investigation of Islam and its heresies going on in much of this music, and the Taqwacore kids have brought something to the table in a decade when the public conversation about Islam, if deeply flawed, has had at least the merit of existing. Knight's original novel, in which many young Muslim Americans have found something to recognize, respond to, or laugh with, stemmed from his own manic whirlwind of faith: a working-class white kid from a broken home finding structure through conversion at sixteen; a Saudi-style hyper-orthodox phase, alienating people around him and ultimately himself; and deep sorrow at learning of Islam's early and recent divisions, internal racism and conflict, all the half-truths and hidden histories. All this turned Knight into a collector of Muslim heresies—"queer alims, drunk imams, punk ayatollahs, masochistic muftis, junkie shaikhs, retarded mullahs and guttermouth maulanas"—with a scholar's attention to their forgotten antecedents in Islamic history.

His quest—recorded in his second book, the memoir *Blue Eyed Devil*—also made room for the self-styled, mostly African-American movements that sprang up in the last century invoking Allah or Islam: the Moorish Science Temple, the Nation of Islam and its mysterious prophet W. D. Fard, the Five Percenters, the Nuwaubians, and more.

If there was any music capacious enough for all of this, it had to be punk—with its embrace of contradiction and its zest for the absurd, the historic and cultural references making energy out of collision like bodies in the mosh pit. The Kominas' 2008 debut album, *Wild Nights in Guantanamo Bay*, has it all: intra-Muslim-American religious beefs, Punjabi tradition, Five Percenter numerology, foreign policy, anti-consumerism, terrorist jokes. Al-Thawra's "Who Benefits from War?" bellows largely indecipherable lyrics into a heavy crust-punk storm, but the agenda is political; it ends with "Taqsim," guitar improvisation in the spirit, if not the style, of Arab classical music. Omar Waqar of Sarmust calls his music "rooted in angst but ultimately about activism." He's as much singer-songwriter as punk rocker; on the side, he also plays a mean sitar.

Taqwacore is still a subculture. Despite all the high-end media attention, there aren't a lot of bands and the fan base is underground. Still, the movement is fleshing out. Both the documentary *Taqwacore: The Birth of Punk Islam* and the feature film of Knight's novel, *The Taqwacores*, directed by Eyad Zahra, have enjoyed a warm reception at the festivals. Zahra's film is slated to open commercially in the next few months. The Kominas and al-Thawra have recently returned from a tour of the United Kingdom and Scandinavia that saw them perform not only for the London hip set but also in Muslim and immigrant-heavy English cities like Bradford. The new album from the Kominas, *Escape to Blackout Beach*, shows a broader stylistic range and a growing melodic emphasis with ska, reggae, and Punjabi and Sufi song all in the mix.

But whether Taqwacore grows into a major pop movement doesn't really matter, least of all to its participants, who tend to be self-deprecating and highly wary of labels in the first place. The music's real contribution is to feed into a broader phenomenon in which young Muslims in the diaspora—together with non-Muslim friends—are crafting their own adjustments to the faith and its culture, and documenting the results in literature, art, music, and politics. Some are experimenting with women-led prayer; others are forming queer Muslim communities. Student groups, spoken-word poets, bloggers, lawyers, and activists are all working it out their own way.

Amid this ongoing reinvention—which is partly about Islam, partly about migration, but mostly just individuals finding a path—Taqwacore blows in with its raucous sounds, eclectic supporters, and bizarre affinities. Its hi-jinks aren't for everyone; nor is its irreverence and freedom. But that's punk rock, right? All noise and possibility. ...

Michael Muhammad Knight, "Muhammad Was a Punk Rocker," from *The Taqwacores* (Brooklyn: Soft Skull Press, 2004).

Siddhartha Mitter, from "Taqwacore: Salat, Angst, and Rock & Roll," MTV Desi, posted Thursday, August 12, 2010.

LOS CRUDOS, INTERVIEW IN *MAXIMUMROCKNROLL*

At the risk of hyperbole, Los Crudos and their label Lengua Armada Records were among a handful of bands and labels that shaped what punk rock was in the 1990s and what it would become in the 2000s. As a band that sang almost exclusively in Spanish, and wrote songs about political concerns in their local Chicago Latino community and in Latin America at large, they were never simply a punk band

playing for the punk community, but a punk band purposefully *of,* *within,* and *for* the Latino community. Punk rock wasn't a way to escape the strictures of their ethnicity; instead it was another way to embrace it. Los Crudos saw punk rock as a way to undo the cultural, political, and economic conditioning that had forced them to repudiate their own language and culture, and used punk to reclaim this Latino identity. The question of "assimilation" never interested them, yet they were colossally influential with the larger punk scene anyway. But there are problems with this position, as the band remained aware: Los Crudos sang in Spanish about issues particularly germane to Latinos and immigrants but their audience remained primarily White punks who relied upon lyric sheets to understand what they were singing.

MAXIMUMROCKNROLL: How long have you been together?

LOS CRUDOS: One year.

MRR: How come you guys started a band?

MARTÍN SORRONDEGUY: Well it was about a year ago, I had an idea. I saw Oscar and José at a festival called Fiesta del Sol that we have in our neighborhood on 18th St. I talked to my brother and he told me that they already were in a band called Fuck the Bureaucracy. Well I thought, these Latinos here, they're already in a band and I saw them at the festival so I told them I wanted to start a band that would sing in Spanish, a hardcore band but something more serious … I don't know … protest songs but in Spanish not in English. They liked the idea and we started practicing. …

MRR: Do you consider yourselves a political band at some level?

SORRONDEGUY: Uh … yeah.

JOSÉ CASAS: At "some level."

MRR: What level?

SORRONDEGUY: Depends. Every song of ours has something to say. We don't sing a song just to sing a song, we don't sing stupid stuff (*no cantanos bobadas*). We sing songs that affect us in our life in one way or another, but it depends on the song, there are different songs that say different things. "Crudo Soy" was the first song we wrote. It talks about all the problems that our Latino community has, the problems of gangs, racism, inner-racism …

OSCAR CHÁVEZ: … who they are, that they are Latinos, and they try to hide …

SORRONDEGUY: Yes, it has a lot to do with shame about who you are, a lack of sense of identity or pride, and it has to do with racism, inner racism in our own community, the murders from gang violence, it talks about a lot of stuff in one, and it's basically saying *Crudo soy* ... *crudo* means raw but we also use it for hangover and we're hungover on the bullshit, basically is what we're saying.

JOEL MARTÍNEZ: It's like when you're hung over, you're not in your right state of mind, you can't think, you can't really react the way you would normally react, your state of mind isn't there to say, "Well this isn't right, this is wrong," and this is a hangover ...

SORRONDEGUY: It's hungover ... we're stuffed (*rellenos*). ...

MRR: Do you think the community around here is really politically conscious?

CHÁVEZ: No, not at all. I mean, the kids are interested in having a good time, going to the clubs and dancing to deejays and ...

MARTÍNEZ: ... Self-centered ...

CASAS: I think they're all assimilated, that's what it is ...

MARTÍNEZ: Yeah, they're trying to find their niche because as kids, you know, the people whose grandparents were already here like say, not to generalize, but say, Anglosaxons, their parents were here for three or four generations already ... Okay there may be Polish, Irish, Italian ... the thing is that they had already found their niche—"We're American," you know—and when these second-generation kids got here, they didn't know how to fit in, because they didn't speak English, they didn't look like the people ...

SORRONDEGUY: They can't fit in, that's the thing, the whole point is that you can't fit in, it's very difficult because you can try to act as gringo as you want, but you know whether it be in the workplace, in the political field or whatever, you still look different so you'll never get to that level that they're at ... let's be for real, why don't you just be proud of who you are, you know there's nothing wrong with supporting and helping your community, don't leave it behind and try to ignore it. And that's what a lot of politicos or whatever do.

CHÁVEZ: I was really surprised to find out, I was doing shows and going along and meeting people, I was surprised to find out that a lot of people who I saw as Hispanic or Mexican, not know a word of Spanish. We did some shows for a friend of his, and I was totally shocked when I found that he didn't know a word of Spanish. I was totally shocked.

SORRONDEGUY: That's becoming more and more common these days.

MARTÍNEZ: He's what? Like third generation here, born here?

SORRONDEGUY: They've been here a long time, his family. But they dealt with a lot of major racism in their lives, a lot.

MARTÍNEZ: A lot of bullshit.

CHÁVEZ: That just reinforces the fact that he's been here, what, like four generations, and people still treat him like shit.

SORRONDEGUY: Yeah, you know, it's funny, I'd talk to him. He'd realize what's going on but he's also told me stories about stuff that's happened to their family …

CASAS: Exactly. The point is even if you don't know a word of Spanish they still treat you like shit.

MRR: How have people treated you in the scene? I'm talking the punk scene, I'm not talking the Mexican kid who listens to heavy metal who has heard there is a band called Los Crudos who sing in Spanish, I'm talking about the punks, the ones who go to, like …

SORRONDEGUY: … Screeching Weasel shows …

MRR: And like Econochrist, because they know who Econochrist is …

SORRONDEGUY: I think for the most part we've gotten a pretty good response here. It could be because I've been around for a while, I know a lot of people … Maybe if we were all new to the scene people wouldn't pay attention to us. Although in Milwaukee and Madison …

MARTÍNEZ: … They totally loved us.

SORRONDEGUY: They were great … and I only knew two people in Milwaukee.

MARTÍNEZ: Exactly. And that's the point.

MRR: So what's the response of the non-punk community to the band?

SORRONDEGUY: It's been really good. People who can only tell you about punk rock as the Sex Pistols, that's all they know, will come out and see us. People who don't even know what punk rock is, artists, or just people from the neighborhood that know me, or something, they'll come out and see us, we give them lyric sheets, and they're totally into what we're doing. They're like yeah, let us know when you're playing again. They've been very supportive.

MRR: Who get into what you guys have to say?

SORRONDEGUY: Yeah, totally, totally. I mean, José's parents come out to the shows, and they're really into it. They worry a bit, but they're really into it.

MRR: Do you have a lot of, like a combination of both, a lot of like, Latino punks…

SORRONDEGUY: The Latino community, for the most part, like the younger community, there's not very much of a punk scene yet. We're the first punk band around that's doing this stuff. So maybe after us they'll get more into it, take more of an interest. There's a big new wave scene, new wave, techno, rave scene, whatever you want to call it, there's a big scene for that, and a big house scene, but we're something new, it's something totally new in the neighborhood, and I think people are now starting to pick up on that. Who knows it'll be maybe five years down the line, 90% of them won't even know what's going on and there'll be 5 or 10% who stick around, and you know, explore more within the punk scene which will be weird …

CHÁVEZ: I ran into some guy earlier this week, and he was asking me questions about recording a demo because he had formed a band and stuff, and he was telling me that he wanted to do a few songs in Spanish, which is kinda odd, because if he had never heard of us or had never seen us, he probably would have never done that.

SORRONDEGUY: I think you have to, like I was telling you earlier, there's three bands as far as I know on all the coasts, there's Huasipungo, there's Dogma Mundista in California and Los Crudos in the Midwest. It's like, us three, we have to like pave this path, you know, so then like maybe other bands will say oh man, and start doing stuff, or I don't know, who knows how it will end …

CASAS: Don't be all important and shit, man …

SORRONDEGUY: No, not that we're important, but we're the ones who will be the first ones to take the shit and deal with it. …

MRR: So now, to talk about political involvement. I didn't know who you were, basically. The first thing I heard about Martín was the band, Los Crudos, and I called you up because of that. And then, a lot of people started telling me, "Oh yeah, I knew him from two years ago," everybody knew you, Martín, as a scenester. So what's your involvement with the scene? I know you're starting to set up shows here or something?

SORRONDEGUY: I've set up a couple shows. We've been doing shows a lot. A long time ago I did a show at a place called Casa Aztlan and that was the first show I ever put on. That was some local bands like the Bhopal Stiffs, Generation Waste … it was the first punk show ever in our neighborhood, it was kinda wild because like 300 people showed up, on 17th and Racine, which is a pretty gang-infested neighborhood. And the gang members were getting all freaked out and walking by with bats and I thought maybe something was going to happen, but they left everybody alone. A lot of white people came into the neighborhood to check out the show, but then a lot of local kids came out too, and you know it was kind of funny because at one point, there were all these cholos who walked up with their flannels and the bandanas, and they were like, "OK, how much is the show," and they all went into the show and were totally into it. You know, and I thought, wow ... and they were totally into like Suicidal Tendencies and stuff like that but they came out, went to the show, and I thought maybe they were going to start trouble but they were like into hardcore, you know. ...

MRR: But what brought you to the point where you decided, "I want to do a band that sings in Spanish"? Because your zine, that you were doing before that, was in English, right?

SORRONDEGUY: Yeah, it was in English.

MRR: Did it deal with what it's like to be Latino?

SORRONDEGUY: No, it didn't.

MRR: So what was the catalyst for each of you personally?

CHÁVEZ: Probably self-identity or something.

SORRONDEGUY: It could have been that. Yeah ...

MRR: How did the change occur?

CHÁVEZ: It's kind of hard to say, you know, because we see a lot of things going on, and we think about them, but often times you don't say much, and like he said, when we do finally have some kind of outlet, like this band stuff, that's when we really start letting loose, that's when we kind of sit back and say, "Yeah, you know there is a problem with this, there is a problem with that ..." Otherwise, we just sit at home and think about it but we don't say anything.

SORRONDEGUY: And a lot of the kids don't. It's a lack of communication. Personally for me, OK, I just had a lot of things as my life, my past experiences, growing up here, coming here to this country with my family, we only spoke Spanish. How, when I went to grammar school, it got taken away like you don't speak Spanish here, you're not in Mexico. You speak English, you're an American now. It was that type of thing, right? You don't realize it ... Oh, you're from Uruguay? Where's that? See, they're brazers but you're a spic, so it's different ... just all this bullshit. And then like, later on as I'm growing up ...

MRR: Brazers?

SORRONDEGUY: Brazers. Like the Spanish, bracero.

CHÁVEZ: But in English it has a different ...

SORRONDEGUY: Yeah, it's a very derogatory name that people use for Mexicans. But anyways ...

MRR: It's like levels ... They're being derogatory to me but I can be derogatory to you...

SORRONDEGUY: Well it's kind of like what happens and I realize that here I am, I'm 17, 18 years old. My family speaks Spanish, but why can't I communicate? Why have I lost ... ? It's like a self-identity ... you realize that you or I have been a product of this. And now, as I'm getting older, I realize what the hell was happening and what went on, and I'm fucking clawing to get back, or get what I can back that was rightfully mine and was taken away. You understand?

CASAS: That's a fucked up feeling when you're like, "Why can't I talk to my parents?" Or at least very well ... I know when I'm pissed, I think in Spanish ... Spanish cursing ...

MRR: That's a good thing. Because supposedly ... let's say you're hammering something and you hit yourself with the hammer, the first thing that goes through your mind, it's the language that's inside you.

CASAS: "Oh darn!"

SORRONDEGUY: *¡Hijo de la gran puta!*

CASAS: *¡Hijo de la muy chingada!*

MARTÍNEZ: I'm victim of exactly what we're saying about. To me, I had no idea of anything of what was going on around me, what politics were going on behind my back. The only politics I heard about were my dad complaining about how fucked up the Republican party was, not that he's pro-Democrat, but he's always been into like the smaller man, or the lower class people, because that's where all my family came from, you know, grandparents, were mostly lower-class families, low-income. The thing is when I started listening more and more to different bands and what they were saying as far as politics go, and then ran into these guys, and then when I found out about more, about what he was singing as far as like being a Latino, I found myself being guilty of all the things we were singing against. And I'm thinking, no one hipped me to it. No one told me, this isn't a good way to think, you're degrading everybody, what you are. ...

SORRONDEGUY: And if there's punks out in other parts of the world that read this: we're fucking here and we try to keep up and we know what's going on there and we are fighting here for you and for our cause and everything. And we didn't forget anybody. People think we come here and our families came here to forget. That's bullshit. We didn't forget anybody. It's like, we're still in here and we're still here and we're still fighting for that. It's not that we left to forget. We didn't leave to forget because you can never forget. It's a part of us. ...

Jane Guskin and Esneider, from "Interview: Los Crudos," *Maximumrock-nroll* no. 117 (San Francisco, February 1993).

MARTÍN SORRONDEGUY, INTERVIEW IN *MAXIMUMROCKNROLL*

By 1999, Los Crudos had disbanded, and in this interview the vocalist Martín Sorrondeguy gives his own postmortem on the band. He speaks directly of the responsibility he felt in developing the band as an explicitly political project, and although Los Crudos performed many songs about explicitly "political" subjects like war, imperialism, immigration policy, and the like, it's the politics of presence that occupies Sorrondeguy's reflection. He speaks of a video project under way (released as *Beyond the Screams: A U.S. Latino Hardcore Punk Documentary* in 2004) that would chronicle the Latino influence on punk, of singing in Spanish and bringing the concerns of the Latino community to punk scenes across the country and the world, and being an example of how Latino or Chicano kids get into punk to explicitly live a race identity, not reject it in favor of some new kind of neutrality. Sorrondeguy wants to rewrite punk history, rejecting the prevailing mentality that the history of non-white punks is that of "punks being punk," a vision subjected to far too much whitening. "It's basically about making our own history," he argues, "and letting people know we exist." Perhaps not coincidentally, Sorrondeguy came out as gay while still with Los Crudos and later went on to form the queercore band Limp Wrist.

The End of Los Crudos

MAXIMUMROCKNROLL: Was there a sense of responsibility that accumulated, over the years, where people expected [Los Crudos] to keep going? Did you feel that way?

MARTÍN SORRONDEGUY: Yeah, a lot of people didn't want us to stop. I think a lot of people did (want us to stop), but then a lot of the younger kids didn't want us to break up. I think the older kids were more like, give it up already.

But a sense of responsibility? I don't know, I guess I always thought there was a responsibility with Crudos ever since the beginning, that we had something to do and that there was a reason and a purpose behind what the band was, why we started and why we did what we did. There was always that sense of it being a project and that we had this work to do, that was definitely there from the beginning.

It's kind of exhausting as a band and as a person, but it was great, and there's no regrets.

MRR: What were the goals you set out with, do you think you accomplished them?

SORRONDEGUY: Yeah, I think we definitely accomplished them, I mean the main goals we came up with from the beginning, I think when anybody starts a band they have ideas and really want to take their ideas as far as they can go, and really push things. We never thought we'd be as popular as we turned out to be, and the support we were never expecting that, we just thought it was going to be more of a project kind of band.

But doing the songs in Spanish and being in the US, you know doing stuff in another language we just didn't think it was going to be very popular at all, and one of our main goals was to talk about the things we were experiencing, being from a different community. Where we come from is not a typically punk background or community—expressing our ideas in our language to young kids in our neighborhood. That was our main goal, and yeah, we did that and it went a lot further than we thought it would go, and it opened up different paths for us to take, to try and go with it, and a chance to take it beyond our neighborhood.

But a band singing in a different language and talking about things that are going on in a certain community, and then going to other areas and parts of the country where kids have never experienced anything like that with them, that was a very powerful thing. ...

MRR: You said the other night that you had another project going?

SORRONDEGUY: I'm working on a video project about the Latino and Chicano punk scenes in the US. It's a project that I tried to do through photography, but it wasn't really working out, so I got myself in a couple of video classes, and I decided that that was how I wanted to do this, that video would be much more effective and have much more life if it was done through video.

So on our last tour I started on it. I bought a camera and started interviewing people and taping bands playing live, including Huasipungo in New York and Subsistencia and Kontra Attaque in Los Angeles. Now I have about sixty hours of tape, and I gotta start editing it. I think it'll probably be about an hour long.

It's basically about making our own history and letting people know we exist, we always existed in the punk scene in the past, but we had a kind of transparency. Especially coming out of the LA scene, there were always Chicanos and Latinos involved but it was never an issue that was talked about, so the documentary is saying that in this era, the nineties, we really went full force and trying to document that and say look this happened and this is what it was about. ...

MRR: ... Los Crudos and Huasipungo were the first two bands that I ever saw who really brought that identity of being Latino to the forefront, do you feel that Crudos was an important force in bringing that to light?

SORRONDEGUY: I definitely think so. We knew that bands existed, because when you look at punk rock and you look at the resources that we have, our documentation of punk rock, there's a certain image that comes up. People often think of punk as being very suburban these days, but in the beginning it was something that was very urban and very city. Now people seem to think of it as this suburban teenage anger towards their parents and that really wasn't where we were coming from. So we knew as a band that there was history of Chicanos and Latinos in punk rock, especially in California and in the South West because obviously historically those people have always been there, so there was bound to be a lot of involvement by those kids, and especially in Los Angeles.

So people never think of things like the first Black Flag singer, that guy Chavo [aka Ron Reyes], who was Puerto Rican. That was never really talked about, or that Alice Bag from the Bags, she's Chicana. You know you have the Zeros, the Plugz, the Adolescents, the list goes on. Still nobody would talk about that. It was transparent and nobody was talking about that, you know, it was punks being punk.

MRR: It seems that while those bands had members that were Chicano or Latino it wasn't brought to the forefront. It was invisible.

SORRONDEGUY: Yeah, the only band to really touch on it in the language was the Plugz when they did their cover of "La Bamba." Besides that though, it really didn't seem like there was much, and it really seemed like there wasn't much else like that. Everyone talks about Black Flag, but who talks about the first singer (who I thought was the best singer) being Puerto Rican? It's just not brought up.

Then there were bands in Los Angeles like Emperismo who really went full force and sang in Spanish, but the thing was, nobody outside of LA ever heard of them, unless you went to Mexico.

Then Huasipungo and Crudos started to tour and bring this to a lot of people, and started bringing it out of the cities and into smaller towns and we really started to push it. There were a lot of new issues that started to get talked about as well, besides "oh, they're gonna drop the bomb." We were talking about propositions, immigration and racism. Ironically of course, that was just what was happening in the early nineties politically with the propositions.

So it was a reaction to those things that were going on politically, and it gave the bands a lot of things to talk about and a lot of us as individuals things to be pissed off about.

MRR: Obviously, you brought these ideas to people who had never heard of them before, in places that these early bands from LA never played, but do you think you brought Chicano and Latino kids into punk rock who wouldn't have been otherwise?

SORRONDEGUY: Yeah, in Chicago, sure, and maybe in some other places if kids just walked into some show and saw us singing in Spanish I'm sure it sparked interest. Then there's been people who have been very supportive of the band who really didn't have any interest in the punk scene, yet really supported and liked the band. Because of what it was about and that was something we always found as a band. Especially in our neighborhood in Chicago from the non-punks—we don't live in an area with a high density of punks but there was always the support.

It would be too easy to form a band and isolate yourself, but that wasn't what we were about. It was too important. ...

Sean Sullivan, from "The End of Los Crudos," *Maximumrocknroll* no. 192 (San Francisco, May 1999).

AFRO-PUNK: THE "ROCK 'N' ROLL NIGGER" EXPERIENCE, FROM THE FILM SCRIPT

At the outset, *Afro-Punk* was, simply, a documentary film by James Spooner chronicling the experiences of U.S. Blacks in contemporary punk rock. It has now grown into something else entirely, spawning a yearly film festival at the Brooklyn Academy of Music and a thriving international community, both online and face-to-face. These selections from both the film and an interview with Spooner available as a DVD extra touch on several of the film's major theses, the overarching one being: despite punk's racial shortcomings, it has provided an avenue of identity articulation for certain Black men and women. That is, there is *something* in punk—how it operates and what it does—that provides effective tools for social organization and the negotiation of racial identities. The punk vocalist Tamar-Kali Brown sees punk aesthetics as a way of reconnecting with aspects of a Native American and African heritage, and hopes that through her music she can reach "jiggy negroes." And Cypher, singer for an otherwise White Long Island hardcore band, finds punk as a temporary means of articulating and expressing his own Black nationalism on the way to finding a more flourishing Black community. But this community is not always a given, for if punk, at its core, is about opposition to the mainstream, then where does this leave punks of color vis-à-vis their own racial and ethnic community? What's clear from Spooner's own assessment of his film is that in giving voice to the myriad voices of Black punks from across the country—with an explicitly Black audience in mind—*Afro-Punk* ends up facilitating something approaching the very community sought by its participants.

TAMAR-KALI BROWN: Growing up, people used to be dissing me in the street a lot. I had this World War II antique US army coat, and you know, my combats or whatever, so I would get a lot of people harassing me, calling me "bull dyke," or "dyke bitch," and you know just I felt a lot of just like really violent, hateful energy towards me: "What the fuck is that shit you're wearing," you know, or "You have that shit in your lip like a white bitch?" Then, I remember coming into my identity as a young African-American woman feeling my culture and recognizing how I grew up kind of hating myself to a certain degree, and coming out of that, and when I embraced my culture, that's when I really started getting called "white." You know in my mind, me and my whole crew, we were on some hardcore black nationalist type shit, but to the average person, we was just doing some white shit. When I'm wearing a mohawk, I really feel it. There's cultural validity in it for me, it's not just a trend or a style. I have Mohawk blood as well as Cherokee blood, and West African blood, being a descendent of enslaved people from West Africa. I remember one time I had a Bantu knotted mohawk and I was like, Ooh, how interesting, I just manifested the fusion that exists in me genetically in my hairstyle. So, it's on that level; it's not a trivial thing. ...

The reason why I think punk rock appealed to me moreover was because of the aesthetic, that's the thing that got my attention first. And that now, as an older woman, considering myself somewhat culturally aware, I'm aware of the direct influence of African peoples as well as the indigenous peoples of America on the punk prototype image. But in hindsight I realized how it drew me in because growing up I had access to these images of, you know, folks in the bush, tribal peoples, what have you, and I remember them being really striking and moving me, just because I really saw just the stark beauty in it all. And so, when I first started seeing images of punk, this really bright colored hair, and safety pin piercings and things like that, it was pretty much on that same level, just like a contemporary Eurocentric version of what people in the bush were doing. All these things that you know existed before, and now because I know exactly who I'm being and I'm like, I have no fear around it, I'm very clear, my choice to look the way I do is just based on me relating to a traditionally African aesthetic, but it was through punk initially that I had those senses reawakened. ...

There's a community that's going to be hard for me to reach, and they're black, you know what I mean? It's not the indie rock scene ... I can't imagine that being an issue or a problem because I've seen how supportive they've been with a lot of different artists. But, the "jiggy negroes," I want you! You know what I mean? [Laughs] I want to turn your ass out, you know what I mean? Open up your mind. Because all this music, this so-called black people's music, it's getting sold in the Midwest. A bunch of white kids are buying it, they're at the hip hop shows. It's never hard to get a white audience, I don't feel. You know what I mean? History has shown that. It's ministering to our own community that's the hard part. And not the bohemian negroes, or the artists, you know, a lot of artists come to see me too. It's folks on my block! You know what I mean? Those are the people that need to hear my music. That's going to be the hardest sell. You know, they be blasting Ashanti, let me hear them blast Tamar-Kali, you know what I'm saying? The world would change if we could get it to those folks. That's going to be the hard sell. ...

CYPHER: After high school I went to Howard and it initially, absolutely, was a reactionary move. I wanted to leave Long Island, where the white people were, and go to Howard, where the black people were. Throughout my journey at Howard, I discovered an organization known as Ubiquity, which is the oldest afro-centric [organization] at

Howard. I became president of the organization. I'm an alumni now, but it's a lifelong commitment. I still try to contribute, when I have some free time: take a drive back to DC and attend a program. I really feel blessed about those type of experiences, coupled with the fact that I do the hardcore thing. But I think what distinguished me, and what distinguishes me from a lot of white kids in that scene is, I don't identify primarily as hardcore. I'm African, that's how I identify myself as. Because, at the end of the day, those are the people that are going to have my back and when revolution comes those are the people that I'm going to be fighting for. There's not going to be a hardcore contingent, unfortunately.

And I have to say on the flip side, if it wasn't for my friendship with these guys [in my band], who are like my closest friends, I think I would have a different, maybe even less developed, understanding of white America and white people, and things of that nature.

I could've been like, I have a bunch of cool black friends and dashikis and ankhs around, so like "Peace guys!"—you know what I'm saying? By having close white friends, but also espousing the beliefs I have and being open and very true to both of those things that are a part of my life, I think it makes my life more challenging, but it also makes me a more developed human being. …

JAMES SPOONER: I remember, I did a screening in Chicago, right? After the screening, there was, like, a line of kids waiting, just waiting 'cos they wanted to say "Thanks" or tell me their story, or whatever it was, you know? And, after about the fourth kid who came up to me to say, "Man, that's totally my story. I'm the only one!" I was like, "Dude, turn around! There's, like, twenty-five people here who are the 'only one'! You know, you guys are here, in Chicago, together; say 'Hi,' meet each other." So, I thought that it was important, that I needed to have a way to connect these people. The obvious way was the internet, so I put together a message board and just started … I got a couple of kids, and then those kids got a couple of kids, and so on and so forth. Next thing you know, it was, like, a-thousand-plus strong. It's just this place where everyone's just super-excited to not be alone anymore and to be able to talk about whatever it is that they want to talk about, and ultimately to have a safe space to be a creative, boundary-pushing black individual.

I started having shows, and I started this thing called the Liberation Sessions, which is basically providing a safe space for talented artists to share their work with an open-minded, open-armed black community.

It's become this thing that, when the film started, I never thought that I would ever go to a hardcore show, or a rock show, or anything like that, and look out at the crowd and see, like, six hundred people, five hundred eighty of them being black, you know what I'm saying? It's nuts, every time it happens—and we do it every time there's a three-day weekend, so it happens, like, eight times a year—every single time, it's just like ... it's amazing, you know?

On the Fourth of July, we had a four-day film and music festival, which went phenomenally. *Afro-Punk* did a really good couple of days at BAM, the Brooklyn Academy of Music, and, when we were in a film festival there, we had a sold out show. So, I e-mailed the guy and was, like, "Hey, I'd like to show my film again. We had a sold-out show before, I'm sure we could do it again." And they're like, "Well, why don't we do it bigger? Why don't we try to make a festival out of it? You can pick the movies, and we'll help advertise ..." I was like, "Okay, this is perfect." Kids flew in from all over the place ... from as far as England, people from Florida and Chicago and LA and San Francisco. It was just amazing. For them to come to a show and see that, you know, like, a kid who's from Florida, to come to a show and see more than just him, but to see the whole crowd, and, like, "Oh my god, I'm in an all-black mosh pit!" It was amazing!

I'm really proud of what's happened, and I can only look forward to what will be the future. You know you've accomplished something when somebody says back to you what you were thinking while you were making it, you know? I was thinking, I need to make the movie that I needed to see when I was fourteen to be able to verbalize what I was thinking. And this guy came up to me, and he was like, "Man, I've been trying to say that for twenty years! I need that movie to come out, because now if anybody asks me, I can be, like, *here!*"

And now it's out.

James Spooner, dir. *Afro-Punk: The "Rock 'N' Roll Nigger" Experience*, 2003 (DVD, 2004).

SEVEN

RACE RIOT

when Kathleen Hanna screamed, "SUCK MY LEFT ONE!"
and nailed the Punk Rock to the wall,
and when the core soon after went queer,
I jumped for joy because it was about time.
But still I'm waiting for my race riot.
                                        —Mimi Nguyen

Why begin this section with writing from a zine rather than lyrics of a song? Because this is how Race Riot played itself out: in the letter exchanges and columns of fanzines rather than in words sung on a stage or recorded in a studio. Arising in the late '90s and early 2000s, and taking place mainly in the United States and Canada, Race Riot was more a literary explosion than a musical movement. It started first in the letters columns of "mainstream" punk zines like *Maximumrocknroll,* moved to the pages of zines created by punks of color themselves, and came together in compilations like Mimi Nguyen's *Race Riot.* Like their White counterparts, these fans and musicians found something in punk rock that spoke to them, something they found lacking in the mainstream. But in this subculture these punks of color frequently found something else: the racism that they thought they had left behind, that their fellow White punks simply refused to acknowledge. Though taking their cues primarily from the personal narratives characteristic of most zine writing, these punks articulate their anger and disappointment consistently in a register of structural critique, taking aim at a culture that prides itself on being alternative yet in issues of race and ethnicity often ends up reproducing the status quo while sporting a mohawk.

These punks represent a second generation, coming of age in a scene perhaps no more racially diverse than the one that came before, but with aspirations and expectations of diversity. At the same time, as inchoate rage and nihilism gave way to more self-consciously progressive and positive ethos, this very ideal of diversity was undermined by the continued insistence that punk was somehow above and beyond all that. One thinks, for instance, of the huge stenciled block letters on the wall in the front entryway of Berkeley's famed punk club, 924 Gilman Street, which read "No Racism, No Sexism, No Homophobia," a sign that signifies that upon entry one leaves one's prior identifications at the door and enters into what aspires to be a punk rock Utopia. The problem with such idealism, as the writers in the following section point out, is that it leaves no room for the questioning of punk's own racism, sexism, and homophobia. We're punk, the logic goes, and that's all that matters.

The letters and rants that follow represent a new chapter in the race and punk discussion. They are not declarations of racial identity expressed in and through punk, but assertions arising out of punk and in opposition to it. Some of the selections in this chapter are angry and heartbroken rejections of punk and its seemingly intractable, and often unrecognized, racism. These punks are tired of waiting for their race riot and this is their parting farewell before leaving the scene entirely. But other writings are an attempt to connect and build community: letters that end with calls for more letters, for exchanges, for networks of punks of color and indeed a truly antiracist punk culture. Punk is *at one and the same time* the hopeful possibility for creating alternative infrastructures to negotiate oppositional racial identities for people of color *and* the abject failure of such a project due to the ways punk rock has constructed itself, mythically, as a White Riot.

MIMI NGUYEN,
"IT'S (NOT) A WHITE WORLD:
LOOKING FOR RACE IN PUNK"

For both her writing and her zine compilations, Mimi Nguyen is one of the central figures of the Race Riot that took place within the punk rock scene in the 1990s. This piece, widely reproduced, began as a *Punk Planet* column and lays out Nguyen's criticism of, as she puts it, the "'whitestraightboy' hegemony [that] organizes punk." It was this very "'whitestraightboy' hegemony" that gave

rise to both queercore/homocore and the even more widespread Riot Grrrl 'movement' earlier in the decade, and these alternative punk positions provide inspiration for Nguyen. What is troubling, however, is that while queercore and Riot Grrrl ended up taking hold as punk rock identity options in a firm way, with the latter even celebrated in the mainstream media, race has yet to mark punk with the same impact. This isn't to undermine the revolutionary ways that Riot Grrrl and queercore destabilized punk hegemony— but doesn't it seem like everyone, at one point, waves the Riot Grrrl flag? So why do so few, even today, line up behind the Race Riot banner?

Everyone knows it. Every once in a while, if I'm lucky, someone will say something definitive about it: *yes, it's true*. But then it just sits there, untouched.

I'm a girl who likes to lay it all on the table, so here it is: *"whitestraightboy" hegemony organizes punk*. And I'm not just talking about its dominant demographic.

Wait. I'll back up.

Race, in punk, is like outer space: this distant constellation of "issues" clustered way, way out there. This isn't to say, for instance, that punks haven't produced some shrewd analyses of US foreign policy (a perennial punk favorite), effectively organized huge protests against apartheid or the Persian Gulf War. In fact, punks seem to be pretty good with political economy; I first learned about the World Bank/IMF from the zine *Assault (With Intent to Free)*, ferchrissakes.

But somehow the p-rock backyard got disconnected from the world on the other side of the fence and what happens "out there" is rarely reflected "in here." So when Kathleen Hanna screamed, "SUCK MY LEFT ONE!" and nailed the Punk Rock to the wall, and when the core soon after went queer, I jumped for joy because it was about time.

But still I'm waiting for my race riot.

Take the way in which travel gets talked about in punk. It reveals all kinds of assumptions we make about privilege and social mobility. Travel is almost always about leisure, self-discovery, "freedom," and rarely ever about immigration, refugee movement, or exile. It's never about how some people—white, heterosexual, middle-class, male—often travel in more comfort than others—nonwhite, queer, poor, female. Don't mistake me, I'm not suggesting we chuck that new *Cometbus* out the window. My point is this: we need to examine our categories, *the words we use and how we use those words*, for the exclusions we make when we oh-so casually invoke them.

This essay tells several stories. The first admits to a motive. That is, it begins with my cynicism, my disappointment and my anger. The second story is half-formed: it's the story of writing a critical analysis of a set of communities—grouped under the umbrella of "punk"—with which I have a sordid past, an ambivalent present and a mutual love-hate relationship. The third and most obvious story is about those communities and what gets circulated under the sign of "race" there. Unfortunately, this is also the most complex story.

So let's map out some of the ways the punk scene deals with race and break down some of the assumptions and problems involved with these particular approaches. I'll just give a general overview—there's a lot more ground to cover. So rather than present a laundry list of specific examples of racist statements or misdeeds, overt or otherwise, produced under the name Punk Rock, it might be more useful to try to understand the "why" and "how"—the politics and attitudes that *make room* for those acts and misdeeds.

And remember: I critique because I care.

I got your theory right here, whiteboy.

I'm going to say something blasphemous: there's something really "American" structuring the rhetoric of punk rock citizenship. When the social critic Joan Copjec wrote, "If *all* our citizens can be said to be Americans, this is not because we share any characteristics, but rather because we have all been given the right to *shed* these characteristics," she could've just as easily been talking about punk. Somehow punk is a quality that's understood as transcending race, gender, sexuality, or whatever.

To get our official membership card, we're supposed to put certain parts of ourselves aside—or at least assign them to a secondary rung. Differences are seen as potentially divisive. Some—like race or gender—are seen as more divisive than others. The assumption is that somehow "we"—because punk is so progressive, blah blah—have "gotten over" these things. But when something earth-shattering like riot grrrl ruptures the smooth surface of p-rock, punks scramble to "unify" again. Appeals are made to a "common culture"—whether as "Americans" or punks (dude)—in order to flatten, soothe, or (if those don't work) bang out those erupting differences.

Of course, this "common culture" is not really that common at all. Whiteness falls into a "neutral" category, and race is a property that somehow belongs only to "others." (How many times have you heard, "Yeah, this girl said" with the assumption that she's white taken for granted?) So this abstract, conformist citizenship offered by punk to someone like me is a one-handed affair—it all depends on how I want to narrate my raced, sexed, and gendered body into these supposedly democratic communities. If I keep my mouth shut and don't "make an issue" of it, I'm told that I'll get along fine—and never mind the psychic erasures I might have to endure.

That's the paradox: some kinds of "individuality" are valued according to punk's "common culture" while others, well, aren't. This is what I mean when I say "whitestraightboy" hegemony organizes punk, and this is why I make a point of my "Asianqueergirltomboy" specificity.

So while race *everywhere else but punk* is understood as institutional, structural, within the scene it gets talked about in terms of often isolated, individual attitudes. So racism in the scene is then commonly understood as something that irrational extremists (you know, good ol' boys in white sheets or marching around with shaved heads) and maybe the Big Bad State do, while "ordinary" people occasionally indulge in individual acts or attitudes of "prejudice." Racist, sexist or homophobic individuals are usually denounced as detractors from "real" punk principles, as if punk were *inherently* anti-racist, -sexist, or -homophobic. But both blunt-object and garden-variety racisms are only part of race as it's understood as a *system of classification*, one that overdetermines all our institutions and intersects with other social categories (gender, class, sexuality) and capital.

Simply put, racial hegemony is big, scary, and messy.

This is not me pointing fingers and saying, "You're a racist! And so is he! And her, too!" When I say "whitestraightboy," I want to invoke how the category is socially constructed with all kinds of privileges attached. I don't mean to indict everybody who "fits"—why, I have a number of friends who are white boys! (She said, batting her lashes in innocence.) This is me, however, confronting a widespread phenomena in punk called Dodging Accountability for My Privilege(s). That is, I want to insert the idea of "power" into the conversation.

And power isn't always obvious. We can point to the State and say, "Now, that's power, sonny!" But where, or *how*, do we locate oppressive ideologies? This is where power gets slippery because it seeps into everything—even in our language.

That is, we have to look at race not as something as simple as "color" discrimination, but as a system or structure of power that's deployed—in any number of ways—within any given historical moment. (I'm going to say the word "power" again and again, so get used to it.)

That said, how exactly *does* race get talked about in punk?

The "dude, punk is equal opportunity!" syndrome

Reading *Maximumrocknroll* is like dredging sewers for corpses; the stink is something awful. *MRR* tends to epitomize the "angry white male" knee-jerk response so popular to the national neurosis, only with spikes and three chords. Trading on crude stereotypes and slurs, the typical *MRR* fan (or columnist, for that matter) will usually assume he (because it's usually a white, hetero "he," but often enough a white, hetero "she") is pushing the envelope—"ohhh, I just called that guy a fag, tee hee!"—and then wave his little fist in the air, triumphantly taking recourse to the First Amendment and the Constitution to defend his speech acts. Alternative, my ass.

This is known as "equal-opportunity offensiveness"—although if you dare say anything about white straight men and their pencil pricks, you're just being plain mean. Poor babies.

But it's not particular to *MRR* (which may or may not evolve under new editorship). Punk luminaries from any number of other venues, whether Fucktooth or AK Press, have learned their lessons well at the knee of free-market (hi, capitalist) ideology: punk is an open emporium of ideas and you, the supposedly savvy shopper, are "free" to pick and choose. It's a perspective that assumes each individual is happily "rational," "objective," and handily armed with "common sense." Yeah right. You don't go to the mall with no clothes on and everyone shops the open marketplace of ideas with certain social logics intact. What gets called "rational," "objective" or "common sense" is always, *always* shaped by the ideological baggage someone brings with them (i.e., it's "common sense" that men fuck women and women give birth to babies, and it's "non-sense" that men fuck men, women fuck women, and babies come from test tubes).

I make this point to reiterate how problematic punk's "rugged indi-vidualism" is for any expression of politics because of the ways in which it ducks the question of power. The artist Jenny Holzer wrote, "The idea of transcendence obscures oppression," and punk is not an excep-tion. From punk's hyper-individualism it's a slippery slope to the kinds of neo-conservative political arguments suggesting, among other things, that affirmative action is "unfair" (like structural inequalities aren't) and why don't more of "those people" (welfare recipients, immigrants, whatever) just pull on those boot-straps? You know you've read those kinds of opinions in the pages of many a fanzine.

Talk about American mythologies. It's the punk version of Manifest Destiny and the Lone Ranger, re-imagining the Wild West for disaffected and mostly white youth. It's a privilege to believe that you can extract yourself from the context of social relations and imagine yourself the sole shaper of your fate. It's the kind of attitude that puts big obstacles in the way of asking the critical questions about *why* punk is largely white, heterosexual, and male, and *why* punk's politics look the way they do.

Invisibility rules (not), okay?

The most famous liberal response to the question of race is compounded by the shrug—the color-blind approach that would have us believe "we're all just human" or, in this case, "we're all just punk." Color-blindness suggests that race is *only* skin-deep; that beneath race is something more fundamental. It's a typically power-evasive move, one that pretends that individuals don't operate within the context of uneven social relations.

The call to transcend differences obscures the material and psychic effects of living in a maligned body—of racial, sexual, or national not-belonging.

And of course, it's always those of us who are "other"—non-white, non-Western, non-hetero, non-male—who are called upon to "transcend" these to become generically "just human," to enter a neutral state which presumably white straight men have got down pat *without even trying*.

Even on the most surface level, the process of making sure everybody is "just human" glosses over histories of people of color in punk because, so the story goes, *it doesn't matter what "color" they are*. But of course it *does* matter—the reasons why I got involved with punk have everything to do with my refugee-queer background, the way I came to understand myself as "alien" in a white working-class neighborhood in central Minnesota. And it might be hugely significant for kids who are otherwise wondering what the hell this white Punk Rock has to do with them, anyway.

But worse, this insistence that "we're all the same" leads to all kinds of equivalences that just make no sense at all. That is, "blue hair" discrimination *does not* even come close to rivaling racism. And if one more punk asks me to explain the difference between calling someone a "whiteboy" and calling someone a "nigger" or "chink," blood is seriously gonna flow. It's called history, people.

As Minor Threat's "Guilty of Being White," Black Flag's "White Minority," the Avengers' "White Nigger," or even Heavens to Betsy's "White Girl," aptly demonstrate, not all states of alienation are alike or "equal." That is, *mine does not match up neatly with yours.*

Where's the riot, white grrrl?

And yeah some of you say we are "out to kill white boy mentality" but have you examined your own mentality? Your white upper-middle-class girl mentality? What would you say if I said that I wanted to kill that mentality too?

Would you say: "what about sisterhood?!"

—Lauren Martin, *You Might As Well Live* no. 4 (Spring 1997)

When it first delivered a good, swift kick to the masculinist punk paradigm where it counted most, riot grrrl marked the not-so-generic-after-all "whitestraightpunkboy." That is, riot grrrl confronted the popular illusion of the "abstract (punk) citizen" and forced punk to examine its given categories of ex-/inclusion. And while previous—and, I think, less radical—manifestations of feminist politics in punk went the way of grim assertions of equality, *riot grrrl made you look.* That is, riot grrrl practiced an unabashedly *embodied* polemic, exercising an oppositional body politic that ruptured the foundation myth of punk egalitarianism.

Now, I truly believe that riot grrrl was—and is—the best thing that ever happened to punk. Please, quote me on that. Riot grrrl critically interrogated how power, and specifically sexism, organized punk. Unfortunately, riot grrrl often reproduced structures of racism, classism, and (less so) heterosexism in privileging a generalized "we" that primarily described the condition of mostly white, mostly middle-class women and girls. For students of feminist history, the so-called second wave—also white-dominated—stumbled over the same short-sighted desire to universalize what weren't very universal definitions of "woman," "the female condition," and "women's needs."

Again, all differences are not created equal. In the hey-day of the second wave, Euro-American feminists caught a lot of flak for comparing (white, middle-class) housework to (black) slavery and riot grrrls are hardly innocent—I've read work by white grrrls abusing the loaded symbolism of black skin to describe the condition of fat discrimination. Hierarchizing oppressions isn't the point, but historicizing oppressions and accounting for material inequalities *is*.

"A friend of color equals better living!"

Once race finally came up in conversation, a deluge of white punk/grrrl confessions flooded the arena. Suddenly everyone was "working" on his or her privileges. Because I'm a demanding girl I'm not impressed—the ways in which "accountability" gets defined and expressed are really problematic. So when p-rock individualism meets riot grrrl's insistence that we take it in the backyard, sometimes not-so-revolutionary things happen. The result is often self-referential, guilt-stricken confessions, broken record-style. (Evil Mimi pipes up, "I blame emo!") I read in one white girl's zine, "I work on the racist thoughts and actions that are just totally subconscious, but I still feel weird about everything. I don't have any friends who are of color. I don't know how to react to people of color." Um, what? Just who was this written for, anyway?

From another emo-zine: "I'm working on my sexism, classism, racism. My revolution deals with me. These are things I am doing to make myself feel better."

And another: "[She] told me that if I wanted to understand and work on my racism, classism, sexism that I need to actively pursue intimate relationships with less privileged people and prove that I can be a real ally to them."

Revolution narrowly defined as individual self-improvement ("I'm doing this for me!") isn't much of a revolution. Again, it's a national phenomena: social change shrinks to fit. It's a popular "band-aid" liberal response to structural inequalities, something akin to "love sees no color" or "I have black friends." I've even read zines that define racism as a "lack of love," easily remedied once "we all recognize each other as family." (This is me, puking.)

The original feminist maxim "the personal is political" registered a transformative logic. Certain personal experiences, like rape, were reinterpreted as social phenomena with histories and political consequences. This was—and *is*—still a revolutionary concept that grounds politics in our everyday lives. But when all politics become only personal, they become removed from both history and immediate social realities so that "race" is acknowledged only as this frozen thing "we" (a conditional, white-ish "we") have to be "more sensitive" to. Meanwhile, social change on any other level is put off and rarely addressed. God knows I'm the first girl to utter all kinds of blasphemies about the ways in which we organize or "do" activism, but getting down to brass tacks, I still think social justice is, you know, *important*.

Moreover, the whole "pursuing friendships with the less privileged" has a real creepy paternalistic vibe. Like other liberal approaches to race, it not only commodifies the "racial other" ("How many friends of color can you collect?") but again denies individual deep complicity with the systematic structures of race and racism. What's uniquely annoying here is the whole "it'll make me a better person/I'm working on my racism" confessional spin—it's ultimately self-serving, self-referential, and, really, arrogant. As a friend of mine put it, "It makes befriending folks of color sound like a pottery class: personally enriching."

In/appropriate behavior

Uh huh I see / Mm-hmm oh I see / You So aware / but my I.D. is your novelty
—Sta-prest, "Let's Be Friendly with Our Friends," *Let's Be Friendly* EP

Appropriation is easy—it supposedly lets "us" off all kinds of hooks, as if the desire to be near, speak for, or even be the Other, was in itself an antiracist strategy. A few years ago in a zine called *Wrecking Ball*, two girls conducted an interview with one another that neatly "ate the Other," to paraphrase black feminist bell hooks, taking the notion of "colonizing blackness" to new levels. Citing a "possible Ethiopian ancestor," a white girl shared with the reading public her decision to "claim" blackness. This was framed as a big antiracist breakthrough. She then went on to speak about an "us" that was defined as "African people all over the world," ignoring the *enormous* material privileges of being nationally and racially Euro-American. Romanticizing blackness and black oppression, she of course doesn't have to actually *live* in a black body. And the emphasis here on a depoliticized "love" (she insists "we are family") performs a kind of amnesia—disguised as something utopian—by abandoning an analysis or engagement with structural inequalities for a privatized, individualized solution.

The Make-Up—with their white-ish gospel thing—kinda bother me. Not that I have anything invested in authenticity. I don't believe that "culture" is or should be understood as static or unchanging, but call me cynical, I'm suspicious of Western avant-garde (including punk) claims to

transgress bourgeois banality channeled through acts of cultural confisca-
tion. So can the Make-Up exist without referencing Elvis's gift to rock 'n'
roll—making black music safe for white folk? This isn't a judgment call as
much as it's a demand to critically examine the dynamics of any so-called
exchange.

There's always room for leftovers.

Other ways to not account for (racial) privilege, or, at least, do it badly?
Out-and-out condescension is an option; there's always talk in punk of
"making room" for the voices of people of color, talk that never quite
examines the power relations involved, i.e., who's making the room
anyway?

And we can't forget the "my great-grandmother was an Irish immigrant" narrative that romanticizes the past in order to evade complicity
and privilege in the now.

Or the "voice of the voiceless" syndrome: rich white kids talking about
people of color or Third World revolutions while avoiding their own complicity in systems of domination. That is, avoiding—for one thing—the
power implicit in presuming to become the "voice" for a population
assumed to be otherwise "voiceless."

And there is, of course, the increasingly popular "race traitor" card—
anarchists really like this one. Called the "new abolitionism," the formula
is pretty straightforward. If enough individual whites voluntarily *decide*
not to be white, creating some sort of critical mass of "ex-white" people,
racial inequality will be toppled by their collective sacrifice and we can all
rejoice. Saved by the white, oops! I mean, "ex-white" people.

Of course, we have Howard Winant to put a damper on proceedings:
"[The new abolitionists] fail to consider the complexities and rootedness
of racial formation. Is the social construction of whiteness so flimsy that
it can be repudiated by a mere act of political will, or even by widespread
and repeated acts at rejecting white privilege?"

Do I need to say it again? You know the drill, but here's the buzzwords:
"rugged individualism," accountability, uneven power relations. *Go.*

"What the hell now?" Coalition politics for a punk age

There are lots of zines that do good—often amazing—work on cultural politics and the social and psychic relations of race: Keyan Meymand's *Kreme Koolers*, Bianca Ortiz's *Mamasita*, Kristy Chan's *Tennis & Violins*, Rita Fatila's *Pure Tuna Fish*, Lauren Martin's *You Might As Well Live*, *Chop Suey Spex*, *The Bakery*, just to name a few. And again, there are always those writers and activists who are doing a lot of important work around institutional racisms—interrogating the nitty-gritty structural issues and ideological underpinnings of urban underdevelopment, environmental racism/toxic dumping, the prison-industrial complex, welfare reform, affirmation action, and yes, U.S. foreign policy. And they can and do write responsibly, accounting for their social location, aware of how that might position them in relation to the subjects about which they're writing.

Punk doesn't exist in a vacuum. Even on the most superficial level, recruitment, while fun, isn't a solution. Diversification of our membership rolls is way different than effecting critical transformations at the analytic level—and in any case hardly addresses the people of color who are in or around punk now. (And yes, we're here, thanks. Banging our heads against the wall, maybe, but we're here.) What needs to happen—on a punk-scale and a large-scale sort of way—is a revolution in the ways in which we frame ourselves within social, psychic and political relations. If you can read Noam Chomsky, you can also read Chandra Mohanty, Andrew Ross, or Lauren Berlant. If you don't know who they are, *find out*.

What all this doesn't mean is, "I can't talk about anything because I'm a white, straight male." That's too easy—too often an excuse not to do your homework. I don't believe that the specific plot-points of your social location have to determine your conscious political agenda (i.e., there's no one-to-one correspondence between the two) and I'm way over the "more oppressed than thou" calculus. I'd like to think my praxis is more complicated than that. And no, I'm not "just like" you but hey, coalitions are risky—and hopefully productive—that way.

So if you're white, own your whiteness. (And yes, I realize that people live their whiteness differently according to how it intersects with gender, class, sexuality, et cetera, within their personal context.) Don't assume whiteness describes the world. Challenge others when they do. My friend Iraya—Aloofah of the sadly defunct multiracial multisubcultural queer pop ensemble Sta-Prest—calls it "doing the white on white."

You (and I mean everybody now) can be accountable to your social location. Interrogate and historicize your place in society, punk, whatever, and be aware of *how* you talk about race, gender, sexuality—it's political. Examine all the categories you're using at least *twice* for hidden assumptions, exclusions, erasures. Recognize power in all its forms, how it operates. Engage it, even use it strategically. And work *with* me, not for me.

Actively creating a public culture of dissent—punk or not—will have to involve some self-reflexive unpacking of privileges/poverties and their historical and political contexts. Here's my bid, where's yours?

Mimi Nguyen, "It's (Not) a White World: Looking for Race in Punk," *Punk Planet* no. 28 (Chicago, November/December 1998).

"JUST ANOTHER NIGGER," LETTER EXCHANGE IN *MAXIMUMROCKNROLL*

Before Mimi Nguyen explicitly named the "Race Riot," punks of color were expressing their alienation in exchanges like the one reproduced below. The letters section of zines truly exemplifies the way punk works, or rather works itself out. These exchanges provide a platform for engagement among zinesters, bands, labels, collectors, activists, and fans. As a result, it is not surprising that here we might see a debate surrounding the issues of race and racial identity in punk take place. In August 1990, a letter appeared in *Maximumrocknroll*, a zine well known for its lengthy and often contentious letters section, eviscerating punk for its casual and overt racism and its implicitly White identity and power structure. The author signs the letter "Just another nigger," and concludes by advocating for all Black participants to leave the scene. Needless to say, thereafter came the stimulus response, some of which we have included here. The first puts forth a dream of integration; another sees punk rock as a place for "misfits," and thus a natural setting to find a community outside and against the feeling of being the racial outcast fostered by culture at large. Still another finds in Skrewdriver's racist "Oi!" a way to articulate his own racial and cultural pride in being Chicano, while another posits that race does not exist and that "J.a.n." (as the author comes to be called) merely did not feel enough attachment to or affection for the music; in other words, all things being equal, "punk will out." Finally, the last letter gets at the ambivalence of the problem, walking the line between

rigorous critique of punk's racism and heartfelt hope for the scene.

Maximumrocknroll, August 1990

Dear MRR,

I recently disassociated myself with the hardcore/punk scene, but I still feel that I have some feelings for your magazine that I want to come to terms with, and like many of the letter writers I have a story/philosophy to tell. The reason why I was probably attached to MRR was because of the columns. Those editorials had a way of making me personally attached (the objective of my entering the scene) to the publication more than the shows or anything else the scene had to offer. So I couldn't throw off my attachment to the mag as easily as I did away from the scene.

The main reason I had to get out of the scene was because I was a black kid. The reasons why my blackness was relevant will be discussed later. I first got into punk when I saw *Sid and Nancy.* The punk culture seemed like an interesting aspect of white culture that I wasn't aware of, being entrenched (not unhappily) in the world of the black ghetto. When I moved into the white suburbs I decided to expose myself to that form of white culture if I was going to be involved in any form of white culture (I didn't want to become a close-minded recluse).

Never Mind the Bollocks seemed like the only punk record I was ever going to like, and I bought a sufficient amount of Sex Pistols memorabilia, I decided to get involved in what I considered the existing form of punk which was Hardcore. It was necessary to do this because since I started living my life off of the Sex Pistols in the frighteningly dull suburbs, I needed something else to live off of since the Pistols was becoming a dead end.

The first Hardcore record I bought was the first Millions of Dead Cops LP just because the cover looked like what I conceived hardcore as being. It proved to be a wise choice as it turned out to be ultimate extremism, attitude wise and musically, I had hoped for. But the raised expectations I received from that record failed me as my dollars wasted away on Spermbirds, Didjits and Kissin' Cousins' records. I decided that I had to attach myself to a genre of HC that wouldn't let me down.

This genre became the straight edge scene. I got into it because my neighbor convinced me that Ray of [Youth of] Today's anti-racist lyrics overrode any perceived threat I had of the nazi skinheads who were in the scene. I engulfed myself in the scene and began to see the attitudes behind the lyrics. Some bands seemed to be as sincere on the subject of racism as they could be, but it seemed like just another well needed song concept for a lot of bands who didn't really have anything to say.

After my pal began to hang out with a nazi crowd, the nazis' attacking blacks became evident to me, and the attitudes of the scene became apparent, my disillusionment increased rapidly.

First off, I couldn't really say the music got to my pleasure senses. As I implied before the main attraction was the social involvement. I could tell when a band was good, what kind of way they had to play so they would be "really Hardcore," but I always thought that I never really had the love for the music that I should have had if I really enjoyed it. Subsequently after an attempt to create an international HC correspondence newsletter failed, I created my own "zine." It came out extremely soulless.

Soon the social side turned out to be a bust. Do not get the assumption that if I wasn't in the SE scene everything would have been okay, I feel the major problem stemmed from the differences, social and otherwise of black and white. The non-racist SE kids seemed to have a way of liking Skrewdriver which puzzled me, and just the plain attitude in which I was dealt with by most whites, even the people I considered sincere, made me see that for some reason that whites, in a totally white dominated arena such as the hardcore scene, had a way of relating to blacks that I did not appreciate. It was like every show somebody did something to piss me off, and it was usually the supposed non-racists.

To any slight received from my white comrades, I didn't respond because I felt it served me right for entering a white dominated social set. I never was conditioned to hang around whites like many black hardcore kids so I felt I always had the option of leaving. This was their thing and if I didn't like it I should get out. I saw and admired militant blacks in the scene but because of the scene's nature they seemed to be constantly fighting an unwinnable war. I also really didn't like the fact that since I was a black in white scene I had to become a staunch integrationist, always ready to run off some garbage about how blacks should mosh along with whites, some of whom would subsequently kick the asses of our brothers and sisters.

Please don't take this as a letter saying "you hypocritical straight edge bastards" because I don't care to indict anyone of any racist thought. I don't blame the non-racist kids for being jerks because I understand that it is the nature of America to breed that kind of mindset, plus it is just the nature of groups. When you get a group of people that think they have something in common it is natural for them to treat perceived outsiders of that group differently and callously. Since I understand that fact I do not intend to start a civil rights movement within the hardcore scene. I am attaching myself, and I think all other blacks should attach themselves to the rap scene (which I grew up on and always have loved), and hardcore should be left to the whites. This process will definitely separate black kids from white kids more, but if no one is going to create a better solution for all of the black kids that get fucked up in the scene then why are we staying or listening to the people that say stay? ...

There should be no black kids in the hardcore/punk scene or any white dominated area of American life (if they can help it), and if you remain in it you deserve every ass kicking you receive from it.

Just another nigger.

Maximumrocknroll, September 1990
Duh, this is in response to Mr. "just another nigger" from MRR #87,
OK, first off, let me state I'm black. I don't know, maybe that gives me some kind of credibility to you. Second, I've been known to be totally naïve on most issues, so if I'm completely wrong in thinking you're out of your mind, let me know.

The black separatism you endorse is merely another way of playing into the hands of a society that thrives on keeping people separated. Take your view on punk for example: you see problems with racism in it and your solution isn't to confront it and render it obsolete by getting more blacks into the scene, but to leave it and let it fester by encouraging all black kids to listen to rap! You went on and talked fatalistically about how we'll never get "white domination" out of rock, but ain't it worth a try? Wouldn't that be better than running off to our own little ghettos, not even bothering to try to communicate with one another (and then of course there'd be the inevitable interracial fighting)?

Now if I may slag black supremacy: yes, America was largely founded and is still controlled by greedy whites, but separating blacks from whites only leaves whites who aren't supremacists stuck in the same place they were in before. And who sez if blacks got away from all white influence everything would be better? Hell, tribes in Africa were slaughtering and oppressing each other before any of 'em had even seen a white person. Black separatism is an almost understandable reaction to oppression by rich (not all) whites, but it's also wrong. You're perceiving all white people as being part of some giant conspiracy to oppress all blacks, but what about the poor whites? Your solution to the problem of racism achieves nothing except making it worse.

Check out this insane dream: we all share each other's cultures and a person could, of his or her own free will, decide which culture or subculture he/she wants to identify him/herself with. Wouldn't it be great if we could take the whole "us vs. them" thing and toss it? And still get along with each other? Of course we could still take into account the struggles of various peoples to attain their rights, but instead see them as struggles to, in the long run, bring us humans together as one species, diverse yet tolerant. Alas, it's only a dream. Well, if you let it be…

Jai Smith, geek / Ettrick, VA

Maximumrocknroll, October 1990
Dear MRR,
This is in response to "Just another nigger." Let's get something straight up front. I am black, male, 24 and SE [straight edge]. The comments or actions of any number of racist assholes cannot change that. Dude, why are you so negative? If you didn't like the music, why did you get into it?

From growing up in an all-white suburban town (Pleasanton, CA) to going to an all-white school in Hayward, I know the kind of prejudice and hatred that white people can inflict on minorities. I spent many of my younger years wishing I was white. That is the worst thing to ever happen to me. I'm sure I wasn't the only one this happened to. Of course I felt like a misfit so by the time I got to high school I hung out with the other misfits who didn't fit in with the blond haired, blue eyed barbie doll malibu Ken jock and cheerleader types. For once I was accepted for who I was instead of what I was.

In saying that black people should not be in hardcore, you are making a racist statement. Anybody who wants to can be into any type of music or life style that they want. Don't limit yourself because of the ignorance of others. The only limits on you are the ones you set yourself. I will always do exactly what I want. I don't see myself as anything except a person. Find inner strength in that and don't black society or the scene.

Think about it.

Eric Fortner / Hayward, CA
P.S. Any black str8 edgers or punks write to me. I know you're out there. Tell me about your life and scene. XXX

Dear MRR,
In response to the guy who wrote about leaving the HC/punk scene in issue #87. I find similar conflicts facing me at this moment in the not

so active S. Cal Oi-punk scene. I found many things he had to say to be factual and discouraging to ethnics in the underground scene. You find that some "so-called" anti-racist groups or organizations, get so involved with themselves they form a type of gang that admits no new persons and attacks them. Sure, if you find ethnics in these organizations, but what's more pathetic is that people of your own race attack you on the grounds that you don't measure on an economic scale to them!

But I've learned to live with this bullshit for some time now, from almost every angle of my social structure, I live in south-central L.A. a few blocks from Watts (which is a black "so-called" ghetto) but which I proudly call home. Before I lived in a mostly dominated Hispanic side of Oxnard, CA and that's where the Oi music influenced me.

At Manual Arts High (from which I graduate this year) I would get all this bullshit from black kids who are paranoid to see a shaved-head and boots kid around the neighborhood, until some took time and began to know me and respect me, and not assume or relate all shaved heads with Nazism. But my Mexican counter-parts continue to call me a "Tio Tomas" (Uncle Tom) and other bullshit, 'cuz their "cholo scene" (Mexican gang shit) wasn't my taste. And they can't understand why a low class (true working class) mex would shave his head and listen to punk music, maybe all he wanted is to be with and around white people. That's all they assumed since they are so fuckin' busy killing their and my own race!!

I don't consider myself an Uncle Tom since I ask nothing of my Anglo friends. I hang around no one for the simple fact that I know they (either side, Mex or whites) will not accept my way of life.

I do listen to Skrewdriver but I don't agree with most of their thoughts, instead I try to change them around to fit my views. I don't think the anglos are a master race, I find that saying in every group just that these anglos repeat it more. I think it's fine to love your race, but not to Skrewdriver's point.

But they (white supremacists) don't understand or act as if they don't understand that America has never been and will never be a pure white country! And we ethnics should and must stay in the scene to show these humans that we may be of different cultures and both praise our own race with the words of Skrewdriver. (Like "Don't let them pull you down, Mexican" in my view). We are in neither of our fatherland. We are in the land of the Sioux, Mohawk, Navajo, etc …

When you go back to England, Germany, I will go back to Mexico. But all this bigot shit come from middle class suburbia, remember "Oi" (true skins in England came from the poor working class) and who is the working class here in America? Yes, illegal Mexicans (mostly Indian Mexicans or cross breeds). But did this government ask the legal land owners permission to form a government in their land? America was formed by illegal English *Mayflower* people—they have no right to say who is illegal or not. So I hope the Afro-American who wrote the letter views my point. I would much rather fight a white supremacist for a cause, than a person of my own race for the color of my pants. Wake up, stupid Chicanos, you don't kill anyone else but your own race!

Francisco Sanchez

Dear MRR,
I'm writing in response to a letter signed "Just another nigger," issue #87. I'll just call him J.a.n. for short. ...
    Your letter hits me hard because like you I'm a black kid in a mostly white scene and I try to make it a point to visit other scenes as often as I'm able to, and in those scenes I've made lasting friendships with other minorities that are in the same shoes as I am. Although we would agree with some of your points I can speak for them also when I say that your "all blacks should leave their scenes and listen to rap music" attitude disgusts me. Why not enjoy both forms of expression at the same time? Is that something that you are unable to do?
    Another reason that I feel that your little experiment with "white culture" failed is because it seems to me that you lacked a genuine love for the music itself. The love for the music is the common bond and one of the main elements that keeps us together. That might sound a little corny but being addicted to the music itself is in my opinion the prime requisite because if a genuine love of the music is missing then your chances of appreciating the whole subculture will be very low.
    Like I said before I do agree with some of your points like your comments about the characteristics of a racist society. And your comment about how it's impossible to reason with a nazi. And how fairness is not a dominating element in the nazi mind. It also seems like common sense is not a quality that fascists have. The problem lies in the fact that their way of thinking does not leave open the forum of debate or argument in which one would be able to show them how their philosophy is full of holes or how their ideology is bankrupt. That being the case, the only way to have a successful debate with a nazi is by talking to him in a language that he will understand. On this issue I tend to side with the militant anti-nazi organizations that refuse to tolerate it on any level. If they can't understand

the language of reason then we must resort to the language of violence, which by the way seems to be much more effective in the battle against the nazis. They must be told in a language that they can understand that their ignorance will not be tolerated and that they are not welcome.

Jan, I fell sorry for you because you were open-minded enough to venture out and try something new, too bad it didn't work out but the next time you think of saying something as stupid as what you said in your last paragraph, think of the few black punk bands and bands with minorities in them that have stayed true to the cause and didn't give up when the going got rough. Think of the ones that make songs that sing out against racism so that people like you and me can be better accepted in our scenes. Also think of the minorities that have suffered verbal or physical abuse at the hands of bigots but never considered leaving the scene because for them their involvement and the music was more than an experiment and had become a way of life.

Good luck with your rap music and don't lose that open mind.

J.P. / Louisville, KY

Maximumrocknroll, November 1990
Dear MRR and readers,
Normally I wouldn't take the time to type out a letter to nobody, but since I respect your zine and all … I've written plenty of letters to y'all in my head, but I figured there were more than enough "I hate Ben Weasel" letters, and letters of the "punk's not dead" variety, so I trashed most of them before even getting to the typewriter. So why am I writing this time?

I want to respond to a couple of letters from the last two issues (87 & 88). Both were written by African-American men, "Just another nigger" and Jai Smith. In the letter from "Just another nigger" the situation for African-Americans in the hardcore scene is made very clear: IT SUCKS! This ain't no whitebread perspective. I have floated in and out of the hard-core scene, and sundry disillusionments mainly cause of all the hassle I got for being African-American (and an out dyke). The Chicago scene is notorious for its extremely brutal, racist, fascist skins. In those days there were no anti-fascist skins. I don't know how I feel about a bunch of bald white boys protecting me and THE SCENE from another bunch of bald whiteboys anyway. Having been in enough fights, physical and verbal, with racist skins, I can completely sympathize with "Just another nigger"'s change of heart. It gets colder and harder. When I see the racist crap that [*MMR* columnists] Mykel Board and Ben Weasel write I feel just as abused. Mykel: KEEP YOUR RACIST TURN-OF-THE-CENTURY TERMS OFF MY PEOPLE! "Negro" went out with segregated buses, get it? It ain't even a matter of being hip to the terms. "Negroid features" was a lie constructed by white colonialist "anthropologists." As for the mugging qualities inherent in "Negros" it should be obvious that this is a bullshit stereotype forced on African-Americans by an inherently racist and classist system of oppression. As for Ben Weasel's Neanderthal views on racism—grow up or read a book or something. Shit, some of the folks out there might find it surprising that punks of color aren't too pleased with their role in the punk scene.

The second letter that I referred to by Jai Smith seems to be along the lines of the surprised category. Jai, you are a bit naïve. I would agree that the punk scene doesn't necessarily have to be completely abandoned by people of color. There's a lot of worthwhile music and people in the punk scene. I could never totally give up. BUT, I think Jai, that you do a lot of overcompensating and explaining for a group of people who generally couldn't care less about racism (meaning white middleclass boys). You'd have to do a fuck of a lot of dreaming to make Tawana Brawleys and Eleanor Bumpers of this decade disappear. This is why the whole unity scam isn't gonna click so easily in the punk scene. If punks of color really want to get something out of the scene they need to be vocal. They need to be seen. THE SCENE ain't no different from the mainstream when it comes to racism. We got to respond the same way. We've already learned that self-determination/radical action is a means to tearing racism down. Malcolm X and Angela Davis taught us that. We can't wait 'til white punks get it together; we got to move together now. This ain't separatism. Black nationalism ain't my thang. Doin' our own thang within the punk scene is possible.

As far as rap being the "better" alternative ... No! When the rhymes are "bold, politically cold" that's fine, but most aren't. The rappers that do know what's up (Public Enemy, Jungle Brothers, BDP) can't get beyond all the sexist, homophobic, and, yes, classist crap this society feeds them. I get bored with all the macho bullshit and pretty soon I'm disillusioned by that scene too. So maybe punks of color should start thinking about the D.I.Y. principle that built this scene.

I better quit before this turns into a book. But some last comments. I think the MRR folks better take a closer look at their definition of racism. If they're truly committed to keeping racist stuff out of their zine they'll stop with white liberal apologist angle and also think about the next time they let Mykel Board run a column. African-American punks, if you're interested, I'd like to put together a zine with a *real* anti-racist point of view. I'd especially like to hear from African-American wimmin, or other wimmin of color. Write me if you're into it. In the meantime—Fight The Power and Keep The Faith. This beat is DONE!

Ayassa /Solon Springs, WI

Letters from *Maximumrocknroll* nos. 87–90 (Berkeley: 1990).

KELLY BESSER, "WHAT HAPPENED?"

We don't think it mere coincidence that the "J.a.n." debate took place in 1990. The '90s marked a generational shift in punk rock, a passing of the torch from the often nihilistic, frequently inchoate, and always oppositional punk politics of the first waves of New York, London, and California punk rock to a more self-conscious, articulated, and "positive" politics that grew to dominate the scene. Here Kelly, one of the editors of the zine *Chop Suey Spex*, takes us directly into the punk rock generation gap by writing about an interchange between herself and the punk legend Exene Cervenka of X. Exene represents a time when the purpose of punk was to, in Dick Hebdige's words, "perform the decline," and bring to light ugliness as "art." The problem is that said art remains ugly, and the performative irony that once served as its justification makes little sense to a new era of punk kids raised on Clash-style earnestness and authenticity that ended up winning out in punk's politicization. Whereas Exene likely understood her Chop Suey Specs as kitschy commentary on the racism of American popular culture, Kelly sees them as simply racist.

Tribe 8 just finished their set at You've Got Bad Taste, a store in Silverlake co-owned by Exene Cervenkova (formerly known as Exene Cervenka from a band called X). I was wandering around the store with Lala and Karla, looking at a lot of old stock merchandise and the old school punk rock flyers and photos that cover the walls. One minute we were looking at harmless popsicle stick houses and the next we were staring at these fake glasses with "Oriental" eyes (read: slanted slits) molded into the frames.

They were sick and fucked up and we couldn't understand why Exene would want to stock them. We saw her walking by so we stopped her to ask. Lala pointed to the Chop Suey Specs and asked, "Do you think I need these?" Exene maintained a borderline blank stare. Then Karla told her we thought the glasses were racist. Exene reminded us that the store is called You've Got Bad Taste. We told her that this was not an issue of Good Taste–Bad Taste. Then she told us that her store specializes in Americana. Karla argued that the Specs were alienating to Asian customers. This comment got us dismissed. Exene shook her head and said, "Whatever. I don't care. Steal them." Then she walked away.

Kelly Besser, "What Happened?" from *Chop Suey Spex* no. 1, eds. Kelly Besser and Felix Endara (New York: c. 1997) reprinted in *Evolution of a Race Riot* no. 1, ed. Mimi Nguyen (Berkeley, 1997),

MADHU KRISHNAN,
"HOW CAN YOU BE SO COLD?"

While it may not have been embraced in the same way as Riot Grrrl or queercore, the Race Riot did spread. In 2000, the Canadian political activist Helen Luu put together her own Race Riot–inspired zine called *How to Stage a Coup*, bringing together people of color's voices from both the punk scene and the activist community. In her short piece from that zine Madhu Krishnan brings to light punk's replication of an assimilation-based neutrality. That is to say that punk covertly insists that its members take up "punk" as their dominant identity. This impulse often comes from a good place—a rejection of those things that divide us in an effort to emphasize what unites us—but its practice often ends up producing the same discourse of assimilation that structures American and European conceptions of citizenship, overwriting cultural and racial difference and producing what Krishnan identifies here as a kind of psychic split, or placelessness for people of color—outside of every circuit of attempted identification, out in the cold.

"How can you be so cold? You are the meanest girl I've ever met. What makes you so cold?"

I remember the night my old friend said those words to me. I remember looking around whatever dark club, reeking of smoke, that we were in and thinking that my friend was absolutely right, and that I was absolutely caught—cold, mean, and hiding behind fast growing walls of nihilism and cynicism, I felt like I'd been found out, revealed. And I remember thinking that there couldn't be a single person in that steamy, crowded room who stood half a chance of smashing the brick wall I kept wrapped so tight around me into the million pieces I was dying for it to fragment into.

I remember some other things, too.

It's the same old story. You know it, so I'm not going to waste anyone's time by repeating it. Trust me, it's probably better this way. Let's just keep it simple—disaffected (pre)teen in the throes of mental anguish and some precocious form of existential angst finds solace in the fabled fairy tale land of American subculture, where everyone is embraced, loved, and respected, simply by virtue of their existence within said subculture. Everyone is equal. Everyone has a voice, and everyone counts, no matter what the majority or minority may say. The only thing is, that's not quite the whole story. In fact, it doesn't even come close, all because of one simple but so fundamental difference: I am not white.

My "disaffected youth" was one that, on the surface, was replete with every privilege one could hope for, and I admit that quite a bit of that privilege went far deeper than just the surface. Rich, suburban Boston, huge front lawns to run and play in, and one of the best public school systems around characterized my childhood. I, as an Indian child, was one of perhaps three non-white students in my school, throughout all thirteen years that I spent in public education, from K to 12. This had the curious side effect of making any and all discrimination and racism that I experienced all the more implicit, insidious, and hurtful in its nature: to everyone else I was an "honorary white kid," and any non-white/non-homogenous aspects of my home life that leaked into my social life were either swept away completely, or subtly filed away as some kind of joke. And so in the end, it, and I, just turned back to that old story: I ran to subculture to find my own place in the world as me, not just some token-assimilated-quasi-white kid/novelty figure.

What I thought I would find in punk rock was some intangible thing that would let me find appreciation (or, at very least, understanding) for myself. What I thought I would find in punk rock was something to thaw the coldness I felt so acutely, both towards my own culture (and the parts of me forever touched by that culture) and towards the rest of the world, which I felt could never understand that or do it for me.

What I found in punk rock, however, was more of the same. I found, in place of outright ignorance or avoidance of race and gender politics, the requisite, tired PC rhetoric about how "racism is bullshit" and "everyone is equal," etc., only to see the same kids who touted those ideals turn around and worship the pale-skinned, red-lipped ideal of beauty in the next breath. I found a whole lot of talk and self-congratulating "discourse" on how great it is that punk rock has evolved past the rest of the world because of course, none of the problems of racism exist in the punk world, and then I found the same person who claimed these things exclaiming on how the whitest of skin and light, light hair are the loveliest traits in a person. I found that when I brought up the discomfort this made me feel, I'd be hastily brushed off, told I was being too sensitive, simply humored or patronized, or even that I was trying to strip away other people's right to their own standards of (white) acceptability. In short, I found myself exposed to the same old backhanded, ingrained racism I had grown up with. I found myself referred to as the "honorary white one" again.

And so again, I grew cold. And now still, I grow cold, and colder with every action, word, or look that reinforces the same mantra that I grew up with: that I, as a woman of color, do not count. That my identity is not as important as my assimilation would be to ease the discomfort of others. There is a responsibility to educate, but when education and communication turn into cycles of beating my head against the wall, I think it's time to cut my losses and pack my bags.

The main problem with the duality of being a person of color involved in subculture is that the nature of many subcultures is so strong that the members of said subculture are expected to completely identify within it, and only it, primarily even at the expense of every other facet of their identity. Even when you try to identify as both, you're still qualified as the "_____ punk kid." You are neither here nor there, and not fully accounted for in either place.

So my friend wanted to know how I could be so cold, and this is how: I cannot be a "true" Indian because I was/am involved in subculture (which is a whole other story—the stereotypical notion of the typical, preppy semi-conservative Indian girl in modern America). I cannot be a "true" member of subculture, in my case punk rock, because I do not want to ignore my culture, because I want to hold it in my life as more than a fashion accessory or occasional pastime. Much like I cannot be a true member of mainstream culture because I do not fit any of the typical prerequisites for mainstream American culture. I am neither here nor there, outside in both cases. How can you be stuck outside for so long without turning cold?

Madhu Krishnan, "How Can You Be So Cold?" *How to Stage a Coup*, ed. Helen Luu (Scarborough, ON, September 2000).

TASHA FIERCE,
"BLACK INVISIBILITY AND RACISM IN PUNK ROCK"

A peculiar phenomenon of Race Riot–inspired zine writing is that certain pieces, through reprinting and anthologizing, take on lives of their own beyond their original context. This piece, for instance, written by Fierce for her *Bitchcore* zine, was reprinted recently in a Pensacola, Florida, zine called *Finger on the Trigger* (Nguyen's *Punk Planet* essay has found itself making similar travels). In it, the author develops the theme of "invisibility" as it operates in punk rock, providing a significant analytic for the treatment of both subtle and overt racism in the scene. The author argues that racism in punk has more to do with subtle assumptions while pointing out examples of prejudice that sound much more like overt, explicit racial antagonism, but this gets at a deeper point: in order for punk rock in its most recent iteration to lay claim to itself as antiracist, it disappears race from its understanding of itself. Insofar as punk sees itself as neutral or overarching, racial subject positions *are simply not allowed to exist.* You are a punk, not a person of color, and thus white—ostensibly raceless—punks feel free to indulge in subtle and not-so-subtle racist jokes, stereotyping, and the like. You really can't be a racist if no one cares about race, right?

Who woulda thought? How white supremacy still exists inside the punk rock bubble.

I'd always get pissed when, on IRC, in a punk chat room, people would just ASSUME I was white. Or, even when I gave them my pics, they'd think of every ethnicity but black to guess as my race. Then when I would tell them, "Well, I'm half black and half white," they'd be shocked. "You're BLACK???" would invariably be the reply. "Wow, I've never met a black punk." I guess eventually I learned to take it in stride but I also started to think about the subversive racism contained in that reaction. It's as if when I state my race as being black, automatically a taste in music, a style of clothing, and a type of speech come with it. I'm sure most of these punk rock revolutionary kids don't even notice that they're prejudiced the way they are. I'm sure they believe they are totally open-minded and that there is nary a racist thought in their liberty spiked head. I'm sorry to say that this is not the case.

To like punk is not joining a whites-only club. But when you get involved in the "scene," when you come in contact with other people who like punk, when you go to shows and do zines—you're stepping neck-deep in an institution steeped with subverted racism. It's subtle. It's not like I'm going to go to a Peechees show and find myself swimming in white power skinhead girls testing out a tree to lynch me on. It's the kind of thing that I described earlier when talking about my appearance—really hard to put a finger on, yet there nonetheless. Maybe a group of "friends" will make some racist jokes and then laugh; because "it's all in good fun." Maybe when I comment on how I need to relax my hair they'll go off on how black people smell funny. Or as I talk about how clipart depicting black people costs money whereas clipart depicting white people is widespread and free, they'll launch into an hour long tirade about how black people should have to pay for their clipart because white people are better. And then they'll call me militant for disagreeing with them.

This was supposed to be about black invisibility in punk. But invisibility is doubled with racism, because once I got here, they had insults waiting. The invisibility means that they didn't even know a black person could like punk. The racism means that although I have that one thing in common with them, I still am an alien being. Maybe it's because punk hasn't been infiltrated by blacks for as long as some other forms of music, and they don't know how to act around a black person who likes anything other than rap or R&B. Maybe all they know of black people are the stereotypes they've been force-fed by popular culture. You can't turn on a TV today and see many black people doing anything but what white people think they're supposed to do. It's like a caricature, and in all my encounters with people in the "scene," they are operating off of this caricature. And I don't fit. They pay lip service to stopping racism yet it's not racism when they say "1000 black men at the bottom of the ocean is a good start" and then laugh. Saying "nigger" isn't appropriate but nothing is said when I'm called, disparagingly, a Rastafarian because I have braids. Because we're all fighting for the same cause, right? We all hate the government and we all love punk, and what does it matter that I feel outed because I never see another black face and you're constantly telling me I'm an aberration. This isn't about "fuck punk." It's about fuck you and your racist attitudes. It's about you waking up and realizing that you're not some kind of revolutionary while you continue to support this institutionalized racism that has even poisoned your precious little PUNK ROCK COMMUNITY.

I am ostracized by the black community and I am only partially accepted by the punk rock community as a token of punk's "fight against racism." Even other minorities are more accepted in punk than blacks, simply because they are perceived as being "more white." Other minorities don't have a pre-defined style of music that they should listen to; therefore it is more believable that they could like punk. I am in no way saying that racism doesn't exist for these minorities in punk. I am simply saying that there is less of a musical stereotype for them, and that facilitates their acceptance. The idea of punk rock as some kind of beacon of open-mindedness is bullshit. Most white punk rockers like to consider themselves absolved of their privilege simply because they publicly denounce racism and don't attend weekly KKK meetings. Let me reiterate: JUST BECAUSE YOU THINK RACISM IS WRONG DOES NOT MEAN YOU ARE NOT A RACIST. Whites will always have internalized racism, and that applies as much to the punk rocker as it does to the redneck. People will always have the need to feel superior, and for whites one area that they have been made to feel is superior about them for so many years is the color of their skin. This does not change when you start to like punk rock. Yes, you can recognize that white superiority is false. Yes, you can work to change it and yes, you have all made such wonderful progress. But shreds of memories of being number one, even if it wasn't in your lifetime, will always haunt you.

This is what causes my invisibility in your punk rock world, and this is what causes you to believe that it is O.K. to say one thing, and do another.

Please take note that I don't hate whites. I completely recognize that even my mother's family, who I love dearly, also bear the burden of racism. They are white, and they are privileged. I, as my mother's daughter, am more privileged than many black people. That is one reason why I am as accepted as I am in the punk rock community. My manner of speech, my pale skin, my house in suburbia—all of these things cause me to gain points of acceptance. But yet, I am not fully in the door, nor will I ever be. But I will not stay invisible. I will not stand idly by while you assume stereotypical things about me that do not apply. Punk rock is mine, too. I am not a black punk—I am black, and I like punk. The two are mutually independent of each other, and if you must use one, don't use the other.

I seriously doubt the issue of racism/invisibility in punk will ever be resolved, much like the issue of racism in society. I just want it to be known, although punk rock claims to be fighting the larger war, it must first win its own internal battle before any progress will be made.

Tasha Fierce, "Black Invisibility and Racism in Punk Rock," *Bitchcore* no. 1 (San Gabriel, CA: 1999), reprinted in *Finger on the Trigger* no. 3, ed. Adee (Pensacola, FL).

VINCENT CHUNG,
"I AM COLORBLIND"

In a piece from *Race Riot* no. 2, Vincent Chung, a zine writer for both *HeartattaCk* and *Punk Planet*, pushes the confessional, perzine format by injecting a heavy dose of well-aimed sarcasm. His target here is a typically White, typically liberal attitude on race and racism that proclaims it does not see racial difference—that it is, as it is often put, "colorblind." The deficiencies of such a position are obvious: race is a lived reality whether you "see" it or pretend not to and such claims further serve to erase the identities of people of color, in punk and in society at large. Chung, however, sees something else in the progressive punk pretension to be colorblind: a status move on the part of the White punk to assert his or her antiracist cred, that perversely relies upon the reality of racism. Doing this, the author charges, is "using my birth given disability as a vehicle for upward mobility." In this way the antiracist positions and politics taken on by punks can be understood as partly tools for identification and prestige, just like, as Chung puts it, so many band-logo badges.

I am I am I am. Seriously, though … toss me a collectable green NYHC record and I might think it's yellow. Or brown depending on the shade of green. During a recent forage in a second hand store, I picked up a shirt and exclaimed, "What a score on this rad white T-shirt!!!" David quickly set me straight on my fumble by retorting, "No, Vince, that shirt is hot pink." With much chagrin, I placed the shirt back on the rack as clerks and customers snickered at my comprehension of what you "normal" people adhere to colors. My face turned a deep shade of T-shirt. I'm sure it looked cute but it's not funny.

At some workshop, some fest ago, some straight edge vegan sensitively emo white liberal boy proclaimed that he was colorblind. He sees color just fine, but for some reason, everyone who has different colored skin is pretty much on an equal level to him. Obviously, I called this bluff on by using my disability as a metaphor for his pseudo PC "I'm at this fest to get chicks" punk rock persona. Seriously, PC points are just as important as what cool band buttons you have on your gain station jacket lapel. So I think to myself, "Dude! This guy is a poseur!" which automatically warrants a 17 punk point markdown.

I mean, he's using my birth given disability as a vehicle for upward mobility? That's so wrong. Just as low as fronting that handicapped pass on your car so you can run today's marathon. As if this fest workshop boy knows what it's really like to be colorblind. The only thing he probably can comprehend are screen printed lyric sheets and this *GENERAL (conformist) RACE* that all these pseudo (mind you, not even quasi- or semi-) colorblind kids like to imagine in their idealistic white liberal world.

This is a call to action to those real colorblind kids out there. The hardcore ones who think camouflage was the worst thing ever invented. The ones whose wardrobes are a wee bit eccentric. The ones who thought for all their life that on Chinese New Year, you got little *brown* pouches filled with money. Take back what was taken from you. Show your true colors, you know what's up.

Vincent Chung, "I Am Colorblind," *Race Riot* no. 2, ed. Mimi Nguyen (Berkeley, 2002).

TAINA DEL VALLE,
INTERVIEW IN *HEARTATTACK*

In this interview, originating in a special issue of *HeartattaCk* on "Punk and Race"—to which many of the zinesters we've already met contributed—and reappearing in *Race Riot* #2, the vocalist Taina Del Valle of the crust band Anti-Product details her own pathways into punk rock and subsequent attempts to negotiate her relationship with that scene as a Puerto Rican woman. We were tempted to include this interview with the narratives of the previous chapter, as it follows the contours of the sort of punk biographies detailed in *Afro-Punk* and elsewhere: punk becomes a place for a (nonwhite) misfit to fit in. But Del Valle also tells another story: that of being a misfit *within* the scene of misfits. When she brings up Puerto Rico in a show, plays congas instead of a drum kit, or reads poems

instead of screams she feels that she steps outside the—White— boundaries of punk. Indeed, in order to find other women of color to bond with Del Valle finds that she has to leave her primarily White punk scene. This, in the word's truest sense, is the very *radicality* of these transgressions: they reveal the ethnic frontiers which demarcate the scene that are all too often invisible to the (White) eye.

HEARTATTACK: What is your ethnic background and where are you from?

TAINA DEL VALLE: I am Puerto Rican. I was born in Binghamton, New York (up-state for all of those who think that New York is just NYC).

HaC: Who or what influenced you into being a punk?

DEL VALLE: I think that in order to answer this question it is important for me to describe the area in which I grew up. It was a predominately white middle class area, so much so that I was in fact one of the only people of color in my entire school. This had a lot of consequences for me and my family.

From the day I entered that school I suffered severe racism, reflecting in physical, verbal, and emotional abuse almost every day by students and teachers. This actually was the main catalyst in my involvement in punk, or my push to rebel against the norm. Like many young womyn involved in the punk/hardcore scene, I was introduced to punk through a guy that I was dating when I was 16. I later became friends with a womyn named Little Chris (who is now a roadie for our band) who really helped me to find an identity in punk of my own. We would listen to music like Minor Threat and dance in my basement. We also tried to challenge the middle class dress code in our school by wearing clothes that we had either made or recreated ourselves, and by dying our hair different colors. More importantly, however, we began to really challenge staunch middle class ideas that were existing in our area, and because of these things we really suffered a lot of abuse at the hands of our community. The punk community became a very important community for me to be a part of and feel accepted by. I did, however, have trouble relating and communicating with other people in the punk scene in relation to the racism that I was experiencing. Fighting against racism was displayed on a patch more than it was talked about.

HaC: Was it difficult to, not only find women that you can connect with, but women of your own race involved in this? Did it matter?

DEL VALLE: Since there really weren't womyn of color in my area besides myself, that was pretty much out of the question, and in the beginning of my involvement in the punk scene I didn't really think about it because it was just what I was used to. I did have an extremely small network of friends that were womyn in the punk scene. They were fundamental in finding myself within and outside of the very male dominated punk scene and patriarchal world. As a matter of fact, I believe Little Chris is one of the main contributors in helping me to find the strength within myself to be in a band with men. I eventually found womyn of color to connect with, but they mostly have not been in the punk scene. Although it would be great to see more womyn of color in the punk scene I think that it is also important to recognize that punk is not the end all be all of the world, and it is important to connect with all sorts of people, and to not look to the punk scene as your only means of making personal and revolutionary connections.

HaC: Have you ever felt alienated by punk in any way? Directly or indirectly?

DEL VALLE: Definitely. It happens every time I talk about Puerto Rico or any other issue during a set that doesn't address one of the many token issues that are usually addressed in the US punk scene. It happens when I read a poem instead of scream a song. It happens when I don't fit certain dress code standards. It happens when I'm caught listening to hip hop or any other genre of music, or when people find out that I also sing for another non-punk group. It happens when I play a conga instead of a drum kit. It happens when I don't collect, know, or care to know every punk record that comes out. It happens when I am called a "spic" or a "feminazi" by a punk. It happens when I am called racist for dedicating a song to Latinos. It happens all the fucking time.

HaC: When I was in junior high and high school in my neighborhood I would be criticized by my own people for listening to punk and wearing Black Flag shirts and stuff. They would tell me I listened to "white boy rock." Did you get any similar treatment in your town? Would you say this criticism is true in a sense?

DEL VALLE: I didn't really get that feedback in my town, but I certainly felt that from my cousins that grew up in NYC, who for many reasons, felt that I was too "cracker." I'm not sure if I can really speak to the historical reasons that punk really grew in the US as a white dominated scene, because I don't think that I know enough about the history of that music/culture. However, I do feel like bands like Ricanstruction and Huasipungo, just to name a few, have really been successful in breaking out of this mold, musically and lyrically.

HaC: Is it important to bring in part of your culture or background, whether it's done lyrically, musically, subject matter or any other way, into your band and your involvement in punk? If so, in what ways do you do this?

DEL VALLE: I think that the more I understand who I am and the history of Puerto Rican people, the more I become passionate towards bringing out certain issues into the scene. Many of these issues have to do with Puerto Rico. The colonization of Puerto Rico by the US has affected not only my country, but who I am today on a very deep and negative level. I want to bring about the truth about what is going on in relation to Puerto Rico and the US. For example, I might discuss the struggle to get the US military out of Vieques, PR, where the land, ocean and people are being destroyed due to their bombing. Also, I tell people about the Puerto Rican Prisoners of War who are unjustly lying in our prisons for fighting, in different forms, for the freedom of our country. Most of these issues are spoken about during and after our set. We do have one song called "The Power of Medusa" that talks about my feelings of frustration with feeling like I had to fit certain white standards of beauty and the ways that I have found to begin to resist that.

HaC: Some people would argue that when you do this (e.g., talk about your roots, sing in a different language, take pride in your culture, talk about other peoples' struggles), that you are separating yourself from other people in the scene thus creating barriers and alienating others. What's your take on this?

DEL VALLE: I think that many white people who feel this way are very used to having the world catered to them. It's as if they are saying that we should all conform to white amerikkkan culture, and that anything else is extra, invalid and unnecessary. Fuck that shit! It just goes to show how deep white privilege really goes. It shows the white centering of this country, and accentuates the need for people of color in the scene to continue doing what they are doing.

HaC: When does pride in your own culture ever become too much? How can we get our message across to different types of people without shutting them out?

DEL VALLE: I don't think we need to baby people into understanding who we are, where we come from, and how we feel about it. I am tired of being the other and I don't think that we should be worried about hurting other people's feelings by being proud of who we are. However, I do think it is important to acknowledge the relationship amongst many different struggles. Ultimately, we have all been duped by the system in one way or another.

HaC: Is the US hardcore/punk scene ready to burn down this image of the "middle-to-upper class, white heterosexual male" dominant subculture? Or is that still what this truly is?

DEL VALLE: I don't think that we can separate the problems from this subculture with the problems of mainstream culture. This scene does not exist in a vacuum. As long as racism, sexism, homophobia, and class struggles exist in this country, they will in one form or another exist in punk. As long as there are people resisting against these things in this country, there will be people resisting in punk. Mos Def says in one of his albums, "We are hip hop. Me, you, everybody. So hip hop's going where we going. So the next time you ask yourself where hip hop is going ask yourself, 'Where am I going?' 'How am I doing?' and you'll get a clearer idea." I think the same could be said for punk.

HaC: If you like, add anything you feel is important and missing from this interview.

DEL VALLE: *Un gran abrazo a todos quienes me inspiran a luchar para la liberación de toda la gente y de la tierra.*

Mike Amezcua, "Interview: Anti-Product," *HeartattaCk* no. 26 (Goleta, CA, May 2000) reprinted in *Race Riot* no. 2, ed. Mimi Nguyen (Berkeley, 2002)

KRISHNA RAU,
"TRY NOT TO THINK: FORGETTING
THE FORGOTTEN REBELS"

We've already seen one aspect of the "this-is-morally-reprehensible-but-it-fucking-rips" problem—the Skrewdriver T-shirt on Majority of One's record cover—and one version of the resolution: throw the record away! Here, in our final *Race Riot* reprint, Krishna Rau gets at the issue in a different way, revisiting a once-loved band—Canada's Forgotten Rebels—who just happen to sing about bombing immigrants. How, he wonders, can one continue to have a relationship to these songs? Rau rejects the usual punk rejoinder—it's ironic!—by pointing up the problem of context and the fact that in a fist-pumping, moshing crowd there may not be any room to explain whatever the original meaning or intention of the song might have been. Music, because of its emotional

**resonance and prominent place in identity formation and identifica-
tion, cannot afford complex semiotics and performative play—not
when it comes to things like race and hate. "Mick was wrong," Rau
writes, "It's not 'only' rock 'n' roll." Nevertheless, the author decides
to keep his Forgotten Rebels albums.**

Too much thinking can spoil your enjoyment.

So, standing in a dingy Toronto nightclub, I try to shut my mind off
and travel back a decade to a time when I didn't think about music, a time
when I just took pleasure from it, a time when the band on stage—the
Forgotten Rebels—had provided me with hours of casual enjoyment. It
doesn't work. My mind insists on having one question answered: How
could you have ignored what they were singing?

It was a cold night in November of 1996, and I had traveled down to
Queen Street West to confront my memories and my record collection,
and to do some research for a book I'm writing on racism and homophobia in rock music. A Forgotten Rebels concert seemed a logical place to
gather impressions. The Rebels—originally from Hamilton—were one of
Ontario's earliest punk bands, along with such groups as the Viletones,
the Diodes and Teenage Head. They were also one of punk's most glee-
fully racist bands.

When the Rebels hit the stage, I barely have time to notice that singer
Mickey DeSadest looks much older and fatter than I remember before
he launches into the band's traditional opener, "Bomb the Boats," their
tribute to the '70s refugees who fled certain death to escape by sea to
Canada. Within seconds, the audience is transformed from a bored crowd
to a pogoing crush pumping their fists and singing along: "I don't want
no foreign pricks to take my job away from me / My tax dollars paid their
ransom / Would they do the same for me? / I don't, I don't want them in
my home / I don't want them around so let them drown / Bomb the boats
and feed their fucking flesh to the fish."

The audience obviously knows the lyrics, and they don't seem concerned about them, just as I wasn't when I started playing Rebels' albums.
Caught up in the band's tight, melodic, undeniably catchy, Ramones/
Pistols sound, I had abandoned myself to enjoyment of the music. I, too,
had known the lyrics and sung along to them, without really pausing
to think about what a repulsive message a song like "A.I.D.S." is really
sending: "You wonder what he did to get him in that awful way—in an
oxygen tent singing glad to be gay / AIDS, now you're gonna die / AIDS,
in hell you're gonna fry."

That's the problem with rock music. If the music is good, if you can tap your toes, or bob your head, or play air guitar to it, the lyrics are all too often ignored or excused. If they could be controversial, then that just adds a little extra fillip of enjoyment to the music. It might shock your parents or your teachers or your uptight friends. It's cool, man, lighten up. And you do. "I know it's only rock 'n' roll," sang the Rolling Stones, "but I like it." Mick was right, rock 'n' roll is just fun. Racist lyrics are intended simply as a joke. None of those bands—the Stones, Sex Pistols, Black Flag, X, Fear, Viletones—actually meant what they were singing. Right? Right.

Well, sometimes, as on this night, when the band is loose and sloppy and the sound system comprehensively sucks, you actually have time to seriously contemplate what rock singers are saying so much of the time, and however hard you search for the joke, it scares you. …

There's no room for irony in rock 'n' roll. It isn't film or literature. When you record or sing a song, the song is all there is. There's no context, no explanation, no space to say "I don't really mean it," there's just the performance. Mickey DeSadest may say, as he has in various interviews over the years, that his songs are jokes, merely part of a persona. And some of those songs are genuinely funny, in a tasteless, twisted sort of way, like "Elvis Is Dead": "The big fat goof is dead, dead, dead / Millions of assholes mourn his death / I'm gonna steal his body from its place of rest"; or "Fuck Me Dead," their ode to necrophilia: "A pillow in a coffin's just as nice as a bed." But these songs, with their obvious jokes, make it even harder to discern the slightest trace of humor in "Gulls peck flesh from rancid stiffs decaying on the deep blue sea / Bits and pieces here and there, bomb them far from my country / Do you, do you want them in your home? / Do you want them finding you alone? / They're commies, subhuman subversives / They're commies / human living curses … / I don't want them around so let them drown / Bomb the boats and feed the fish." Whether DeSadest has any sympathy for the Heritage Front or not, the sentiments in his songs, especially early ones like "3rd Homosexual Murder" ("I got away with a 3rd homosexual murder, and you might be the 4th") are uncomfortably close to those expressed in white supremacist literature found in Canada.

You see, Mick was wrong. It's not "only" rock 'n' roll. Rock music is an indelible part of our common cultural discourse. Even those who hate and despise every power chord ever played know about rock music. It's part of our lives, it's part of our socialization, it's part of the way we think. And in attaining this cultural ubiquity, rock music has also obtained a unique power, especially over young people, who through various musical eras and heroes, have screamed, fainted and lost control over their idols. Some fans not only faithfully buy the albums, watch the videos, wear the T-shirts and go to the concerts, but also find in the music a degree of sympathy and understanding they cannot find anywhere else in their lives. When Seattle's grunge-rock leaders, Nirvana, released their first major-label album, millions of people turned their songs of angst and misery into a world-wide, and highly profitable, phenomenon. And since Nirvana singer Kurt Cobain killed himself, at least a dozen of his fans have been distraught enough over his death or their own lives to follow his example. Cobain is, of course, an extreme example of the influence rock musicians wield, but he does serve to illustrate that much of that influence is not necessarily salutary. Mickey DeSadest may reach only a limited audience, but when Axl Rose sings, millions of people listen. And Axl sings: "Immigrants and faggots, they make no sense to me / They come to our country and think they'll do as they please / Like start a mini Iran or spread some fucking disease." These songs have an effect, serving at an absolute minimum to further justify the acceptance of casual racism and stereotyping within our culture of social discourse.

And, of course, while I'm considering the semiotics of race and music, the Rebels are playing on regardless. In between further songs about race relations like "I Left My Heart in Iran" ("That Ayatollah really must be a whore / Filth eating camel sweat, he's a sickie Moslem ... / Bring back the Shah, that's where it began / Should have dropped some bombs and watched how they ran") and tender-hearted paeans to women ("Shit for Brains" and "Autosuck"), the band crashes into "White Riot" by the Clash.

This is interesting. Since its release in 1977, the song has frequently been criticized as racist, and has been adopted as a rallying call by various white supremacist groups. However, the Clash, the original lefty punks, certainly didn't intend it that way. Joe Strummer says he wrote the song after witnessing a black riot against police in London, and intended it as a call for dispossessed whites to stage their own fight against police and state in solidarity with black activists. The song's lyrics, though, are disturbingly open to misinterpretation. "Black men gotta lot of problems / But they don't mind throwing a brick / White people go to school / Where they teach you how to be thick / White riot / I wanna riot / White riot / A riot of my own." But whatever Strummer's intentions, they are completely obviated by the Rebels' performance of his song. Coming, as it does, in the middle of a set punctuated by frequently offensive numbers, "White

Riot" loses any progressive meaning, sounding instead like the calls of the Heritage Front or the Klan for "white patriots" to fight fire with fire in defense of Aryan nationhood. The crowd, once again, goes into their fist pumping sing-along, and my internal debate deepens.

The song demonstrates exactly how slippery issues of race can be when it comes to rock music. And it becomes even more complex when one realizes that even at a Forgotten Rebels concert, I am not the only person of color in attendance. In part, that's because rock music has become a factor not only in the formation of a person's social identity, but in the formation of a person's racial identity within society. Rock music has a long history of being a part of a rebellion; indeed, the music was largely based on rebellion, and still is, to a large extent, even if only as an illusory image. But rock music has also gained such wide-spread acceptance, such popularity, that it has also become a potent part of mainstream society and even a defender of the status quo. To know and enjoy rock is to be part of that mainstream society. For whites, rock music confirms one's place in the mainstream, while allowing the continued tang of thinking of oneself as a rebel. For people of color, rock music often represents a far more concrete rebellion against one's ancestral culture and expectations, but an acquaintance with rock music also provides an entrée into mainstream, white-dominated society. It means, however, that when rock songs attack difference in race, gender or sexual orientation, it is necessary to develop a studied ignorance of the fact that such attacks may also focus on you. It means, in other words, ignoring your heritage in some crucial ways; even, perhaps, developing some degree of self-hatred. ...

By the time the show ends, after one rather perfunctory encore, my head is spinning with all these complexities, and I cannot remember what in the hell I ever saw in this band. Could I ever have been as naïve or downright ignorant as all these fervent Rebels fans? When I get home, I put on some of their albums, looking for answers, and then it all comes back to me. They wrote good songs. Live, they may now be old and fat and sloppy, but on vinyl they still sound as young and tight and tuneful as ever, and even though I've thought extensively about how repulsive they are, the music still attracts me. So, almost against my will, I decide I'm going to keep my Forgotten Rebels albums. I know my enjoyment of those albums will never again be innocent, but I also know that I will continue to derive a guilty pleasure from them. I reach what is really a rather unpleasant conclusion: I can't change rock music, and I can't stop listening to it. The music and I will simply have to reach a new understanding.

Krishna Rau, from "Try Not to Think: Forgetting the Forgotten Rebels," *Broken Pencil* no. 7 (Toronto, ON, Spring 1999), reprinted in *Race Race* no. 2, ed. Mimi Nguyen (Berkeley, 2002).

EIGHT

I'M SO BORED WITH THE USA (AND THE UK TOO)

I'm so bored with the USA
But what can I do?
— "I'm So Bored with the USA," the Clash

Want to know where punk is really happening? It's not in London, New York, or Los Angeles, nor in Manchester or Minneapolis either. Arguably, the most vibrant punk scenes in the world are in places like Mexico City, the big urban centers of Brazil, and Jakarta, Indonesia. Though it is often overlooked in popular treatments of the genre, punk is a global phenomenon. This has been the case since the late 1970s when punk began to circulate throughout the world via tape trades and zines containing comprehensive "scene reports" on international music. The global circulation of punk has only increased in recent years with interlinked economies and advances in technology and communication.

This globalization of punk raises some interesting questions. If punk, as we've argued, constituted itself around whiteness, and a whiteness primarily articulated in interrelationship with blackness, then what happens when punk rock migrates to places that don't operate along that racial axis? Does punk lose its, albeit problematic, ethnic and national identity? Or is the identification with punk as initially a White Riot of the Global North something capitalized upon, reconfigured, and transformed in the process of punk's global spread? Exactly how does the Clash's "White Riot" translate in Indonesia?

The answers to these questions are complex. Punk rock is, without a doubt, just another cultural export of the Anglo-American world. Indeed, part of the global attraction to punk is this very Northern, Western "otherness." And exported along with the music and the mohawks are certain assumptions about racial identification. In this way, globalization reinscribes the Anglo-American whiteness of punk. A punk in Mexico may be so bored of the USA, and the UK too, but when the language, aesthetics, and ethos of the culture all come from the north, what can they do?

But they *do* do something; they make punk their own. Like all culture, punk, in order to be meaningful to its participants, adapts to local conditions and is transformed in the process. Because one of the things exported with punk is its oppositional ethos, there is a certain built-in *space* in the culture to take on regional rebellion, be it simply youth-based or more explicitly ethnic or political. It's in this process of adaptation that punk stands a chance of becoming more than just a White Riot, and it is through these acts of transformation that punk lives on.

VÍRUS 27,
INTERVIEW IN *CHICLETE COM BANANA*

Here, in an interview with the 1980s Brazilian Oi! band Vírus 27 in a local magazine, *Chiclete com Banana*, we get a glimpse of what happens when White Power skin culture travels to a largely mixed-race country. For Vírus 27, "nation" appears to have little to do with race. This is in marked opposition to their bro-band Skrewdriver, who, as we saw, conceived of nationalism according to a transnational conception of "whiteness" that included working-class Brits, mystical Norse Aryan, U.S. Klansmen, and others. In fact, the group asserts that due to the diversity of Brazil, "racial purity" punk would be simply impractical. "From Rio up, everybody's dark," they argue, so "we can't be racist." This vision of racial unity under nation does not immunize them from certain varieties of hate—see, for instance, the nervous and vile references to AIDS and "black music discos" that bookend the conversation—but it does at least offer a picture of the way that certain notions, such as "pride," become salient in different ways according to the cultural, ethnic, and racial dynamics of the contexts in which they are taken up and developed.

CHICLETE COM BANANA: The virus is really spreading. It even became the name of a band. But in your case it's Vírus 27, not 24, why? *(In Brazil, 24 means gay, so it's a reference to AIDS.)*

JOE: It has nothing to do with today's fashionable virus. By the way, it has nothing to do with fashion at all. The name is old, it's because of the founder of the band, who was a Dead Kennedys fan.

CCB: What about you, were you already called Joe 90 in '80?

JOE: That's something older than the band. It's a nickname from home, because of a cartoon from TV.

CCB: In the beginning the band was punk, right? But the first LP (*Parasitas Obrigatórios*, from '86) is already dedicated to punks and skins, and the second one is exclusively Careca. *(Careca is the Brazilian variety of right-wing/nationalist nonracist skinhead.)* Nowadays punks and skins don't get along. What happened? Did this audience choose you or did you choose this audience?

JOE: We are the audience. We are real suburbans *(in Brazil, "suburban" means working class)*, and nowadays the suburbs are more skinhead than punk. Punk has been commercialized, became a fashion. Skinhead is not about fashion, it's about reality.

CCB: You've managed to record 2 albums already, and of all bands that say "Oi!" in their songs, only you and Garotos Podres have made it onto vinyl. Was that out of luck?

JABÁ: It was out of willpower. There are other Oi! bands with records out, like Histeria. But each has their own way to struggle, their differences

…

EDMILSON: Garotos Podres don't play for free. We don't live off the money we make from gigs, we all have jobs. We even pay for our own tickets (when we travel to play). Besides that, Garotos Podres don't believe in "Order and Progress." *(The motto on the Brazilian flag. Garotos Podres have a song where they say "I don't believe in order and progress," and have always been a left-wing Oi! band.)* We are nationalists. Only the music is the same, the lyrics are not.

CCB: If they are anarchists, are you nazis?

JOE: There are people who label us nazis just because we talk about Brazil, the fatherland … Then, Milton Nascimento *(Brazilian black folk singer)* is a nazi!

EDMILSON: What about the Americans, don't they love their flag? Every American movie shows their flag with a lot of pride. So, the American people are nazis, then …

JOE: All the suburbans from the 'hood here like our lyrics. After the first record we became more aware. I won't do like Lobão *(Brazilian junkie rock star)* and write a lyric that makes a kid want to use drugs.

CCB: But, like it or not, part of the audience is nazi. And a nazi band would have to be openly racist, which would burn a lot of bridges in Brazil. Here, any band with lyrics like Skrewdriver's would be confined to garage gigs and could only dream about putting something out through some European label. In this sense, you got along fine, since you could spread your message here in Brazil. Was it planned?

JOE (emphatically): Nothing was planned. We write lyrics for the movement in Brazil and we live among this huge mix of races. It would be unrealistic to discriminate races in a country of immigrants. Blacks and whites are all the nation's children. Look: we have Skrewdriver's records, we read about Holocaust revisionism, and we know that history hasn't been well told. We're not misinformed. But nationalism is not racism, at least in Brazil. From Rio up, everybody's dark, we can't be racist. Or separatist. *(In southern Brazil, the Nazis' main platform is separating the mostly European southern region from the rest of the country, and they hate the people who come from the racially mixed northeastern region and are the majority of the poor population in the more industrialized south.)* Most of the Carecas have a northeastern background. Our drummer's nickname is Jabá. *(Jabá is a typical northeastern food, and it's a common nickname for northeastern men, just like "Tex" is for Texans.)*

CCB (being careful): What about that story of a band from ABC *(region of industrial towns around São Paulo)* called Poder Branco *(which means White Power)* that considers themselves as the only nazi band in Latin America and discriminates [against] you guys for being "mongrels"? How do you deal with this kind of stance?

JOE: It can only be envy. They want promotion and to make a name for themselves quickly.

EDMILSON: We've been around for almost ten years, slowly making a name for ourselves. We're not a fanzine band. Even punks respect us. We play twice a year in other states. Nowadays it's even easier to play outside of São Paulo.

CCB: In your first record you say that your music is for punks and skins, "and not for rich kids." Of course, you're not a rich kid band, and that's why you're here, and not in mainstream newspapers or music magazines. But how has the press reacted to you? Has anyone said anything good or bad about you?

JOE: We don't give a damn about the press. We don't give interviews to anyone. We're only here to defend ourselves from some stupid things

that have been said about us. We've been called by mainstream magazines and have been invited to play on TV. But we didn't go.

JABÁ: And we don't regret it. I prefer to play in schools around here.

CCB: In the first record the songs were signed, while in the second one
the lyrics are more explicit, but it doesn't say who wrote them. Why?

JABÁ: Collective creation. Each one has his own opinions, but in the
band it's everyone's message.

CCB: Wasn't there a party thing? FNB? *(Frente Nacionalist Brasileira—
Brazilian Nationalist Front.)*

EDMILSON: We used to like some of their ideas, but as time passed, the
FNB has been swallowed by another party. Movements with political
parties don't work.

JOE: You shouldn't mix movements with politics, bands with politics.

JABÁ: The audience wants to have fun. Speeches are for rallies, our thing
is music and our commitment is only to the movement. *(The movement
in question is the Carecas.)*

CCB: What about the skinhead audience, are they fanatical? Do they
follow you wherever you play? Are they really into aggro, do they really
kick ass? Or is that just gossip?

JABÁ: They lack options and go wherever there's a gig. If it wasn't for us,
they would even go to black music discos. They just want to have fun.

"Vírus 27: Interview," *Chiclete com Banana* (Brasil: 1990), reprinted
by Chris Hubbard in the webzine Kill from the Heart. Translation by
Pedro Carvalho—everything in italics is an explanatory note from the
translator.

ALAN O'CONNOR,
"PUNK AND GLOBALIZATION:
MEXICO CITY AND TORONTO"

**The anthropologist Alan O'Connor has become one of the primary
scholarly voices on punk rock and globalization. In this essay, he
melds autobiographical and ethnographic elements to develop a
theory of how punk travels along subcultural networks of exchange.
Punk's horizon has been, in many ways, global from the start (think
of the minutiae-filled scene reports that filled the pages of so
many zines), and O'Connor uses this notion to think through the
differences between his own experiences growing up in Toronto's**

hardcore scene and contemporary accounts of scenes in Toronto and Mexico City. He argues that these differences, across both space and time, reflect preexisting political and cultural commitments and values that then interact with transnational "punk" ideals—an insight borne out by our previous reading of Vírus 27's peculiar brand of skinheadism.

La Tocada/The Show

In both cities, the show (*la tocada*) is the central collective expression of hardcore culture. To be a punk means to go to shows—and in Mexico to participate in *el slam*. In Toronto and Mexico City the entrance charge is low and commercialization of the scene is energetically resisted. Bands that demand guarantees and seek to make money from the scene are strongly disliked. Promoters are expected to cover their costs but not to profit personally from putting on shows. Bands and promoters gain respect and popularity for their efforts. It is a system of mutual aid that has as its aim the creation of a strong scene.

It's July 1994 and there is a show in a well-established but poor *barrio* built on hills to the south of Mexico City. I go by the metro and then by bus with a sixteen-year-old Mexican punk kid who is presently living on the streets. The show itself is on a flat piece of ground, like a small basketball court, beside a house. It has an earth floor, and a tarpaulin protects the equipment and part of the audience from the afternoon rain. There are about 150 punks at this show and the entrance fee is N$12 (about US$3.50). It is collected at a narrow entrance. Bands receive food and travel money only. The public address system is good. At shows like this all the bands usually share the same equipment. There's one drum kit, one bass amplifier, and one guitar amp. Most bands even share the same electric guitar and bass. Among the bands Desviados are very popular. They make me think of punk in London in 1977—they even have a "No future" song: "No hay futuro, no hay solución." I like Ley Rota (Broken Law), who are crazy punks and play good fast songs. Vomito Nuclear and Estrudo play fast generic hardcore (punk music played fast and loud). There are lots of political statements and lyrics. Songs are about school, unemployment, the police and the military—there is even one funny song about Christmas.

This show is in a very remote *barrio*. Some people pool their money and buy industrial alcohol, which they dilute with bottled fruit drinks.

Others stick to beer, also bought in a nearby general shop. There is quite a bit of glue sniffing. A young punk woman reads out a letter about somebody who was attacked last week. Many people sign. She asks me to sign even though I'm not Mexican. Luis approaches me and we have a conversation about punk in Mexico and in Canada. He's a bit older than most people here, plays in his own band, and takes courses in social science and politics at the university, where there are no tuition fees. Then he takes me around and introduces me to a lot of people. One is an Afro-Caribbean man who lived for a while in Montreal and who speaks perfect English. "Now you know everyone," Luis says. This would never happen at a show in Canada. Mexican punks don't applaud but make an energetic pit or *el slam* (part of the stage where everyone dances together) for bands they like. As the show builds up steam, a vigorous pit happens with bodies and elbows flying. It goes in a circle and speeds up and increases force with the pace of the song. No women participate and neither do I. Luis teases me about this. "Are you punk or not?" he says. Canadian punks don't often make pits like this anymore. This is like California in the mid-1980s. The late afternoon turns into early evening and I look out from under the tarp at the flickering lights of the small houses built on the surrounding hills.

Many shows in Toronto take place in the suburbs, where the scene is contemporary hardcore. Shows in downtown Toronto are usually in clubs or restaurants and the scene is more punk: people have weird hair, dress in black with spikes or patches. It is more of a drinking scene. A hardcore show in the suburbs is held in a rented hall, a gym at the YMCA, or the basement of the United Church. These spaces have to be negotiated (having parents on the church committee helps) and the rent of $250 for the evening is not cheap. In addition, you need a PA system. Either the space has one or you rent it or acquire it through benefit shows. This is a temporary space, negotiated and supervised. No drinking or smoking is allowed. The space can easily be lost because of graffiti in the washroom or if someone is caught smoking a joint outside. But in general this is a young and non-drinking crowd. Many are straight edge. The style is more skater than classic punk. Most people dress in loose pants and oversized T-shirts with underground band logos or a political message (often vegan). Sometimes people wear service-job shirts (not their own). There are a lot of wallet chains, some stylishly long. Hair is usually short, sometimes bleached, rarely dyed. Jeans, leather boots, Mohawk hair, and T-shirts for bands like the Sex Pistols are not what this scene is about.

At the entrance there is a table staffed by friends of the kid who is putting on the show. You pay and get your hand marked. It's usually $5 unless there is a justifiable reason (such as several touring bands to pay). Promoters are not allowed to make money from the shows. Local bands might expect $50–$100 and touring bands $100–$200 from a successful show. Sometimes bands get a lot less. There are no agreed fees or guarantees and no written contracts. The system works on trust. Around the hall there are tables where bands sell their tapes and records. They might have home-made silk-screened T-shirts and patches. The T-shirts are often recycled, bought by the pound from Goodwill stores. There might be an animal rights table or an Anti-Racist Action information table. Sometimes, Who's Emma [a punk/anarchist bookstore] will set up a table with records and books from its storefront. A big black Who's Emma banner is taped to the wall.

There are five bands to play. They are almost all boys, aged seventeen to twenty-three years and mainly white. The audience is mostly white too. Some of the bands have expensive electronic equipment: drum kits costing $3,000 are not unheard of. Between sets each band takes down and sets up its own equipment. Occasionally, a band will lend another a bass amp or drum kit, but this is something that results in special thanks: "We'd like to thank Ian for putting on the show and Shotmaker for letting us use their drums." Broken strings during a performance do result in mutual aid. "Does anybody have a spare string? This will just be a minute." A successful show requires popular local bands. Touring bands do not draw a crowd unless they are very well known but they get paid more to cover their travel costs. The audience mostly consists of boys (perhaps 80 percent) and they are very young. There is only a handful of people over twenty-five years old. The band plays on the floor right in front of the audience and is expected to mix with people before and after their set. Mostly the audience stands still, moving their bodies a little to the music. Sometimes there may be a small pit of faster dancers but "moshing"' (mass dancing) is looked down on. That's what people do in music videos or at commercial rock concerts. There is a high value on safety and respecting other people's space. Everyone has the right to enjoy himself or herself. The scene turns over rapidly: after two or three years one suburban school crowd replaces another. The faces change.

Bands play quite loud. Quite a few band members and some of the crowd use brightly coloured earplugs to reduce the decibel damage. Bands tend to sound fairly similar, following a limited number of styles. At any show there may be one or two good bands out of five or six. Bands may have limited musicianship, with not enough practice behind them, or they be too similar to others. Lyrics are most often poetic and vague.

This is the land of emo, a subgenre initiated by bands such as Rites of Spring and Fugazi in Washington, D.C. Where lyrics are political they usually work along well-worn themes: animal rights, against rape, against violence. Shows are sometimes benefits, e.g., for a women's shelter (probably the most popular cause), animal rights, anti-racism, a community centre, or Food Not Bombs. However, most never move beyond this to engage with a more explicit kind of politics. There are never benefits in support of striking workers, political prisoners, or socialist or anarchist organizations. Friends often hug on meeting each other. This includes boys and so there is a fairly conscious progressive gender politics at work here. But there are a few queer boys who are out and they almost never find boyfriends in this scene. The hugs and greetings have an emotional importance. Sometimes one hears of an absent emotional life at home: divorced or busy parents, lack of communication and understanding or hurtful remarks from siblings. ...

Global Networks: Los Crudos on Tour

It is not clear that postmodern theories of global flows[1] are needed in order to explain how punk travels around the globe. Punk is an international movement and the conduits are fairly obvious. Zines such as *Profane Existence* almost always have articles on scenes in various countries and lists of contact addresses. Records and tapes are sent in the mail. Punks are great letter writers and travellers. Visitors are generally welcomed and often helped with meals and places to stay. There are occasional international gatherings such as the "Encuentro Punk" in Uruguay in January 1998 that attracted participants from Mexico and the USA. But probably the most important contacts are through bands on tour.

The Chicago-based band Los Crudos toured Mexico in 1994. The band is very popular in both the "crusty" and emo/straight-edge scenes in North America. They play fast, energetic hardcore and their lyrics are all in Spanish. The singer is a Latin American teacher and photographer and the bass player and guitarist are Mexican. In part, because the songs are in Spanish, the singer developed a breathless style of speaking after every few songs in order to explain what the songs are about. Their best-known song is "Asesinos," which speaks about the disappearances of radical youth during military dictatorships in Latin America. Los Crudos' first show in Mexico City was on 12 July 1994, and was advertised by a very small number of posters in El Chopo and by word of mouth. The show was on the outskirts of the city, a long bus ride from La Paz metro station. It was organized by anarchist punks and was a benefit for the Zapatista convention in Chiapas to be held in August. Most people paid in bags of rice and bars of soap for the convention. The show was in a basketball court and the entrance was only opened wide enough for one person to squeeze in at a time. There was a quick body check. Once inside, there were several large anarchist banners on the walls and an information table. One woman had a questionnaire for youth enquiring about what issues concerned this group with respect to the Zapatista convention (for example, the issues of compulsory military service). There were about 100 punks at 4:30 p.m., and later about 250. It rained as usual in the afternoon and a large tarp kept the PA system and guitar amplifiers dry. It seemed to be an open stage for whatever bands wanted to play. Unlike North American shows, all the bands shared the same equipment and drum kit. Everyone used the same electric guitar and bass. The audience stood expressionless for the Mexican bands but started a vigorous pit when Los Crudos performed. Mexican punks do this for bands they like. They knew the words of the songs from the first 7-inch record. Musically, Los Crudos were noticeably tighter than the local bands, which were mainly straight-ahead fast hardcore. All the bands were highly political in their introductions and their songs. However, some people in the audience were restless with the Los Crudos singer's political monologues. They wanted to dance. Overall this was a well-organized show and political event. The young organizers had arranged not only the space and the equipment but also political information, leaflets, and vegetarian food. Many people left after Los Crudos finished. It was getting late and was about to rain again. Many people faced a long journey home across the city.

Los Crudos were enormously popular in Mexico. Their largest show was organized by a Mexican promoter and advertised by huge posters pasted on the walls of El Chopo market. There was some controversy because admission was N$30 (about US$9), whereas the usual admission to punk shows was N$10. Many kids could not afford the 30 pesos. When Los Crudos realized what was happening they negotiated with the promoter to lower the price. The show was on a Sunday afternoon in the large ex-Olympic swimming pool building and required a fairly large PA system. Many of the bands playing had been around for many years, and some were criticized for attempting to make money from the scene. What happened on the day of the show was that at the start people were charged N$30. But after about three hundred people had paid that price and several bands had played, the price was lowered to N$20 and at about 3:30 p.m. to N$10. A large group of more political punks held out on principle until it reached N$10 and only then entered. Then we heard Desviados, and my friend Pedro jumped onstage and sang into the microphone for their song "No hay futuro, no ha solución." The next band was unpopular because it was too commercial. The criticism was less about its sound than that it was trying to make money from punk. A very cool anarchist punk band played with an energetic but rudimentary sound. When Los Crudos finally played, the band didn't go over as well as at the small shows it had done. There was barely a murmur for an encore and fewer than half of those present participated in the slam. There was the usual impatience from some people with the singer's political statements and a broken string interrupted the show until it was replaced. Many people here at this big show wanted fast music and a good time. Los Crudos were paid almost nothing for playing. It would seem that the promoter made quite a bit.

Punk in the 1990s: Local Scenes and Global Networks

Punk exists in the form of local "scenes" in different cities and as networks that extend beyond the local.[2] Writing about global cities, Eade et al.[3] stress that community extends beyond locality. For example, people who live in Toronto may have significant links with the Caribbean. In turn, Toronto hosts a major Caribbean music festival each year that attracts tens of thousands of visitors from the islands. This type of space-time compression is certainly the case for punk, with international conduits formed by zines, record distribution, letters, travel, and touring bands. Most parts of the punk scene (but not all) have little interest in the nation-state and welcome contacts with punks in different parts of the world. The contemporary hardcore scene is a good example of a global movement.

But the different aspects of globalization do not mean the erasure of the social. The multisite ethnography proposed here examines contemporary punk and finds that it is articulated differently in Mexico City and in Toronto. Each scene is not self-contained locally. ... Los Crudos is a good example of the cultural dimensions of globalization, both in Chicago and on tour in Mexico. Yet at the same time the scenes in Toronto and Mexico City are articulated according to social and political patterns that need to be theorized differently. Punk in Mexico City is obviously not a matter of U.S. cultural imperialism. The argument made here for the Mexican scene is that proposed by [Guillermo] Bonfil (1996) in *México Profundo*.[4] There may be an element of romanticism in this, but it is not in any way an appeal to a primordial Mexican identity. Bonfil's work is clearly a political intervention into debates about Mexico as a "developed" nation, against the political and economic project of the Mexican elite. His invented phrase is now used quite widely in Mexico. However paradoxical it may seem, my argument is that Mexican punk patterns itself after the *México profundo*. The ethnographic evidence clearly shows a politics that is against the state and its development project and that demonstrates strong support for the issues raised by the Zapatista uprising in 1994. It would be reductionist to argue that practices such as low admission charges and shared equipment at shows are explained only by poverty and a lack of resources. Mutual aid and disapproval of personal gain are central to the subculture.

Whereas punk in Mexico City is involved (in complex ways) with El Tianguis del Chopo, in Toronto we find an example of a North American and European punk infoshop. Who's Emma locates itself in anarchist history (near to the street where Emma Goldman lived) but is also situated in a market area shaped by generations of different immigrants to Canada. To some extent, Who's Emma had to negotiate its space within a declining Portuguese neighbourhood. The politics of Mexican punk is explicitly against the state and the ruling political party. Even bands that have little actual political motivation sing songs about police brutality. The politics of the punk scene in Toronto is much more ambiguous. Only a minority of the Toronto hardcore scene is anarchist. Issues of identity politics (such as feminism and access to abortion) are not completely absent from the Mexican scene, but tend to be the central issues in Canada and the USA.

In the north the punk scene has evolved both musically and in terms of different subscenes: especially the difference between "crusty" punks, who drink and so on and who may be involved in the street, and the more suburban emo and straight-edge scenes. In Mexico City this kind of evolution has not happened. Mexican punks simply cannot understand the emo phenomenon. For them punk has to be musically fast, heavy, and straightforward. Their style of dress is more "classic" punk, with black jeans and jackets covered in silk-screened patches. And the Mexican *slam* would have been typical of California in 1985: fast, aggressive, with elbows and bodies flying. This type of dance is frowned upon in many (but not all) parts of the North American punk scene. It is a matter of intense debate, but in Toronto the Mexican slam would be regarded by many punks as inauthentic (copying the "mosh pits" in commercial music videos) and as macho, and as an unsafe space for women.

We do not need to adhere to outdated notions of local culture in order to find evidence of social structure and political struggles. Punk scenes reach out to globalizing networks but also have their own patterns. Los Crudos on tour in Mexico offer an excellent image of these networks. Yet another band (for example, one singing in English rather than in Spanish) would not have had the same reception. And however popular Los Crudos are in Mexico, they also had to negotiate their relationship with the scene there. The consequences of globalization call for new ways of thinking about musical scenes, new ways of doing ethnography. Although this remains worth doing, such attempts need to resist the generalizing visions of modernity and globalization that are often found in cultural studies if they are to provide a genuine ethnography of hidden musical worlds.

Alan O'Connor, from "Punk and Globalization: Mexico City and Toronto," *Communities Across Borders: New Immigrants and Transnational Cultures*, ed. Paul Kennedy and Victor Roudometof (London: Routledge, 2002).

CARMELO ESTERRICH AND JAVIER H. MURILLO, "ROCK WITH PUNK WITH POP WITH FOLKLORE: TRANSFORMATIONS AND RENEWAL IN ATERCIOPELADOS AND CAFÉ TACUBA"

Zine pages have long been filled with ads for bands and record labels, which is remarkable for two reasons: one, they come from all corners of the earth, and two, they basically all look and sound the same. In other words, punk is often in the paradoxical position of constantly looking abroad and in doing so finding only itself—it is globalized but never quite decentered, in a manner similar to much of what passes for "global" culture today. However, under certain circumstances, punk is taken up to critique and refigure local forms, and punk itself gets refigured in the process. In this piece, Carmelo Esterrich and Javier Murillo provide an in-depth analysis of two bands who use punk to transform traditional Latin American musical forms and vice versa. Interestingly, the authors characterize this transformation in quasi-racial terms, calling the result "hybrid, mestizo music." This designation begins to make more sense if we see it in light of the idea, expressed by some, that punk rock's rigid aesthetic policing has a role to play in its continuing whiteness. The

implication, then, is that the relationship between aesthetics and identity may swing both ways, provided that punk opens itself up to transformation: to becoming "punk with folklore."

In the last fifteen years Latin America has experienced a musical explosion: the so-called *rock en tu idioma* (rock in your language), or *rock en Español*. This urban phenomenon is rapidly creating its own space in the popular musical tradition of the continent and is one of the most important musical creations in Latin America this century.

The term "rock," however, is highly problematic. Let us think of it not exclusively as a musical genre, but rather as an attitude, since this is the only way such diverse musical productions can be understood today under a single label. In addition, let us think of rock as a sometimes conscious, sometimes unconscious critical stance, a contestatory musical expression that expresses the dissatisfaction of the young. The Argentine rock singer Fito Páez describes it thus:

> What is important is the will to dislocate, the will to be always on the edge, of not following the establishment in a complacent way. The day when rock doesn't disturb anymore, "cagó."[1]

In this essay, we consider rock as a space of criticism in Latin American urban culture, and one displaced from normative social expectations. Rock is the musical shout of the young generations.

Rock became popular in Latin America in the sixties, when many cities were losing, or had already lost, their provincial character. The city was no longer the gray world opposed to the color and life of the countryside, but a place where the diverse Latin American cultural and socioeconomic strata interacted, clashed, and exploded. Slowly, rock became part of that place and acquired a symbolic resonance with the young. As Jesús Martín-Barbero explains this phenomenon in *De los medios a las mediaciones*, one of the most important books written in Latin America on popular culture:

> Music constitutes a key exponent of what is the urban popular. From one extreme to the other: from "chicha" or Peruvian cumbia to "national rock" in Argentina. In both cases the musical appropriation and elaboration is linked or responds to movements towards the constitution of new social identities: the Andean migrant in the capital or the youth in search of expression. And in both, the new music is created not due to abandonment but to "mestizaje," caused by the profane deformation of "the authentic." It is not

strange, then, the condemnation or disdain that this music usually receives from those who, from the left and the right, cultivate "high" and "low" authenticities.[2]

It is precisely in Argentina that rock became an oppositional, critical phenomenon in the midst of a military dictatorship (1976–83), a "time during which the youth struggled for their symbolic survival and the bulk of the repression was visited upon them."[3] But what makes Argentine rock interesting is that it not only adopted Anglo-Saxon rock instrumentation and characteristic musical forms, but also blended Anglo-Saxon rock with other musical forms, from social protest music to blues to Argentine pop music.

In the mid-eighties rock surfaced again as a strong musical attraction for Latin America's youth. Eighties pop groups such as Menudo, Parchis, Los Chicos, and later Flans—along with rock, pop, and new wave bands imported from Spain (e.g., Mecano and Alaska y Dinarama)—created a market and paved the way for Latin Americans to begin to listen to pop/rock-influenced music not in English but in Spanish.

But eighties rock has different roots from the more Anglo-imitative Latin American rock of the sixties and seventies: it was seduced by the lure of punk.

Punk created a unilateral position against the establishment and was out to break traditions of any sort. Punk was musically and visually aggressive. Thus, its image was purposefully shocking. Clad in black and metal, or in recycled fashions discarded by the consumerist elite, punk rockers established an image of violent opposition to or defense against the social fashion, in order to break all established codes. Technically, punk is very simple, and this became an attractive factor for bands that could not afford the paraphernalia of the "Art Rock" of the late seventies.

Punk arose in the late seventies in England and the United States out of the dissatisfaction of the young facing high unemployment and underemployment, especially in the working and lower classes. It embodied a statement against the establishment (in its many definitions and incarnations) and normative bourgeoisie behavior.[4] The aggressiveness and violence of its rhythms adapted easily to the Latin American urban atmosphere, and rapidly became a symbolic response, authentic and proper, to the social and economic hardships of the growing marginal groups in Latin American cities. The aesthetic and musical project of these Latin American bands was to create a voice within the complex periphery that limited and defined the urban elite societies.[5]

In Latin America, this attraction to punk has been accompanied since the late eighties by the appropriation of traditional and popular music. More and more rock bands are blending Latin American popular and traditional music with rock. Take, for instance, Caifanes from Mexico and the hit "La Negra Tomasa," a mix of Mexican cumbia and salsa, or the Argentine group Los Fabulosos Cadillacs, who have added mambo and salsa rhythms to their typical ska sound in the album *Rey Azúcar* (1995). This is "mestizo" rock.

What is happening is the appropriation of the Latin American musical tradition but not necessarily its destruction or disappearance. These groups adopt musical structures and themes from traditional and popular music to transform and renew these traditions. There are two bands in Latin America today that are making this transformation part of their musical style. Colombia's Aterciopelados and Mexico's Café Tacuba transform Latin American music tradition through rock and punk. Originating from punk, both groups have moved into playing with and absorbing popular and traditional forms into their musical language. In this way these groups adopted the contentious stance of punk to transform traditional genres of music in Latin America. It is a popular musical form that neither forgets Latin America's rich popular and folk traditions nor adapts them passively. These groups adopt and adapt mambo, bolero, cumbia, and carrilera, but they do so critically.[6]

Aterciopelados's first album, *Con el corazón en la mano* (1993), is a classic punk album and not only musically—the lyrics constantly describe the daily violence of the city, as in "La gomela" and "Mal castigo." However, already in this album Aterciopelados began to appropriate the urban musical tradition of Colombia with the song "La cuchilla," an extremely popular song of the carrilera genre.[7] The instrumentation and arrangement is punk, but the song uses the rhythm of the original carrilera and its typical coda. Needless to say, the violence of the lyrics fits the punk style perfectly.

Andrea Echeverri explains in an interview:

> We have two principal sources. Hector comes from very hard rock groups; he was in La Pestilencia [The Stink] and loves hard rock. And I have a more folkloric background: my mother taught me to sing and play the guitar when I was little, like boleros and rancheras.[8]

As she says in another interview, they absorbed "what we listened to and what we were brought up with."[9]

In the case of Café Tacuba, their irreverent punk stance is evident from their first album. The liner notes warn us:

> Any similarity of the characters with reality is coincidental. Any offense committed against the Royal Academy [of the Spanish Language] was deliberate.[10]

The lead singer of the band is described in the album as "the one who acts like he can sing." The album deals frequently with the punk life in Mexico City ("Chica Banda," "Pinche Juan," "Noche Oscura"), but as with Aterciopelados, the album contains the germs of the urban popular music tradition. The lyrics of the song "María" are illustrated in the liner notes with a photo of Café Tacuba done up like a bolero trio. In "Noche Oscura," the band yells out at the end of the song their double identity—punks and "charros";

> Dark night at Garibaldi[11]
> We're all dressed in black.
> Dark night at Garibaldi
> And like good "charros" we sing.
> Drunk charros in black
> Dizzy charros in black
> Drowned charros in black
> Drunk charros in black.

Transforming the Bolero

One of the musical genres that both Aterciopelados and Café Tacuba adopt in their music is the bolero, a form which has Cuban origins but that was popularized in Latin America in the 1940s. The bolero is essentially romantic—in the melodramatic, twentieth-century sense of the word—and both bands are very aware of that. Their treatment of bolero, however, is miles apart.

Café Tacuba's "Madrugal" (*Café Tacuba*, 1992) is, musically, a Los Panchos style of a bolero through and through. The band uses acoustic guitars, maracas, the typical requinto of the traditional bolero, and harmonic voices:

> The city of palaces gives way to dawn,
> Calm is lost when the sun rises.
> All splendor diminishes, people take the streets.
> The cathedral disappears among smog and pigeon shit.

The lyrics could not be farther from the romantic themes of the bolero. There is no unrequited love, no retaliation, no begging, no rejection. The title alludes to another form, the madrigal—a musical genre from sixteenth-century Europe, known, like the bolero, for its love themes—but at the same time it is an allusion to the Spanish word "madrugar" (to wake up early). The song describes a dawn in Mexico City (baptized the "City of Palaces" by Alexander Von Humboldt), with its stinking pollution and its overpopulated streets. Café Tacuba has turned one of Latin America's most romantic musical genres into an urban chant. The lyrics could easily fit in a rock song—pollution, cars, smog, pigeon shit—but they insert them within a tradition that is completely disconnected to rock (the bolero).

Besides that, the bolero "Madrugal" is polluted with dirty words, which boleros, as racy or sexy as they may be, would never have. The last line shocks us, precisely because we are listening to a bolero. The transformation is greater because nothing happens, nothing changes musically; only the lyrics dismantle our expectations.

In contrast, Aterciopelados's "Bolero falaz" (*El Dorado*)—"Deceitful Bolero"—is a song whose beginning resembles a bolero, reconstructed with an acoustic guitar. But that is the end of the resemblance. After this introduction, the song changes completely, yet maintains the musical structure of the first phrases. Aterciopelados uses the bolero as a musical point of departure, then later delves into rock. But the lyrics of the song do not forget the bolero.

> You look in my pocket
> For proof of another love.
> Hair on my lapel,
> This smile exposes me.
> Lipstick on my shirt;
> My alibi has fallen apart.
> I've been found out,
> To deceive is a science.

Here, as opposed to in "Madrugal," we have jealousy, anger, and retaliation. The song is sung with two narrative voices: a man who plays around and is fed up with his woman's jealousy, and the woman who tells him to his face that she know he is being unfaithful and in a typical machista stance blames the other woman ("*esa infame*" [that woman]) for the actions of her man ("If I find here I'll slap her silly"). She is also fed up with the situation, and the chorus ("I'm not myself anymore / You've driven me out of my mind") could be applied to either of them.

Traditional boleros use an elegant, lofty style of lyrics recalling nineteenth-century melodramatic and "modernista" language. In "Bolero falaz" the theme of love and dissatisfaction continues as in a bolero, but now with the colloquial language of the younger generation:

> I've had it up to here
> You're not my other half
> Nor the eighth wonder.

"Bolera falaz" is an updated bolero, with an introduction that pays its dues musically to the traditional romantic song, and language with which the young can identify. But the song is not all reverence—the last lines say:

> I told you "No more"
> And you shit yourself laughing.

As in Café Tacuba's "Madrugal," dirty language ends the song. Here, however, it is repeated again and again and again. The bolero is profaned with punkish irreverence.[12]

Another important point about this song, as with all Aterciopelados's songs, is the fact that it is performed by a woman, a rarity in Latin American rock with very few exceptions.[13] This makes the critical dismantling of popular music even more powerful. Andrea Echeverri, the lead singer of Aterciopelados, is really the one who is "shitting herself laughing."

Tradition and Misogyny: Mexican Ranchera and Colombian Vallenato

Popular culture has the potential to create spaces for contesting normative cultural practices, but it can also perpetuate traditional values that belittle and insult displaced or marginal subjects. In music, Latin America has a long tradition of misogyny from bolero to Mexican ranchera to Colombian vallenato, not forgetting merengue, bachata, and salsa in the Caribbean. Part of the musical project of Café Tacuba and Aterciopelados is to use this type of music to reveal the misogyny in all its disgusting splendor.

"La Ingrata," from Café Tacuba's second album, *Re* (1994), is their most popular song. In "Madrugal" the lead singer, Rubén Albarrán—who in the first album is called Juan, in the second Cosme, and in the latest one Anónimo (Anonymous)—sings with a gentle, melodic voice (he is, after all, imitating the bolero voices of the 1940s). In "La Ingrata," however, he sings with his typical screechy, annoying voice, rough and unmelodic.[14] In this song Albarrán purposefully sings badly.

The song is an interesting homage to the Norteña tradition in Mexico, where the accordion—believed by some to to have been brought to the region by Bohemian immigrants—and rolling drums are characteristic of this music.[15] This is really a *ranchera norteña*, however, and it is from the ranchera aspect of the song that the tradition of misogyny comes: those countless songs about bitter and melancholic men abandoned by women (just think of the song "Ella" by José Alfredo Jiménez). "La Ingrata," though, is the next step of that natural machista disappointment: the man insults the woman for having rejected him. The song is, thus, one of retaliation: "Don't tell me you miss me because I don't believe you anymore … your tears are false."

The song does not contain anything in its lyrics proper that criticizes the misogyny hinted at in the text. What makes us think again is the exaggeration of his retaliation. It is hard to take it straight. The end of the song moves into delirious violence in teary, loaded, appalling eleven-syllable [in Spanish] lines:

> That's why I will have to shoot you
> A couple of times to hurt you
> And even though I'm sad because I won't have you
> I will be with you at your funeral.

The parody in these last lines is revealed in full. Along with this, the vocal performance of Cosme is overtly melodramatic and spiteful, so full of indignation that it ultimately parodies the desperation of the macho and "La Ingrata" turns into a critique of itself.[16] What seems superficially to be a misogynous song is in fact a song against the misogynous standpoint of so much ranchera music.

In northern Colombia the vallenato is a type of popular music from the Upar River Valley.[17] Vallenato lyrics are either about love treated sentimentally and melancholically or based on stories from Colombian folklore. Recently, the vallenato has become popular throughout Colombia, especially after its resurgence under Carlos Vives in the early nineties. This has made it pertinent for Aterciopelados to use the vallenato in their albums: this is music heard—now—by almost everyone. Vallenato is now "play," that is, "cool" in the jargon of Colombian youth. In addition, the vallenato is not only sung exclusively by men in Colombia, but the songs are typically a dialogue between men, which makes the appropriation of this music by Aterciopelados and its female vocalist even more pertinent.

"Baracunátana" was a popular song in the Colombian vallenato repertoire of the seventies[18] which, like "La Ingrata,"[19] deals with a man reproaching a woman, this time because she's going out openly with other men: "You left with the blond guy in jeans, overalls, and jacket." His frustration turns into pure insult; the chorus is literally a list of them: "*Por eso, tú eres vergaja, fulera, guaricha, baracunátana, garosa, morronga, farisea, gorzobia, retrechera, garulla, baracunátana, cucharamí, baracunata, baracunátana.*" All these words are insults of some sort, but all are roughly equivalent to "bitch."[20]

What makes Aterciopelados's cover so fascinating is how, even though Andrea keeps the woman as the object of reproach throughout almost the entire song, the band dismantles the song at the very end. At the end of a traditional vallenato the singer (a man, let us not forget that) finishes with a "*Sí, señor.*" In vallenato, the communication is between a man—who sings, because he has experience—and another who listens, either because he wants to learn from the singer's experience, or because he had the same experience and identifies with the singer. But in Aterciopelados's version, Andrea ends with a "*¡Sí, señora!*" Changing the gender subverts the vallenato tradition. The last two words of the song frame the entire lyric, written by Leonidas Plaza, and the text becomes a mere quote. We have before us an exercise in mimicry: "Almost the same, but not quite."[21] Now the song is a dialogue between women (the female singer and the women who listen to her, the women who feel themselves included in the "*¡Sí, señora!*" at the end of the song). As in much popular music of this kind, the voice of the woman never appears in the original song; she is never allowed to respond, criticize, or contradict what the man says about her. Aterciopelados is able to insert a woman's voice into "Baracunátana" without taking a single word out of the man's text. Andrea Echeverri takes possession of the man's words, like a disturbing poltergeist.

From Pop to Punk: "No Controles"

The transformations that Café Tacuba and Aterciopelados undertake are not exclusively of traditional and popular music; they also include the immense corpus of pop music that has filled the radio airwaves of stations all over Latin America since the 1960s. Café Tacuba's latest album, *Avalancha de Exitos* (1996), is a series of eight covers bringing together the most diverse popular music: Leo Dan, Juan Luis Guerra, Botellita de Jérez, Bola de Nieve. One of the songs is "No Controles" by the Mexican group Flans, a group absolutely pop, with light and catchy lyrics and music. Flans is, to use Mexican jargon, *"fresa,"* that is, frivolous, and happy to be the fashionable ones—thoroughly establishment.

At a superficial level, "No Controles" (Don't Control) hints at rebelliousness against an authoritative voice of control, "Don't control my way of dressing ... Don't control my way of thinking." However, on listening to the song more carefully, it is really about being accepted: "Don't control my way of thinking because it is cool and everybody likes me." The catchy tune reminds us of shopping, pajama parties, and fashion. "No Controles" is really the anthem of the "fresas": do not question our way of dressing, dancing, and talking, because we are the trendsetters, we are beautiful and everyone falls in love with us, we are "fresas" and nothing but. The supposed opposition to a controlling voice does not exist to produce a critical posture, but rather to enforce social acceptance of their tastes and preferences ("because it is cool and everybody likes me"). Café Tacuba, of course, turns "No Controles" upside down.

In their hands, "No Controles" becomes a punk manifesto: do not control my way of talking, dancing, thinking and looking. All lyrics having to do with being beautiful and the center of everyone's attention are ripped out in Café Tacuba's version.[22] Albarrán's voice is scratchier than ever, on the verge of the grotesque. The arrangement of the song, and the angry, fast tempo of the cover dissolves any "fresa" elements from the Flans version. (The song is, interestingly enough, produced by David Byrne, an American rock singer and composer with definite punk origins.)

But Café Tacuba's transformation of "No Controles" transforms punk itself. The synthesizer arrangement of Flans is substituted with a series of angry guitars. Café Tacuba, however, employs acoustic guitars rather than electric. Here Café Tacuba begins the transformation of the already transformed song: it is a punk manifesto but without the typical discordant sound of the electric guitars of the Sex Pistols and the Clash. This is an explosive hybrid, a parodic play on Mexican pop music charged with the demolishing capacity of punk, and drawing on the long tradition of Mexican string music. This is punk with folklore.

In a television interview, Café Tacuba denied that they were a rock band, perhaps because of their serious interest in absorbing the musical tradition that exists in Latin America. Aterciopelados and Café Tacuba are not groups that absorb traditional music frivolously—"world music" or "world beat," as it is called in CD stores now in Europe and the United States—to make their sound more exotic. Both Aterciopelados and Café Tacuba know this music tradition, and because they know it so well they are able to critique it and transform it. Café Tacuba and Aterciopelados are a crucial part of the process of transculturation in Latin American popular music today. This is hybrid, mestizo music with such a capability for mimicry and adaptation that, by seizing and absorbing the diverse music of Latin America, it creates a new tradition of music. It is, as Martín-Barbero stated, the "profane deformation of 'the authentic.'" This is not merely rock "*en tu idioma*,"[23] a translation of Anglo rock, but something far more interesting, a new musical genre. It is Latin American rock, an urban hybrid formed by the youth in the ever-growing cities of Latin America, music that combines the irreverent sound of rock and punk with traditional and popular musical expressions.

Carmelo Esterrich and Havier Murillo, from "Rock with Punk with Pop with Folklore: Transformations and Renewal in Aterciopelados and Café Tacuba," *Latin American Music Review/ Revista de Música Latinoamericana* 21:1 (Spring–Summer 2000).

JEREMY WALLACH, "LIVING THE PUNK LIFESTYLE IN JAKARTA"

The ethnomusicologist Jeremy Wallach offers us a portrait of a punk scene that did not arise out of tape trading or seeing out-of-town bands in sweaty basements—the subcultural circuits described by O'Connor above—but precisely out of what might reasonably be called American "cultural imperialism": hearing Green Day, Rancid, the Offspring, and other commercial American punk bands with big multinational promotional budgets. Wallach argues, however, that such avenues of introduction need not result in plastic imitations. Rather, such encounters enable young people to explore the history of punk rock and engage primarily with the

"formal stability" that renders it so appealing. Additionally, Wallach suggests that the relative "Indonesian-ness" of punk is less important than how punk works within this specifically *embedded* cultural and socio-political context. As an example he uses the now-familiar appropriation of the swastika. Wallach claims that it is precisely the situated context that made symbolic play with Nazi iconography rapidly untenable: the swastika and its attendant ideology of White Power simply do not "make sense" in Jakarta. Anti-Nazi iconography, however, is adopted and adapted by Indonesian punks to speak to local political concerns.

> How I have disappointed you, Mother, because I don't have the ability to write traditional Javanese sung poetry. The rhythm of my life is bursting forth crazily, Mother; it can't be contained in the song-form of my ancestors.[1]
> —Minke, the young protagonist in *Bumi Manusia*, by Pramoedya Ananta Toer [2]

What interpretive frameworks can we employ to understand punk scenes in non-Western developing countries? Conversely, what can researching these scenes contribute to scholarly understandings of "punk" as a complex cultural and historical phenomenon? In the following discussion, I revisit well-worn claims about the "signifying practice" of the punk subculture in light of punk's global expansion in the decades following its mid-1970s emergence. Drawing upon ethnographic research carried out between 1997 and 2000, I focus specifically on a historical development that 1970s cultural commentators (and ethnomusicologists!) could not easily have foreseen: the development of a dedicated nationwide punk movement in the Republic of Indonesia during the 1990s.

Subculture, Southeast Asian Style: Indonesian Punk and the Meaning of Stasis

In his *Subculture: The Meaning of Style*, Dick Hebdige famously claims, "punk style is in a constant state of assemblage, of flux. It introduces a heterogeneous set of signifiers which are liable to be superceded at any moment by others no less productive."[3] Hebdige's argument, based on his readings of the then cutting-edge French semiological theories of Roland Barthes, Julia Kristeva, and the *Tel Quel* group, was groundbreaking at the time, and has influenced a generation of researchers.[4] Yet in the quarter century that has passed since the publication of *Subculture*, punk music, iconography, and fashion, instead of constantly evolving, have remained unchanged to a remarkable degree, even as they have spread around the world. In fact I would argue that punk's appeal, at least to contemporary Indonesian young men and (to a lesser extent) women, lies not in Hebdige's indeterminate semiotic flux but rather punk's formal stability. Indeed, contrary to what a semiologist might expect, the proud Indonesian punks I met during the course of my research seemed less interested in punk's avant-garde potential than in conserving punk as a sort of living tradition.

The world's fourth most populous country and home to the world's largest Muslim population, Indonesia is seldom a topic of conversation in Western punk circles.[5] Yet—though this fact is usually omitted in Western world music survey classes—Indonesia is home to what is almost certainly the largest punk movement in Southeast Asia, and one of the largest in the world. Following their exposure in the mid-1990s to commercially hyped groups such as Green Day, Rancid, and the Offspring, Indonesian youth in cities such as Jakarta, Denpasar, and Bandung began to build informal grassroots networks of bands, local fanzines, small independent record labels, and merchandisers dedicated to the production and distribution of punk music and ideology.[6] These networks overlapped with those associated with other so-called underground rock genres, including metal, gothic, and industrial, which had surfaced at roughly the same time. The Australian observer Jo Pickles writes:

> Close-knit communities of young people sharing an interest in underground music have emerged throughout Indonesia. Underground youth cultures provide a network of like-minded people to experiment, hang out and jam with. A place of refuge from families who don't understand the aspirations of their youth, and from a society preoccupied with other issues. These groups provide a sense of belonging and family-like support for members who choose nomadic life on the streets in preference to living at home. Distinct from other more segregated social structures, the underground scene is open for all to join and participate in. Money and education are not barriers.[7]

While in most cases Indonesian youths' exposure to punk music began with major-label acts that were heavily promoted through mainstream global media, Indonesian punk tastes quickly turned to less hyped but indisputably seminal bands from the 1970s and early 1980s, particularly the Exploited, the Ramones, and above all the Sex Pistols. Why these particular bands emerged continually in conversations rather than other contemporaneous groups such as the Clash, Abrasive Wheels, Crass, or Discharge, is open to conjecture. I suspect that the Pistols and the Ramones were valued for their supposed origination of the punk style, and the Exploited was celebrated because the band exemplified nearly all the features regarded as canonical by Indonesian punks: Mohawks, musical simplicity, antagonism toward the musical mainstream, and so forth.

The remarkable rise of DIY (Do It Yourself) cultural production devoted to punk music and culture catalyzed the growth of self-consciously local punk "scenes" in urban and semi-urban areas all around Indonesia, and over the last ten years or so these interconnected scenes have mounted numerous performance events and generated several hundred independently produced and distributed punk music cassettes recorded, on shoestring budgets, by local Indonesian bands.[8] These DIY endeavors tended to have very limited commercial reach and even less profit potential. Nevertheless, by the start of the twenty-first century, Mohawked, black-leather-clad *anak punk* (punk kids) were widely recognized figures in the Indonesian popular culture landscape, and in 2003 the Balinese punk veterans Superman Is Dead signed a contract with the multinational conglomerate Sony Music to release their first major label album,[9] a controversial move (given the fervent opposition of Indonesian punks to major labels and commerce in general) that nonetheless attested to the cultural influence that by then was wielded by punk music on millions of Indonesian young people. Ironically, the first song on *Kuta Rock City*, Superman Is Dead's Sony debut, "Punk Hari Ini" ("Punk Today"), denounces punk's dilution by Indonesian mainstream popular culture. Its refrain is a rant that in translation would no doubt be familiar to many punks in other countries:

Kubenci semua yang tak pasti	I hate everything that's uncertain
Rambut spikey dibilang funky	Spiky hair is considered trendy
Mall dipenuhi lambang anarki	Malls are full of anarchy symbols
Yang akhirnya hilang tak berarti	That in the end are lost and meaningless
Cheerleader ingin jadi punk rock star!	Cheerleaders want to be punk rock stars![10]

Responses to the signing of punk bands on major labels (which in this context meant large commercial labels, both national and multinational) among punk scene members were overwhelmingly negative, though sometimes laced with ambivalence. In the words of one Indonesian punk enthusiast discussing Rage Generation Brothers, the first Indonesian punk band to break ranks with their DIY compatriots by releasing an album on the large national recording label Aquarius in mid-2000, "Don't boycott, better to pirate" (*Jangan boikot, lebih baik bajak*), meaning it was better to make unauthorized recordings of the album than to refuse entirely to listen to it. Since punks in Indonesia had long relied on homemade illegal copies of music cassettes, this statement in essence gave this fan's fellow enthusiasts permission to enjoy a "sellout" group's music, so long as they did not pay for it.

The Indonesian punk movement came of age during a tumultuous period in modern Indonesian history. In 1998, in the wake of the Asian economic crisis, the Suharto dictatorship (in power since 1966) was overthrown by a broad-based reform movement spearheaded by student activists. These students were members of the most globally aware generation in Indonesia's history, and the music of choice for many of them was underground rock. Almost from the beginning, musicians in the Indonesian underground movement performed songs attacking the corruption and brutality of the Suharto government, even when it was dangerous to do so.[11] Thus, although Indonesian punk is as politically divided as its Western counterparts, it is not surprising that many Indonesian punks place their movement and their allegiance in the context of the struggle against Suharto. A particularly eloquent punk from Cirendeu, a region on the border between Jakarta and West Java province, stated that he became a punk because of the pain he felt as one of Indonesia's "little people" (*rakyat kecil*) victimized by the oppression and injustice of the Suharto regime. He added that he was a member of a local band named Stainless, which sang about this theme. Our conversation took place in front of a wall of closed-up shops covered with graffiti sprayed by members of the Cirendeu scene, which included a Mohawk-sporting punk stick figure, anarchy and peace symbols, local band names (including Stainlees), and a series of intriguing English-language slogans: *Our Lifestil* (*sic*), *Smash Capitalism*, *Hardcore The Way of Life*, *Punk Not Dead*, and *We Are Not Komunis* (Indonesian for "Communist").

Social Class and Stylistic Conservatism

Punk is the most working-class-identified of the subgenres that constitute the underground music movement in Indonesia, though in reality local punk scenes are composed of both middle-class students and followers from humbler backgrounds who are unable to afford schooling. In this sense, Pickles's idealistic claim that "money and education are not barriers"[12] to membership in the Indonesian underground scene would appear to contain an element of truth. In fact, class differences are often downplayed among Indonesian punks, and the number of homeless runaways from middle-class homes that join their ranks blurs class lines significantly (as they do in scenes elsewhere). There is, nonetheless, a tendency for Indonesian students to become politically oriented "anarcho-punks," whereas working-class kids are more likely to identify themselves as apolitical, hedonistic "street punks" dedicated, I was told, to an ethic of hanging out and substance abuse (summed up for one Jakartan punk by the English phrase "drunk and pogo"). Both subgroups, but particularly the latter, stress the importance of living a punk lifestyle. Their appropriation of the English loan word "lifestyle" (used in everyday conversation far more frequently than the Indonesian equivalent, *gaya hidup*) does not include the ephemerality and consumerism with which the term is sometimes associated in the West. Instead, commitment to a punk lifestyle entails participating in a set of subcultural practices that include hanging out in public places with other punks, attending punk concert events, drinking alcohol (a grave offense in Islam), and wearing punk clothing and hairstyles. The value placed on "living the punk lifestyle" among punks from nonaffluent backgrounds is an example of how global flows have dramatically transformed working-class culture in Indonesia.[13]

Just as class differences between members of the punk scene are deemphasized, so too are ethnic differences. An overpopulated, metropolitan national capital located in the western portion of the island of Java, Jakarta is a city where nearly every ethnic group in the archipelago is represented, though the vast majority of its inhabitants are from groups indigenous to the island: Sudanese, Javanese, or Betawi (native Jakartans, from the Malay for "Batavia," the city's former name under the Dutch colonial government). Despite the Suharto regime's valorization of appropriately presented "traditional cultures" as foundations for identity in the archipelago, such allegiances seemed tangential at best to one's membership in a local punk scene. Even internal rivalries in the scene tend to be based on geography (e.g., South Jakarta versus East Jakarta punks) rather than ethnicity (there are no groups labeled "Betawi punks" or "Javanese punks" in Jakarta). Similarly, the Indonesian punk subculture's relationship to organized religion appears to be one of polite coexistence and avoidance. (I have more to say on this subject later on in this essay.) More research certainly needs to be done in these areas, particularly as the Indonesian scene enters its second decade of existence amid widespread national uncertainty on matters of ethnic autonomy and the separation of mosque and state.

Punk is the most "purist" underground music subculture in Indonesia, and Jakarta punk musicians therefore tend to be reluctant to experiment with writing lyrics in Indonesian.[14] They prefer to sing in English—the original language of punk—even though many working-class punks have little knowledge of the English language. Unlike Indonesian heavy metal and hardcore[15] enthusiasts, punks are also loath to embrace musical innovations, instead maintaining their stylistic allegiance to what they perceive as a classic punk rock sound. Moreover, male and female punks in Indonesia follow the same dress code as their forebears in England and the U.S., and, as stated above, they are the underground music fans most opposed to "major labels."[16] That a punk cassette is produced and distributed independently of the commercial music industry is for punks a crucial mark of its authenticity. Such formal conservatism and ideological purism arguably characterize both punk movements and working-class subcultures around the world, but the question remains: Why does the punk lifestyle hold such strong appeal to a segment of Indonesian youth?

An Ethnographic Vignette: A Punk Show in a Banana Grove

On June 25, 2000, I was invited by Wendi Putranto, then a Moestopo University communications student active in the Jakarta underground scene, to an *acara total punk* (totally punk performance event) which took place in a *kampung* (poor urban neighborhood) located on the unfashionable far southern outskirts of Jakarta. The concert's organizers, all residents of the neighborhood, had obtained permission to hold the event from the kampung's Rukun Tangga, the local municipal official. The kampung was located in a region known as Joglo. Like other working-class areas of Jakarta I had visited, Joglo consisted of a main road lined with simple wooden food stalls, behind which lay a labyrinthine network of narrow alleyways connecting a mosque and a large number of cement single-story dwellings. The event took place near the main road in an open, grassy area normally used as a soccer field by neighborhood residents. At the far end of the field was a makeshift "stage" set up in the shade of a grove of banana trees. The performance area consisted of five small portable guitar amplifiers placed on the ground on either side of a rudimentary drum kit. The amps were connected to a single extension cord that ran into a nearby house. In front of the drum kit stood a microphone stand holding a battered microphone that had been plugged directly into one of the guitar amplifiers. Facing the stage was a narrow wooden bench, which served both as a barrier separating performers from slamdancing audience members, and a place for weary fans to sit and rest.

Unlike numerous other popular music concerts I had attended in Indonesia, including some that had featured punk bands, this acara lacked a professional sound system, video screens, and corporate sponsorship.[17] The daylong event featured fifteen punk and old-school hardcore bands playing two or three songs each, using the drums and amplifiers provided by the organizers. Though the event's "host band" had an Anglicized Russian name, Glasnost, most of the bands had English names like Dislike, Straight Answer, Street Voice, Ruthless, Total Destroy, and Error Crew. The groups (the members of which were all male) played in front of a small but enthusiastic audience, and their music, with its headlong rhythms, shouted/barked vocals, and three churning, distorted guitar chords, differed little from that of the early Western punk groups aside from the strong Indonesian accents of the vocalists.

The concert lasted until *magrib*, the Muslim evening prayer, when the organizers had promised local authorities that the music would cease. The concert also paused briefly for *asar*, afternoon prayers, in order to "respect the religious," in the words of one participant. I did not observe any event participants actually praying during this intermission. Looking back at this, I would argue that this accommodation to religious authority, coupled with the absence of any actual participation in religious praxis, typifies the interactions between music-based subcultures and Islamic orthodoxy I observed in pre-9/11 Jakarta: rather than criticize the strictures of religious fundamentalism, the punks tolerated its rules and hoped in turn that their presence in the Indonesian body politic would be similarly tolerated.

While the bands played, some members of the audience clustered in front of the stage in a sweaty makeshift "pit," while others sat a distance away in the grass or hung out in the sunken area on one side of the stage. A few local kampung residents, married women holding babies, old women, and a group of about a dozen young boys, watched from a discreet distance, their carefully neutral facial expressions occasionally betraying a hint of consternation or bewilderment. The punks in the audience totaled about sixty and were almost all male. Some arrived in full punk regalia—Mohawks, spikes, and leather jackets (despite the intense midday heat); many also wore locally made T-shirts depicting both foreign and domestic band logos. One shirt for a local band called Stupid Bones featured the English slogan "Here's the Punk Rock. We come from our self." Another shirt, for a band called Out of Control, displayed the text, "Stop the hate / Support one another / Still exist for the punx."

My presence, rather conspicuous at this small gathering, was tolerated by most of the event's participants, though many bands refused to be photographed and one lead singer spat at me from the stage (which I interpreted as a sign of aggression, despite the complex meanings of "gobbing" in other punk contexts). Following this incident, my host explained that punks disliked publicity and did not want to be "exposed" to outsiders (*nggak mau di-expose*). After all, I was told, this concert event was supposed to be "pure underground" and "just for having fun," with no commercial motives whatsoever.

Punk ideology in Indonesia valorizes self-sufficiency and existence on the margins of society. At the concert I was introduced to Amsoi, an especially flamboyant street punk sporting a colorful Mohawk haircut, who explained to me in a combination of colloquial Indonesian and badly fractured, obscenity-laden English that he survived on the street by working as a *tukang parkir* (freelance man who helps motorists park their cars and exit from Jakarta's parking lots for a modest tip) and as a *pengamen* (roving street musician). He showed me the two tools of these respective trades: a whistle (to direct traffic) and a very large *gicik* (homemade percussion instrument made from a wooden dowel with punctured and flattened bottle caps nailed to it). Instead of carrying around a battered guitar like other pengamen, Amsoi resembled an overgrown punk *anak jalanan* (street child), singing with his gicik on the streets of Jakarta for spare change. Amsoi was rumored to be the son of a civil servant and was the lead singer of a band called Civil Disorder, which, I was told, was about to release a cassette.

A handful of women wearing punk rock regalia were present at the event; they smoked openly and laughed and talked with the men— atypical behaviors in mainstream Indonesian society. One of my companions referred to them as *pecun underground* (underground sluts), which suggests that feminism's impact on this particular scene was limited, though his choice of words was later criticized by a fellow punk, who stated that as a rule he avoided misogynist language. Berta, one of the young women present at the event, was an active member of the punk scene in the neighboring West Javanese city of Bogor.[18] She mentioned to me that she played in an all-woman punk band called the Hookers. While Berta assured me that she knew what the English word "hooker" actually meant, she said that the band's name was merely intended to be humorous and was not intended to suggest sexual impropriety. Berta admitted that punk music was "difficult to understand," but claimed that while punks' outfits were *brutal*, their *jiwanya* (souls) were not. The neighborhood children present at the concert agreed: no, punks did not scare them, they were humans, after all, not monsters. Furthermore, they told me punks were definitely preferable to the neighborhood *preman* (thugs, criminals). The children did not seem to mind the music being played, but nonetheless expressed a strong preference for *dangdut* (a national popular music genre influenced by Indian film songs and Western hard rock) over punk music, adding that dangdut was the only other style of popular music they had ever seen performed in their neighborhood. When I asked them if they thought about adopting a Mohawk-type hairstyle in emulation of the punks, they laughed and one boy remarked that they could not wear their hair that way because "at school we'd get scolded."

As at many other kampung concerts I attended where solitary physically or mentally disabled men danced freely to the music regardless of its specific genre or the skill of the performers, an older blind man holding a cane and wearing a clean white shirt and a *peci* (black Muslim cap) was present at the punk acara.[19] He stood alone in the field in front of the stage dancing, his gyrating movements, executed with both of his feet planted firmly on the ground, expertly following the rhythmic contours of the punks' music. When I asked one of the local residents about him, she said, "Oh, he likes any kind of music!" (*O dia suka musik sembarangan!*) The blind man, seemingly oblivious to everything but the sounds emanating from the makeshift stage, smiled radiantly as he danced. During the breaks between songs and band sets, he shouted "*Musik!*" impatiently, but otherwise seemed quite content. The other audience members, both the punks and kampung neighbors, paid very little attention to him—like the tall American ethnomusicologist with the camera and notebook, he was just another participant in an event that, despite its subcultural affiliations, was inclusive and fully embedded in the everyday realities of the neighborhood.

Indonesian Punk and the Authenticity Question

How can one account theoretically for events like the one described above? Absorbed in the documentation of the cultural particulars of specific genre-based music movements, it is all too easy for the ethnographic researcher of global music subcultures to forget the still-dominant, trivial-izing perspective toward such phenomena, both inside and outside the academy. For many observers, the existence of punks in Indonesia exem-plifies the tragic "mimesis" of Western culture by a formerly colonized people.[20] In this view, the Indonesian punk movement is little more than a latter-day cargo cult of cultural dupes in the thrall of imported commodi-ties and the aura of global consumer culture. Punk music in Indonesia therefore cannot be anything other than derivative and inauthentic.

In a similar way, sociologist Hilary Pilkington uses a perhaps overly literal interpretation of Hebdige's arguments about punk in Britain to describe the punk scene in late-1980s/early-1990s Moscow: "In some ways Soviet punk is one of the clearest examples of 'imitation' of Western subcultural forms—there can after all be no social base for a movement subverting consumerist lifestyles in a society where a safety pin or a dustbin bag is an article of deficit not abundance."[21] Such a view suggests that punk symbols can only be meaningful in particular societal contexts. Outside those contexts, the appropriation of those symbols can only be construed as "imitation" without a "social base" in actual lived experience. In order to respond to the logic of those who would dismiss the punk phenom-enon in Indonesia, it is instructive to compare the Indonesian punk music movement with Indonesia's most celebrated "authentic" musical export: gamelan, a traditional orchestra composed of gongs, drums, bronze xylo-phones, and other indigenous instruments.

As the brilliant work of Sumarsam,[22] Michael Tenzer,[23] and others makes clear, the development of gamelan music traditions on the Indone-sian islands of Java and Bali over the past two and a half centuries resulted from an intensively collaborative process involving local musicians and composers, native aristocratic elites, European colonists, Indonesian government officials, and Western musicologists, performers, compos-ers, anthropologists, and ethnomusicologists. The cooperative efforts of these various social agents have helped develop gamelan music along the lines of decontextualized, formalist Western art music traditions. Thus, while gamelan's original musical materials—its instruments, performance practices, tuning systems, and the like—were assumed to be purely indig-enous, gamelan's subsequent creative development, contextualization, and institutionalization cannot be understood apart from continuous contact with and direct influence from powerful cultural outsiders.[24]

In contrast, while the fundamental musical materials of punk are indisputably imported from the vast elsewhere of global cultural com-modities, the expansion and development of the punk music movement in

Indonesia was largely an autonomous affair, unknown to and unexplored for the most part by Western musicians or researchers. My ethnographic research in Jakarta as well as in the cities of Bandung, Surabaya, Yogyakarta, and Denpasar suggests strongly that Indonesian punk scenes emerged in those places with minimal interference or direct influence from Westerners. Instead, the scenes crystallized via often-idiosyncratic interpretations of imported cultural forms (fanzines, sound recordings, album artwork, etc.) and local replications of those forms informed by such interpretations. These interpretations and replications were then disseminated through highly efficient patterns of social organization and group formation derived from indigenous notions of sociability. Hence, contemporary Indonesian punk rock could be viewed as nearly the opposite of gamelan music: Indonesian punk is a Western, imported musical form framed by local agents, whereas gamelan is an indigenous musical form framed in large part by translocal agents employing an imported Western ideological category, namely that of "classical art music."

Despite this contrast, a striking similarity exists between classical gamelan and punk music in Indonesia: both are formally conservative and place high value on musical continuity with the past. Hebdige's theories aside, punk's post-1980s traditionalism happens to be a remarkable strategy for resisting co-optation by the culture industry, which is concerned with distinctiveness, novelty, and innovation when searching for sounds to introduce into the mass market. Despite the current global popularity of "pop punk," "true" punk music is perhaps safe from total commodification because, in a sense, it is nothing new. But how can we best interpret this stubborn refusal to evolve, and again, what could punk possibly mean in an Indonesia context? To address these questions we must turn to approaches to cultural meaning other than those employed by Hebdige.

In the years since *Subculture* was published, the dyadic, Saussurean model of signification on which Hebdige's study was predicated has been questioned from a variety of angles. Among the most persuasive alternative models of meaning that have been proposed for cultural phenomena are those derived from the semiotic theories of the American philosopher Charles Peirce, which are based on a triadic model of signification in which the "signifier" and the "signified" (in Peircean terms, the "sign" and "object") are always accompanied by an "interpretant," an entity present in semiosis that connects the sign-object relationship to a larger world of signs relevant to the specific semiotic encounter. Above all, Peircean semiotics reminds us that signs do not really operate in an abstract, closed system—they signify to concrete perceivers inhabiting specific locations (or, to use a different lingo, subject positions) at specific moments of encounter.

Thomas Turino, in his pathbreaking essay, "Signs of Imagination, Identity, and Experience: A Peircean Semiotic Theory for Music," argues that it is only through ethnographic research that one gains access to the interpretants of a particular musical community's meaningful encounters with musical signs.[25] Punk music is no exception, and Hebdige's questions about what punk subculture "signifies" cannot be answered without reference to a particular historical moment and from the inside of a specific interpretive community, whether in 1977 London, 1989 Moscow, 2000 Jakarta, or anywhere else.

Turino also emphasizes the creation of musical meaning not through the arbitrary symbolic relation between signifier and signified, but through what Peircean semiotics identifies as indexicality (a non-arbitrary relationship of copresence between sign and object), and iconicity (a non-arbitrary relationship of resemblance between sign and object). Turino argues that the phenomenological immediacy of these non-arbitrary relationships lends music its affective power and anchors musical sound and performance to lived experience.[26] Given these semiotic properties, it is perhaps not surprising that Hebdige paid very little attention to punk *music* in his famous study, for it is rather difficult to detach non-arbitrary signifiers from their objects in the fashion he argues is constitutive of punk signifying practices.

In the case of punk in Indonesia, I would contend that it is the materiality of the sign vehicles themselves that constitutes a stable point of reference for identity. More importantly, the non-arbitrary meanings of musical sound are what ground these signifiers in affective experience. Thus punk in twenty-first-century Jakarta is not a radical signifying practice that treats style as the manipulation of ahistorical, disembodied symbols, but rather a traditionalist discourse rooted in the powerful indexical and iconic meanings of particular sounds and images—distorted guitar chords, pounding rhythms, shouted vocals, English obscenities, Mohawks, studded leather jackets, etc. Furthermore, punks in Indonesia *do* care about history, particularly the history of their movement. An example of this can be found in one of the few changes in Indonesian punk style I observed—one that diverged from the classic 1970s Anglo-American model. This shift involved the use of the German swastika in local punk iconography.

Hebdige holds up early punks' sartorial deployment of the swastika as a prime example of punk's radical resignification of cultural symbols from the so-called parent culture. He claims that the punks' incorporation of the swastika into their fashion and iconography was part of a nihilistic attempt to "willfully detach" even the most potent social symbols from their historico-referential meaning. In his words, the swastika was "exploited as an empty effect."[27]

When I first visited Indonesia in 1997, before the fall of Suharto, I was dismayed, but not entirely surprised, to see swastikas frequently appearing on stickers, T-shirts, and iron-on patches worn by punks. Many, perhaps most, of these punks were not aware of the particular political and ideological history of the symbol they chose to wear, and to them the swastika really was perhaps an empty signifier of punk rebellion as envisioned by Hebdige.[28] But two years later things had changed. As the Indonesian underground punk scene developed, its more intellectually engaged members increased their knowledge of punk history, including the movement's frequent (if not always consistent) opposition to fascism, racism, and neo-Nazism in the West. Many Indonesian punks who had bitterly opposed the corrupt Suharto dictatorship and the brutal tactics of the Indonesian military saw an obvious parallel to their own struggles, and they began to reject the swastika. While some punks in Jakarta still wore the symbol, many more adopted anti-Nazi symbols. By late 1999, anti-Nazi slogans and iconography had become conspicuous at punk shows. Those slogans included "Destroy Fascism—Fight Back!" and "*Gegen* [Smash] Nazis,"[29] as well as the felicitous title of a 1983 song by the leftist California punk band the Dead Kennedys: "Nazi Punks Fuck Off!" More than once I even observed punks wearing swastika patches with lines drawn through them in permanent marker, almost as if after having purchased the patches they had experienced a change of heart.

Such a turn of events cast doubt on the essential, disconnected nihilism of the punk movement posited by Hebdige. Instead, this transformation of the swastika sign resembles what M. Gottdiener[30] calls the "recovery of lost signifieds," a reclamation of the historical significance of particular sign systems that operates as a form of resistance to the decontextualizing commodification of culture under capitalism. Ultimately, however, I want to reiterate that, far more than their semiotic potential, it was the sheer forceful *materiality* of dyed Mohawk haircuts, tight black jeans, shouted English obscenities, painted leather jackets, safety pins, iron-on patches, and punk music's visceral sonic icons of rage and alienation that originally appealed to late-twentieth-century working-class youth in the US and UK as well as their counterparts in Indonesia—where the working class has its own distinct but not entirely unrelated experiences of violence, marginalization, and disempowerment—twenty years after the birth of the genre. While punks in these varied spatiotemporal settings express their opposition to the dominant order primarily through embodied symbolic practices (sartorial, hygienic, kinesthetic, iconographic, musical) rather than through formal involvement in politics, their actions are hardly apolitical. In early twenty-first-century Indonesia, punks themselves could be considered sign vehicles that index the social inequality, corruption, and as-yet-unfinished project of national self-definition that continue to characterize life in their country despite its having successfully transitioned to a multiparty democratic form of government.

Conclusions

The story of punks in Jakarta provides one illustration of how Western-derived musics have become a fundamental component of generational identity for youth around the world. It is evident that cultural globalization has not resulted in a decontextualized, semiological free-for-all but instead is a process entangled with real purposes, real social agents, and real life. We must point out the limitations of non-ethnographic approaches to the interpretation of this phenomenon, for all meaning is situational and dependent on a limited set of interpretants characteristic of a particular interpretive community. Moreover, "… an interpretant can only be grounded or justified in relation to some goal of interpretation."[31] In other words, the interpretation of punk music by Jakarta punks (for instance) is *purposeful*, in this case motivated (I would argue) by their desire to connect specific musical forms with their everyday social experience. But even ethnographers must be careful to avoid oversimplifying the diversity of purposeful relationships between the signs, objects, and interpretants they encounter. Music is powerful because different people invest it with complex meanings at different times, and through its non-arbitrary, sensible features music can amplify those meanings and make them palpably present and experientially true.

The real question, then, from an ethnomusicological perspective is not how Indonesian punk is distinctively Indonesian but rather how punk music and style operate within an Indonesian national youth culture where it is one musical genre alternative among many for social agents struggling to find meaning, community, and self-expression in a complicated, globalized, post-authoritarian reality. For Indonesian punks, the forms themselves, by virtue of their physical stability, articulate a coherent subject position. Furthermore, in addition to possible interpretants such as the opposition to Suharto, the continuing social injustice and inequality of Indonesian society, and the cultural impact of globalizing processes, Indonesian punk's social infrastructure is itself a powerful interpretant. Punk music provides a social gathering place for alienated youth, and in many working-class Jakarta neighborhoods it constitutes a viable alternative to the grim choice young men face between religious fundamentalism on the one hand, and gang membership and criminality on the other. And for many of punk's adherents, the fact that the fundamental stylistic features of punk music and fashion are thought to be unchanged since the dawn of the movement only adds to their potency.

Jeremy Wallach, from "Living the Punk Lifestyle in Jakarta," *Ethnomusicology: Journal of the Society for Ethnomusicology* 52:1 (Winter 2008).

BLIND PIGS, INTERVIEW IN *THE PUNKS ARE ALRIGHT: A PUNK ROCK SAFARI FROM THE FIRST WORLD TO THE THIRD*

One Canadian punk's (almost) trash, it turns out, can be a Brazilian band's treasure. The film *The Punks are Alright* documents the way the music of the Forgotten Rebels, who we met in the last chapter through a disenchanted fan, travels the world. The Canadian band's song "The Punks Are Alright" (itself adapted from an earlier hit by UK's The Who) is covered more than twenty-five years later by a Brazilian band, the Blind Pigs, who then receive letters from Indonesian fans searching for records to trade. Not only does this vividly illustrate punk rock inheritance across borders, it also shows the degree to which punk's alternative infrastructure sets up global shop. Additionally, while there are innumerable bands in scenes all over the world singing in their local languages, the introduction of English is particularly interesting here: not only is it the common language of the documentary itself, but it proves to be, just as Wallach observed, a kind of Latin for punks: pored over and studied precisely because it is the language in which punk primarily arrives. And while we could, and should, be critical of the importation of Anglo cultural norms, the key moment comes at the end: after punk has been invested in and puzzled over in its English format, the Blind Pigs write an anti-imperialist song for a transnational Latin

American audience of punks. English verses and Spanish choruses, sung by a Portuguese-speaking band, add up to a hybrid punk internationalism.

Blind Pigs, Henrike and Mauro

HENRIKE: My dad, he's fifty-five and a Brazilian naval officer, he's a captain in the Brazilian Navy, he's also a nuclear engineer [who worked in the US and the UK]. ... One day my Dad came up to me with this tape. The first band on the tape was the Forgotten Rebels. He gave the tape to me and said, "Hey, Henrike, what you listen to isn't real rock 'n' roll. I'm giving you this tape and this has some real rock and I think you'll like it." And being a little kid I said: "Give me that tape—whatever." And I got that tape and I played it and I was blown away. I could feel honesty; I could feel energy flowing out of the speakers, you know?

MAURO: Henrike was the one who introduced me to punk rock, and the first tape he recorded for me was the Forgotten Rebels on the A side and Stiff Little Fingers on the B side. I used to sit with Henrike in classes and we would have a Forgotten Rebels lyric and I would translate it into Portuguese, and wouldn't see the meaning. One day we did the "Fuck Me Dead" lyrics, in the English class I have with him. And I was like: "What is rigor mortis?" I don't know what is that. "What is stiff?" I was like learning English with "Fuck Me Dead" lyrics. ...

We're, like, simple guys. We have day jobs where we work and we don't make a living off the band because there's no such thing making a living off a band in Brazil. I'm always thinking about the band; it's like making something out of nothing, you know?

It's a challenge to us. We come from the honest place to have a punk rock band. We love making music and really believe we can do something great, something unique. That's what really motivates me: to show people, and to show myself, that I can make something good. Because sometimes you have that dilemma, like: I'm from the Third World, maybe I'm not meant to do punk rock, because we don't have a rock 'n' roll history in Brazil. You ask yourselves: Are we good? Are we really making a good sound?

I get mail from everywhere. From Indonesia there's a guy who wrote to me. He's like, "Please give me your CD. I have no money to buy CDs here. There's no way of buying your records here."

HENRIKE: We were like, whoa, man, Indonesia! Fuck man. Let's send him a CD.

MAURO: We know that Indonesia is even a poorer country than Brazil. He wrote me this huge e-mail …

HENRIKE: "Thank you so much. Thank you so much." Just for sending him a CD. "It's great. We are such huge fans of the Blind Pigs." And then a few months later, man, check this out, we got these fucking patches from Indonesia. Blind Pigs patches. Imagine that. [Henrike points to a patch on his pants that reads Blind Pigs, in English].

MAURO: We reached the heart of this guy. He's like really touched by our music. That's what music is all about. You can reach someone on the other side of the world. You're successful, you know? You can't be any more successful than that …

HENRIKE: It's great to see how punk rock's so universal. Like you're here in Brazil and you've been influenced, not by a Brazilian band; you've been influenced by a Canadian band. That's weird, you know? It just shows you that borders don't exist in punk rock …

I wanted to write a song that anybody from Mexico all the way down to Argentina could relate to. Because it's actually a song about Latin America, the Latin American situation with the puppet dictatorships that the CIA helped set up back in the sixties and the early seventies when you had people disappearing because they were considered to be subversive or left-wing sympathizers. That was really a dark time for Latin America. And the sad thing is that America helped with all of that.

The chorus is in Spanish. It goes something like this:

> Patria libre o muerte
> El grito de la nacion
> Patria libre o muerte
> Por la revolucion

So it means:

> Free state or death
> The scream of our nation
> Free state or death
> For the revolution

It's in Spanish because Brazil is the only Latin American country that speaks Portuguese. I was trying to do a song to reach kids in Latin

America, so that's why it's in Spanish. The rest isn't in Spanish because I don't know how to speak Spanish, so I did the other lyrics in English.

Douglas Crawford, dir. *The Punks Are Alright: A Punk Rock Safari from the First World to the Third*, 2004.

ESNEIDER OF HUASIPUNGO, "MIGRAPUNK"

One often hears that punk rock is "borderless," transcending nation. This is, of course, a corollary of the claim that punk rock transcends race. The question that needs to be asked in both instances is: For whom? Here, Esneider of the U.S.-based, Spanish-singing band Huasipungo—who we previously met interviewing Los Crudos—details the route by which he came from Colombia to the United States: smuggled across the Mexican border, captured and detained by the Immigration police, and then jumping bail before finally making his way to New York. In the New York punk scene he finds a home, albeit a home with all kinds of borders that many punks don't even realize are in place, like those of ethnicity, language, class, and political circumstance. Esneider sets about remodeling his punk home, getting involved in the scene, forming a Spanish-language band, and catching "the DIY bug," rearranging punk's frontiers in the process. As Esneider points out, the size of the world is, in many ways, decreasing, and as people and cultures flow and combine, sometimes with ease and at other times with great difficulty, but ineluctably nonetheless, the ideal of racial, national, and cultural purity is increasingly hard to sustain, not only within the dominant culture but its punk opposition as well. Esneider's closing emphasis on maintaining difference—and not in the usual punk way, as a unified punk difference from the mainstream, but rather as difference within punk—may represent the scene's best hope for transforming its complicated, contentious racial politics by ensuring that punk is never experienced as merely a White Riot.

I came to the USA with a visa once. Fine country but not for me—never wanted to live here. I went back to Colombia and went on with my life. I went to shows. Mostly metal shows as there were no punk shows back then. There were very few punk bands. Metal ruled. I was finishing high school, I was part of the swimming team, went to shows, and helped organize a small student movement. Things, it seemed, were good. Then the political situation of the country started to go from bad to worse. A country with an open civil war (promoted and financed by the USA), an extensive drug trade (promoted and financed by the USA). The so-called drug cartels started organizing their own private armies. The government and the army started increasing their dirty war now to include paramilitary forces.

Everyone around me started to get into one faction of the war or another. In the middle of all this I decided I needed to leave the country. That if I stayed I probably would not be alive for a long time. I did not want to be drafted into the army (it is compulsory) and because of political reasons I was at this point in serious danger. I got out... .

I arrived in New York ... For the next couple of years I did my best to adapt. Got really depressed, gained some 50 pounds and wanted to kill myself. Not a pretty picture. I attended language classes and learned as much English as I could. I made the decision not to become like some immigrant cases. The ones that worked sixteen hours a day, save all their money only to get robbed their first day back to their home country. Or the ones who do not learn English, "'cause I am leaving or getting kicked out any second," etc. So I started to get out a little more. Learned to navigate the limbo world of having no documents. Attended Queens College, got a job and eventually found the HC/punk scene. I lived in Queens but eventually found myself making my way to the Lower East Side for shows. CBGB's, squats, Tin Pan Alley, Lizard's Lounge, etc. I started writing to people, buying records, and trading via mail (there was no email then) but did not meet anyone really. I mostly stayed by myself. I talked to some people briefly but did not really make any friends.

One day someone sent me a letter asking me to meet some guy named Freddy Alva. His address was three or four blocks from mine. I was a little scared due to the realities of the NYHC scene back then. But I walked over anyway. He was of Peruvian origin and we soon became friends. Through him I started to meet people and eventually we all went down to ABC No Rio for its first set of punk matinees. I started to get involved. Around this time I also met Neil Robinson, an English punk who was an engine of Squat or Rot, setting up shows, doing a band, etc. I caught the DIY bug more and more. But this scene was not very aware of what was going on outside the USA, let alone in Latinoamerica. Most of the anarcho punk and/or hardcore punk scene was mostly white, while the violent, homophobic skin scene was actually anti-racist and very diverse. It was very confusing. One day at ABC someone came up to me and told me that there was some kid who was Latino and spoke no English. I went to meet him. He was Peruvian and his name was Ivan and with his brother Francisco we eventually started a band called Huasipungo. The idea was to sing in Spanish about the things that affected us—documents, violence, imperialism—and that we would do it in the language we would feel more comfortable with. We expected to receive at least the same amount of respect as any other band in our small scene.

Yet it became really hard to be taken seriously in the scene. It seems that singing in Spanish and talking about what we were talking about was a joke to them. We struggled to keep the band going, do records, and tour like everyone else, though it became really hard to do anything and figure out who was genuinely helping us and who was just jerking us around. Our flyers were ripped off of walls, our records were hidden in the bins so they would not sell. Despite this, some people threw their support behind us and we kept going. Ivan finally threw in the towel. He was tired of being in the USA away from his wife and kid and went back to Peru. Francisco moved with his family to San Francisco and I kept the band going. New people came in. Eventually we met Los Crudos, did a split EP and went on a national tour. All done with the effort of a group of wetbacks doing DIY punk. … When touring we stayed away from the border, avoided towns even though we would do well there just so that we could avoid checkpoints. I stopped doing Critical Mass when they started arresting people. The band members who were citizens always kept an eye on things. If we went through a checkpoint, only the white Americans would get in the driver and passenger seat; the rest of us would sit in the back.

So, Jane [my partner] and I went through all this legal bullshit. And I had a chance. We saw so many cases where people did not have a chance and they would get detained, deported … just for lacking a piece of paper or just because *la migra* did not believe part of their story. But we stuck it out and eventually I became a green card holder or a "legal alien resident," got a social security card, and got on the books at work. Now at least I could get some of my tax refunds. Because if you pay taxes but you do it under a fake number or any other such thing you get no refunds—then on top of that you have to take shit from the racists saying that you don't pay your taxes. When I became legal we started to dream big—touring outside the USA. We did the Mexico tour, went through a lineup change, and went back to having band members with legal document problems. So we have not been able to tour outside the USA since.

Things come and go, people come and go. But we keep fighting for what we believe in and talking about who we are. I am a USA citizen now (dual citizen of USA and Colombia, actually) but I am always dealing with the immigration system. I petitioned to legalize my mom. The INS claimed my mom was *not* my mom because her first name was missing from my birth certificate. It took more than a year to get it all sorted out. All my family members have had to deal with this ridiculous system. My partner Jane has always stuck it out and fought side by side with me and my family every step of the way and has been fighting for other immigrants' rights for years.

To tell you the truth, people who want to end immigration are fighting a lost war. People moving around has always and will always happen. Borders are fallacies made up by politicians, wars, landlords, racists, and imperialists. Borders make no sense. Countries, their flags, their maps are irrelevant. If those who hate immigrants so much really wanted to make a difference they should fight to end free trade agreements, to promote fair trade, to end imperialist intervention of first world countries, to end the IMF and the World Bank, to promote fair and just unions, fair wages everywhere. They should refuse to buy sweatshop clothes, CDs, cars, food, etc., etc.

The world is becoming smaller and smaller—we can take planes anywhere more easily than ever before. Now I can buy a $2 phone card and call anywhere in the world for up to two hours. The internet has brought us closer to each other, anywhere in the world. It is really a scary time for racists, imperialists, and the sort. The working-class people of the world get to know each other, communicate, and support each other more easily than before, while they consolidate their elitist power. Fear is one of their few weapons and stirring fears around a group of people who want nothing more at times than to work and live is a desperate attempt to distract from real problems and to keep us divided and fighting each other.

We are punks, we are every day more and more. The world is not a homogeneous place. We are all different, speak many languages, sing about different issues that affect us. We just happen to have had to move around.

Esneider, from "Migrapunk," *Maximumrocknroll* no. 293 (San Francisco, October 2007).

NOTES

Duncombe and Tremblay: White Riot?

1 W. E. B. Du Bois, *The Souls of Black Folk* (New York: Dover Publications, 1903/1994), p. v.

2 Jeff Chang, "Overpowered by Funk," *San Francisco Bay Guardian* (January 1, 2003), on the Web.

3 Greil Marcus, "The Last Broadcast," in *Ranters and Crowd Pleasers: Punk in Pop Music 1977–92* (New York: Doubleday, 1993), p. 304.

4 John Clarke, Stuart Hall, Tony Jefferson, and Brian Roberts, "Subcultures, Cultures and Class: A Theoretical Overview," in Stuart Hall and Tony Jefferson, eds., *Resistance Through Rituals* (London: Unwin Hyman, 1976), pp. 47–48.

Waksman: Kick Out the Jams!

1 John Sinclair, "White Panther Statement," *Fifth Estate* 14 (November 14–27, 1968), p. 8.

2 Ibid.

3 Ibid.

4 This program is reprinted in Eric Ehrmann's profile of the Five, "MC5," *Rolling Stone* 25 (January 4, 1969), pp. 16–17. Archie Shepp is profiled in Amiri Baraka's *Black Music* (New York: William Morrow and Company, 1967).

5 Marianna Torgovnick, *Gone Primitive: Savage Intellects, Modern Lives* (Chicago: University of Chicago Press, 1990), p. 228.

6 Donald Lowe has a meticulous analysis of the mind/body split in his

History of Bourgeois Perception (Chicago: University of Chicago Press, 1982), pp. 85–108. On the civilizing process, see Norbert Elias, *The Civilizing Process, Vol. 1: The History of Manners* (New York: Urizen Books, 1978).

7 Barbara Ehrenreich, *The Hearts of Men: American Dreams and the Flight from Commitment* (New York: Anchor Press, 1983), pp. 99–116.

8 Todd Gitlin, *The Sixties* (New York: Bantam Mooks, 1993) p. 228. Much of Gitlin's account is drawn from Abbie Hoffman's description of the same episode in *Revolution for the Hell of It* (New York: The Dial Press, 1968), p. 35. Hoffman himself was certainly in the same category of radicalism as Grogan and Sinclair; indeed, the White Panthers were a branch of the Hoffman and Jerry Rubin–led Yippies.

9 Gitlin, p. 349.

10 Sinclair, "Coat Puller," *Fifth Estate* 7 (August 1–14, 1968), p. 5. This is a reprint of the original article to commemorate a year having passed since the riots. Sinclair's enthusiastic response to the riots was echoed, albeit with a more cynical inflection, by Peter Werbe, editor of *Fifth Estate*. In a 1969 article by John Burks on the underground press, Werbe was quoted as saying: " 'When it was burning, man you could get up on the rooftops and see the flames in all directions. It was *beautiful*. So beautiful. You've never seen anything like it.' He thought about the fires for a minute, then added—just to make sure I hadn't missed the point—'I hate this fuckin' town so much … I've lived in the Motor City a long time—long enough to really know what it's about, and, you know, I really hate it.' " Burks, "The Underground Press: A Special Report," *Rolling Stone* 43 (October 4, 1969), p. 13.

11 Gitlin, pp. 234–35.

12 Ehrmann, p. 16.

13 Gitlin, p. 245. The phrase "What should whitey do?" is taken from a letter to Gitlin by Carol McEldowney.

14 Eric Lott, *Love and Theft: Blackface Minstrelsy in the American Working Class* (New York: Oxford University Press, 1993), p. 18.

15 Ibid., pp. 49–50.

16 Ibid., p. 52.

17 Rob Tyner had one of the most impressive Afros to adorn any public figure in the 1960s and 1970s, especially among whites. Whether his hair was naturally that way, I am not sure; but the issue of the Afro's association with naturalness is provocatively treated by Kobena Mercer in "Black Hair, Style Politics," in *Welcome to the Jungle: New Positions in Black Cultural Studies* (New York: Routledge, 1994).

18 Sinclair, "Separation Is Doom," *Guitar Army*, (New York: Douglas Book Corp., 1972) p. 110.

19 David Walley, "MC5 Interview," *The Age of Rock 2: Sights and Sounds of the American Cultural Revolution*, edited by Jonathan Eisen (New York: Vintage, 1970), p. 283.

20 Norman Mailer, "The White Negro," *Advertisements for Myself* (New York: Signet, 1960), p. 310.

21 Ibid.

22 Sinclair, *Guitar Army*, p. 12.

Hebdige: Bleached Roots

1 The implicit "threat" to traditional British values is of course most clearly exploited by the National Front. Indeed, Rastafarianism seems to have been identified as a kind of black bacillus by the N.F. For instance, an N.F. poster depicting a black face, framed in dreadlocks, "melting" onto a Union Jack, interprets the black presence as a literal "sullying" of British culture.

2 André Breton, "Introduction to an Anthology of Surrealist Poetry," in Lucy Lippard, ed., *Surrealists on Art* (Englewood Cliffs, N.J.: Spectrum, 1970).

3 As well as providing a stimulating gloss to Genet's work, Sartre's famous essay (1963) contains many insights into the psychology of subculture in general. Sartre interprets Genet's willful elevation of crime into art as a truly "heroic" act of self-transcendence. Born a bastard, adopted by a peasant family, and named a thief at the age of nine, Genet systematically contravenes civic, sexual, and moral law, aspiring towards the condition of the utterly abject "which turns out to be next door to saintliness." In Genet's own words (1967) "... we arouse pity by cultivating the most repulsive of wounds. We became a reproach to your happiness." As Kate Millett writes in *Sexual Politics*, in Genet's "mortification, both in the flesh and the spirit, lies the victory of the saint."

4 The punk look was essentially undernourished: emaciation standing as a sign of Refusal. The prose of the fanzines was littered with references to "fat businessmen" and "lard-ass capitalists." Paul Weller of the Jam flatly refused to take the more recent music of Roger Daltrey (lead singer of the Who) seriously because "you can't play rock 'n' roll with a beer-gut" (*New Musical Express*, 7 May 1977). The movement from metaphorical to literal frames of reference seems a crucial part

of the process of 'magical resolution' (see pp. 77–78) common to all spectacular subcultures.

5 See Richard Hell, *New Musical Express*, 29 October 1977, on the significance of being rechristened a punk: "One thing that I wanted to bring back to rock'n'roll was the knowledge that you invent yourself. That's why I changed my name." Punks in pursuit of an "immaculate" identity often adopted aliases—Paul Grotesque, Sid Vicious, Johnny Rotten, etc.

6 One punk assured me in October 1977 that punk's only claim to political significance lay in the fact that "we're like *that* with the blacks," indicating by clasping his hands together that the interests of the two groups were inseparable.

7 Listen for instance to Elvis Costello's "Watching the Detectives," which has a strong reggae rhythm. Punk dub consists of a series of independently recorded tracks, superimposed one on top of the other without being perfectly synchronized. Without stretching the point too far we could say that dub alienates the listener from the prevailing aesthetic of unobtrusive naturalism (i.e., the polished product). It leaves the studio door open.

8 R&B groups like the Yardbirds, Them, the Animals, the Pretty Things, and the Rolling Stones readily acknowledged their black American sources. Jagger frequently claimed to have modeled his celebrated dance routines on the stage act of James Brown. Groups like the Small Faces, the Who, Zoot Money, and Georgie Fame and the Blue Flames—all extremely popular with the mods—did cover versions of soul classics (particularly numbers originally recorded by Bobby Bland, James Brown, Otis Redding, and Wilson Pickett). See Charlie Gillet's excellent *Sound of the City* for a thorough account of black American music in the 1950s and 1960s.

9 The subcultural styles of these periods in particular were "scrambled" in the punk ensembles and the lyrics and self-presentation of some of the American punk groups (especially Mink DeVille and Blondie) reiterated in a quite deliberate way the theme of "crazy mixed-up" adolescence firmly associated with the earlier periods (c.f. the Shangri-Las).

Beeber: Hotsy-Totsy Nazi Schatze

1 *Editors' Note:* Endnotes from the original.
Author Interviews: Thomas Erdelyi, Neil Gaiman, Gyda Gash, Debbie

Harry, Richard Meltzer, Glenn O'Brien, Martin Popoff, Genya Ravan, Peter Robbins, Camilla Saly, Frank Secich, Andy Shernoff, Sylvie Simmons, Chris Stein.

Web Citations: Suggs, "Hell's West talk on CD, and more," http://www.richardhell.com/cgi-bin/forum/showmessage.asp? messageID=7492 (accessed April 19, 2011); Krassner, "Paul Krassner Reviews *The Trials of Lenny Bruce*," http://www.deepleafproductions. com/wilsonlibrary/texts/krassnerlenny.html (accessed April 19, 2011).

Dylan, Bob, "With God on Our Side," *The Times They Are A-Changin'* (Columbia, 1963).

Gainsbourg, Serge. *Rock Around the Bunker* (Universal/Polygram, 1975).

Hell, Richard, On Jewish-American novelist Nathaniel West (talk, Teachers & Writers Collaborative, December 7, 2005).

Simmons, Sylvie, *Serge Gainsbourg: A Fistful of Gitanes* (Cambridge, MA: Da Capo Press, 2002).

Sontag, Susan. "Notes on 'Camp'," *Partisan Review*, 1964.

Meadows: Pistol-Whipped

1 *Editors' Note:* Meadows not only misreads the politics of punk, but also makes a number of factual errors: England isn't an island, Richard Hell wasn't in a British band, most bands were not pro-NF, etc.

Sabin: 'I Won't Let That Dago By'

1 It's risky to concur with the stereotype of a fanzine as an arena where contributors could say whatever they wanted, unhindered by the restrictions prevailing in the mainstream media. For many this was true, but some were heavily edited (for various reasons), and some cultivated their links with the music biz in order to secure interviews, advance copies of records, etc., and were therefore open to "persuasion." Nevertheless, for this chapter, I have found them very useful. I researched my own collection, that of Teal Triggs (with thanks), and that of the Victoria and Albert Museum Library (thanks to librarian Simon Ford).

2 A word on terminology. Any usage of the words "race," "racism," and "anti-racism" is controversial: within Cultural Studies, race is understood in terms of social construction rather than biological difference. Other terms are equally difficult. Here, "Asian" is used to describe

the diaspora from the Indian subcontinent (including those born in Britain); "Afro-Caribbean" for the diaspora from the Caribbean islands (including British-born); and "black" for "Afro-Caribbean" (as opposed to the definition of the National Union of Journalists, for example, which encompasses all people of color on a "strategic" basis). The best theoretical background to race politics, for our purposes, is Paul Gilroy, *There Ain't No Black in the Union Jack* (London: Century-Hutchinson, 1987).

3 A useful recent history of the NF can be found in Richard Thurlow, *Fascism in Britain* (Oxford: Basil Blackwell, 1987, revised 1998), especially chapter 10. The most detailed earlier text is Martin Walker, *The National Front* (Glasgow: Fontana, 1977).

4 On the role of the Conservative Party, see Martin Barker, *The New Racism* (London: Junction Books, 1981). For useful perspectives on racism in the media during this period, see Phil Cohen and Karl Gardner *It Ain't Half Racist Mum* (London: Comedia, 1982) and the accompanying video of the same name, made in 1978, which contains footage of an RAR carnival. On racist humour, see Stephen Wagg, *Because I Tell a Joke or Two* (London: Routledge, 1998: chapter 15).

5 Some readers may be surprised to see the name of Garry Bushell in the list of "left-wing" journalists. But, despite his later association with the Oi! movement and his subsequent employment on the right-wing *Sun*, his views at the time were often socialist: he had just left the SWP, and some of the most impassioned anti-racist articles of the period were penned by him.

6 For example, Julie Burchill and Tony Parsons, *The Boy Looked at Johnny* (London: Pluto, 1978), and Caroline Coon, *1988: The New Wave Punk Rock Explosion* (London: Omnibus, 1978).

7 Dick Hebdige, *Subculture: The Meaning of Style* (London: Routledge, 1979) p. 69.

8 Hebdige has since disowned many of the points in his book, and his theories have been questioned elsewhere—see, for example, pp. 148 and 180 of Roger Sabin, ed, *Punk Rock: So What?* (London: Routledge, 1999) and Anne Beezer's impressive critique in Martin Barker and Anne Beezer, eds., *Reading into Cultural Studies* (London: Routledge, 1992: chapter 6).

9 Ostensibly, RAR and the ANL were separate groups, the former being an "independent" organisation, the latter an offshoot of the SWP. However, both shared members and organisers, and worked very

closely together—the union being made official by their joint Carnival, in April 1978, in Victoria Park, London.

10 David Widgery, *Beating Time* (London: Pluto, 1986), p. 117. For more critical perspectives on RAR/the ANL see Simon Frith, "Rock Against Racism and Red Wedge: From Music to Politics, from Politics to Music," R. Garofalo, ed., *Rockin' the Boat* (Boston: South End Press, 1992), Jon Savage, *England's Dreaming: Sex Pistols and Punk Rock* (London: Faber & Faber, 1991: 480–85), and Gilroy (1987: 115–35).

11 Dave Laing, *One Chord Wonders* (Milton Keynes: Open University Press, 1985), Savage (1991), and Stewart Home's—admittedly ragged— *Cranked Up Really High: An Inside Account of Punk Rock* (Hove: CodeX, 1995) among them.

12 As well as "racial" enemies, other NF targets included feminists, gays, Communists, anarchists, and anybody associated with the Irish Republican movement.

13 The nearest Asian musical equivalent to reggae was bhangra (a mix of folk melodies—often Punjabi—and rhythmic dance beats), which was growing in importance among Asian youth, but which was totally ignored by both punk and RAR. (The meshing of Asian and [white] "alternative" music did eventually happen, with encouraging results: this chapter is being written at a time when Cornershop are having their first taste of success with "Brimful of Asha.")

14 Anon., "Talking Clash," *Record Mirror*, 1 July 1978.

15 Frith (1992), p. 69.

16 Lindsey Boyd, "Interview with Mark Perry," *Sounds*, 24 December 1977.

17 Robin Denselow, *When the Music's Over* (London: Faber & Faber, 1989), p. 144. The Stranglers were another contradictory band concerning racism. Singer Hugh Cornwell was notorious for goading audiences with racist comments, but the group was also known to take on fascists in fist-fights. Their song "I Feel Like a Wog" was written as a comment on RAR/the ANL—and was immediately misinterpreted by the NF (see David Buckley, *The Stranglers: No Mercy* [London: Hodder & Stoughton, 1977]).

18 See, for example, *Bulldog*, "The Newspaper of the Young National Front," no. 10, November 1978: 5.

19 Punk's relationship with the skinhead movement was a symbiotic one, though with tensions. Skins tended to see themselves as "hard punks," distanced from what they saw as a middle-class influence within punk, and followed certain bands (though never exclusively)—e.g., Sham

69, Skrewdriver, Menace, Cocksparrer, etc.—many of which were later co-opted by the Oi! movement (see below).

20 There was also, for a very brief period, an "Anti-Paki League," though what form this took organizationally is unclear.

21 Vivien Goldman, "Interview with Siouxie and the Banshees," *Sounds*, *3 December* 1977.

22 *NME*, 30 July, 1977.

23 This was the man who co-wrote the lyrics for the tasteful "Belsen Was a Gas" (released 1979).

24 Anonymous writer (probably "Skid"), *Ripped and Torn*, no. 7, August 1977. The piece goes on to warn against the dangers of wearing "Nazi paraphanalia" [*sic*].

25 The lyrics to "Puerto Rican" are from a bootleg of 1977–78 session recordings entitled *Madam Stan* (c. 1986). The song has been interpreted by Stewart Home (1995, p. 72) as being ironic. However, the song may have been "humorous," but not ironic, and its suspect nature was reinforced by Adam's gleeful introduction to it during gigs: "Light a beacon with a Puerto Rican!"

26 Alan Lewis "Review of 'Television Screen,'" *Sounds*, 7 May 1977.

27 Recent histories that have stated the swastika was for shock, without going further, include: Erica Echenberg and Mark P, *And God Created Punk* (London: Virgin, 1996, p. 118); Adrian Boot and Chris Salewicz *Punk: The Illustrated History of a Musical Revolution* (London: Boxtree, 1996, p. 33); and *Arena*, "Punk and the Pistols," BBC TV, 1995.

28 Where I grew up, in Ilford, there was a big Jewish population and a rising Asian one. The NF and BM would hold meetings in local halls, and groups of flag-carrying NF-ers would try to sell us newspapers and "debate" with us on our way home from school. Here, the meaning of a swastika could be very different to that in a trendy London club. It would have been different again, of course, in a (white) rural area.

29 "At a Later Date," Joy Division, on the LP *Short Circuit: Live at the Electric Circus* (Virgin, 1978). Curtis is quoted elsewhere saying ridiculous things, e.g., calling Hess "the Prince of Peace" (Ward 1996, p. 157).

30 Sandy Robertson, "Interview with Sham 69," *Sounds*, 29 April 1978.

31 For example, on the *Arena* documentary "Punk and the Pistols."

32 Tony Wilson, quoted in Dave Simpson, "Torn Apart," *Uncut*, December 1997, p. 75.

33 Robertson.

34 Savage (1991), pp. 242–43. Siouxsie was, of course, a Bowie fan.

Black Flag: Interview

1 Jon Lewis, "Punks in LA: It's Kiss or Kill," *Journal of Popular Culture* 22:2, Fall 1988, pp. 87–97, 94.

Traber: LA's 'White Minority'

1 Lawrence Grossberg, "Another Boring Day in Paradise: Rock and Roll and the Empowerment of Everyday Life," in *Dancing in Spite of Myself: Essays on Popular Culture*, pp. 29–63. (Durham, N.C.: Duke University Press, 1997).

2 Barry Shank, *Dissonant Identities: The Rock'n'Roll Scene in Austin, Texas* (Hanover, N.H.: Wesleyan University Press, 1994), p. 122.

3 My bookends encompass the points from which punk becomes a recognized scene in Los Angeles to its transformation into hardcore and final wane into cliché. There is typically a line drawn between punk and hardcore that places the latter in the 1980s, depicting it as faster, more violent, and less interested in the artistic motivations of the first phase. Hardcore is all of these in its different guises, but several of the so-called later punks had been interested and active in the scene well before any official demarcation was imposed. Black Flag is a band associated with hardcore that existed since the beginning; in fact, "White Minority" was first recorded in January 1978, well after the Germs' first single but *before* Dangerhouse issued the *Yes L.A.* compilation of "properly" punk bands. Stories of the changing scene—that hardcore pushed out Hollywood art-rockers with younger, dumber, rougher suburban kids—rarely mention that hardcore bands had been blocked out of the scene by the key clubs, so it did not occur as suddenly as historians tend to frame it. Thus hardcore is best understood as an emerging culture within an emerging culture.

4 In *Resistance Through Rituals* (London: Routledge, 1993) John Clarke et al. establish a theory of subcultures as a symbolic response to social contradictions with political limits: "The problematic of [a subculture's] experience can be 'lived through,' negotiated or resisted; but it cannot be *resolved* at that level or by those means" (p. 47). The notion of the popular as an imagined solution to problems is limited; the actions of L.A. punks who moved to the sub-urban were influenced by the music and subculture. To expect no more of a subculture than that it be a symbolic reaction to social problems, and a realistic perception of the odds for failure, underestimates what can be achieved.

In short, L.A. punk's *very* material act deserves a critique that takes it more seriously.

5 That there are boundaries determining the kind of marginality one is allowed to pursue is another level of contradiction and complicity in L.A. punk rebellion. For a counterhistory of punk and racism see Roger Sabin's essay " 'I Won't Let That Dago By': Rethinking Punk and Racism" in *Punk Rock: So What?* ed. Roger Sabin (New York: Routledge, 1999). In terms of gender, the subculture remained determinedly masculine despite the increased opportunities for women to express their own critique of gender roles. The very interest in a life typified as "tough" is indicative of punks accepting the stereotype of virility attached to certain racial (most commonly African-American) and lower-class identities, which then posits suburban males as more feminized, domesticated, and sensually reserved; see Frith's *Sound Effects: Youth, Leisure, and the Politics of Rock'n'Roll* (New York: Pantheon, 1981) for a discussion of sexuality in punk in comparison to disco. See also Lauraine Leblanc's *Pretty in Punk: Girls' Gender Resistance in a Boy's Subculture* (New Brunswick, NJ: Rutgers University Press, 1999) for a fuller analysis of female participation in punk as a masculine subculture. Furthermore, there was a distinctly homophobic sensibility during this time; refer to Jeff Spurrier for some fans' comments on this issue (p. 124); also see D. Robert Dechaine's "Mapping Subversion: Queercore Music's Playful Discourse of Resistance," *Popular Music and Society* 21, no. 4 (1997), pp. 7–37 on how this changes with the later "queercore" movement.

6 Peter Belsito and Bob Davis, *Hardcore California: A History of Punk and New Wave* (San Francisco: Last Gasp Publishing, 1983), p. 17.

7 *Subculture: The Meaning of Style* (London: Methuen, 1979), p. 120.

8 Belsito and Davis, p. 22.

9 Jeff Spurrier, "California Screaming," *Details*, December 1994, p. 122.

10 Greil Marcus, *Ranters and Crowd Pleasers: Punk in Pop Music, 1977–92* (New York: Anchor, 1993), p. 134.

11 See Mike Davis's *City of Quartz* (New York: Random-Vintage, 1992) on the development and political mobilization of L.A.'s suburbs, especially chapter 3. In *The Possessive Investment in Whiteness* (Philadelphia: Temple University Press, 1998) George Lipsitz gives a detailed history of the Federal Housing Administration's racist practices in making home loans that resulted in the overwhelming white demographics of postwar suburbs.

12 Spurrier, p. 126.

13 Henry Rollins, *Get in the Van: On the Road with Black Flag* (Los Angeles: 2.13.61, 1994), p. 8.

14 Ibid., p. 11.

15 Katherine S. Newman, *Falling from Grace: The Experience of Downward Mobility in the American Middle Class* (New York: Free Press, 1988), p. 21.

16 Frederick R. Strobel, *Upward Dreams, Downward Mobility: The Economic Decline of the American Middle Class* (Lanham, MD: Rowman & Littlefield, 1993), p. xiii.

17 Davis, p. 7. See Edward Soja's "It All Comes Together in Los Angeles" in *Postmodern Geographies: The Reassertion of Space in Critical Social Theory* (New York: Verso, 1989), pp. 190–221 for further discussion of the economic shifts during the 1970s and 1980s in Los Angeles and how these reflect and construct special spatial sites that then affect the relationship between subjects and power.

18 Barney Hoskyns, *Waiting for the Sun: Strange Days, Weird Scenes, and the Sound of Los Angeles* (New York: St. Martin's Griffin, 1996), p. 293.

19 Spurrier, p. 126.

20 Paul Fryer, "Punk and the New Wave of British Rock: Working Class Heroes and Art School Attitudes," *Popular Music and Society* 10, no. 4 (1986), p. 1.

21 In *Sound Effects* Simon Frith claims that punk "was *about* the relationship of individualism and collectivism," and while he does not discuss this point in detail it does open up the question of how these two forms of social interaction are configured in the punk ethos (p. 267). Punk strives for a reconciliation between the individual and the group. It understands that a collectivity is necessary even to have a music scene, but this does not require a containment of the individual by or within that group. In terms of a political collectivity there are many instances of punk acting as a part of a group: the antinuclear movement, the Rock Against Racism concerts in England, and the D.C. punk scene of the 1980s, which often organized political events. A localized list could go on ad infinitum; still, I contend that the individual is the privileged element in the majority of punk rock and that it places more value on the ultimate freedom of that individual and his/her personal means of agency in and against society.

22 The details of punk as a style (fashion, music [form and performance], dancing, etc.) and approach to cultural production have been dealt

with at length. See Hebdige, Tricia Henry's *Break All Rules! Punk Rock and the Making of a Style* (Ann Arbor: UMI Research, 1989), Laing, Neil Nehring's *Flowers in the Dustbin* (Ann Arbor: University of Michigan Press, 1993), and Shank as sources attending to this topic with more depth than I have space for here. For more general histories and commentaries on L.A. punk specifically, see Belsito and Davis, Hoskyns (pp. 291–330), David E. James, "Poetry/Punk/Production: Some Recent Writing in LA," in *Postmodernism and Its Discontents*, ed. E. Ann Kaplan (New York: Verso, 1988), and Lewis.

23 Elaine K. Ginsberg, ed., *Passing and the Fictions of Identity* (Durham, N.C.: Duke University Press, 1996), p. 15.

24 Eric Lott, *Love and Theft: Blackface Minstrelsy and the American Working Class* (Oxford: Oxford University Press, 1993), p. 51.

25 David R. Roediger, *Towards the Abolition of Whiteness: Essays on Race, Politics, and Working Class History* (London: Verso, 1994), pp. 3, 12.

26 Greil Marcus attacks "White Minority" as a song about hatred of the Other, that person or thing which is the not-I (p. 185). His censure is based on misunderstanding the song's lyrics: what he reads as "breed inferiority" is actually "feel inferiority" (p. 184). This is not an attack on the Other, it is a call to *become* the Other, to "hide anywhere" you can so as to escape that center legitimizing itself through "white pride." Discarding social centeredness for a life on the periphery allows one to sidestep the dominant power formations and to forestall being incorporated into their system of reality.

27 Roediger, p. 189.

28 Spurrier, p. 124.

29 Lawrence Grossberg, "Identity and Cultural Studies—Is That All There Is?" in *Questions of Cultural Identity*, ed. Stuart Hall and Paul du Gay (London: Sage, 1996), p. 102.

30 Belsito, p. 31.

31 Gayle Wald, "One of the Boys? Whiteness, Gender, and Popular Music Studies," in *Whiteness: A Critical Reader*, ed. Mike Hill (New York: New York University Press, 1997), p. 158.

32 Norman Mailer, "The White Negro: Superficial Reflections on the Hipster," in *The Portable Beat Reader*, ed. Ann Charters (New York: Penguin, 1992), p. 602.

33 Wald, p. 153.

34 Robert N. Bellah, Richard Madsen, William M. Sullivan, Ann Swidler, and Steven M. Tipton, *Habits of the Heart: Individualism and Commitment in American Life* (New York: Harper, 1985), p. 335.

35 Stephen Duncombe's *Notes from Underground: Zines and the Politics of Alternative Culture* (New York: Verso, 1997) raises similar concerns about the likelihood of collective action and enervated dissent in relation to zine publishers of the 1990s. Like punk, zines privilege an ethos of individuality and otherness but entangle themselves in a logic of us versus them. They form a network based on a valorization of being "losers," but a collective response to the systemic problems they critique becomes difficult since the publishers are often so preoccupied with avoiding co-optation that they descend ever further into cliques of obscurity.

36 Craig O'Hara, *The Philosophy of Punk: More Than Noise* (San Francisco: AK Press, 1995), p. 69.

37 Zygmunt Bauman, "From Pilgrim to Tourist—or A Short History of Identity," in *Questions of Cultural Identity*, p. 33.

38 Stuart Hall, "Notes on Deconstructing 'the Popular,'" in *Cultural Theory and Popular Culture: A Reader*, ed. John Storey (Athens, GA: University of Georgia Press, 1998), p. 447. Johan Fornäs argues that debating authenticity is pointless. Authenticity should be seen as an act of contextualized self-reflexivity such that it "appears as an option and a construction rather than as a given fact" (quoted in Nehring, *Popular Music*, p. 63). Identity is formed according to localized "rules" that create the boundaries defining authenticity, and sense is then freed from a romantic conception of "natural" origin or purity.

Clarke: The Skinheads and the Magical Recovery of Community

1 Susie Daniel, and Pete McGuire, eds., *The Paint House: Words from an East End Gang* (Harmondsworth: Penguin, 1972), p. 67.

2 Ibid., p. 68.

3 Ibid., pp. 21–22; author's emphasis.

4 Ibid., pp. 21, 31.

5 *Editors' Note:* "Ends" means the parts of stadia associated with particular groups of fans or gangs.

Brown: Subcultures, Pop Music & Politics

1 More than one genre of music has been infiltrated by right-wing and racist beliefs. The 1990s have seen the emergence of Nazi techno and Nazi folk to name just two. See the essays in Devin Burghardt, ed.,

Soundtracks to the White Revolution: White Supremacist Assaults on Youth Subcultures (Chicago, 1999).

2 Indeed, the Oi! genre is home to a number of self-consciously anti-racist and even socialist-leaning bands that place themselves in open opposition to racist and Nazi bands. See George Marshall, *Spirit of '69: A Skinhead Bible* (Dunoon, Scotland, 1991), p. 143.

3 See Dick Hebdige, "The Meaning of Mod," in Stuart Hall and Tony Jefferson, eds., *Resistance Through Rituals* (London, 1993), pp. 89–96.

4 Dick Hebdige, *Subculture: The Meaning of Style* (London and New York, 1979), p. 55; Stanley Cohen, *Folk Devils and Moral Panics: Thirtieth Anniversary Edition* (New York, 2002).

5 See Hebdige, *Subculture*, chapters 3–4; Marshall, *Spirit of '69*, pp. 44–49. Roger Sabin has recently argued that the claims of the affinity between punks and skinheads and blacks in Britain have been overstated; Roger Sabin, "'I Won't Let That Dago By': Rethinking Punk and Racism," in Roger Sabin, ed., *Punk Rock: So What?—The Cultural Legacy of Punk* (London and New York, 1999), pp. 199–218, 202. Jack Moore makes a similar but less nuanced argument in his *Skinheads Shaved for Battle: A Cultural History of American Skinheads* (Bowling Green, Ohio, 1993), p. 57.

6 Frank Cartledge has emphasized, with respect to punk rock, the highly contingent nature of "authenticity"; see Frank Cartledge, "'Distress to Impress'?: Local Punk Fashion and Commodity Exchange," in Sabin ed., *Punk Rock: So What?*, pp. 143–53, 149.

7 Phil Cohen, "Subcultural Conflict and Working Class Community," *Working Papers in Cultural Studies* 2 (University of Birmingham: Centre for Cultural Studies, 1972).

8 Marshall, *Spirit of '69*, p. 136.

9 See the caricature in ibid., p. 142.

10 Hebdige, *Subculture*, p. 31.

11 Murray Healy, *Gay Skins: Class, Masculinity and Queer Appropriation* (London, 1996), p. 197. For a different reading of the gay-skinhead connection see Ashley Dawson, "Do Doc Martens Have a Special Smell: Homocore, Skinhead Eroticism, and Queer Agency," in Kevin J. H. Dettmar and William Richey, *Reading Rock and Roll: Authenticity, Appropriation, Aesthetics* (New York, 1999), pp. 125–43.

12 With emphasis on "relatively"; as Frank Cartledge points out with regard to punk, "style ... cannot be [reduced] to a single simple paradigm," but must be recognized, even in a given historical moment, as the product of "difference, change and evolution related to both

individual and physical space;" Cartledge, "Distress to Impress?,"
p. 149.

13 Keith Negus, *Popular Music in Theory: An Introduction* (Hanover and London, 1996), p. 134.

14 Ibid., p. 135.

15 Ibid.

16 See Sabin, "'I Won't Let That Dago By.'"

17 See Roger Sabin's excellent discussion of the prominence of racial humor in this period in ibid., p. 200; see also Stephen Wagg, *Because I Tell a Joke or Two* (London, 1998), chapter 15.

18 Stan Taylor, *The National Front in English Politics* (London and Basingstoke, 1982), pp. 15–19; Paul Gilroy, *"There Ain't No Black in the Union Jack": The Cultural Politics of Race and Nation* (Chicago, 1987), pp. 44–50.

19 This was the so-called "Rivers of Blood" speech delivered in Birmingham on April 20, 1968.

20 Kenya, Uganda, and Malawi. Sabin, "'I Won't Let That Dago By,'" p. 203. A similar scare was cooked up by the tabloid press in 1976 over the expulsion of Asians holding British passports from Malawi.

21 The National Front was founded in 1967 by Arthur Chesterton and John Tyndall, both former members of Britain's interwar fascist party, Oswald Mosley's British Union of Fascists. The NF achieved at one point a membership of 17,500, and reached its peak in the national elections of 1977, winning close to 250,000 votes. On the National Front's place in the English radical right see Richard Thurlow, *Fascism in Britain* (Oxford, 1987). On the issue of racism and racial violence in British society see P. Pataya, ed., *Racial Violence in Britain in the Nineteenth and Twentieth Centuries* (London, 1993); Robert Miles and Anna Phizacklea, *White-Man's Country: Racism in British Politics* (London, 1984); Zig Layton-Henry, *The Politics of Immigration: "Race" and "Race" Relations in Post-War Britain* (Oxford, 1992). The NF was particularly interested in gaining recruits from the working-class youth subcultures; see Roger Sabin, "'I Won't Let That Dago By,'" p. 200.

22 Marshall, *Spirit of '69*, 19.

23 Dick Hebdige, "This is England! And They Don't Live Here," in Nick Knight, *Skinhead* (London, New York and Sydney, 1982), pp. 26–35, 31.

24 Marshall, *Spirit of '69*, p. 125. The British Movement, founded in 1968, was successor to the National Socialist Movement (1962–1968). It

made little attempt to gain mainstream support, focusing instead on terrorism and street combat. The British Movement profited from the collapse of the National Front after 1979; see Cronin, ed., *The Failure of British Fascism* (London, 1996).

25 Steve Silver, "Echoes of the Past," *Searchlight*, July 1999.

26 Skinhead supporters protest that not only skinheads but punks and so-called "normals" (fans with no obvious subcultural affiliation) were at the gig, and that the bands involved were not right wing; see Marshall, *Spirit of '69*, p. 108. But the shock of the bully suddenly finding himself on the receiving end of the "boot" comes across clearly enough in skinhead complaints about the result of Southall.

27 Healy, *Gay Skins*, 124.

28 See the photo of a pre-skinhead Skrewdriver in punk regalia (with swastikas) in Sabin, "'I Won't Let That Dago By,'" p. 214.

Duncombe and Tremblay: Punky Reggae Party

1 Jeff Chang, "Overpowered by Funk," *San Francisco Bay Guardian*, January 1, 2003.

Simonon: Interview

1 Greil Marcus, "The Last Broadcast," in *Ranters and Crowd Pleasers: Punk in Pop Music 1977–92* (New York: Doubleday, 1993), p. 304

Widgery: Beating Time

1 *Editors' Note*: The show Widgery refers to was on Thames Television (London), not Granada (Manchester); and it was Steve Jones, not Rotten, who called Grundy a "dirty fucker" (*not* "fuck off") after Grundy had propositioned Siouxsie ("we'll meet after, shall we?"); none of which changes the validity of Widgery's point that punk had received national notoreity.

Gilroy: Two Sides of Anti-Racism

1 D. Hiro, *Black British White British* (London: Eyre and Spottiswoode, 1971); M. Abdul-Malik, *From Michael DeFreitas to Michael X* (London: Sphere, 1968); Pryer; A. Sivanandan, *A Different Hunger* (London: Pluto Press, 1982).

2 M. Glean, "Whatever Happened to CARD?" *Race Today*, January 1973.

3 Hiro, 1971.

4 N. Fielding, *The National Front* (London: Routledge, 1981).

5 Lord Justice Scarman, *The Red Lion Square Disorders of 15 June 1974*, Cmnd. 5919, HMSO (London, 1975); R. Clutterbuck, *Britain in Agony: The Growth of Political Violence* (Harmondsworth: Penguin, 1978).

6 B. Nicholson, *Racialism, Fascism and the Trade Unions* (London: Transport and General Workers Union, 1974).

7 *Melody Maker*, December 9, 1978.

8 *Evening News*, September 20, 1977.

9 *Sounds*, August 28, 1976.

10 R. Huddle, "Hard Rain," *Socialist Review* (July/August 1978).

11 Michael Gray, "Elvis," *Temporary Hoarding*, no. 3, 1977.

12 D. Hebdige, *Subculture: The Meaning of Style* (London: Methuen, 1979).

13 Ibid.

14 *Searchlight*, May 1981.

15 C. M. Young, "Rock Is Sick and Living in London," *Rolling Stone*, October 20, 1977.

16 C. Coon, *1988: The New Wave Punk Rock Explosion* (London: Orbach and Chambers, 1977).

17 October 20, 1978.

Tate: Hardcore of Darkness

1 Michael Azzerad makes a similar point in his impressive volume *Our Band Could Be Your Life: Scenes from the American Indie Underground 1981-1991* (New York: Little, Brown, 2001), cf Brian Cogan, "Beyond the Clash: The Post-Punky Reggae Party," unpublished manuscript, 2010.

Jones: Black Culture, White Youth

1 *Black Echoes,*, 26 June 1976, p. 12.

2 Dave Laing, *One Chord Wonders: Power and Meaning in Punk Rock* (Milton Keynes: Open University Press, 1985).

3 Dick Hebdige, *Subculture; The Meaning of Style* (London: Methuen, 1979); Laing 1985.

4 Hebdige, 1979.

5 Sue Steward and Sheryl Garratt, *Signed, Sealed and Delivered: True Life Stories of Women in Pop* (London: Pluto Press, 1984).

6 Simon Frith, *Sound Effects: Youth, Leisure and the Politics of Rock'n'Roll* (New York: Pantheon, 1981), p. 20.

Habell-Pallán: "¿Soy Punkera, y Qué?"

1 Considering the importance of the Bags in the L.A. punk scene, it is curious that Alice Bag/Alicia Armendariz Velasquez is minimally quoted in the collected interview in Marc Spitz and Brendan Muller, *We Got the Neutron Bomb: The Untold Story of L.A. Punk* (New York: Three Rivers Press, 2001).

2 Pop music markets have undergone enormous change since the 1970s. Given the changes in the music industry and the "boom" in Latino pop music in the 1990s, a Latina performer like Shakira can become mainstream—although it must be taken into account too that Shakira is considered a rock singer, not a punk singer who pushes rock conventions. See Maria Elena Cepeda's insightful article, "Shakira as the Idealized, Transnational Citizen: A Case Study of Colombianidad in Transition," *Latino Studies* 1, no. 1 (July 2003): 211–357, to understand how and why Shakira translates to U.S. and Latin American audiences.

3 See José E. Muñoz, *Disidentifications: Queers of Color and the Politics of Performance* (Minneapolis: University of Minnesota Press, 1999), p. 93.

4 Ibid.

5 See Richard Durado's silkscreen poster for X's performance at the Punk Prom held at Self-Help Graphics in 1980, in the catalogue for Chon Noriega, ed., *Just Another Poster? Chicano Graphic Arts in California* (Santa Barbara: Regents of the University of California Art Museum, 2001), p. 59.

6 For photo, see Don Snowden and Gary Leonard, eds., *Make the Music Go Bang: The Early L.A. Punk Scene*, photographs by Gary Leonard (New York: St. Martin's Press, 1997), p. 76.

7 The Official Alice Bag Website, "Biography," http://alicebag.com/bio .html, accessed July 17, 2004.

8 Angie Chabram-Dernersesian, "I Throw Punches for My Race, but I Don't Want to Be a Man—Writing Us Chica-nos (Girl, US)/ Chica*nas*—into the Movement Script," in *Cultural Studies*, ed. Lawrence Grossberg, Cary Nelson, and Paula Treichler (New York: Routledge, 1992), 81–95.

9 David Jones, "Destroy All Music: Punk Rock Pioneers of Southern California," forthcoming.

10 Kristine McKenna, "Female Rockers—A New Breed," *Los Angeles Times*, June 18, 1978, Calendar sec., 78–82.

11 Ibid., 78.

12 Ibid.

13 Ibid., 82.

14 Ibid., 78.

15 The Official Alice Bag Website, "Violence Girl," http://alicebag.com/violencegirl.html, accessed July 16, 2004.

16 Sincere thanks to Jim Fricke, former senior curator at the Experience Music Project, for allowing me to access the *Yes L.A.* compilation. For more on the rise of British punk, see Dave Laing's classic *One Chord Wonders: Power and Meaning in Punk Rock* (Philadelphia: Open University Press, 1985).

17 See Spitz and Mullen, *We Got the Neutron Bomb*, for varied testimonies of Canterbury's history.

18 A City of Los Angeles Cultural Affairs Department press release for the Gamboa 84 exhibition opening on April 15, 1984, at the Los Angeles Photography Center, documents that the Odd Squad, the Brat, and ASCO performed on the same program. Marisela Norte and Daniel Villarreal performed *Exito*. Harry Gamboa's *Shadow Solo* was performed by Sean Carrillo and Humberto Sandoval. *Pseudo-turquoiser* was performed by Gronk. Diane Gamboa provided *Cold Blooded* paper fashions. See flyer held in the Tomás Ybarra-Frausto Research Material, 1965–1997, collection at the Archives of American Art, Smithsonian Institution.

19 Lysa Flores "starred in critically acclaimed indie-film, *Star Maps* (1997) by Miguel Arteta, and served as the film's musical director and soundtrack producer. She played the lead in *The Furthest Room* by Paul Saucido, a play based on her songs. She runs her own record label, Bring Your Love. She has been a member of legendary performance-artist El Vez's band since 1996." See Lysa Flores Official Website, "Biography," http://www.lysaflores.com/bio.html, accessed July 16, 2004.

20 I do not mean to suggest that Alice Bag and Teresa Covarrubias were the first Chicanas from East L.A. to participate in local music scenes. See Dionne Espinoz, "'Tanto Tiempo Disfrutamos …': Revisiting the Gender and Sexual Politics of Chicana/o Youth Culture in East Los Angeles in the 1960s," in *Velvet Barrios: Popular Culture and Chicana/o Sexualities*, ed. Alicia Gasper de Alba (New York: Palgrave

Macmillan, 2003), pp. 89–106, for a discussion of Chicana participation in the East L.A. music scene in the 1950s and 1960s. In fact, in Reyes and Waldman, *Land of a Thousand Dances*, Covarrubias recalls refusing requests by her manager to rerecord a version of Rosie and the Originals' 1961 classic oldie "Angel Baby" because she wanted to create a new sound. Rosie and the Originals, although from San Diego, California, are often associated with the East L.A. sound.

21 Teresa Covarrubias, interview by author, East Los Angeles, August 8, 1998.

22 Covarrubias, interview by author.

23 "Chicanas in Tune," produced by Ester Reyes, broadcast on KCET, Los Angeles, 1994.

24 McKenna, "Female Rockers," p. 82.

25 Reyes and Waldman, *Land of a Thousand Dances*, p. 139.

26 "Chicanas in Tune"

27 Las Tres, *Live at the LATC*, Panocha Dulce-Black Rose-Bhima Music, 1993, audiocassette. "Happy Accident" was written by Alicia Armendariz Velasquez. Thanks to Antonia Garcia-Orozco for inventing the notion of Chicana Trova in relation to Nueva Trova; Chicana Trova is sung in English and lyrically calls for consciousness raising through a form of folk music that can be played on accessible instruments.

28 See Tiffany Lopez, *The Alchemy of Blood: Violence as Critical Discourse in U.S. Latina/o Literature* (Durham: Duke University Press, in press), and Angela Davis on incarceration and women of color in her recording *The Prison Industrial Complex* (AK Press, 2000, compact disc).

29 Reyes and Waldman, *Land of a Thousand Dances*, p. 136.

30 Ibid.

31 Teresa Covarrubias to M. Habell-Pallán, personal e-mail, February 24, 2003, bio for Chicana Punk Aesthetic Conference. According to a flyer announcing a night of ASCO performances on June 24, 1982, Teresa Covarrubias was one of the participants in *Random Rumor* (her name was spelled as Therese Covarrbuias). Other performers in the piece included Humberto Sandoval, Lorraine Ordaz, Diane Gamboa, Daniel Villareal, Sean Carrillo, and Harry Gamboa. See flyer archived in the Tomás Ybarra-Frausto Research Material, 1965–1997, collection at the Archives of American Art, Smithsonian Institution.

32 Reyes and Waldman, *Land of a Thousand Dances*, p. 140.

33 Sean Carrillo, "East to Eden," in *Forming: The Early Days of L.A. Punk*, ed. Sean Carrillo, Christine McKenna, Claude Bessy, and Exene

Cervenka (Santa Monica: Smart Art Press, 1999), p. 42. In addition to participating in the West Coast punk scene, Latinos were also part of New York's emerging hip-hop scene, which developed during the same time period. See Raquel Z. Rivera, *New York Ricans from the Hip Hop Zone* (New York: Palgrave, 2003).

O'Connor: Punk and Globalization

1 Arjun Appadurai, *Modernity at Large: Cultural Dimensions of Globalization* (Minneapolis: University of Minnesota Press, 1996).
2 In his study of youth gangs in Tijuana, Jose Manuel Valenzuela Arce, *A La Brava Ese! Cholos, Punks, Chavos, Banda* (Tijuana: El Colegio de la Frontera Norte, 1988) argues that punks are much less tied to their local *barrio* than *cholo* youth. Nonetheless, many punks do live with their families, much harassment from police happens near home, shows depend on local contacts to secure a hall or basketball court, and there is a huge punk scene in Ciudad Neza, an extension of Mexico City with high youth unemployment. The punk use of space in Mexico City goes against the grain of the pattern described by Néstor García Canclini and Mabel Piccini in *El consumo cultural en México*, Néstor García Canclini, ed. (Mexico City: Consejo Nacional para la Cultura y las Artes, 1993), in which because of economic crisis and pressures of life in a big city many people retreat to their home, television, radio, and recorded music.
3 Guillermo Bonfil Batalla, *México Profundo: Reclaiming a Civilization*, trans. Philip A. Dennis (Austin: University of Texas Press, 1996).
4 John Eade, ed., *Living the Global City: Globalization as a Local Process* (London: Routledge, 1997).

Esterrich and Murillo: Rock with Punk with Pop with Folklore

1 "Cagó," from the verb "cagar" (to defecate), can be translated as "is finished," "is over." The complete phrase is "cagó fuego." Pablo Vila, "Argentina's Rock Nacional: The Struggle for Meaning," *Latin American Music Review* 10:1 (Spring/Summer 1989), p. 1.
2 Jesús Martín-Barbero, *De los medios a las mediaciones: communicación, cultura y hegemonía* (México: G. Gili, 1987), pp. 219–20, authors' translation.
3 Vila 1989, p. 2.

4 John Beverly, "The Ideology of Postmodern Music and Leftist Politics," *Against Literature* (Minneapolis: University of Minnesota Press, 1993), p. 137.

5 In an issue of the Colombian *Cambio 16* dedicated to rock, the weekly magazine stated in the editorial page that "rock is booming because the recent bands, in general, are much more attuned to the national reality. They are not looking for stardom with catchy tunes and bland lyrics of adolescent love or with the typical themes from 'rock in Spanish' of 1988–1989, the 'Say No to Drugs' type" (Eduardo Arias, "Florecita Rockera," 1995, p. 3: authors' translation).

6 This article was written before the release of Aterciopelados's fourth album, *Caribe Atómico* (1998), and therefore does not examine songs from it. It is important to point out, however, that the trend we are discussing here continues in the new album, toying with an Argentine bandoneon and the tango tradition in "Maligno," and sampling old recordings of Colombian popular music in the first hit of the album, "El Estuche."

7 Carrileras are Colombian songs from the Medellín and Pereira regions. They are spiteful, vengeful songs. The first two stanzas of "La Cuchilla" give an accurate idea of the carrilera sentiment: "*Si no me quierés / te corto la cara / con una cuchilla / de esas de afeitar. / El día de la boda / te doy puñaladas, / te arranco el ombligo / y mato a tu mamá.*" (If you don't love me / I'll cut your face / with a blade / for shaving./ The day of your wedding / I'll stab you, / rip out your belly button / and kill your mom.) (All song translations are ours.) "La Cuchilla" was popularized by the Calle Sisters.

8 Lawrence La Fountain-Stokes, "Aterciopelados: Interview," *Claridad* (Puerto Rico, July 11–17, 1997), p. 23, authors' translation.

9 Sonia Bandenas, "Los Aterciopelados: la bendición llegó de alguna parte," *El Universal* (Venezuela, August 6, 1995), sec. 3:30, p. 30, authors' translation.

10 This and all other lyric translations are the authors'.

11 Plaza Garibaldi is the famous plaza in Mexico City where mariachi bands play, especially at night.

12 It is important to note here that "Bolero falaz" hit the top of the charts in Colombia. "Cagar" [to defecate] is not a word that is often heard on Colombian radio, and its shock value increased because it was played for everyone to hear, not necessarily in the privacy of a Walkman or a stereo at home.

13 Santa Sabina and Tijuana NO, both from Mexico, have female lead

singers. More recently, new bands are forming with female singers and musicians, e.g., Julieta Venegas and Aurora y la Academia.

14 This screechy, scratchy voice is not new in *Re*. In "Rarotonga," "Pinche Juan," and "Las Persianas"—all songs from their first album—Albarrán distorted his voice like a typical punk or hard rock singer.

15 Mary Farquharson, "Over the Border: Mexico Is a Lot More Than Mariachi," *World Music*, ed. Simon Broughton, Mark Ellingham, David Muddyman, Richard Trillo, and Kim Burton (London: Rough Guides, 1994), p. 442.

16 The parody continues in their liner notes: the page containing the lyrics of this song (curiously incomplete) includes an illustration probably taken out of a "Libro Semanal"—stories with romantic plots loaded with gender and racial stereotypes published weekly in the style of comic books and sold throughout Mexico and in many other Latin American countries. In this illustration a man melodramatically slaps a woman.

17 Vallenato's original instrument is, like Mexican Norteña, the German accordion, which joined the "guacharaca" (of indigenous origin) and the "caja" (an Afro-Colombian drum) in the 1920s to produce an absolutely "mestizo" sound.

18 This is not, in fact, a traditional vallenato. The song is from a recording by Lisandro Diaz, a famous vallenato singer of the late seventies and early eighties, especially popular among the working class. Even though the origins of vallenato lie in the northern provinces of Colombia, the constant migration to the central cities popularized this music in Bogotá's and Medellín's lower classes. The use of words like "chicle" (chewing gum), "jeans"—"Lees" in the original version—and "motoneta" (moped) are clear evidence of the urban character of this vallenato.

19 It is important to stress that while Aterciopelados' "Baracunatana" is a cover or remake, Café Tacuba's "La Ingrata" is an original Café Tacuba song.

20 All these words are very colloquial, Colombian words; a few of them appear in regular Spanish dictionaries. "Vergajo/a" (scum); "fulero/a" (a liar, someone who tricks others, a useless person, also someone tacky; *Gran diccionario de la lengua española* 1996, p. 768); "guaricha" (a derogatory form for woman, like "broad" or "wench" in English, also a prostitute; *Diccionario hispánico universal* 1962, p. 1457); "garoso/a" (a glutton; *Diccionario hispánico universal* 1962, p. 702); "morrongo/a" (colloquial for cat, by analogy a really seductive woman; *Gran*

diccionario de la lengua española 1996, p. 984); "fariseo/a" (colloquially, a hypocrite, a suspicious person; *Gran diccionario de la lengua española* 1996, p. 726); "retrechero/a" (someone who can easily evade obligations, also attractive, seductive; *Gran diccionario de la lengua española* 1996, p. 1528); "garulla" (a good-for-nothing, *Gran diccionario de la lengua española* 1996, p. 787).

21 Homi K. Bhabha, "Of Mimicry and Man: The Ambivalence of Colonial Discourse," *The Location of Culture* (London: Routledge, 1994), p. 86.

22 Café Tacuba deleted the following lines: "*porque es total que a todos les encanta*" (because it's cool and everybody loves it), "*que a todos les excita*" (and excites everybody), and "*que a todos enamoro*" (and I make everybody fall in love with me). Café Tacuba substituted these lines by repeating "*porque es total y a todo el mundo gusto*" (because it's cool and everybody likes me) (authors' translation).

23 "Rock en tu idioma" (rock in your language) is actually a slogan created by the record company Ariola International to group all the albums they produced from Mexico, Argentina, and Spain.

Wallach: Living the Punk Lifestyle in Jakarta

1 My translation of this quoted passage differs from other published translations.

2 Pramoedya Ananta Toer, *Bumi Manusia* (Jakarta: Hasta Mitra, 1981). p. 292.

3 Dick Hebdige, *Subculture: The Meaning of Style* (London: Methuen, 1979), p. 126.

4 This influence has rarely gone uncontested, however. For recent critical appraisals of the semiological approach to subcultural forms that characterizes the work of Hebdige and other scholars associated with the Centre for Contemporary Cultural Studies in Birmingham, see the essays in Andy Bennett and Keith Kahn-Harris, eds. *After Subculture: Critical Studies in Contemporary Youth Culture* (New York: Palgrave, 2004), and David Muggleton and Rupert Weinzierl, eds. The *Post-Subcultures Reader* (New York: Berg, 2003).

5 For a notable exception see Jan Johannsson, *"Indonesian Punk Underground,"* Missing Link Newsletter (2003). Writing for an Australian punk webzine, Johannsson starts by acknowledging possible objections his readers might raise regarding his chosen subject:

I know that at this stage some of you will be rolling your eyes and thinking "Sheesh! Why would I want to know ANYTHING about the music scene in a Muslim country ... don't they hate Westerners over there anyway?" Well, here are a couple of reasons why you should:

I remember that even at the start of the '90s, most "underground"-type cats around town would just laugh at the thought of Japanese underground music. These days most of us know that in fact Japan had an amazing scene even back in the early '70s stoner days of the Flower Travellin' Band and Speed, Glue, and Shinki, and now Japanese bands are probably more popular than ever in worldwide independent music circles. Now, I'm not saying that Indonesia is the "new Japan." But if you really want to be, as Julian Cope charmingly puts it, a "forward-thinking motherfucker," you should open your mind to the idea of rock'n'roll from non-European cultures.

We live in pretty screwy times, where nuts like Osama bin Laden, George W. Bush (the guy, not that band with the ex-Mindsnare drummer in it) and John Howard conspire to keep people divided on the basis of their religion, race and culture. Therefore the fact that people in two very different cultures can share a common love of ripping punk rock and a common hatred of shitty corporate pop is a very, very good thing.

A lot of Indonesian bands just flat-out rock anyway. (Johannsson 2003)

The presupposition here that members of Australia's well-established, long-standing punk scene would be wholly unaware of the enormous punk movement in one of Australia's closest neighbors underlines a point I make later in this essay regarding the relatively autonomous development of the Indonesian punk movement.

6 Emma Baulch, "Punks, Rastas and Headbangers: Bali's Generation X," *Inside Indonesia* 48 (1996), online edition: http://www.insideindonesia.org/edit48/emma.htm (June 18, 2003); "Alternative Music and Mediation in Late New Order Indonesia," *Inter-Asia Cultural Studies* 3 (2002), pp. 219–34; "Creating a Scene: Balinese Punk's Beginnings," *International Journal of Cultural Studies* 5:2 (2002), pp. 153–77.

7 Jo Pickles, "Punks for Peace: Underground Music Gives Young People Back Their Voice," *Inside Indonesia* 64 (2000), online edition: http://www.insideindonesia.org/edit64/punk1.htm (June 18, 2003).

8 Marc Perlman, "The Traditional Javanese Performing Arts in the Twilight of the New Order: Two Letters from Solo," *Indonesia* 68 (1999),

pp. 31–32; Jeremy Wallach, "Exploring Class, Nation and Xenocentrism in Indonesian Cassette Retail Outlets," *Indonesia* 74 (2002), pp. 98–101.

9 Jason Tedjasukmana, "Bandung's Headbangers," *Time Asia*, June 16, 2003, http://www.time.com/time/asia/magazine/article/0,13673,50103 0623-458837,00.html (June 19, 2003).

10 Superman Is Dead is one of the bands featured in the recent documentary film *The Punks Are Alright: A Punk Rock Safari from the First World to the Third*, by the Canadian filmmaker Douglas Crawford (2006). A version of the film was shown at the Jakarta International Film Festival in December 2005 (Taufiqurrahman 2005).

11 Krishna Sen and David Hill, *Media, Culture, and Politics in Indonesia* (New York: Oxford University Press, 2000), pp. 177–85; Jeremy Wallach, "'Goodbye My Blind Majesty': Music, Language, and Politics in the Indonesian Underground," in *Global Pop, Local Language*, ed. Harris M. Berger and Michael T. Carrol (Jackson: University Press of Misissippi, 2003), pp. 53–86; Wallach, "Underground Rock Music and Democratization in Indonesia," *World Literature Today* 79:3–4 (2005), pp. 1–28.

12 Pickles, 2000.

13 See Tod Jones, "*Angkutan* and *Bis Kota* in Padang, West Sumatra: Public Transport as Intersections of a Local Popular Culture," paper presented at the Arts, Culture and Political and Social Change since Suharto Workshop, Launceston, Australia, December 16–18, 2005. Available from http://www.utas.edu.au/indonesia_workshop/abstracts.htm (August 13, 2006).

14 The Indonesian standardized variant of Malay is spoken as a second language across the archipelago. It is the language of public performance, formal politics, education, the mass media, and pop song lyrics, and its role as a relatively neutral communicative vehicle that transcends ethnic boundaries seems neither to be resented nor questioned, at least not in Java or Bali. In addition to having some command of formal Indonesian, residents of Jakarta may also speak slang-filled Malay speech variants closely related to nonstandard Betawi Malay as languages of everyday socializing.

15 Punk and hardcore are considered related but separate genres in the Indonesian underground movement. The latter is divided into "old school" and metal- and rap-influenced "new school" variants, and in general hardcore music is stylistically more diverse than punk. Old-school hardcore bands like Jakarta's Straight Answer occasionally play

at punk concert events such as the one described later in this essay. Significantly, Indonesian hardcore bands are far more likely to sing songs in Indonesian (instead of English) compared with Indonesian punk groups (Wallach 2003).

16 This bias does not apply to canonized Western punk groups such as the Ramones and the Sex Pistols who recorded on major corporate record labels.

17 See Martin Richter, "Grounded Cosmopolitans and the Bureaucratic Field: Musical Performance at Two Yogyakarta State Institutions," in *Sojourn: Journal of Social Issues in Southeast Asia* 21:2 (2006) and Wallach (forthcoming) for discussions of the sponsorship of live music events in Indonesia by agents of the state and by large corporations.

18 Berta also gave me the URL of the Bogor punk scene's official website. Unfortunately, as of July 2006, that URL (http://www.geocities.com/bogoriot) was no longer functioning.

19 I did not observe any handicapped women playing this role, and I suspect such behavior would not be as well tolerated as it is with men.

20 Peter L. Manuel, *Popular Musics of the Non-Western World: An Introductory Survey* (New York: Oxford University Press, 1988), p. 22.

21 Hilary Pilkington, *Russia's Youth and Its Culture: A Nation's Constructors and Constructed* (New York: Routledge, 1994), p. 228.

22 Sumarsam, *Gamelan: Cultural Interaction and Musical Development in Central Java* (Chicago: University of Chicago Press, 1995).

23 Michael Tenzer, "The Life in *Gendhing*: Current Approaches to Javanese Gamelan. A Review Essay," *Indonesia* 63 (1997), pp. 169–86.

24 Wallach, "Of Gongs and Cannons: Music and Power in Island Southeast Asia," *Wacana Seni Journal of Arts Discourse* 3 (2004), pp. 1–28.

25 Thomas Turino, "Signs of Imagination, Identity, and Experience: A Peircean Semiotic Theory for Music," *Ethnomusicology* 43:2 (1999), pp. 224–25.

26 Turino pp. 234–37. See also Naomi Cumming, "Musical Signs and Subjectivity: Peircean Reflections," *Transactions of the Charles S. Pierce Society* 35:3 (1999), pp. 437–74.

27 Hebdige, p. 117. The reality was likely more complex than that. See Jon Stratton, "Jews, Punks, and the Holocaust: From the Velvet Underground to the Ramones – The Jewish-American Story," *Popular Music* 24:1 (2005) for a subtler, more historically grounded examination of the complex, contradictory meanings of fascist imagery in early punk and heavy metal music in the United States. For a journalistic but

fascinating account of the close relationship between Jewish culture and the early punk movement and 1970s punk's fraught relationship to Nazi symbols, see Steven Beeber, *The Heebie-Jeebies at CBGB's: A Secret History of Jewish Punk* (Chicago: Chicago Review Press, 2006), especially Chapter 13. Beeber states bluntly, "No Holocaust, no punk" (ibid., p. 164), and given what is known about the early history of the genre, it is difficult to dispute such a statement.

28 A number of readers of this essay pointed out that the swastika is also an ancient Hindu symbol. While I did not encounter any evidence that this fact was at all relevant to Indonesian punks' decisions to accept or reject the symbol, it could be in some cases, particularly in Hindu-dominated Bali—home to Superman Is Dead and known around the region for its punk scene—where Hindu swastikas are fairly common. The association of the swastika with anti-Judaism, of which Jakarta's punks, being predominantly Muslim, presumably approve (though I would take issue with such an assumption), was also suggested as a factor in its adoption. Again, in my research I found no evidence for this hypothesis, and would argue that for most Jakarta punks in 1999–2000 at least, the association with a fascist regime outweighed any appeal the symbol might have had for other reasons.

29 The sticker slogan "Gegen Nazis" is actually German for "Against Nazis"; "Smash Nazis" in Indonesian (which is probably what most people in Jakarta thought it said) would be "Geger Nazis."

30 Mark Gottdiener, *Postmodern Semiotics: Material Culture and the Forms of Postmodern Life* (Cambridge, MA: Blackwell Publishers, 1995), pp. 233–52.

30 Thomas L. Short, "Life Among the Legisigns," *Transactions of the Charles S. Peirce Society* 28:4 (1982), p. 285; see also Short, *Peirce's Theory of Signs* (New York: Cambridge University Press, 2007), pp. 108–12, 172–74.

PERMISSIONS

Alien Kulture, interview with the BBC, reprinted with the permission of the artists.

Anonymous, "Not Just Posing for the Postcard," *Clamor #2,* reprinted with the permission of the anonymous author.

James Baldwin, "The Black Boy Looks at the White Boy," copyright 1961 by James Baldwin. Copyright renewed. Originally published in *Esquire.* Collected in *Nobody Knows My Name,* published by Vintage Books. Reprinted with the permission of the James Baldwin Estate.

Lester Bangs, "The White Noise Supremacists," reprinted with the permission of the *Village Voice.*

Steven Lee Beeber, "Hotsy-Totsy Nazi Schatzes: Nazi Imagery and the Final Solution to the Final Solution," reprinted with the permission of the author and the Chicago Review Press.

Kelly Besser, "What Happened?" *Chop Suey Spex #1,* reprinted with the permission of the author and editors.

Timothy S. Brown, "Subculture, Pop Music & Politics: Skinheads and 'Nazi Rock' in England and Germany," reprinted with the permission of the author and the *Journal of Social History.*

Simon Jones, from *Black Culture, White Youth,* reprinted with the permission of the author.

Michael Muhammad Knight, "Muhammad Was A Punk Rocker," reprinted with the permission of the author.

Madhu Krishnan, "How Can You Be So Cold?" *How to Stage a Coup,* reprinted with the permission of the author.

Norman Mailer, "The White Negro," reprinted with the permission of *Dissent* magazine and the Mailer Estate. Copyright © Norman Mailer 1957, used with permission of the Wylie Agency LLC.

Greil Marcus, "Crimes Against Nature," reprinted with the permission of the author.

Maximumrocknroll: Bob Noxious interview; Vic Bondi, Dave Dictor and Ian MacKaye discussion; Majority of One, review and letter exchange; Kieran Knutson interview; Los Crudos interview; Martín Sorrondeguy, "The End of Los Crudos"; "Just Another Nigger," letter exchange; all reprinted with the permission of *Maximumrocknoll.*

Edward Meadows, "Pistol-Whipped," *National Review,* reprinted with the permission of the *National Review.*

Siddhartha Mitter, "Taqwacore: Salat, Angst, and Rock & Roll," reprinted with the permission of the author.

Mimi Nguyen, "It's (Not) a White World: Looking for Race in Punk," *Punk Planet #28,* reprinted with the permission of the author.

Otto Nomous, "Race, Anarchy, and Punk Rock: The Impact of Cultural Boundaries Within the Anarchist Movement." "Feel free to read, copy, and distribute this article as often as your heart desires."

Alan O'Connor, "Punk and Globalization: Mexico City and Toronto," reprinted with the permission of the author and Routledge, Inc., part of the Taylor & Francis Group.

Joel Olson, "A New Punk Manifesto," *Profane Existence #13*, reprinted with the permission of the author.

Jimmy Pursey, interview in *Sounds*, reprinted with the permission of Rock's Backpages.

Krishna Rau, "Try Not To Think," *Broken Pencil #7*, reprinted with permission of the author.

Daisy Rooks, "Screaming, Always Screaming," *HeartattaCk #3*, reprinted with permission of the author.

Roger Sabin, "'I Won't Let that Dago By': Rethinking Punk and Racism," reprinted with permission of the author and Routledge, Inc., part of the Taylor & Francis Group.

Jon Savage, from *England's Dreaming*, reprinted with the permission of St. Martins Press.

Paul Simonon, interview in *Search & Destroy #7*, reprinted with the permission of V. Vale and *Search and Destroy*.

John Sinclair, liner notes to MC5's *Kick out the Jams!*, reprinted with the permission of the author.

James Spooner, "Foreward," original essay, rights reserved by the author.

James Spooner, dir. *Afro-punk*, from the film script, reprinted with the permission of the director.

Greg Tate, "Hardcore of Darkness," reprinted with the permission of the author and the *Village Voice*.

Daniel S. Traber, "LA's 'White Minority': Punk and the Contradictions of Self-Marginalization," reprinted with permission of the author and University of Minnesota Press.

Steve Waksman, "Kick Out the Jams! The MC5 and the Politics of Noise," reprinted with permission of the author.

Jeremy Wallach, "Living the Punk Lifestyle in Jakarta," reprinted with the permission of the author and the Society for Ethnomusicology.

The editors have made every effort to obtain the proper permissions for all the selections printed in this anthology. If we have inadvertently neglected any we will be pleased to make full acknowledgement in subsequent editions of this book.